KING YESHUA'S VISITATION

KING YESHUA'S VISITATION

AWAKING to HIS PAROUSIA as a THIEF in the NIGHT

CARMEN SAUNDERS

LitPrime Solutions
21250 Hawthorne Blvd
Suite 500, Torrance, CA 90503
www.litprime.com
Phone: 1 (209) 788-3500

© 2021 Carmen Saunders. All rights reserved.

No part of this book may be reproduced, stored in a retrieval system, or transmitted by any means without the written permission of the author.

Scripture quotations taken from the New American Standard Bible* (NASB), Copyright © 1960, 1962, 1963, 1968, 1971, 1972, 1973, 1975, 1977, 1995 by The Lockman Foundation Used by permission. www.Lockman.org

Published by LitPrime Solutions   03/05/2021

ISBN: 978-1-953397-83-6(sc)
ISBN: 978-1-953397-84-3(e)

Library of Congress Control Number: 2021900917

Any people depicted in stock imagery provided by iStock are models, and such images are being used for illustrative purposes only.

Certain stock imagery © iStock.

Because of the dynamic nature of the Internet, any web addresses or links contained in this book may have changed since publication and may no longer be valid. The views expressed in this work are solely those of the author and do not necessarily reflect the views of the publisher, and the publisher hereby disclaims any responsibility for them.

The voice of an angel once told me, "You waste time contemplating." Time is quickly running out. Everything I sense concerning this old earth will soon be no more.

> The Pharisees and Sadducees came up, and testing Jesus, they asked Him to show them a sign from heaven. But He replied to them, "When it is evening, you say, 'fair weather, for the sky is red.' And in the morning, 'a storm today, for the sky is red and threatening.' Do you know how to discern the appearance of the sky, but cannot the signs of the times? An evil and adulterous generation seeks after a sign; and a sign will not be given it, except the sign of Jonah." And He left them and went away. (Matthew 16:1–4)

> Therefore be on the alert, for you do not know which day your Lord is coming. But be sure of this, that if the head of the house had known at what time of the night the thief was coming, he would have been on the alert and would not have allowed his house to be broken into. For this reason you also must be ready; for the Son of man is coming at an hour when you do not think He will. (Matthew 24:42–44)

> Therefore, be on the alert—for you do not know when the master of the house is coming, whether in the evening, at midnight, or when the rooster crows, or in the morning—in case he should come suddenly and find you asleep. What I say to you I say to all, "Be on the alert!" (Mark 13:35–37)

> Be dressed in readiness, and keep your lamps lit. Be like men who are waiting for their master when he returns from the wedding feast, so that they may immediately open the door to him when he comes and knocks. Blessed are those slaves whom the master will find on the alert when he comes; truly I say to you, that he will gird himself to serve, and have them recline at the table, and will come up and wait on them. (Luke 12:37)

> They will not leave one stone on another, because you did not recognize the time of God's coming to you. (Luke 19:44)

The same can be said of our current generation, except the signs given to us are different with the passing away. We must read the signs given throughout history and on the earth and recognize His Parousia (visitation upon us). We must be on the alert and awake to open the door because He has knocked, so we must open it or catch the thief who has arrived and entered. How can we open the door to Him if we are not alert and awake to hear Him or do not know the signs to watch for? A thief is not always so obvious for all to see, making himself easy to catch. Why be alert if it is going to be so obvious for everyone to see? I don't have to be alert if it is obvious.

Contents

Galaxy Center, Large Cloud in Sagittarius.
Acknowledgment... xiii
Preface.. xv
Introduction xix

Part I: Preterism: A Type of Watchman

Chapter 1. Lift Your Eyes to the Heavens, Look on the Earth
            Beneath...1

Chapter 2. Kingdoms (Daniel 2:24–45 and Revelation 20:4–10) . . 20
   - Peace and Safety during the Roman Empire............20
   - The Seventy Sevens 21
   - Worldly Kingdoms in Daniel's Prophecy 26
   - The Kingdom of Heaven Is Near! 27
   - The Rock..32
   - An Age to Come after Christ's Coming and after the
     Roman Empire 33
   - Time Line of Kingdoms..............................34

Chapter 3. Revelation: The Beast 35
   - Four Clues..37
   - Ten Kings of Daniel (The Beast/ Roman Emperors).....39
   - Ten Kings of Revelation 39
   - The Ten Hebrew Kings/Tetrarchs or Rulers or the
     Ten Horns with the Ten Diadems.....................40
   - Seven Heads of the Beast/Ten Horns with Crowns......42
   - Julio-Claudian Dynasty 43
   - Civil Wars 43
   - Nero..44
   - Flavian Dynasty.....................................52

- Feasts 54
- The Order in Revelation. 55

Chapter 4. The Tribulation. 57

Chapter 5. The Two Reigns of the Saints or the Continuance of One. 63

Chapter 6. Kingdom Takeover/Day of the Lord 72
- Hades or Gehenna (Lazarus and The Rich Man) 73
- The Sun. 74
- Supernova Explosion 74
- Meteors/Fireballs 74
- Super Volcanoes. 75
- Lake of Fire or a Super Massive Black Hole 75
- Spontaneous Combustion. 84

Chapter 7. The Recognized Comings and Visitations of God 97

Chapter 8. Every Eye Will See Him (Zechariah 12 and Revelation) 100
- Zechariah 12 and Revelation 100
- Dual Fulfillment of Zechariah 12. 102
- First Point 108
- Second Point 113
- Third Point 118

Chapter 9. Zechariah 14: The Day of the Lord and the Nations of the Crusades 120

Chapter 10. The Prophecy of the Plague of Worldwide Drought Is Now Fulfilled 139

Chapter 11. Blessed Is He Who Comes in the Name of the Lord . . 145

Chapter 12. The Time was Shortened—Not Lengthened 149

Chapter 13. The Visitation. 151

Chapter 14. The Temple as the Center of Jewish Life (The End) . . 159

Chapter 15. The Great Commission Then and Now (Matthew 28:16–20; Mark 16:15) 161

Chapter 16. The Imminence of His Coming in the First Century . 164
- The Complacency of the Church 170
- Questions to Ponder. 172

Chapter 17. An Explanation of 2 Thessalonians 2 and 2 Timothy 2 175

Chapter 18. Was the Resurrection Fulfilled? (Luke 24:39–43;
2 Timothy 2:15–21; Revelation 20) 178

Chapter 19. The Passing Away, Destruction, and Hell 182
- Kingdom Takeover. 186

Chapter 20. Addressing Futurist Arguments against the
Preterist View 188
- Time Texts. 188
- When Revelation Was Written by Apostle John 188
- Not One Stone of the Temple. 190
- The Great Commission Fulfilled, yet Continued 190
- The AD 70 Tribulation Was the Worst for That
  Generation 193
- The Tribes of the E°arth Seeing the Son of Man 195
- This Generation. 195
- When You See 200
- Nero the Antichrist 202
- Isaiah 13:6 203
- Matthew 23:34–36. 204
- Jeremiah 29:1, 10 205
- Judgment of Humankind during and after the
  King's Arrival. 205
- Time Line of Harvest and Judgment 208
- Other Points. 209

Chapter 21. The Two Hands 212
- The One Hand. 212
- On The Other Hand 215

Chapter 22. A Warning from Two Signs. 217
- Titanic. 220
- Schindler's List. 224
- The Comparison 227

Part II: A Visitation of a Different Kind

Chapter 23. The Witnesses: Body, Blood, and Spirit. 237
- Points of Contact or Bridges between Two Dimensions . 237
- The Body and Blood of Yeshua. 242
- Spiritual Intake of His Flesh and Blood 245

- The Blood's Active and Continuing Testimony over Us . 247

Chapter 24. The Water as a Witness........................259
- God Works through Water........................259
- The Importance of Water as a Witness..............260
- Crossing Over through Water in the Spirit..........263
- Biblical and Nonbiblical Examples of Water as a Contact/Bridge................................265
- The Power of Water in Creation...................269

Chapter 25. The Biblical Pattern of Contacts 270

Chapter 26. The Lord's Prayer (Matthew 6:8–15)..............273

Chapter 27. The Gun and the Bullets: The Scripture and the Sword 277

Chapter 28. The Warning and the Blessed Hope 287
- Enlarged Time Line of Kingdoms 296

Glossary 299
Bibliography 301
Catastrophes and Crises....................................303
Index..313

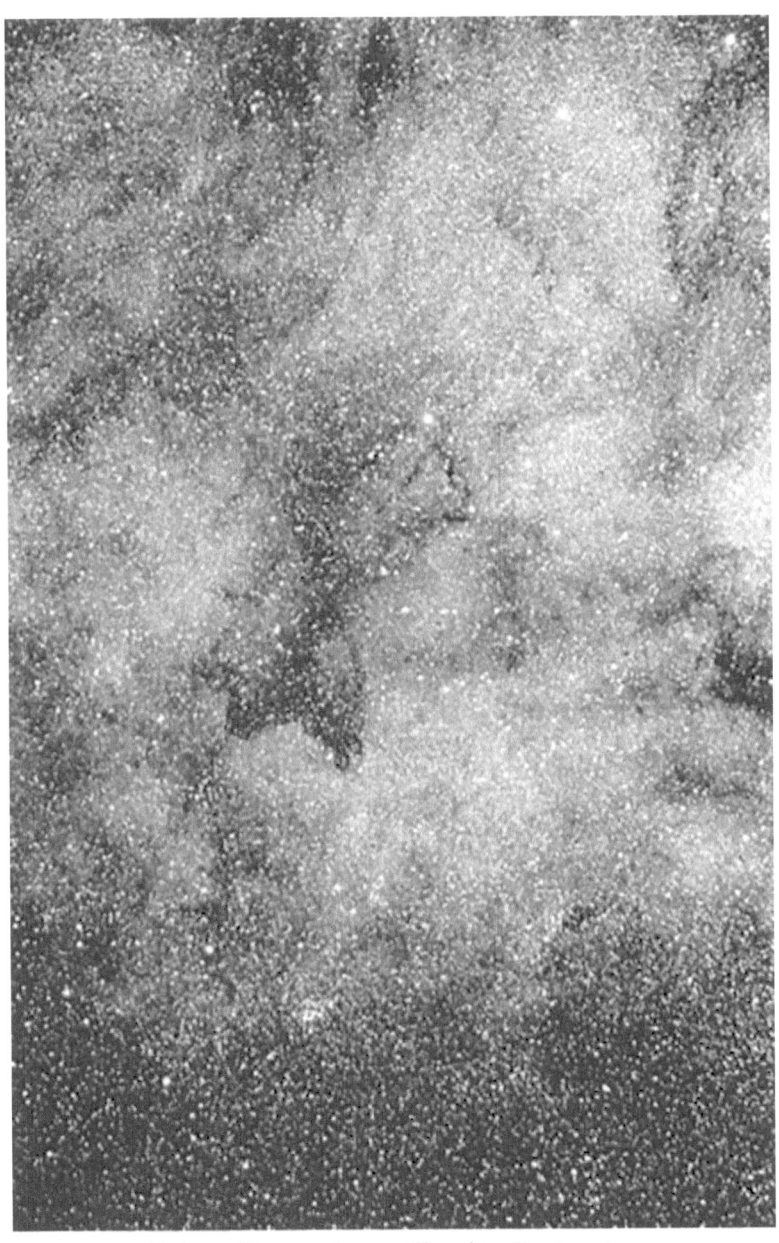

Galaxy Center, Large Cloud in Sagittarius.
Could this be the sign of the Lion of Judah?
Turn photo sideways to capture the face of
one whose face shines like the sun
and whose hair is white like wool with eyes of fire.
Photo by Chris Cook.

Acknowledgment

Blessed are You, O Lord, our God, creator of the heavens and earth.
Blessed are You, O Lord, our God, who brings
forth food and drink from the earth.
Blessed are You, O Lord, our God, who gives
the bread of heaven, Yeshua.
Blessed are You, O Lord, our God, who gives
the water of life, the Holy Spirit.
Blessed and holy is Your name.

Thank you, Yeshua, for Your mercy and redeeming me through Your sacrifice. I thank You for Your blessings upon my life big and small. Thank you for guiding me in my life and being a shield around me. Thank You for allowing me to share my faith in what I know and believe with others for Your glory and their edification. Thank You for making this book possible so others may consider prayerfully what is written and according to Your word they begin to make preparation for what You are bringing to pass.

Preface

My understanding in the fulfillment of biblical prophecy started between 2000 and 2002. Despite what the majority of Christians believe, as a preterist, I knew in the time line of prophetic fulfillment we were currently at the passing away of heaven and earth. However, I did not understand exactly how. Everything seemed peaceful and normal. Somehow, the earth's end was at hand, but I didn't understand specifically in what way it was happening. I couldn't see the connections until news about the deteriorating state of the earth began to become known and the massive die-offs of various species of life started to occur and increase at an alarming rate.

The Jewish Messiah returned again to Jerusalem in the first century:

> And they will see the Son of Man coming on the clouds of the sky with power and great glory. (Matthew 24:30)

> Then the Lord will appear over them, and His arrow will go forth like lightning; and the Lord YHWH will blow the trumpet, and will march in the storm winds of the south. (Zechariah 9:14)

The picture of the large cloud in Sagittarius makes me wonder if He, in another form, in a sort of dual fulfillment, is still in those clouds of heaven in power and great glory even after the fulfillment almost two thousand years ago. It reminds me of the description in Zechariah 9:14.

A cloud *appears over* the earth, looking *south* in the night sky, and it is near the center of the galaxy. There is an image of a man's face. He gazes toward earth. His hair is as white as wool, and His face shines like the sun.

His eyes are like fire, and he bears the scars of a man who was beaten. He sees all the deeds of humankind through the millennia. He looks on like a thief in the night as the inhabitants of earth live their lives unaware of the danger they are in. They sleep, unaware of His arrival.

As He looks toward the earth from the center of the Milky Way, peering through the gaseous, nebulous clouds, things begin to flee from His presence. Perhaps, in a sort of cyclical pattern, His Word finds its fulfillment again. As there was mourning among the tribes of Israel around AD 70 in fulfillment of Zechariah, there too is the sound of mourning to be heard from the tribes of the global earth from the nations almost two thousand years later before it passes away.

The body of the Messiah should be made aware of the signs unfolding in our time. A partial preterist is a type of watchman, and more people in the body of the Messiah should pray about the signs occurring globally and prepare. If scientific data, videos concerning the deterioration of earth, and people's testimonies of the changes they are seeing in their regions are not convincing enough, consider that a passing away or *extinction* was prophesied in scripture.

Consider prayerfully how humankind in history has come to this point since the worldly kingdoms in Daniel. We should not see these signs in isolation but as the big picture, as a whole, and as a sign of what is happening right now and what is to come in the next few decades.

According to scripture, it is certain the end of heaven and earth is imminent—if not in my lifetime then in the generations that follow.

Scripture may not be specific about exactly how earth ends; the only detail given is that everything heats up, is on fire, and melts, which is what we are beginning to see with wildfires, glaciers, and some asphalt streets. Scripture may not label it "climate change" or "environmental destruction" or a "super volcano," but Yeshua knew humankind would not change quickly enough to save earth due to greed, riches, preeminence, blindness, and pride.

It is not just the passing away of earth, but also the heavens above when the stars change and diminish and the sky rolls up like a scroll. How does earth escape if the heavens in which it exists pass away around it?

How does the heavens pass with a roar, but earth is left untouched? It is like running from a snake inside the house, only to meet the bear outside.

Even if we kill the snake (save and cool planet earth), the bear is waiting or approaching us (from the heavens). According to His word, there is no escaping judgment and destruction. It is at the door.

> Alas, you who are longing for the day of the Lord, for what purpose will the day of the Lord be to you? It will be darkness and not light; as when a man flees from a

lion and a bear meets him, or goes home, leans his hand against the wall and a snake bites him. Will not the day of the Lord be darkness instead of light, even gloom with no brightness in it? (Amos 5:18–20)

Humankind will understand too late, like Noah's generation. It would do us good to take heed to it and prayerfully consider what is actually happening. Ignoring it or denying it might hurt us. We might miss what God is going to do. This might be why an awakening and outpouring of the Holy Spirit is coming. At such a time as this, we really need Yeshua. We need to be more united as His body—not just locally but globally. The connection between biblical prophecy and this landmark of prophecy wasn't made until between 2007 and 2009.

Introduction

He waited until the activity of the street died down. The cars stopped going to and fro. A dog was barking in the distance, and a stray cat walked across the street. Bugs began to flitter around the streetlight across the street. He had planned for a long time and knew every step of how he was going to enter and carry out everything he wanted. He knew the layout of the house; he had been inside several times before. There was no alarm system.

The owner of the house did not seem strong, and the thief could take him out easily. He would have the element of surprise and catch him unaware of his presence in his territory. He would catch him off guard.

The owner would not be expecting the thief's arrival, and it would be dark outside and inside. People were less likely to witness him stalking and breaking into the house at nighttime than during the daytime. The last time he attempted a break-in was years ago, and it was daytime.

The neighbors who were on neighborhood watch grew suspicious of his activities. At the time, he thought he would get away with it because everyone would be at work. Not so—he was seen by several people, was caught, and was apprehended.

The lights went off, and the house became silent. He waited and came up to the house after midnight. He broke the glass of the back door, turned the lock, and unhooked the latch. He entered slowly and went to the master bedroom where the valuables were hidden. He entered the bedroom and stood over the husband and wife.

They were sleeping very deeply. The husband was snoring.

He stared at them and brushed his hand over the lovely woman's hair several times.

She didn't feel him, didn't move, and didn't stir.

He went quietly into the drawers and closet, took the precious jewelry out of the beaded box, and slipped it into his black bag. He went through the purse and wallet and took the checks, cards, and cash. It all went into his bag. He kept stopping and checking to see if they were awake.

They were in dreamland, completely unaware of his presence. They were unaware that he was walking around their bedroom, standing over them for minutes at a time.

How can people be so out of it when their life is in my hands now? I can spare them or kill them in an instant. They are at my mercy. They do not know they are being visited. They are unaware that their time is quickly running out. This is their last day, last night, last breath. They did not see this coming. If they had, they would have taken precautions.

As he left the house, the flames were getting bigger. They did not have a chance to fight. He came, he saw, he took; he conquered the master of the house.

***

Yeshua's coming is much like this thief in the night. His coming was sudden, unexpected, unrecognized, and unknown. Yeshua knew *the generation* He would return to, but He and the angels did not know *the day or hour within that generation* (Mark 13:30–37).

A thief, who comes during the day, like at a bank, is sudden and unexpected too, but he is recognized and known at the bank. A thief in the night comes as the world sleeps—as they live, move, and work. They are out of it and at His mercy. Just as a thief in the night can be inside a house without the owner knowing it because he sleeps, Yeshua can be here in the earth without the nations aware that He has been here because they sleep and are blind. If the owner's life is not taken, the only way the owner knows a thief has been in his house is by looking at the changes, the signs, the footprints, and things that are missing or out of place that indicate he was present in his midst as he slept so soundly. The world's time is quickly running out. It is their last day, hour, night, and breath. They don't see it coming. They haven't taken precautions.

He has been here for a while, and now their house, earth, is on fire. The flames are growing bigger. He has conquered the master of the house; he has conquered them. He stood over them and watched them; taking out His people over time and the world never suspected or knew.

Who is the one who sees His coming? Who is the one who knows? It is the one who is in the light and is awake. It is the servant who is a gatekeeper, watchman, and girded to serve the one knocking on the door. It is the one who has the Spirit poured out on him who sees as He wills him to see. The world cannot receive his Spirit; therefore, most likely, they will never see Him. However, there are some exceptions.

A *preterist* is one who believes part or all biblical prophecy has been fulfilled, including the Second Coming of the Messiah. A preterist believes the Lord is zealous for Zion and bringing His Word to pass. In scriptures, there are clues to the generation and era Yeshua was referencing in the fulfillment of His return: the first century. He did not tarry for long; His return was only delayed for a short time, about a generation or less.

A *futurist* believes much is still yet to be fulfilled and that we are in a pause in the prophecy with little progress in the fulfillment of the Lord's Word. In their view, the Lord tarries for almost two millennia.

Figuratively there are two perspectives about His visitation: the futurist doesn't believe the dinosaur ever lived on this earth because they have never seen the dinosaur alive with their own eyes. They either don't know there are signs, evidence and clues in history to support fulfillment or they know it, but choose to set it aside and ignore them. A preterist doesn't need to see the dinosaur to believe it once was present here on this earth. They just look at its footprints and bones that seem to say, "I was here". They don't have to see it to believe it. There is an element of faith here. So basically, the futurists want to see the dinosaur or Yeshua come again. The preterist sees the footprints, or signs, left behind and draws a conclusion that the dinosaur, or Yeshua, was here at some point or may still be present. The futurist says, "The dinosaur wasn't here, I want to see the dinosaur". The preterist says, "The dinosaur was here, look at the signs of its presence here in the past".

It is also like finding footprints at your window which is a sign that someone has visited you. They are watching you, they are much closer than you think, and someone is causing all these strange and unusual things to happen on your property that they wrote to you they were going to do. A preterist looks at the signs that were written in scripture to us about what would happen and says someone was here, but a futurist ignores them and doesn't believe someone was here until they see the person in flesh.

> It is the glory of God to conceal a matter, but the glory of kings is to search out a matter. (Proverbs 25:2)

This book is like an investigative study into how in prophecy we arrived to this state of our planet and how it could be God bringing to fulfillment the passing away right before us. There has to be an explanation as to what has occurred in history, the footprints. If believers, of these latter generations, are to rule in the new earth, then we as possible kings and queens should seek to understand this. We can connect these footprints or clues to His presence here.

> You will seek Me and find Me when you search for Me with all your heart. (Deuteronomy 4:29; Proverbs 8:17; Jeremiah 29:13; Matthew 7:7; Luke 11:9; Acts 17:24-28)

This book draws the parallel between fulfillment of biblical prophecy and the increasing signs the world is seeing in the impending extinction of this earth: earthquakes, powerful storms, super volcanoes, climate change, diminishing food supplies, and increased populations. Many call what they are witnessing "biblical" or "Noah-like," and it literally is when we look at how much of the prophecy has been fulfilled.

Yeshua's words are coming to pass and have not been fruitless or empty. This book is not an attempt to go in-depth with the scientific explanation of climate change. I write about two controversial issues that are aligning with scripture. This book does not scratch "itching ears," telling people what they want or like to hear or what they are used to hearing.

It is not so much "the Lord is coming soon" as it is that He has visited this place unbeknownst to many as a "thief in the night" as they sleep. Even now, He visits without the world knowing or recognizing the time of God's visitation to them—just as He has done several times before in scripture. He is more present than we think. His coming was not once and then gone; but His coming was an extended visitation in the Day of the Lord.

According to Wikipedia.org, the word *Parousia* means "the physical presence of a person" and "the prospect of the physical arrival of that person, especially the visit of a royal or official personage and sometimes as an extension of this usage, a formal occasion." Yeshua's Parousia, or visitation, is spiritually physical. The spiritual can be physical, but it has a different substance and a different ability or power than what we understand as naturally physical. It can be sensed only through the Holy Spirit with our spirits and not the flesh. There are natural signs that stem from the spiritual realm. The Day of the Lord can span thousands of years: "With the Lord a day is like a thousand years, and a thousand years are like a day" (2 Peter 3:8–9). In this Day of the Lord, King Yeshua has visited in fulfillment of the Word of God.

KING YESHUA'S VISITATION

Luke 19:44 speaks of Jerusalem not recognizing His visitation in flesh and blood. Most of Israel did not recognize His coming in flesh to earth. They were blind and hardened. He lived among them and worked many miracles, but was rejected and pierced. His message ignored, dismissed, and distorted among them to keep others from believing. Many Jews in the first century missed His coming in flesh and blood as He dwelt and walked among them. It is possible to not know of or miss His visitation to earth.

The wise men from the east knew a king was coming to Israel by observing the shining star as it led them. How did wise men from the east know and understand this sign, but Israel in the first century missed this sign of the coming of their own anointed one, Yeshua Hamashiach? The shining star moved across the night sky unhidden from the world below, so how did Jews and other nations miss something that glorious and unusual occurring above them? How was an unusual star not noticed or understood? Were they so consumed with their own lives not to take notice until it was pointed out to them? Maybe they saw the sign and didn't know what to make of it. They did not know how to interpret the sign. *That star, or object, was a sign hidden in plain sight. That star was a footprint of someone great and renowned in the heavens arriving to earth, yet so few knew and understood it. The star, so visible and obvious, yet it was hidden like a thief in the night. Those few people who are alert, wise, and believe see it and make a correct interpretation of Scripture. Among His own people, Yeshua was hidden in plain sight.*

Likewise, there are signs in history, or footprints, believers today must recognize to know He has been here, even in glory, throughout the centuries in accordance with Scripture which mark a fulfillment. These are historical accounts that are clues or signs hidden in plain sight that indicate someone great and renowned in the heavens arrived and visits. He is hidden in plain spiritual sight as a thief in the night. If we fail to recognize and interpret the signs correctly, we may never know He was here and we could miss His visitation. Just as many Jews in the first century failed to recognize His visitation in flesh and blood, many others fail to recognize Him in Spirit in the following centuries.

> And He was also saying to the crowds, "When you see a cloud rising in the west, immediately you say, 'A shower is coming,' and so it turns out. And when a south wind blowing, you say, 'It will be a hot day,' and it turns out.

You hypocrites! You know how to analyze the appearance of the earth and the sky, but why do you not analyze this present time?" (Luke 12:54–56; see also Matthew 16:1–4)

This same question should be asked of today's generation, *why do you not analyze this present time* correctly? How come you don't know what's up?

He made visitations to earth before in the Old Testament, unknown to the world, but only to a select few (see chapter 7). His Parousia can be understood as either one visitation or three visitations as He traverses between heaven and earth. There was one around AD 70–96 in accordance with Zechariah 12 and Matthew. There was another visitation around AD 1096–1291 after the millennial reign in battle and judgment against the nations around Jerusalem in accordance with Ezekiel 38-39 and Zechariah 14. Another separate visitation could happen imminently in deliverance of His people out of a dying earth, which is prophesied to pass away or go extinct.

According to a futurist viewpoint and interpretation, there is hardly any time left to fulfill everything that will be fulfilled according to their view. It doesn't fit. The door to spreading the Gospel is closing, and this extinction has already begun. There is a calling of humankind to death and judgment in this "fleeing" of heaven and earth in His presence or visitation. Believers should rethink their interpretations and see how out of line they are. It is getting to the point where the holy remain holy and the wicked remain wicked because no one else can be saved after He shuts the door.

"Heaven and earth fled from His presence" (Revelation 20:11). The word *fled* is important because that is what scientists are observing with climate change. It is also what could happen when the heavens begin to display strange things and passes away with planet earth. It is happening faster, stronger, and worse than they had anticipated. What they thought would take centuries or decades is happening in much less time and at a rapid rate. This is the *fleeing* they are witnessing, which concerns and frightens many people. The Bible speaks of this rapid end.

- Flee. To run away or escape from danger or unpleasantness. To pass away swiftly; vanish. To go rapidly, go swiftly.

- Rapid. Moving, progressing, or occurring with speed; swift; fast; quick.

- Swift. Moving with great speed, rapid, fast; coming or happening or done quickly or suddenly, undelayed.

This happens in the presence of the Lord. Heaven and earth flee from Him, but there is no place for them to go. If we are witnessing earth going through extinction (passing away), it is a sign that He is present because heaven and earth flee from His presence. The passing away happens very quickly, and it accelerates.

- Vanish. To go or pass suddenly from sight; disappear; to decay or fade to nothing; pass gradually out of existence; to cease to exist; come to an end.

Scientists are noticing more holes in the ozone. They will notice more strange things disappearing in our atmosphere and in the night sky, including the stars. Isaiah 51:6–7 says the heavens will *vanish* away like smoke. Going by this definition, the heavens will pass suddenly from sight, disappear, fade to nothing, cease to exist, and come to an end. This doesn't sound like just a purging, but destruction.

I agree with preterists about some things, but there are other things I don't agree with them: that God is finished with the Jews, that their return to their land has nothing to do with Bible prophecy today, that the church can replace Israel or be the New Israel, that God can't work with Israel today because they have rejected Him, and that the fall of Babylon was the destruction of Jerusalem by the Romans. I don't accept those viewpoints at all.

The fall of Babylon was the end to the prophesied kingdoms that were mentioned in Daniel. When a tall tree is cut down near the root, everything on top and within the tree falls too. The rock of Daniel, God's kingdom, brought down these worldly kingdoms. His kingdom brought an end to the earthly ones that no longer exist.

The prophecies that have been fulfilled include the Second Coming, the first resurrection, the beast, millennial reign/the Day of the Lord, Gog and Magog, and Satan's defeat.

The prophecies that are currently being fulfilled include the passing away of heaven and earth, the Day of the Lord, the beginning of second resurrection, sheep and goats/wheat and tares, the kingdom in the midst of us, Yeshua's presence during the fleeing, and the Jews gathered in Israel.

The prophecies that are still to come include the end of death, the passing of heaven and earth in fire, judgments, the completion of the second resurrection, Israel seeing Yeshua as the Spirit is poured out, Him being revealed to them in spirit, and a new heaven and earth to come.

Knowledge is power, and truth is freedom. Many speak of having seen Yeshua. How does Yeshua come before His Second Coming unless He came already? There seem to be no progression or advancement in prophecy or faith accordingly. There is a first-century mentality and understanding.

It is like Apollos in Acts who preached John's baptism but didn't know of Yeshua's baptism. There is a veil or a sense of being uninformed.

In this seemingly hidden divine visitation, the understanding of contacts or bridges across dimensions is lost on the churches. What idols, unholy objects, and poles are to the unsaved, and what the Ark of the Covenant, articles, and elements in the holy temple were to Israel, the water, Spirit, and blood of Yeshua are to believers today since His first coming. Many don't see a hidden law at work in bridges or contacts between the natural world we dwell in, the spirit world, and heaven. The church's understanding of it has been lost and darkened over time. They are reduced to symbols that hold no power. Water, Spirit, and the body and blood are the God-established bridges or contacts between this realm and heaven, which is where the Father's throne is by faith.

Many in the world and in the church do not believe the signs of climate change are real or are unaware. They see life as business as usual. They don't understand that they are witnessing the last century and the last decades. Many people think this is false or made up. Some even go so far as to mock it and criticize those who are concerned and care about this issue. Noah was the preacher of righteousness. The people of the world did not believe him or understand him. Lot's sons-in-law did not believe the angels or Lot. What happened to them? By the time they saw what Noah, Lot, and the angels said was coming to pass, it was too late for them. They all perished.

We must be careful not to neglect what was said by the prophets of God, what is being said by the scientists who observe the signs, and by the Word of the Lord, which spoke of these things long ago. Science is confirming what was written in scripture thousands of years ago. They are just uncovering what God said would happen long ago.

When referring to climate change deniers, one scientist said, "You can say you don't believe in gravity, but the apple is still going to hit you on the head. You can say you don't believe in climate change, but it is not going to stop it from getting hotter." You could also say, "God does not exist," "Yeshua is not the Son of God," "Climate change is not true," or "He has not returned," but it is not going to stop the Rock, Yeshua, from crushing those who sleep if they are in His way. It is not going to stop His Word from coming to pass at the appointed time.

This takes precedence over anything else; this dominates after the preaching of the Gospel of the kingdom. This crisis is a sign that the door to salvation is closing. People talk more about politics, the economy, their personal lives, business, and money, but this mammoth problem has no place—or only a small place—in their lives. Many people don't give it much thought. They are not seeking the Lord about this.

The time when no more souls can be saved is quickly approaching. This is it.

Concerning climate change, Michael Ruppert said, "It is high time we turn our full gaze and attention to this. This is a culminating event of all of what we have called history. It's here, it's now, it's what we came here to witness and be a part of. There's no game left to play, but to face it. Not facing it will produce … a fire in a madhouse."

One should read this book prayerfully, with an open mind, and without listening to any gut feelings, which could stem from the flesh. Listen to what the Spirit is saying. We must hear what the Spirit is saying. Many people, I realize, won't take this seriously and will think it is foolish or heretical. Many people will reject this message despite the explanations and descriptions of the signs. The easiest thing to do is ignore the reality of the catastrophe unfolding and the peril the earth and its inhabitants are in. It is easier to say, "I don't agree with this" or "I don't believe this." This would be easier than facing the reality of the truth.

This book is a wake-up call to everyone as a watchman to open the door to the King in humility and greet Him. The time of this earth and its inhabitants' existence is short. All must take heed that the ancient King renowned in the heavens traverses to and fro. He is displacing the powers and principalities in high places as the conquering King and causing the nations of the world to be displaced as well. Could this be why sightings of UFOs are on the rise? They too flee from Him when they have nowhere else to go?

Many have witnessed visitations during this time. The heavens above, the earth below, and below the earth—in every dimension—are affected and impacted by His presence. No one and no thing can escape His judgment. The natural world as we know it is being stripped away, the old is passing, and the new is coming in. Will we adjust and proceed with Him—or will we not proceed with Him, turn back, and be destroyed?

To be saved, we must have the testimony of the God-established witnesses over us. This is written about later in this book. We must not become as those in Noah and Lot's generations were before their destructions: so busy with our lives that we become unaware, indifferent, hardened, asleep, and not ready for departure. We must recognize the time of His visitation upon us: the visitation of the great King, Yeshua, renowned in the heavens.

PART I

Preterism: A Type of Watchman

Chapter 1

Lift Your Eyes to the Heavens, Look on the Earth Beneath

Heaven and earth pass away according to the Word of God:

> Lift up your eyes to the heavens, and look on the earth beneath, for the heavens will vanish away like smoke, the earth will grow old like a garment, and those who dwell in it will die in like manner, but my salvation will be forever, and my righteousness will not be abolished. (Isaiah 51:6; see also Isaiah 66:22–24)

> From whose face the earth and the heaven fled away. (Revelation 20:11)

> And I saw a new heaven and a new earth, for the first heaven and the first earth had passed away. Also there was no more sea. (Revelation 21:1)

> Heaven and earth will pass away, but My words will by no means pass away. (Matthew 24:35)

> Of old You laid the foundation of the earth, and the heavens are the work of Your hands. They will perish, but You will endure; yes, all of them will grow old like a garment; like a cloak You will change them and they will be changed. (Psalm 102:25–27; see also Hebrews 1:11, 12)

> But the day of the Lord will come as a thief in the night, in which the heavens will pass away with a great noise, and the elements will melt with fervent heat; both the earth and works that are in it will be burned up … looking for and hastening the coming of the day of God, because of which the heavens will be dissolved being on fire, and the elements will melt with fervent heat? Nevertheless we, according to His promise, look for new heavens and a new earth in which righteousness dwells. (2 Peter 3:10, 12, 13 NASB)

Extinction. How did we come to this in prophecy? This is exactly what the above scriptures are talking about, yet there are signs of it already beginning to come to pass. Scriptures coincide with what is now being witnessed with extinction (or passing away). It is underway right now.

The following are species that have disappeared, never to be in existence again. These animals' DNA is forever lost. It is irreversible. They will never come back apart from God's will. The following are some species that have gone extinct in the last 150–200 years: the Northern White Rhinoceros in March 2018, the Spix Macaw, the Thylacine or Tasmanian tiger or wolf, the Passenger Pigeon, the Quagga, the Pyrenean Ibex in 2000, the Golden Toad in 1989, the Zanzibar Leopard, the Po'ouli, the Madeiran Large White butterfly, Carolina parakeet, West African Black Rhino, Tecopa Pupfish, Falkland Islands wolf, Javan Tiger, Round Island Burrowing Boa, Pinta Island Tortoise in 2012, Dutch Alcon Blue Butterfly, Schomburgk's Deer, the Dodo in 1662, Baiji White dolphin in 2002, Heath Hens, Caribbean Monk Seal in 2008, Caspian Tiger in 1970, Alaotra Grebe in 2010, Formosan Clouded Leopard, the Liverpool Pigeon, Christmas Island Pipistrelle (bat) in 2009, Madagascar Hippopotamus in 2014, Yangtze River Dolphin in 2006, Japanese River Otter, Stellars Sea Cow, the Great Auk in 1844, the Bramble Cay melomys in 2016. As stated before, they have disappeared, never to be in existence again. These animals' DNA is forever lost. It is irreversible. They will never come back apart from God's will.

The following is a list of animals that is on the precipice of extinction, their numbers are too low. Once gone, they are gone forever. In Australia, there are wombats, sharks, possums, frogs at risk of extinction. Some other endangered species are the African Wild Dog, Amur Leopard, Amur Tiger, Asian Elephant, Bengal Tiger, Black-Footed Ferret, Black Spider

Monkey, Blue Whale, Bluefin Tuna, Bonobo, Borneo Pygmy Elephant, Bornean Orangutan, Chimpanzee, Eastern Lowland Gorilla, Fin Whale, Galapagos Penguin, Giant Panda, Green Turtle, Hawksbill Turtle, Hector's Dolphin, Humphead Wrasse, Indian Elephant, Indochinese Tiger, Indus River Dolphin, Javan Rhino, Leatherback Sea Turtle, Loggerhead Sea Turtle, Malayan Tiger, Mountain Gorilla, North Atlantic Right Whale, Pangolin, Snow Leopard, Sea Lions, Sei Whale, Sri Lankan Elephant, Sumatran Elephant, Sumatran Orangutan, Sumatran Rhino, Sumatran Tiger, Western Lowland Gorilla, Yangtze Finless Porpoise, and many more to come.

According to scripture, everything is passing away unless He mercifully reserves and preserves a certain amount as He did in Noah's day to preserve the species and repopulate the new earth under a new heaven.

According to *The Conversation.com*, many Australian species are disappearing:

> The thylacine is the most recognized and mourned of our lost species, but the lesser bilby has gone, so too the pig-footed bandicoot, the Toolache wallaby, the white-footed rabbit-rat, along with many other mammals that lived only in Australia. The paradise parrot has joined them, the robust white-eye, the King Island emu, the Christmas Island forest skink, the southern gastri-brooding frog, the Phillip Island glory pea, and at least another 100 species that were part of the fabric of this land, part of what made Australia distinctive.
>
> And that's just the tally for known extinctions. Many more have been lost without ever being named. Still others hover in the graveyard – we're not sure whether they linger or are gone.
>
> The losses continue: three Australian vertebrate species became extinct in the past decade. Most of the factors that caused losses remain unchecked, and new threats are appearing, intensifying, expanding. Many species persist only in slivers of their former range and in a fraction of their previous abundance, and the long-established momentum of their decline will soon take them over the brink.

> They represent failures in our duty of care, legislation, policy and management. They give witness to, and warn us about, the malaise of our land and waters.

This could be said of other animal species and the way humankind stewards the planet in other continents now and in the near future. Even now there are massive die offs of animals on land, air, and water. There have been thousands and millions of species falling from the sky or washing up from the oceans dead in various regions on earth.

Futurists don't make the connection between this increasing trend and scripture. This sign is not taken into consideration among them. I have not heard any futurist teachers speak to this in their interpretation of prophecy. Its place in their prophetic teachings is thousands of years from now, but how can that be when it is happening now and for the last two centuries? It is not acknowledged right now. Many prophets and teachers in the church, but none or few of them acknowledge this. Yet this was prophesied in scripture to happen and it is now occurring in the last two centuries and in our lifetimes. Their focus is not extinction, but *a beast is to come to defile a third temple, Yeshua is coming soon to Jerusalem to take us away in fulfillment of Zechariah 12, and we return to rule the planet for one thousand years, then Satan deceives the nations and there will be World War III as the nations surround Jerusalem in Armageddon.* All these things have been fulfilled. How do the saints rule on a dead, burning planet? The visible millennial reign on this present earth can't happen if there is near or complete extinction.

We are much further along in prophecy than they realize. We can't ignore the fact that there are many species of animals that are no longer here on earth or they have very low and decreasing numbers and then say *extinction and endangerment is not happening.* We can't ignore this increasing trend that there is a dying in process according to the word of God. If we do ignore this, we set His word aside and reject the truth of His word.

We are to proclaim the good news and the great news of the kingdom of heaven. This book is not intended to destroy people's faith or cause division; it is meant to increase the faith of the saints and edify the body of Yeshua. Believers in Yeshua must come into alignment with reality and prophecy. An increase in knowledge and wisdom brings an increase in faith and the expansion and takeover by the kingdom of heaven over what remains of the defeated and vanquished kingdom of darkness.

It is my desire that others become watchmen as they witness the fulfillment of God's Word, the passing away of this earth, and the visitation of a Great King. Our conquering King will take over the kingdom of darkness and everything in it. This writing is not meant to turn hearts away from God—unlike those of 2 Thessalonians 2 and 2 Timothy 2, which were not in line with the truth in that era. It will draw them even closer to Him in the fulfillment of the truth. It is not meant to go into the science of climate change or extinction, but it will bring awareness to how the signs that scientists now observe are the signs of scripture fulfillment.

When it comes to interpretation and fulfillment of prophecies such as the Second Coming, the millennial reign, the beast, Gog and Magog, and the defeat and judgment of the devil, it must not be interpreted from just a natural perspective and not with the eyes of the flesh. Interpret them with faith, with eyes of the spirit, and from a spiritual perspective. Many Christian interpretations are metaphorical and symbolic and have no power to them. Many Christians do not believe very much has been fulfilled, and they are still waiting for God to fulfill His Word. He's already been there and done that. They are sleeping when they should awaken to the times we are living in.

The increase in the knowledge of truth brings an increase in faith that is accompanied by the power of the Holy Spirit. God confirms and endorses faith in the knowledge of truth with His presence, power, and works. This increase brings a rise above the level of jurisdiction that many believers are already in. According to the level of knowledge and faith one has in the spiritual realm, it is manifested in the natural realm (Hebrews 11:1; 2 Corinthians 5:7; 4:13–18).

It takes faith to be a preterist today. A preterist in the first century would be a liar because he was not aligned with the truth. He went ahead of the truth at that time. A believer's faith must keep pace with the truth and the knowledge of truth: Yeshua. A futurist today relies on the eyes of the flesh to "see the coming" and not on the Spirit. As a preterist, I do not believe my faith was destroyed as those in 2 Thessalonians 2 or 2 Timothy 2 believed. As faith grows, one is encouraged and drawn nearer to Him.

Scientists have a certain type of faith that there are things that exist unseen by the human eye: bacteria, virus, light and sound waves, gases, evaporation in the water cycle, and radiation. However, there are manifestations and evidence that make it appear as though something is there. A virus is unseen to our natural eye, but there are manifestations of its presence, which can be called its footprint or clues. Astronauts took a leap of faith to go to moon for the first time. They did the calculations, understood how laws worked, theorized, and tested. Without knowing exactly how successful it would be, they figured out how to build a rocket to launch into space and make it come back to earth safely. They asked for support from the government, the people, and their leaders. Their faith was in the knowledge of the truths they discovered. They built and acted on that knowledge, and with courage and a type of faith they had, a great thing was accomplished for humankind.

Climate change, environmental destruction, and other kinds of unforeseen disasters are bringing about the extinction of the inhabitants of the earth—and that was prophesied in scripture. Other kinds of disasters that are coming are plagues, super volcano eruptions, and asteroids. Scripture doesn't label it as such, but it is written that heaven and earth will pass away, which is synonymous with extinction. Earth has been blessed to avoid major devastation for many centuries. During the existence of the human species, earth and its inhabitants have been protected and shielded from destruction by divine providence. According to prophecy, everything is to perish before the judgment of the dead. This is how the first earth ends, and many of the dead will stand before the "great white throne" in the book of Revelation. The death of many people and all species of animals will result from some form of destruction in the end of the first earth. It is here; it has arrived.

In decades to come, shortly, believers must prepare for the test of their faith and courage. If the Lord wills we stay in the old earth, things will get really competitive with earth's resources. Persecutions might increase because of this. Believers must know what to ask, seek, and knock on heaven's door.

Noah, Lot, and the Hebrews had to act to show their faith when they had to build an ark, pack their belongings, and migrate to a new region that was unfamiliar to them. Some believers today think we won't have to do anything, but we might have to act in obedience to the Lord's direction. Why do we think Noah's, Lot's, and Moses' generations and the first-century believers had to act according to knowledge and faith, but we are somehow exempt and excluded?

A spirit of complacency and assumption pervades Christians today. We must not assume the King will do everything, but we never ask Him about it. We need to be praying. Are we ready? Will we obey Him or doubt and deny what is happening, causing us to shrink back to destruction like those in Noah's and Lot's day? Are we going to seek to save our lives for His sake or lose it? Is your heart on the old or the new? There may be nothing we will have to do; the King may take care of everything for us. However, what if it is required that we act by faith? Are we going to argue, doubt, question, debate, deny, ignore, remain ignorant, and waste time? Will we obey Him when there is a call for action?

In Elohim's time, in just over an hour (150 years), earth has been polluted and destroyed. Violence has increased, and all kinds of species are vanishing at a rapid pace. According to the Word of the Lord, heaven and earth will die and burn. It has already begun, and it is inevitable. There is no time for all the things futurists believe to be fulfilled in prophecy to happen. We all must draw even nearer to Him. Jews have a veil over them and do not recognize the First Coming of the Messiah. Most believers today have a veil over them and do not recognize the Second Coming. I pray that this veil will be lifted so they can understand and keep step with Yeshua.

We must wake up to what is happening on earth and wake up to the Spirit of prophecy in the Messiah. We are under a visitation of a great King. The heavens and earth will pass away in His presence (Revelation 20:11). The phrase "from whose face" indicates in His presence or Him being present and not distant. This indicates a visitation.

It is bittersweet that animals, babies, and children will suffer. Everything will perish and be swallowed up in death—and then death in the lake of fire. We will be in the presence of a great and renowned King. In this takeover of one kingdom over another seen and unseen kingdom, His holy saints can look forward to a new heaven and new earth, which will be an upgrade.

We get to be a part of this and witness whether this first earth will be renewed, recycled, or purged. Will the new earth be another completely virginal planet, untouched by death, evil, curses, sorrow, corruption, and wickedness? Will we witness another virginal planet earth that is untarnished and never knowing any form of dark deeds or wickedness?

Many people of the world are depressed because all it has ever known is being taken away from them. They want to keep the out-of-date, old, broken earth, but His faithful will inherit an upgraded new earth. People of the world are being evicted because they can't pay the rent or the wages for their sins. The King is requiring payment they cannot give.

Everyone loves upgrades—even the King! The Master wants a new footstool, and He shall have a new footstool. Should He keep an old, broken one? How will anyone convince Him to save or keep the old, defiled, worn-out, dilapidated, broken footstool? We must keep in step with the King and follow His lead.

The signs of earth's deterioration are called a landmark because it is a huge sign that cannot be ignored anymore. The signs can be seen, heard, and felt all over the planet. Some in the church deny climate change by quoting Genesis 8:22: "While earth remains, seedtime and harvest, and cold and heat, and winter and summer, and day and night shall not cease." They believe this earth will remain forever, but that is not what this verse suggests. It does not say, "The earth shall remain forever" or "Without end the earth shall remain." It says, "While earth remains," its *function* shall not end. As long as the earth lives, this is the order in which it shall function. This implies that when earth dies or does not remain, these functions or its order will change and cease. With earth's existence, there is a ceaseless set of functions; without earth's existence, the functions will cease.

This is what is already started happening in many areas of earth—even in California. Heaven and earth's passing away is the same as an extinction (Isaiah 51:4–6; 66:17–25; Psalm 102:25–26; Matthew 24:35; Hebrews 1:11, 12; and Revelation 20:11). With this passing, we are gradually witnessing a change in seedtime and harvest, cold and heat, winter and summer. In parts of the world, winters are shorter, and summers are longer. Every summer has been "hottest summer" for a few years now, and global temperatures are increasing. Blossoms bloom earlier, and birds migrate earlier than usual. Farmers are losing their harvests due to severe drought, famine, or disease. Crops are affected by the extremes in heat, cold, and moisture. Droughts in 2010–2013 had a global affect, especially in Egypt. According to the Megan Detrie, with *Egypt Independent* in 2012:

> Egypt might have to look beyond the world's biggest wheat exporter to feed its hungry nation, after the worst drought in more than a decade has wilted US grain crops.
>
> Egypt imports more than half of its wheat supplies . . . and almost a quarter of that amount comes from the US.
>
> The rising cost of wheat could leave Egypt, which is the world's top consumer of the commodity, scrambling to find affordable sources of it.

Most of Egypt's wheat is imported from the US, Russia and Australia, making the country particularly vulnerable to potential wheat price shocks caused by extreme weather this year. This problem was highlighted when Russia stopped wheat exports in 2010 after a drought and a series of wildfires devastated it harvest. About half of Egypt's imported wheat comes from Russia.

Chapter ten is about the prophecy of the plague of worldwide drought written in Zechariah 14. This is fulfillment of prophecy.

> Then it will come about that any who are left of all the nations that went against Jerusalem will go up from year to year to worship the King, the Lord of hosts, and to celebrate the Feast of Booths. And it will be that whichever of the families of the earth does not go up to Jerusalem to worship the King, the Lord of hosts, there will be no rain on them. If the family of Egypt does not go up or enter, then no rain will fall on them; it will be the plague with which the Lord smites the nations who do not go up to celebrate the Feast of Booths. (Zechariah 14:16–19)

While Canada had too much water, which destroyed its crops, droughts hit China, Russia, and the Ukraine. Russia's drought affected Egypt since they get their supply of wheat from them. There are the signs of the Lord's Day in certain parts of the earth that are not normal.

Insects are slowly disappearing. In the seventies, when my dad was driving through the country or taking a long drive, there were a lot of insects on the front of his car. Nowadays, many people notice that there has been a decrease of insects on vehicles after a long drive. Where are they going?

In an article in *The Guardian* written by Kris Holt, insects are beginning to disappear rapidly:

> Insects are dying so rapidly, they could disappear within 100 years.
>
> "It is very rapid. In 10 years you will have a quarter less, in 50 years only half left and in 100 years you will have none,"

> co-author Francisco Sanchez-Bayo, an environmental biologist at the University of Sydney, told the *Guardian*. "If insect species losses cannot be halted, this will have catastrophic consequences of both the planet's ecosystems and for the survival of mankind."

According to an article published on February 11, 2020 by Marlow Hood, scientists give a "warning to humanity to stop killing insects now before it's too late".

> Half of the 1 million animal and plant species on Earth facing extinction are insects, and their disappearance could be catastrophic for humankind, scientists have said in a "warning to humanity".
>
> "The current insect extinction crisis is deeply worrying", said Pedro Cardoso, a biologist at the Finnish Museum of Natural History.
>
> The disappearance of bugs that fly, crawl, burrow, jump and walk on water is part of a gathering mass extinction event, only the sixth in the last half-billion years.
>
> The main drivers are dwindling and degraded habitat, followed by pollutants – especially insecticides - and invasive species.
>
> Over-exploitation – more than 2,000 species of insects are part of the human diet – and climate change are also taking a toll.
>
> Many animals rely on abundant insects to survive.

Since many animals rely on insects to survive, when insects disappear, there begins a collapse in the food web. Animals that depend on them begin to starve and die off too.

Farmers in Kansas and California in recent years have had to wait for rain to come to water the seeds they planted to take root and produce a harvest, but some are finding a weak crop that is barely there. Crops are not flourishing or healthy.

Bees are vanishing, and they are essential for pollination and the production of food. In this *bee colony collapse*, the bees go out to pollinate, but they never return to the hive. They disappear or die somewhere. They attribute this to be caused by a man made product. In part this is true.

Georgia Slater in the article titled, "Scientists Warn Bumblebees Might Be Going Extinct Due to Climate Crisis":

> Bumblebee species are drastically declining—possibly risking extinction—due to the world's heightened climate crisis.
>
> Findings suggest that due to climate change, the odds of seeing a bumblebee in North America and Europe have declined by an average of 30 percent.
>
> "If decline continue at this pace, many of these species could vanish forever within a few decades," first author Peter Soroye said.
>
> "We found that populations were disappearing in areas where the temperatures had gotten hotter," Soroye explained.
>
> Scientists discovered that the bees preferred cooler, wet conditions and variations in seasons. As the rising temperatures are drying out habitats, this could be raising the risk of extinction and lack of colonization.

Penguins in the polar regions have to search farther and harder for food due to the icebergs melting. Penguins, for the sake of their colonies, will leave on suicide marches in search of food and get lost. They never return to their colonies.

As the earth dies, its functions begin to cease. According to many scientists, we are now in the sixth extinction. The extinction rate is about two hundred species a day, and that is likely to dramatically increase in the next few decades. About half of wildlife populations are only half of what they were four decades ago. Land animals are dropping dead in the fields by the hundreds and thousands. Dead crabs, whales, and fish wash up on the shore, and birds—for no reason—fall from the sky dead.

The oceans are dying, including the coral reefs and the life that depends on it. Oceans are acidifying. In the video, *Years of Living Dangerously*, marine biologist Hoegh-Guldberg states that

> Eighty percent of coral reefs disappeared in the Caribbean since the 1970's and forty to fifty percent of coral was lost across the planet in the last fifty years. Within twenty to thirty years time, you don't have coral anymore.

It will cease to exist at the rate of stress we are putting on it.

Species of lizards can no longer be found; they are becoming extinct. Sequoia trees in California are beginning to die.

Saiga antelopes are one of many endangered animals. In 2015, the *Los Angeles Times* reported on the mysterious mass deaths of the saiga antelope.

> More than 120,000 critically endangered saiga antelopes—more than one-third of the worldwide populations—have died in Kazakhstan since mid-May, and the cause of the "catastrophic collapse" is unclear, officials said. Not a single animal survived in the affected herds ... Pasteurella and Clostridia bacteria exacerbated the die-off, but they are not lethal unless the animal already has a weakened immune system, so experts are still trying to identify the underlying cause.

Some have speculated that the increase in global temperature is causing the bacteria naturally found in them to turn against them and kill them. Coral reefs are dying all over the ocean floors. People can't breathe the air in certain parts of China, and some young children have never seen a blue sky or a star.

Glaciers, seas, lakes, rivers are disappearing. There are water shortages occurring in parts of the world, including the United States. Wells are running dry. Islands, Florida, and Louisiana are just a few areas on earth that are beginning to sink into the ocean. There are countries and nations that will no longer exist because they are sinking underwater. Leaders are searching for real estate for their island nations.

Huge amounts of methane are being released in the Arctic as the permafrost melts, which causes earth's temperature to rise even more quickly. There is a depletion of fisheries. Plastic is found in abundance, polluting the Pacific Ocean, which much of marine life consumes and then perishes. The oceans are becoming warmer and more acidic, making it nearly impossible for marine life to survive and thrive.

God spoke about what 97 percent of scientists are discovering, confirming what was already written and spoken of. Many believers in Yeshua, including many preterists, do not make a connection between the two. Some scientists are losing sleep at night and are terrified by what they observe happening. Some have resolved themselves to an end to life. Believers say it is a sign of an imminent Second Coming, but it's much more than that. It is a visitation that has been happening, unknown to many, and it's a threat of extinction upon this world. While many believe that heaven and earth will pass away thousands of years from now, they don't believe it is occurring right now.

Many people have not recognized the time of God's visitation to earth. It is my opinion, despite what many say, that what the world is witnessing was prophesied in 2 Peter 3:6, 7, 10–13. God controls the temperatures upon the earth, but also it is written that earth will heat up and be on fire. This is the fever the earth is experiencing. According to Peter, at some time in earth's existence, the temperature of earth will increase to fatal degrees.

Whether this is a man-made, a natural extinction, or a combination of the two, this one is happening much faster because of humanity. It is accelerating and worsening. Don't just look at the scientific data, say it's not enough, and dismiss it as just the "wisdom of men" because it is not constantly at your door as it is for other people in the world. Don't think, *It's over there—it doesn't concern me.*

The wisdom of men comes with errors and flaws, but as God allowed it, it has also given us medicine, technology, transportation, and other innovations that believers use in their daily lives. The terrifying changes on earth previously mentioned are not the wisdom of men. When many people observe coral reefs disappearing, that is not wisdom of men. When many people observe the fish are less in quantity and less in quality, this is not the wisdom of men. When various species of animals are dropping dead by the thousands and millions and scientists cannot explain why, this is not the wisdom of men.

When whales, seabirds, and dolphins are autopsied, and their bellies are full of plastic after they starved to death, this is not the wisdom of men. As islands sink and bodies of water (even in Israel) are drying up, this is not the wisdom of men.

There are instances where deer are seen strangely walking hypnotically in circles, around and around, for no reason. They are either rotating in place or revolving around a center as a herd. Birds are flocking in very large numbers in certain places. Strange trumpet sounds and booms have been heard in the sky in various countries, and no one knows where they are coming from. There is no source or explanation.

These are the terrifying observations and signs scientists and people who live in those areas—who may not be educated—have made. This is not normal anymore. Look at the signs they are seeing; they aren't making it up and telling tales. Look at the experiences and testimonies of people in other parts of the world; some of them could be your brothers and sisters in the Messiah. You can't dismiss what they are going through as the wisdom of men. The wisdom of men, though innovative, has its errors and its limits. It cannot save us from the catastrophes that are unfolding.

Other signs to consider in the passing away of earth are economic collapse, nationally and globally, recessions, mass migrations, civil and social unrest, increase in violence in various places, and massive flooding that has killed cattle and devastated farms. Radiation from the Fukushima nuclear plant, which was damaged by an earthquake and tsunami is 2011, is poisoning and killing marine life in the Pacific Ocean. Marine life is destroyed by agriculture runoff, which causes dead zones. Fisheries are almost depleted by overfishing. There is an increase in hauntings and demonic possessions.

A few years ago, whales were stalking fishing ships and stealing their catches. Now there are reports of whales washing up dead due to starvation. Polar bears are traveling thousands of miles to Russia and starving because they can't find food. The fish they eat are dying by the millions, and humans are overfishing what they eat. Also, the Amazon rainforest, which the earth needs, is being destroyed for profit. Forests and polar ice caps are like an air conditioner for the earth. Losing these will only accelerate heating up the planet. For more information, refer to the suggested videos and articles in the Online Resources in the back of this book.

It is happening so fast now that scientists are losing equipment in the polar regions where the ice is melting. Many towns, regions, nations, and cities are declaring emergencies, but there is no action. Indonesia is moving the capital city of ten million people to Jakarta due to the land sinking.

Seven hundred million people in forty-three countries face water scarcity. Desalination of seawater helps people, but it puts a strain on ocean life and still uses fossil fuels. According to *Bloomberg Businessweek*,

> Desalination is a poor solution—it's expensive and energy-intensive and produces more chemical-laced brine than potable water. Much of that brine, which is extra-salty and contains potentially harmful substances necessary for the desalination process, including copper and chlorine, is pumped back into the ocean. There, its density causes it to sink to the ocean floor, where it depletes oxygen and destroys marine life. According to a 2019 UN report, global desalination plants already produce 51.8 billion cubic meters of brine annually, enough to cover the entire state of Florida a foot deep. Last year a study of almost 180,000 people in Israel linked desalinated water to a 6 percent to 10 percent increase in heart disease. Plus, it tastes terrible.

Giant icebergs from Antarctica are being harvested and towed to supply fresh water to people in countries whose groundwater is vanishing. How long will this last with the atmosphere and oceans heating up quickly? Icebergs are quickly melting.

In *Bloomberg Businessweek,* Caroline Winter wrote,

> Meanwhile, more than 100,000 Antarctic icebergs melt into the ocean each year. They range from merely large to country-size (the biggest seen recently was the size of Jamaica), and by some calculations they contain more than the annual global consumption of fresh water. Rather than let that water slip away, several groups are vying for berg-towing funds and know-how. The European Union in 2010 received a proposal to pull icebergs from Newfoundland to the Canary Islands, which have long been short on fresh water; and the United Arab Emirates plans to test its prospects of importing icebergs by bringing one from the Antarctic to Australia or Cape Town by late 2020. In Germany, a company ... spent $2.8 million over the past six years hiring experts to complete a strategy for

getting Antarctic iceberg water to drought-stricken areas, with an emphasis on minimizing environmental impact.

To deny what is happening now is like a pregnant woman, at full term, who will not believe the truth that she is pregnant, just fat, despite the obvious signs that she feels, sees, the changes in her body, and what the doctors tell her. They tell her about the pain she will experience in childbirth and how she needs to prepare, but she stubbornly refuses. She just denies it because it will inconvenience her life. Ignoring the signs and the truth won't make the pregnancy and imminent painful birth go away. The truth is going to happen despite people ignoring it or wishing it away. We would consider a woman like that either dumb or crazy. These increasingly stronger birth pains are biblical (see 2 Peter 3:6, 7 10–13). Scientists are confirming what the apostle Peter wrote almost two thousand years ago (see Online Resources at the end of this book).

There are skeptics who would argue this isn't climate change and laugh at this, but the point is that earth is passing away according to the Word of God, whether the cause is man made climate change or not. The point is not *how* it is happening, but that it is happening. We shouldn't waste time debating on the how. Many Christians would rather deny extinction is even occurring now and place it several thousands of years away from now. This is a venomous snake they are choosing to ignore and pay no attention to. It is a bad sign and many just don't want to interpret the sign correctly. They'd rather believe that this snake doesn't exist, until it fatally bites them. According to the Scripture, it comes true:

> My people are destroyed for a lack of knowledge, because you have rejected knowledge, I also will reject you from being My priest. Since you have forgotten the law of your God, I also will forget your children. (Hosea 4:6) How can Christians be His priests if the priests won't stand in the gap?

How can God allow us to be stewards of the new earth if we don't pay attention to what is happening now to this one? Not that we can save earth for the Word of God shall come to pass. If Christians don't believe the word of God is being fulfilled now, then when holy instruction comes to do something, as it came to Noah, Moses, and Lot, they will not obey it and so be destroyed. What would have happened to Noah and his family if they didn't believe the flood was coming and refused to act and build the arc according to God's instruction? What would have happened to the Hebrews if they did not believe in God's deliverance, refused to obey the instruction of Passover, and then refused leave Egypt through the Red Sea? What would have come of Lot and his daughters if they ran back to the cities after the angels took their hands to lead them out or if they all looked back as Lot's wife did? "None of them would have perished", you say? You are gravely mistaken. The death of Lot's wife should serve as our example today. We can perish in our unbelief and disobedience. They will not *obey* the word of God because they do not *believe* the word of God is coming to fruition now. This reveals the true state of their hearts. They will only blindly continue with their lives like nothing is happening and because they ignore the snake and the word of God, their children will be fatally impacted by this.

A preterist must be in line with the truth and should not run too far ahead. This watchman or gatekeeper realizes that much has been fulfilled as the church sleeps or is unaware. The Great One—an ancient King from another world—has arrived and visited the earth, unknown to many, as a thief in the night. He is present while many sleep—just as the thief is present in the house as the people in the household slept. The gatekeeper and watchman will know when someone is present because they are alert. They know the danger of the passing of heaven and earth, and they know there should be prayers made when many are not praying as they should—and some even deny the warnings.

Noah, Moses, and Abraham were watchmen. They saw God face-to-face. God visited the earth when many of the Hebrews and other nations were unaware that a great King had visited the earth. How many nations at those times knew and understood that the God of heaven came to them and was present in the earth with them? How many Hebrews understood that there was to be destruction? How much of the world knew? Not many. Very few understood and believed. Just because most of the thousands of Hebrews did not see Him like Abraham and Moses did and God remained veiled to the majority of them, does not mean his visitation was less real or did not happen.

He was a thief in the night during the times of Noah, Abraham, and Moses, and now He is a thief in the night again. It does not make Noah, Moses, or Abraham false prophets. Many people did not believe Noah, and many people will not accept a watchman who sees the danger earth and its inhabitants face today. Many Christians believe He comes as a thief in the daytime—when everyone sees with the natural eye. No, He came to a certain generation with the eyes of the Spirit by the Spirit.

I believe God is preparing His people with the outpouring of His Spirit and the breaking down of walls between churches. Congregations, at this time of great crisis, should come together all the more in the name of Yeshua. The time of judgment is already at hand. This is not a time for complacency or competition or lengthy arguments that waste time. We must be ready for God's glory to be revealed in our midst. This is not a time to panic; it is time to act and pray in the Spirit. We must be ready to act in faith to whatever He commands or directs us to do for the remaining time here in preparation for leaving earth. This will be a migration of a different kind. It will help others—be it people or creation.

The tide is coming in, but who can stop it? Billions of dollars can be worthless when there is nothing to buy or sell that is necessary to life. A relationship with God through Yeshua is essential. He is salvation from this deadly tide coming in. We must seek His face and draw nearer to Him.

What do we pray? Pray that He will confirm and power the truth with His presence. Pray that congregations will wake up. Pray for salvation and deliverance from this. Pray for the wisdom to be prepared. Pray that our eyes and ears will be opened by the Holy Spirit so we can see God's kingdom. Pray that His provision of necessary resources. Pray for the earth that is too weak or unable to provide for His sheep.

As long as He wills us to live here—until He decides to remove us—pray that He will not allow the righteous to suffer and be destroyed with this. Pray that His holy name will be glorified and renowned in the world among His people because they notice a mighty presence in the midst of the people who care for them. Pray that He will provide redemption from this place because there is really no place on earth to migrate to. Pray that He will reveal Himself to the members and bodies of churches because we need Him now for comfort and encouragement and words that are seasoned with grace.

Much of the world is in a panic right now. The panic will only get worse when the heavens begin to change. Leaders are trying to figure out what to do. As the world despairs, God will become more and more present for His people. With the outpouring of His Spirit, we will see His face. We will see His salvation. The door to salvation is closing. When no one can be saved anymore, the Gospel can no longer be spread. Creation moans. Why believe Yeshua gave us authority over the earth if we do nothing with it? We let the world destroy the earth. It is His footstool—His Word stands—but it will die. No one can override a King's decree. If everything dies, everything dies. However, "the meek shall inherit the earth," whether it is this earth renewed or a virginal one that is untouched by sin and death. Are these birth pains signs of a return of Yeshua or a sign of One who has returned and in whose presence everything begins to die and flee? Yeshua never said these birth pains would end with His return. They very well could continue in His presence until this old earth is no more.

To understand how we got to this point in prophecy, I must first share—or cast upon the waters—my understanding of how the prophecy was fulfilled. I make the connections between history and biblical prophecy. In part two of this book I go into a different kind of visitation. I will explain contacts, bridges between dimensions, and the witness of water, Spirit, and blood in part two of this book.

If one wishes to get more information and look into more about climate change, there is a list of resources in the back of this book.

In the following chapters, I begin with the worldly kingdoms in prophecy and how events in history run parallel to what was written by the prophets.

CHAPTER 2
Kingdoms (Daniel 2:24–45 and Revelation 20:4–10)

Peace and Safety during the Roman Empire

Peace: 1 Thessalonians 5:3—Pax Romana in Roman times.

> For them, Roman civilization meant a period of relative peace, the so called Pax Romana, in which they could work their fields and carry on their business without interruption. For the townspeople the 'Peace of Rome' meant that the goods they bought were better made and varied. (The Last Two Million Years, 114–115)

Safety:

> The town was guarded by high walls, which were pierced by 4 main gates.

> . . . the 30 legions of the Roman army were stationed at strategic places near the perimeter. Besides the legions, the Roman army included auxiliary troops, recruited in the provinces and fighting with their traditional weapons.

> It was in this spirit of misguided optimism that his mint forthwith produced coins bearing cheerful slogans, such as 'The Security of the Roman People' and 'The Peace of the Whole World'. (The Twelve Caesars, 192).

This was done in a time of great civil war.

The Seventy Sevens

All the worldly kingdoms prophesied by Daniel and the kingdom of God run consecutively one right after the other one. There are no gaps between their existences as some teach. There are no gaps between the iron and iron-clay mix. There are no gaps between the iron-clay mix and the rock.

> Daniel did not imply any huge time gaps in his prophecy, and if he did, the prophecy would be useless. Only people place huge time gaps in prophecy, not God. (Schuldt, 269) In part, I agree. *While the kingdoms prophesied in Daniel run consecutively without any gaps, the seventy sevens have a pattern of gaps.*

It was God who separated the seventy sevens. He didn't say just seventy sevens. It was already broken up into three distinct parts for a reason, but why were they divided up by God?

A consistent pattern exists. There is a forty-year gap (a generation) between each of the seven periods. There is not just one mysterious gap that is unexplained. There are three forty-year gaps that show that the three seven eras signify something. This prophecy was foretold during the head of gold of the statue (Babylon). The seven sevens equal Medo-Persia (chest of silver). Sixty-two sevens equal Greece (abdomen and thighs of bronze). One seven equals Rome (legs of iron). The feet of iron and clay occur during and after the one seven is fulfilled.

If the seven sevens and the sixty-two sevens were consecutive, why did the angel separate the three at all? Why couldn't he just say the sixty-nine sevens and one seven? The seventy sevens are broken up into three parts, which calculate to 490 years alone.

Why are there forty-year gaps? What are they there for? What do these seventy sevens signify? Perhaps they signify important events, prophecy fulfillment, and action that occurred during these periods (Dan. 9:24–27). Could they be high points in the silver, bronze, and iron kingdoms of Daniel 2:38–45? Could they signify highlights and happenings to Israel, God's house, and rebellion? Or both? Are the gaps times of silence or inaction? It seems the gaps are silent, the sevens are high points.

Many futurists teach the one seven occurs two thousand years after

Messiah is cut off in our current age or a future one. *The seventy sevens are not for current or future generations, it was already fulfilled. It applies to past events not current and future. It also revolves around Israel.*

Antiochus Epiphanes was the first abomination of desolation. Some preterists believe the abomination of desolation mentioned in Daniel 9:27, in the one seven, is Antiochus Epiphanes. They take the seventy sevens out of order. Somehow they take the one seven and put it somewhere in the middle of the sixty-two sevens so that Antiochus Epiphanes fits in somehow. He does fit in, but not by combining the sevens or else it is sixty-nine sevens instead of seventy. Antiochus Epiphanes was in the sixty-two sevens, not the one seven. So the abomination of desolation mentioned in the one seven is a second abomination of desolation, not the first one.

The seventy weeks described in Daniel 9 are in order: seven weeks, sixty-two weeks, and then the one week. Many read the seventy sevens and think there is only one abomination of desolation in it. There are actually two abominations in this, though one of them is specifically mentioned. The last week or seven occurs *after* the Messiah is cut off. How is the abomination in Daniel 9:27 Antiochus Epiphanes, who defiled the temple in 167 BC before the Messiah was cut off? *If the abomination mentioned in the one seven is Antiochus Epiphanes, he should have come after Messiah, not before Messiah was cut off. So the abomination mentioned is not him, but another.*

The one seven following the sixty-two seven is suggesting there is another abomination of desolation to come after the Messiah is cut off.

This is what Yeshua was talking about in Matthew 24:15. There was another abomination to come after He died. When He mentioned this, he was nearing the end of His ministry; He was about to be cut off and have nothing. A short time after this, the one seven starts and another abomination comes. This cannot be Antiochus Epiphanes, though these two abominations are similar.

In Matthew 24:15, Yeshua is referencing Daniel (9:27; 12:11) that is another abomination of desolation. Daniel 11 is Antiochus Epiphanes, who cannot come after Messiah dies. There is not just one abomination in the seventy sevens, both are there. One is hidden in the sixty-two sevens and the other is spoken of in the one seven.

- seventy years of Babylonian captivity: (586 BC–516 BC)
- forty-year overlap/gap (536 BC–496 BC) or twenty-year gap (516 BC–496 BC)

- seven sevens equals forty-nine years (496 BC–447 BC)
- forty-year gap (447 BC–407 BC)
- sixty-two sevens equals 434 years (407 BC–AD 27) – Antiochus Ephiphanes, the first abomination of desolation.
- forty-year gap (AD 27–AD 67) or even (AD 33 to AD 73)
- one seven (AD 67–AD 73), which is the Jewish rebellion against Romans and the second abomination of desolation.

"Seventy-sevens are determined for your people and for your holy city."

- This is 490 years of prophecy, not including three forty-year gaps. It is the total scan. Israel, Jews, Jerusalem, and the temple are the focus—and not world events. Israel and the holy temple are the center of this.

"To finish transgression, to make an end of sins, to make reconciliation for iniquity."

- Done through John the Baptist (who was Elijah) and Yeshua: "Repent for the kingdom of God is near."
- Malachi 4:1-6

"To bring in everlasting righteousness."

- The Messiah gave His kingdom over to the Father. God's kingdom is here unseen. Evil and death shall never prevail over His holy ones in heaven and on earth again.

"To seal up vision and prophecy."

- Look at the chart. The fulfillment of Revelation is coming to an end (1 Corinthians 13:8–13). We are at Revelation 21:1. This does not mean God doesn't do miracles or speak to His people about things anymore. God still works; he never retires. Prophecy is being and has been fulfilled. Also, it means to conceal the truth of fulfillment. No truth, no understanding. No one hears from God.

"To anoint the Most Holy."

- This refers to the temple of Jerusalem. It was rededicated twice since captivity: circa 516 BC and 165 BC.

"That from the going forth of the command to restore and build Jerusalem until the Messiah the Prince, there shall be seven weeks and sixty-two weeks ... even in troublesome times."

- There was civil war and little peace. There was violence and destitution, justice thrown down, fields gone to ruin, and homelessness.
- The Messiah is Yeshua.

"And after the sixty-two weeks Messiah shall be cut off and have nothing; and the people of the prince who is to come shall destroy the city and sanctuary."

- The phrase, "And after the sixty-two weeks" suggests sequential order of fulfillment.
- Gentiles take over who are the Romans (Luke 21:24).
- Christ's death, resurrection, and ascension in AD 33.
- The Romans under Vespasian and Titus destroy the temple in AD 70. Nero comes as the beast in spirit years after he has died from a fatal wound in the head (neck).
- Persecution begins under Nero (AD 54). Is Nero the beast to come out of the abyss later? Is he the prince of the people to destroy the temple? Yes, he is.
- War occurs in the natural and spiritual places.

"He shall confirm a covenant with many for one week; but in the middle of the week he shall bring an end to sacrifice and offering."

- This is not Antiochus Epiphanes who defiled the temple in 167 BC. In 164 BC, sacrifice was restored by Judas Maccabeus three and a half years later. Daniel 11 speaks of him. There is another abomination of desolation to come after the Messiah is cut off and has nothing in the one seven.
- Nero had a following though he lost favor with people. Could

he have had made a covenant with them and have a major act in the middle of this one seven? It doesn't actually say he broke a covenant in the middle, it only says he brought an end to sacrifice and offering. Could it be that he made a covenant while he lived, but by entering the temple as a spiritual entity, thus defiling the temple, put an end to sacrifice and offering?

- A Jewish rebellion against the Romans began around AD 66, during the reign of Nero. Nero gave Vespasian the task to quell the rebellion. Vespasian appointed his son Titus as second-in-command. With four legions and with the help of forces from King Agrippa 2 (a Jewish king who is pro-Roman, pro-beast, and pro-antichrist), invaded Galilee. Nero commits suicide in AD 68 which resulted in a head wound. Nero entered the temple as a spiritual entity. In AD 70, over 3 years after the Jewish rebellion began, the temple was destroyed and sacrifices and offerings end, which is in the middle of the seven. The rebellion ended in AD 73, at the end of the seven. This rebellion took 7 years. The Romans trampled the temple and its surrounding area even after its destruction for over 3 years until the rebellion ended. This is not coincidence, but fulfillment of prophecy.
- Revelation 11:1, 2 – The temple is trampled by the gentiles for forty-two months or three and a half years. This begins in the middle of the seven. The gentiles mentioned is the Roman army invading the holy temple in AD 70. They continue to trample the temple area until the rebellion ends over 3 years later. This is fulfillment of prophecy.
- Interesting to note too that from the time of Yeshua's death in AD 33 until the end of the Jewish rebellion in AD 73 is forty years, a generation passes. There is a forty year gap from event to event here as there are between the other weeks.

"And its end will come with a flood; even to the end there will be war; desolations are determined."

- The end spoken of here is the end of the sacrifice and offering in the holy place. This is the same end written in Daniel 12:4, 6, 9, and 13. This is the same end the disciples asked Yeshua about in Matthew 24:3. This is not the end of earth as many believe.

Worldly Kingdoms in Daniel's Prophecy

Gold: Kingdom of Babylon

Silver: Kingdom of Medo-Persia

Bronze: Kingdom of Greece. Antiochus IV Epiphanes defiled the temple (168 BC, Daniel 11:31; 12:11) and Alexander the Great with four generals.

Iron: The Roman Empire

The middle of the seven is AD 70 when the temple is destroyed:

> And he will make a firm covenant with the many for one week (seven years), but in the middle of the week he will put a stop to sacrifice and grain offering (AD 70); and on the wing of abominations will come one who makes desolate, even until a complete destruction, one that is decreed, is poured out on the one who makes desolate. (Daniel 9:27; see also 2 Thessalonians 2:3, 4 and Revelation 13:14, 15)

This is after Nero's death from a fatal head wound and coming out of an abyss as a beast seen with the eyes of the spirit and not eyes of flesh. This is how he enters the temple before its destruction unnoticed—unless the Spirit of God revealed him. This abomination in the holy temple was like an unclean haunting. The sacrifices offered to Nero and idols opened the portal for the beast to enter into the natural atmosphere.

Iron and Clay: Roman and Jewish Rebellion

The Roman kingdom is divided and becomes split. There are many nations within the empire from around the world. There is not a fifth worldly kingdom. There is not a mysterious, long gap in history. This occurs consecutively. The Jewish priests must have seen the beast as the Spirit was poured out.

The ten toes are more likely the ten Jewish kings of the royal Hasmonean/Herodian dynasty, which is Jewish aristocracy during the first-century Roman Empire. Domitian is the "eleventh little horn" of Daniel.

This is the beginning of the end to the Roman Empire. The clay is the Jewish rebellion that is a weakness in the midst of the iron. There is separation due to the difference in the material which could signify a rebellion. The Romans and Jews are different materials. The clay represents the Jews and is of a humble, even weak consistency. God uses those things that are weak and humble in the world, of seemingly no importance, for His glory. He used the Jewish rebellion for His purpose. The coming of the kingdom of God as a rock hits the statue where it is already weak, breaks it apart, and brings down everything else on top. It is a picture of His judgment upon both the Jews and gentiles. He humbles the proud, both Jew and gentile in every worldly kingdom, in every generation, dead and alive. Nobody sees this rock coming at them, they don't believe the truth. They are blind. They never understood what John the Baptist (Elijah) and Yeshua were proclaiming that the Kingdom of heaven was literally at hand.

It wasn't far off in a distant future; it was well on its way or here. The mourning, cries, and screams heard in and around Jerusalem among the tribes that lived there were thought by other cities in Israel to be because of Jerusalem's destruction, but they did not know that as the tribes in that region alone, and some filled with the Spirit, saw Him come and mourned for the One they had pierced as prophesied in Zechariah 12. The horror to think that one believed he was serving the Most High God—and God was with Him—only to find out he had actually rejected and forsaken the One pierced and had Him killed. They see Him coming in glory, but then realize he was left in the hands of an enemy the beast, which no one understood that is who they were actually serving.

The Kingdom of Heaven Is Near!

> Behold, I am going to send you Elijah the prophet before the coming of the great and terrible day of the Lord. (Malachi 4:5)

This was fulfilled with John the Baptist (Matthew 11:14; 17:10–13; Mark 9:11–13; Luke 1:17; John 1:21). Yeshua said he was Elijah—not that he was a type of Elijah as many today say of him. If John denied he was Elijah, Yeshua said He was. John did not realize it at that time. Elijah appeared on the mount of transfiguration, but this was after John's death.

During this period of iron and iron-clay mix, the coming of the kingdom of God is proclaimed as good news or the Gospel. John the Baptist's baptism was one of repentance from sin and the announcement of a kingdom of heaven. He cried out in the wilderness, "Repent for the kingdom of heaven is at hand!" (Mark 1:14, 15; Matthew 3:2; 4:17; 10:7; Luke 21:31; 4:43; 8:1; 9:2; 9:60; 10:9, 11; 16:16; Acts 1:3; 8:12; 20:25; 28:23).

John and Yeshua were dropping a clue here on *the imminent fulfillment of this prophecy in their current generation or century.* There is a connection to be made between what John and Yeshua were preaching to the prophecies in the book of Daniel regarding the kingdom. Many people think John was only making reference to the coming of the One after him who is a King.

Both John and Yeshua are referencing Daniel 2:44 and 7:9–14, the coming of the Rock in Daniel, which is the kingdom of heaven. *These prophecies were about to be fulfilled, and the Rock in Daniel was about to crush to dust the kingdoms of the world and the kingdom of darkness.* In the Lord's Prayer (Matthew 6:10a), He says, "Your kingdom come," which is referencing the Rock in Daniel. Many Jews of that century would understand this proclamation by both John and Yeshua. It was a fulfillment of the prophecy spoken of in Daniel. This would stir many of them up, but Gentiles might not understand it.

"The time has come" or "The time is fulfilled" means the kingdom of God is at hand (Mark 1:14, 15). It is the fulfillment of the Rock prophesied in Daniel.

In Mark 1:24 and 5:7, demons knew of the fulfillment and the time of their end. Even the demons confirmed the fulfillment of Daniel. Yeshua did not come too early; it was time. The coming of the Rock of Daniel brought destruction, crushing, and torment to His enemies. The time of the fall and crushing of His enemy's kingdom on earth and in the spirit realm had come.

It is here that the purpose of the Rock's arrival is to begin to destroy the works of the devil (1 John 3:8b) and the kingdoms mentioned in Daniel's prophecy, which are under the influence of the devil.

They are seeing the Rock of Daniel coming and rolling down a hill so to speak. It is on its way, a huge avalanche with boulders and rocks, which comes with shaking. At this point, one is either a part of the Rock or will be crushed to dust by it. Anything in its path will be destroyed. There is no pausing, postponing, time out, or pushing back on the Rock. There is no line one can draw in the sand and say, "You can't cross this point." God, as zealous as He is for the advancement of His own kingdom, won't pause at this point. Why would any king, even God, want to pause and wait for his kingdom to come and take over the enemies' possessions? Why would God wait to fulfill His Word after sending His servant John to proclaim the kingdom for two thousand years?

What is the good news or Gospel that John and Yeshua proclaimed? The Gospel is the good news of the coming kingdom of heaven (Luke 4:43; 8:1) and entrance into it through Yeshua being born of water, Spirit, and blood, which testify as witnesses (John 3). The coming of the kingdom of God was spoken of in the book of Daniel in that generation, and anyone who repents and believes can enter through the anointed One, the Lamb. Many Christians today focus on the latter and still await the Second Coming of the Messiah almost two thousand years later, but the good news for that generation was about the coming of a kingdom that was prophesied in Daniel in their century. John, Yeshua, and first-century believers preached and taught about it. He said some of His disciples would not die until they saw it coming (Mark 9:1). That was one of several verses that speak to His return to that first-century generation.

If it wasn't about a coming kingdom during and shortly after the fall of the Roman Empire, why did Herod seek to kill the babies? Why were so many Christians persecuted so often? The kingdom of darkness was trying to resist and stop it from happening because it meant their end and destruction were at hand. With the imminent coming of the God's kingdom in the first century, there was the imminent end and demise of another. Satan would hate the idea and summon the beasts to resist and stop it at any cost. He would summon and deceive the nations and powers in the air to fight against the camp of the saints after their reign. What is good news or the Gospel to one is devastating news to another.

Keeping in mind that the good news is also about the coming of a kingdom, why send John, the forerunner, to tell people in the first century to repent and proclaim the kingdom if it wouldn't come for almost two thousand years? Why send him two thousand years ahead of the appointed time? Why make the proclamation of good news that is so far off to humans? Why even tell that generation about something that is good news if no one of that time would ever see in the Spirit? How can the coming of the kingdom be good news when it is not something for them, but for others to see by the Spirit in a distant future? They wouldn't even begin to find fulfillment until after they were long gone.

If that were the case, why not begin to proclaim the good news during any of the previous empires before the Roman Empire began to proclaim the coming of the kingdom of heaven? Why send John if the kingdom was going to be so far off anyway? If the kingdom of God came almost two millennia later, why not just proclaim *the way* to enter the kingdom through Yeshua and not that the kingdom of God is near and at hand?

John and Yeshua both proclaimed, "Repent, the kingdom of heaven is at hand!"

In that first-century generation, the way to enter His kingdom was taught and preached—and the Kingdom had arrived at their door. The prophecy was to be fulfilled; it was coming to that first-century generation.

That is like telling a large group of stranded people on a Godforsaken island the "good news" of a ship approaching and is very close. The captain goes ahead of the ship to see and comfort those stranded and tell them his ship is coming to save them and how they will get on the ship. The people are so excited, pumped, and celebrating. There's preparation, a sense of urgency, but it will arrive many centuries after they are all dead. None will ever see in the Spirit. The captain speeds away into the sunset and waves goodbye from his speed boat, not taking any of them with him. They are left to the wild hogs, venomous snakes, and beasts of the island. How would that be good news to them? That would deflate their hope because none of them or their children or their children's children would ever see salvation in their lifetimes. If you were on that island, your hope would deflate too.

What is the urgency to repent if the kingdom is near to that generation in the first century as John says, but at the same time, it actually is not near? Why preach about the fulfillment coming if there is a two thousand-year gap between the Roman Empire and a kingdom that has not even come in the twenty-first century? Why would John and Yeshua preach the kingdom is at hand, getting the people's hopes high, and then put prophecy on pause? How is it near then if it is on hold? It makes better sense to proclaim it because it was to come sometime in John's century, and God keeps His Word. It was imminent to that generation—not far off from them as many today teach.

The end of the temple and its sacrifices was a major sign that was to usher in the imminent coming of a kingdom to destroy the beast and Satan. When false teachers proclaimed the resurrection past, while the temple was still standing—and so its end didn't come to pass according to the prophecy—how could the resurrection come to pass too? Since one could not happen without the other preceding it, the teachers at that time were in error. They did not interpret the signs correctly.

How do we know a resurrection took place after the temple's destruction?

> Many of those who sleep in the dust of the ground will awake, these to everlasting life, but the others to disgrace and everlasting contempt. But as for you, go your way to the end; then you will enter into rest and rise again for your allotted portion at the end of the age. (Daniel 12:2–3)

This would happen at the end of what? It would happen around the time or shortly after of the end of the temple. There is another resurrection after the Crusades (Gog and Magog) of the wheat and tares.

I have said this elsewhere, but will put it here too: In the preterist view, the apostles' same use of the words "at hand" from AD 35 to AD 69 is about thirty-four years, but from AD 35 to AD 95 is about sixty years. Both are still better than two thousand years. Thirty-four or sixty years are more "at hand" than two thousand years.

But God stands outside of time so that thirty or two hundred years are like minutes or hours to Him. To Him, this is "at hand." He would see fulfillment approaching quicker than humans would. *Eventual fulfillment that is a long way off to humans is literally "at hand" to Him.* A thousand years are like a day, and a day is like a thousand years. "At hand" could be decades or a couple of centuries—but not close to two millennia. This shows imminence of a bringing to pass His Word shortly after it left His lips. The "at hand" can occur within or shortly after a generation's life ends. To Him, it's about to happen. When the coming of Yeshua is "near" or the end is "at hand" or "the kingdom of heaven is at hand," to Him it is about to happen, which could be within or shortly after a generation's life ends. "At hand" here was immediate and imminent, to happen in a short time, not many years off (Mark 14:42, 43; see also the section "Explanation of 2 Thessalonians 2 and 2 Timothy 2").

The people of the first century were so hopeful about the proclamation of John and Yeshua that when these false teachers who ran ahead of prophecy—ignoring the fact that the temple was still standing and the beast had not yet come—said it was already fulfilled. That destroyed some of their faith because there was an expectation that it would all go down in their lifetime—and they had somehow missed it. So why obey Him still since they would be doomed to the second resurrection?

For us in current generations, we have a grace in the second resurrection that they would not have if they forsook Him. They had grace and mercy, but if they rejected Him, they were left for the judgment and second resurrection. That's why Revelation says they (those who did not worship the beast or take his name) are blessed if they rose in the first resurrection and the second death cannot touch them (Revelation 20:4-6). They had one shot and if they missed the first resurrection, they were left behind and doomed in the second. Knowing this would destroy their faith. Our current generations were born of a later time, so "His mercy extends to every generation" (Psalms 103:17; Luke 1:50) including our own. If it didn't, and we are not given the chance to repent as they had, and we are condemned in the second resurrection, He is a liar. As believers, we know He is not a liar. So there is a mercy and a grace given to us in the second resurrection of wheat and tares, the sheep and goats that they don't have.

The Rock

John and Yeshua preached about the kingdom of heaven in the first century. They proclaimed the coming of this "Rock" shortly. Daniel 2:44, 7:9–14, 7:26–27 were fulfilled here and came like a thief in the night. Many sleep and are not aware a thief is in the house. A true watchman or gatekeeper would know this because they are awake, alert, aware, and have their lamps lit.

Even today, there are testimonies of people who die and see Yeshua, heaven, hell, angels, demons, the devil, and judgment and return to share with others. Their testimony tends to confirm a harvest has begun and a kingdom has arrived (Daniel 2 and 7). This Rock was present through the millennial reign (AD 96–1091), the Crusades to the Holy Land or Gog/Magog (AD 1099–1291), and the passing away of the heavens and earth (present and future).

Yeshua comes in the kingdom of the Father in the first century AD. The Rock of Daniel comes and crushes all other kingdoms seen and unseen and the millennial reign begins. "In the days of these kings the God of heaven will set up a kingdom" (Daniel 2:44) correlates with the time in Revelation 20:1–11.

The rock fell on the feet of the image, and God's kingdom has been present for many years now. The rock fell when Yeshua came into the Father's kingdom.

Daniel 2:39–45 correlates with Revelation 19 and the Roman Empire (iron). Revelation 20:4–10 was the Roman Empire and the Jewish revolt (iron and clay). Revelation 11:15–18 is a prophecy about iron and clay. This has been fulfilled. The feet of iron and clay are not Rome and the Byzantine era. If so, how does Christ come during the iron (Roman age), yet the Rock falls hundreds of years later when He sets up His kingdom? If the iron and clay are Roman and Jewish rebellion, the kingdom is divided more in the east and west. The ten toes equal the ten kings from Jewish descent (Hasmonean and Herodian lines). The Rock falls on iron and clay, and God's kingdom is set up. Babylon, thus, is fallen. This all happens during the first century and not our modern age, almost two thousand years later.

There is no large, mysterious gap between the worldly kingdoms and the Rock that comes and crushes them to dust. The worldly kingdoms do not go out of existence by themselves. There is a Rock, an unseen and spiritual kingdom that makes it fall and pass away. There is no gap between the iron and the iron/clay as some teach.

An Age to Come after Christ's Coming and after the Roman Empire

> In the day of these kings, God will set up a kingdom. (Daniel 2:33–35, 41–45)

"These kings" are the Roman emperors. The millennial reign begins sometime after Domitian's reign, the eleventh horn. Note what happened before the Crusades in Jerusalem, which was a time of relative peace around Jerusalem: a sign of an unseen reign without Satan. The rest of the world of that time would not necessarily have peace.

An age to come after the Roman Empire was prophesied in Revelation 20:1–15; Ephesians 1:20–23; Mark 10:29–31; and Hebrews 2:5–9. This age to come is from the Byzantine Era even up until our time.

The kingdom of God did not come visibly or with visible signs (Daniel 2:44, 45; Luke 17:20, 21; Revelation 21, 22). It was not visible; it was invisible. It was among them and within them, but it was unseen.

Many Christians expect to see a millennial reign on this present earth and see the kingdom of God come. The kingdoms of the world have become God's. The kingdom of God has come (Matthew 4:8; 6:10; John 18:36; Revelation 11:15; 12:10; Daniel 2:44, 45).

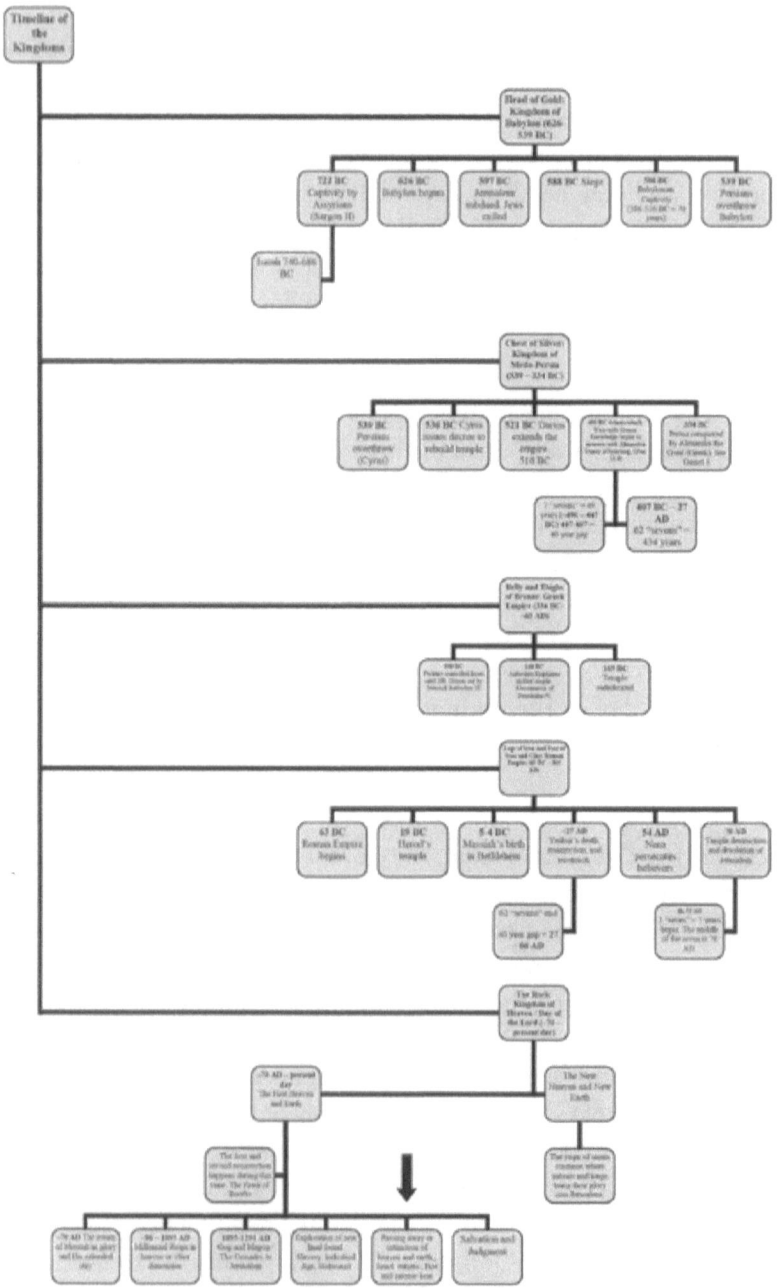

Time Line of Kingdoms
(In prophecy and time, we are at the black arrow.
Enlarged Time Line of Kingdoms on page 296 for clearer reading.)

CHAPTER 3

Revelation: The Beast

Since John wrote the book of Revelation while he was *in the Spirit*, most of the book should be understood and interpreted from the view of the spirit realm, not just the natural. There are a lot of things believers miss today or do not understand. Although they understand some spiritual things, they tend to rely on the natural or what their bodies sense.

According to Revelation 1:1, 19, John was to write about past, present, and future events:

> The Revelation of Jesus Christ, which God gave Him to show to His bondservants, the things which must soon take place;

> Therefore write the things which you have seen, and the things which are, and the things which will take place after these things.

There are things that John had already witnessed in the past, things that are present during his generation, things that were to occur shortly after. The things to occur shortly after were not two thousand years later, but within a few months, years, or even a few decades. Futurist interpretations of some events in Revelation are projected far into the future from John's time when it shouldn't be. They occur near to him as he writes. The only things that were far into the future from John's time are the millennial reign, the Crusades, the passing away of the first heaven and earth, and the new heaven, earth, and Jerusalem.

When it comes to *seeing* the Second Coming, the millennial reign, the beast as the abomination of desolation, or the city of Jerusalem, they tend to go back to the natural understanding and flesh and put the spirit aside. Then they teach an interpretation of prophecy from a natural perspective that does not make sense, contradicts, or gives the sense of tarrying, when it was fulfilled. They don't see the fulfillment because they still wait for it to happen in the natural—with eyes of the flesh—when it actually happened *in the spirit*. Only the signs manifest in the natural. They are asleep or are not watching completely in the spirit as a watchman. A watchman watches in the spirit and interprets the signs manifesting in the natural from the spiritual realm. His kingdom is not of this world; it is a spiritual kingdom that is only detected when the Holy Spirit wills it and comes upon the people.

Could this be the reason Yeshua said in John 3 that one cannot see the kingdom of heaven unless he is born of water and Spirit? He also said in John 4:24 that the Father is Spirit and those who worship Him must worship Him *in Spirit and truth*? Is this why Paul wrote in Ephesians 5:18 to be filled with the Spirit? Jude writes in verse 20 to build yourselves up on your most holy faith, praying in the Holy Spirit. *To understand and see spiritual things, one must be anointed, filled, and walking in the Spirit.* No one can see the *spiritual* kingdom with *natural* eyes. The Spirit must open up our blind eyes. They have eyes but do not see because they are not in the Spirit, and the Spirit of God is not in them (Isaiah 6:10; Matthew 13:10–17). We have spiritual eyes.

An unsaved person gifted as a psychic or clairvoyant can see things in the spirit realm, but they cannot see the kingdom of heaven. They must be born again of God's Spirit to enter and see it. They see the spirit realm from the outside of God's kingdom or in the kingdom of darkness. They might detect or see a holy angel or two—unless God opens their eyes like He did with Balaam. Balaam used sorcery to see God, but the Spirit of God later opened his eyes and ears apart from sorcery to see and hear the angel (Numbers 22:31; 24:1, 2) and Him. Balaam understood that sacrifices opens up doors (Numbers 23:1–5, 14–17, 23:29–30). He offered sacrifices three times to have God give him a word.

Revelation was written around AD 69. There were probably seven or eight handwritten copies of it because it had to go to each of the churches back then. It was written during a time of persecution of believers. The times of Nero and Domitian were major times of persecution of believers in the first century, but believers were persecuted on a smaller scale in between those reigns. There are clues in the book itself that suggest the time the book was written by John.

Four Clues

Clue 1: Revelation 11:1, 2. Temple and altar mentioned. Gentiles trample a temple that *is already present at the time of the writing*. It has to be the last earthly temple (Herod's temple). It was trampled for forty-two months or three and a half years (which equals to one thousand, two hundred and sixty days) which aligns to the middle of the one seven in the book of Daniel. This is from AD 70 to AD 73. John is writing about the sacrifices and offerings ending in the middle of the seven which is AD 70 if the seven is from AD 66-AD 73. He is aligning here with Daniel who wrote about the one seven. The gentiles here are the Roman army as they entered and destroyed the temple. This invasion and destruction of the temple by Titus' army would fulfill these verses. Yeshua also said this would happen in Luke 21:24.

Clue 2: Revelation 12:6. The woman who gave birth to a son taken up to God is Israel. It says she fled to the wilderness. This goes in line with what Yeshua said to his disciples what believers should do when they see the abomination standing where it should not stand, to flee to the mountains of Judea. (Matthew 24:15-22) This was done as the armies surrounded the temple in AD 70, and those who heeded His warning fled to the wilderness. The one thousand, two hundred sixty days are from AD 70 to AD 73, about three and a half years. This aligns with Clue 1 where the gentiles (Roman army) trample the temple for the same amount of time: one thousand, two hundred and sixty days. The two witnesses prophesy for the same amount of time: twelve hundred and sixty days (Revelation 11:3). Somehow these two witnesses appeared from AD 70 to AD 73. This woman, the believers of Israel, was persecuted by the dragon.

Clue 3: Revelation 17:8–11. Seven kings and heads—five fallen. Five emperors were *already dead in John's time of writing*: Augustus, Tiberius, Caligula, Claudius, and Nero. *One is present in John's time of writing* (Galba), and the "other has not yet come" (Otho). *The tenses are important to note here for it tells us this occurs during John's generation as he is writing this book, not a future one.* Julius Caesar is not counted since he was only a dictator and not an emperor.

Clue 4: "Was (of the five who once lived), is not (now dead in John's time), is to come (rose from the dead/appears) is also an eighth." This verse is referring to the Roman emperors in John's generation. Nero's name does calculate to 666, and he is "of the seven." Again, *the tenses are important to note here.*

Nero couldn't have been alive at the time of the writing of the book of Revelation because he was of the five that were dead. The one who is also an eighth comes up out of the abyss because he had already died from a head wound and would be seen by the world again according to Revelation. If we don't count Julius Caesar, Nero did not reign at the time of the writing. Nero had already died by the time John wrote this. Nero could not have been the "one is."

Futurists ignore or fail to notice these tenses and forget that this beast is spiritual like a ghost or an entity with a spirit body because it is written in Revelation that he was of the five and is fallen (already dead). *This would be how after death he could have entered the temple as a beast in the spirit as an unclean spirit.* The phrase "five have fallen, one is, and one is to come for a short time" does not refer to men other than the Roman emperors. *How does John write in these past and present tenses about a distant future and not his own generation? These tenses are in John's time and not our own. If the angel is correct, the book was written around AD 69.*

"Wound in head, fatal, comes back to life" was not a myth (Revelation 13:3). Nero stabbed himself in the throat. He was seen after his death.

Most scholars date the book of Revelation around AD 95. Revelation was not written in AD 95, but circa AD 69—before the temple's destruction in AD 70. Why would anyone believe a man before the angel in the book?

According to John, the beast (the emperors) was already in the world when John wrote this (1 John 2:18 and 4:3). These books were written circa AD 69.

"At the last trumpet" (1 Corinthians 15:52) seems to reference Revelation 11:15–19. This letter was also written around AD 69. What else would it reference?

"With the trumpet of God" (1 Thessalonians 4:15, 16) references Revelation. "We who are alive and remain until the Lord's coming" suggests those of that generation will live to see the coming—not us. We, of this time, didn't exist yet. So "we" is them. Also, "we who are alive and remain shall be caught up." That generation lived until the time of "the Lord's coming." This could also apply to us of this age and generation in a way before the destruction of heaven and earth with fire. He will not destroy the righteous with the wicked. We would have to be changed and removed too.

"Sits as God in the temple of God" (2 Thessalonians 2:1–12) refers to the earthly temple of AD 70 (not the church). Most likely, Nero came out from the bottomless pit as a beast, a spiritual entity, after he had already died. He would enter not in flesh and blood, but in spirit as an entity.

Ten Kings of Daniel (The Beast/ Roman Emperors)

Daniel 7:7–8, 24–25: The ten emperors from Augustus to Titus do not seem to be the same as the ten horns or kings in the book of Revelation. "There was another horn … coming up *among* them," "another shall rise *after* them" and "arise *from* their kingdom (Roman)." This is Domitian, and one little horn equals an eleventh! Domitian subdued three emperors. The three who fell (7:20, "before which three fell") and were plucked and subdued were either Galba, Otho, and Vitellius or Vitellius, Vespasian, Titus.

Daniel 7:11 speaks of the beast with ten to eleven horns and not just the eleventh horn. All emperors were condemned and burned—not just one horn.

Domitian was stabbed, cremated, and interred in the temple of Flavian (Daniel 7:11, 26). He was addressed as "*dominus et deus*" ("master and god"). The little horn, Domitian, "made war against the saints and prevailed against them, until the ancient of days came." This indicates that the ancient of days must have come in the first century when Domitian's persecution came to an end. Yeshua must have been there in AD 96 as a thief in the night.

This is not a fifth unknown future earthly kingdom. This not the Euro currency system used across Europe.

Ten Kings of Revelation

The Hasmonean/Herodian dynasty was a Jewish aristocracy. These kings and the Romans appointed high priests. This is not a fifth unknown future earthly kingdom.

> Accordingly, the number of the high priests—from the days of Herod until the day when Titus took the temple

and the city and burnt them—was twenty-eight. The time that belonged to them was 107 years. . . . as did the Romans also, who took the government over the Jews into their hands afterward. (*The Works of Josephus, Antiquities of the Jews*, X, 1, 426)

The Ten Hebrew Kings/Tetrarchs or Rulers or the Ten Horns with the Ten Diadems

1. Antipater (46 BC–4 BC).
2. Herod the Great, son of Antipater (73 BCE–4 BC. He began to rule in Galilee in the fifteenth and twenty-fifth year of his age; governor of Syria; bribes Marc Anthony; impeached by the Jews, but is notwithstanding made a tetrarch by Anthony; gets the better of the Jews who oppose him; made king by the Roman senate, at the desire of Anthony; solicited to adultery by Cleopatra; makes war against the Arabians by Anthony's order; causes his wife's brother, Aristobulus, to be cunningly drowned at Jericho; promotes his friends; marries the famous Mariamne and puts her to death; afflicted with a kind of madness by divine vengeance; departs from the manners and customs of the Jews by introducing foreign practices including celebrating the Roman games every five years; builds a temple at Samaria and a palace at Jerusalem; builds a temple to Caesar; rebuilds the temple at Jerusalem; impeaches his sons at Rome, before Caesar; rebuilds Apollo's temple, and renews the Olympic games; opens David's sepulcher; becomes mad, bitter, has a terrible sickness; attempts suicide; had his sons Antipater, Alexander, Aristobulus (who, according to Josephus, was king of Chalcis who governed the Lesser Armenia) executed.
3. Phasaelus or Phasael (died 40 BC).
4. Herod Philip 1 (4 BC– AD 34).
5. Herod Archelaus (23 BC– AD 18).
6. Herod Antipas (20 BC– AD 39).
7. Herod Philip 2 (26/27 BC– AD 33/34)—prince of Judea.
8. Herod of Chalcis or Herod V (Aristobulus' son, d. AD 48–49).
9. Herod Agrippa 1 (10 BC– AD 44).
10. Herod Agrippa 2 (circa AD 50–AD 100?).

Satan is the red dragon; the seven heads are the Roman emperors from Augustus to Otho. Julius Caesar was only a dictator, not an actual emperor, and wasn't alive when Yeshua was born into the world. The ten horns with crowns were the Jewish kings (Herods) who ruled with the Roman emperors without having their own kingdom. These Jewish rulers gave their authority and power to the Roman emperors who were the beast (Revelation 17:13). They were pro-Roman. Futurists mistakenly teach these are leaders in our modern or future generation.

- Revelation 12:3: "A great red dragon having seven heads and *ten* horns, and on his heads were seven diadems."
- Revelation 13:1–7: "Then I saw a beast coming out of the sea, having *ten* horns and seven heads, and on his horns were *ten* diadems."
- *Revelation 17:3, 12–18; 18:9: The "ten kings who have not yet received a kingdom, but they receive authority as kings with the beast for one hour."*

The family of Herod was not Roman Gentiles; they were Jews. They are descended from the Jewish aristocratic family of Idumaean or Edomite *descent. Did they not rule with the seven Roman emperors (the beast) over the Jews even though they had no kingdom of their own?*

These three kings were born in the Hasmonean kingdom which is the ruling dynasty of Judea and surrounding regions. The others are from the Herodian dynasty. *These kings of Jewish descent didn't have a kingdom, but they ruled certain areas around Judea for one hundred years (one hour). It seems one hour could equal a century, just like a thousand years are like a day in God's sense of time.*

Antipater was born around 100 BC. The last Herod died around AD 100. These kings, who were of Jewish aristocracy, were to have authority with the beast (Roman emperors) for one hour or about one hundred years. These kings were immoral, and a few of them were known to persecute the saints. Herod the Great killed the children under two to eliminate any other kings.

In Mark 3:6, the Pharisees plotted with the Herodians to destroy Yeshua. Herod Antipas decapitated John the Baptist, and Yeshua stood before him to be questioned and then mocked.

The last one, however, heard Paul speak and declared Paul innocent.

This interpretation seems to fit Revelation. It also seems to confirm the Second Coming of the Messiah in the first century (not our time).

The ten kings in Daniel are not ten nations to destroy Israel as many teachers today teach. They are the Jewish aristocracy, and for the most part, they did not recognize the Messiah. They rejected him. These Jewish kings—who were given authority to govern Jewish matters and over certain regions of nations within the empire—were in cahoots with the beast, the Roman emperors.

Seven Heads of the Beast/Ten Horns with Crowns

Julius Caesar is not counted in the seven heads or the ten horns with crowns since he was only a dictator and was in leadership before the incarnation of Yeshua. The count of the heads and the horns begins with the one reigning as an emperor at the time of the Messiah's arrival into the world.

Some preterists count Julius as the first head. Julius was a dictator, not an emperor, and was not one of the heads of the beast. In comparing other scripture, it would not line up with Daniel's prophecy of the beast with ten horns with crowns, from Augustus to Titus, and an eleventh horn being Domitian. *Julius counts as the first Roman leader in history, but in biblical prophecy, Augustus was the first emperor or head. He was reigning at the birth of the Jewish Messiah, Yeshua.*

Beginning with Julius's reign throws off the heads and the horns with crowns prophecies, and with Domitian's reign ending in AD 96, the millennial reign has to be around AD 96–1095 for the Crusades (Gog and Magog) to begin soon after (for several hundred years).

One thing to note about most these emperors is that if they weren't deified, they claimed to be God. If they did not claim to be God, they were deified and worshipped as one. This is a sign that the beast was the emperors and the emperors were part of the beast. Why do futurists ignore this and still look for a beast to come?

It is not a coincidence that these Roman emperors were either deified as gods or claimed to be gods, and one of them (though not in flesh and blood, but in spirit) I believe, claimed to be God in the holy temple before its destruction in AD 70. It is not coincidence; it is a fulfillment of God's Word.

Julio-Claudian Dynasty

The emperors of the Julio-Claudian Dynasty are Augustus, Tiberius, Caligula, Claudius, and Nero. John wrote what the angel is saying "five fallen" as the Julio-Claudian Dynasty comes to an end with Nero's death. Nero must have recently died:

1. Augustus (later deified; 31 BC–AD 14). Ruling with him over the Jews is, yet without a kingdom of his own, Herod the Great (one of ten kings who ruled with the beast yet had no kingdom) sought to kill Christ as a baby, the slaughter of infants.
2. Tiberius (AD 14–37). Yeshua the lamb sacrificed on the cross/altar. Herod Antipas beheaded John and rejected Yeshua. Yeshua rose from the dead.
3. Caligula (AD 37–41). Claimed to be God and attempted to place a statue of his image in the temple to be worshipped.
4. Claudius. (later deified; AD 41–54)
5. Nero (666 is the number of his name; AD 54–68)—fatal head wound of the sword (Revelation 13:14)—claimed to be God while he lived and after death. The "abomination of desolation" that came later coming out of the abyss as a spiritual entity, the beast. Nero here is "the beast who was." He used to be alive.

Civil Wars

Note that the angel describes the three emperors' reigns during the civil wars as very brief. It is not a coincidence that the angel describes three brief reigns back to back and here are three brief reigns in history back to back. This is fulfillment of God's word. This is a piece of the puzzle. Many miss this footprint.

6. Galba. These books probably written during this time: Revelation, 1 John, Corinthians 15:52, and Thessalonians 4:15, 16 (last trumpet). One not yet come, to come for a short time, remains a little while.
7. Otho.
8. Vitellius. The eighth crown with horns—not the eighth head.

Nero here is the beast who "is not," meaning he is dead when the book of

Revelation is written. He died of a fatal head wound. During Otho's reign, Nero spiritually rose again out of the abyss and is also an eighth beast. He is the eighth in a spiritual sense and is not dwelling in the natural realm anymore. The presence/spirit of the beast, the abomination, in the temple was like a haunting in the temple bringing on the desolation of Jerusalem. This evil presence would defile a holy temple.

Nero

Nero was "the beast who was, and is not, and is about to come up out of the abyss and go to destruction." He is "the beast who was, and is not, is himself also an eighth and *is one of the seven*." Many forget that he is one of the seven emperors or heads. At the time of the writing of the book of Revelation, it was circa AD 69.

There are many who don't believe Nero was the beast, but the beast is either another man from the first century or the future. Whether he is a high priest, priest, prophet, a leader of another country, or a dictator, when someone claims someone other than Nero (or in the least any emperor) was the beast, they forget or set aside what Revelation 13 says about him. They acknowledge the evil character of Nero, but consider other individuals in history with evil characters who had or will have access to the temple as the beast instead. They forget that the beast has crowns; they forget he is a powerful one who rules as a king or emperor. They lay aside what Revelation said about where the beast comes from (Revelation 17:8–11).

Nero is no longer considered because he never entered the temple in the flesh while alive since he died in AD 68. They choose someone who had or will have access to the temple (hence the belief and doctrine of a third earthly future temple by many futurists) in order to claim to be God in the temple, putting aside the fact that, according to Revelation, the beast has to be "of the seven" heads or emperors. Yet none of the other men they believe is or will be the beast is "of the seven" heads or even wore a crown.

The beast is of the Roman Empire cannot be a future person. He is one of the emperors (seven heads equals five was, one is, one is to come), and he is a man of sin and lawlessness. He is a public person, a pagan, and the number of his name is 666. He persecutes believers in Yeshua as some of the other emperors also have, and he is doomed to destruction.

When choosing another one as the beast, they forget some of these things. Nero is all these things as were the other emperors before and after him.

Suetonius writes, "Count the numerical values of the letters in Nero's name, and in 'murdered his own mother': You will find their sum is the same." (*Twelve Caesars*, VI, 39, Penguin Classics) "Nero's full name in Latin was Lucios Domitium Ahenobarborum." (*Twelve Caesars*, VI, 1) This statement by a Roman historian writer suggests the Romans added numerical values to phrases and names back then. This was done in the first century.

"The number of his name was Lucios (50 + 5 + 100 +1) + Domitium (500 +1 + 4) + Ahenobarborum (5) equal 666". (*The Twelve Caesars; AD 79 A Prophecy Paradox*, 175, Son Mountain Press)

When a preterist says it was spiritual, some futurists equate spiritual with being symbolic, allegory, make believe, or not real. Daniel 8:23 refers to Antiochus IV and his rise to power—but not Nero. Antiochus defiled the temple. The beast (Nero) defiled it a second time.

Yeshua destroyed Nero's spirit body in the spirit, which doesn't make it less physical or real because it is not sensed by the flesh or of the earthly realm. What is of the spirit realm is not just symbolic or allegorical; there is a reality and physical element to it. A believer in Yeshua is not unspiritual and merely religious and of this earthly space. They are to believe and have faith even when the body can't pick up on some things. Even their interpretations of some prophecy are based on the body's senses and not the Spirit or spiritual realm.

Even Revelation 19:17–21 seems to be either a battle in the spirit realm or a combination of the two realms. One who doesn't understand or believe spiritual things and tends to lean more on the natural or focuses more with the eyes of the flesh will not understand this and miss it. Futurists don't believe Nero was the beast, but they forget the spiritual nature of it. They are so focused on the natural flesh and blood part of it. There is no faith in what is spiritually true.

Many forget what Revelation says about Nero's "fatal" wound in the head and the beast coming out of the abyss *after his death* (Revelation 13:3, 12, 14; 17:8, 11).

Futurists ask, "When did Nero ever enter and sit in the temple? How can he be the beast? The beast will be destroyed by the King of kings, but Nero committed suicide?"

Nero killed himself as a human, but Yeshua destroyed him as the spiritual beast. If he comes out of the abyss after a death in AD 68, then as a beast, he could enter the temple in AD 70. The mark could be a spiritual mark. His unclean spiritual presence defiled the temple of God, caused the sacrifices and grain offerings to stop, and brought desolation. Priests likely witnessed the Roman ensign and idol and his evil presence, and many even saw him on the wing of the temple in Spirit as He was poured out according to Zechariah. Seeing the abomination caused believing Israel, the woman, to flee to the wilderness or mountains of Judea. They also may have seen Yeshua destroy him.

Hence, the fulfillment of Yeshua's words to Caiaphas (approximate dates of his rule as high priest circa AD 18 – 37) in Matthew 26:64. As high priest of the temple, they would see Him come in the clouds of heaven (Zechariah 12). How else could Caiaphas see Him in the Spirit unless the Spirit was poured out on Jerusalem?

The phrase "from now on" or "hereafter" could mean Caiaphas would have frequent visions and dreams of the Second Coming of the Messiah since the phrase implies something that occurs starting at one point and continuing on until he actually saw it in the Spirit. It is also possible Caiaphas was a very elderly Levite of about seventy to ninety years old when he saw it. The range of years of his life is estimated from 14 BC to AD 46, which is only about fifty-two years, which isn't really elderly. This range of years is only a guess. He could have lived longer. If he lived to AD 70, then he would have been about seventy-six years old and elderly. Why is it hard to believe he could have lived to be that age? If God wanted him alive to see the fulfillment of Yeshua's coming, He could make him live that long. He could have seen the age of eighty or ninety.

Concerning Nero's birth, *The History of the Roman Emperors* wrote:

> Have been sensible of his own depraved character, as well as his wife's; for, when his friends congratulated him upon the birth of Nero, he declared that nothing could be born from himself and Agrippina, that would not be of a detestable and pernicious nature.

Concerning the Romans invasion into the temple, it was recorded:

> Titus, accompanied by his officers, advanced into the most holy parts of the Temple, and was convinced by his own observation, that the fame and beauty and splendour

had not been exaggerated by the credulity of foreigners, or the partiality of the Jews themselves.

Titus and the Roman soldiers were inside the most holy parts of the temple. Josephus wrote,

> The Romans upon the flight of the seditious into the city, and upon the burning of the holy house itself, and of all the buildings lying round about it, *brought their ensigns to the temple*, and set them over against its eastern gate; and there did they offer sacrifices to them and there did they make Titus imperator, with the greatest acclamations of joy.

In the footnote, it says

> Havercamp says here: "This is a remarkable place; the Tertullian truly says that the entire religion of the Roman camp almost consisted in worshipping the ensigns, in swearing by the ensigns and in preferring the ensigns before all the [other] gods." (*The Works of Josephus, Wars of the Jews,* VI, VI, 1)

> The Romans, having expelled their enemies from the temple, reared their idolatrous standards upon the once sacred spot, and offered adoration to them; at the same time they saluted Titus with the appellation of Imperator, in testimony of the joyful success which had crowned his arms.
> *(The History of the Roman Emperors)*

The precious, holy articles of the temple were given or taken away:

> Two of the priests saved their lives by delivering to Titus the golden candlesticks, tables, phials, and other costly utensils of the Temple, together with the habiliments of the sacerdotal order, and stores of cassia, and other aromatic spices.

> The golden table, taken from the Temple of Jerusalem, the golden candlestick with seven branches, and the sacred

volume of the Law of Moses, were exhibited among the spoils; and with these relics of the ancient worship of the true God were mixed statues of pagan divinities, and images of Victory constructed of gold and ivory. The Law, and the purple veils of the Sanctuary, were deposited in the palace of Vespasian; the other spoils of the Temple were destined to adorn a new edifice, which was to be built under Dion. *(The History of the Roman Emperors)*

Bringing the idolatrous ensigns into the temple and sacrificing to the serpent and the head of the beast (emperor) inside the temple were abominations of desolation seen standing on the wing of the temple. When was the beast in the temple worshipped like God? *Through the ensign or standard they elevated, sacrificed to, and worshipped.*

Believers in Yeshua in that generation would see the ensign enter and stand on the wing of the temple where it did not belong *and understand it was the natural sign of something happening in the spirit. Keep in mind entities and spirits attach to objects and can be carried into a place. It happened with the Ark of the Covenant. God's Spirit was with the Ark of the Covenant.* Wherever the Ark of the Covenant went there were signs of His presence, supernatural things would happen, such as a river parting in half, a priest struck dead, battles won/lost, tumors and cancer spread, an idol fallen and broken without humans present, a city blessed or cursed. *There is a dimensional law at work here. This is why there is the commandment not to make an idol in any kind of image; it is a bridge to the other side.* Demons, spirits, and entities attach to them. This can bring trouble into the camp just as Achan's greed and sin did. Idols or cursed objects can cause supernatural activity to occur. It is an open door to an unseen realm. This is true for holy and unholy objects. God knew this dimensional law and commanded the people not to create images and only worship Him.

What is an ensign?

> An aquila (Latin for "eagle") was a prominent symbol used in ancient Rome, especially as the standard of a Roman legion. A legionary known as an aquilifer, or eagle-bearer, carried this standard. Each legion carried one eagle ... The bundle of hay or fern was soon succeeded by the figures of animals, of which Pliny the Elder (H.N.x.16) enumerates five: the eagle, the wolf, the ox with the man's head, the

horse, and the boar. After 104 BC, under later emperors the eagle was carried, as it had been for many centuries, with the legion, a legion being on that account sometimes called aquila. Each cohort had for its own ensign the serpent or dragon, which was woven on a square piece of cloth textiles anguis, elevated on a gilt staff ... Under the eagle or other emblem was often placed a head of the reigning emperor, which was to the army an object of worship or veneration. The name of the emperor, or of him who was acknowledged as emperor, was sometimes inscribed in the same situation. (Wikipedia.org)

It is interesting to note that Revelation 12 and 13 speak of Satan, the devil, as a red dragon or serpent, and the Romans carried the image of the red dragon/ serpent and an image of the emperor's head with his name. They were both on the ensign and worshipped as sacrifices and offerings were given to the ensign/ idol. What was natural represented what happened in the spirit.

It is not a coincidence that the Roman army had a serpent on their ensign. It is not a coincidence it also had the head of the emperor (head of beast). It is not a coincidence that both of these idols were worshipped in the Jewish holy temple as the gentiles trampled the holy place. This is not a coincidence, but fulfillment of prophecy. So why do futurists ignore this and continue to look for a future beast? How come they don't want to see this connection, but dismiss this?

John wrote, "They worshiped the dragon (the devil) because he gave his authority to the beast (emperor's head); and they worshiped the beast" (Revelation 13:3). *The Roman army worshipped the dragon and the beast through their ensigns.*

Revelation uses "heads" to describe the emperors, yet it was the "heads and names of the emperors" on the ensigns and on the coins they used to buy and sell goods back then. To me, this is not a coincidence, but it coincides with the fulfillment of the prophecy in Revelation. "I saw one of his heads as if it had been slain, and his fatal wound was healed" (Revelation 13:3). This is a piece of the puzzle.

Nero killed himself by stabbing himself in the neck with help:

> He applied the dagger to his throat, but even then had not strength and courage to give himself the fatal blow,

until he was assisted by Epaphroditus. (*The History of the Roman Emperors*, 7268)

Nero was worshipped while he lived:

> The month of April was to be called by the name of Nero, and a temple was to be erected to *Sal us*. (*The History of the Roman Emperors*, 6801)

The temple was erected to Nero.

> One of the senators, outstripping the others in blasphemous adulation, proposed that a temple should be erected, as soon as possible, to the *divine* Nero; although it was not customary to deify the emperors until after their death. We learn from an ancient coin, that this most detestable of princes was really steeled *a god* in some of the provinces; and from this fact we may infer to what a degrading state of idolatrous corruption the most civilized nations of the world were then reduced. (*The History of the Roman Emperors*, 6813)

Emperors could claim they were god while they lived, but weren't deified until after death. Nero was deified while he lived.

Also interesting to note is there was a coin in some provinces of the nations of that world that indicated that he was a god to them. People use coins to buy materials, goods, and other necessities. The nations of that era couldn't buy or sell these things unless they used the coin that had his image and name on it, which deified him as a god (Revelation 13:16-18). His name calculates to 666. As they worshipped him, there was a spiritual mark on their hands or forehead. It is like when we are baptized into the name of the Father, Son, and Holy Spirit, His holy names are upon us too, though not visible to the natural eye.

Sacrifices were offered to Nero *after his death* by the Romans according to one account:

> Then he dispelled any doubt as to which of the Caesars was to be his model by sacrificing to Nero's ghost and,

at the subsequent banquet, while a poplar flutist was performing, called for something from the "the Master's book" (Nero) as an encore. When the flutist obliged with one of these compositions, Vitellius jumped up delightedly and led the applause. (*The Twelve Caesars*, 272)

This was done in AD 69—before Vitellius died and before the temple's destruction in AD 70. Since the sacrifices were offered to Nero's ghost, some of the people must have been seeing him after he died. If mediums were defiled by communicating with the dead, then the dead Nero's ghost would defile the temple. Remember that sacrifices open doors to the spirit realm for entities, demons, and spirits to come into our earthly realm. Also, spirits can attach themselves to natural objects as a bridge into this world.

It makes sense that these blood sacrifices to Nero's ghost would open a door. This is how he would sit in the temple. Like other emperors, he claimed to be God while he lived and after he died being worshipped as a god. Nero was a human who became a spiritual entity after his death. As a believer in Yeshua, we must all understand and know this. We cannot be ignorant of it. We must understand spiritual matters and not just what pertains to our natural, earthly human space.

It was written that his image was worshipped and sacrifices were offered to it:

> He consented to deposit his diadem before the image of Nero, and not to resume it except from his hand. A curdle seat, supporting the image of Nero, was placed on an elevation; and Tiridates, after sacrifices had been offered, approached it, and, taking the diadem from his head, laid it before the emperor's effigy. Thus, in the country where the Romans had lately suffered the basest indignities, the brother of the Parthian conqueror paid homage to a statue of their prince, and consented to go to his capital with all the humility of a suppliant. (*The History of the Roman Emperors*, 6416)

Why do so many people believe Satan exists spiritually and unseen with signs in the natural realm, but when it comes to the beast, he is only a natural being and not a spiritual one as well?

Flavian Dynasty

The emperors of the Flavian Dynasty are Vespasian and his two sons Titus and Domitian. They make up the ninth, tenth, and eleventh heads or horns in biblical prophecy. Note here that the angel here brings in the eighth beast "who was and now is not" or an emperor who died at the time of the writing of Revelation, who became a spiritual entity like Satan was. It is the natural emperors of the Flavian dynasty, in the flesh, who destroyed the temple and persecuted the Jews and believers in Yeshua.

There were ten horns with crowns in the book of Daniel. This is where the horns with crowns as written in Daniel continue:

9. Vespasian (later deified; AD 69–79), temple destroyed, Julius Sabinus executed AD 79

Vespasian was against the Messiah, King of the Jews, like Herod was:

> It is also recorded, that Vespasian made a search for those who ere of the race of David, being anxious to destroy the descendants of the royal house ... He might be employed to annihilate all their (the Jews) reasonable hopes of seeing any future king arise from that stock, which they believed was to give birth to their Messiah. (*The History of the Roman Emperors*, 3789)

Titus is one of the heads of the beast worshipped. There were plagues during this time of Vespasian's reign:

> A colossal statue, more than a hundred feet high, was erected in the Sacred Way. It was intended originally for Nero; but on account of the disgrace of that prince, it appears to have been surmounted with the more honourable effigy of the head of Titus. While foreign nations were awed by the power of Vespasian, and the citizens in general were wontedly obedient to his sway, he was engaged in an acrimonious contest with the philosophers. (*The History of the Roman Emperors*, 3868) Among the few remarkable events which distinguish the latter years of Vespasian, Eusebius records, that an earthquake overthrew three

cities in Cyprus, and that a pestilence raged at Rome with so much violence, that for some time it destroyed nearly ten thousand persons daily. *(The History of the Roman Emperors,* 3912*).*

This sounds similar to one of the plagues written about in Revelation 16:18–19.

Josephus wrote that when Jerusalem was taken by the Romans, idols were brought into the temple and placed above the eastern gate, and they sacrificed to them there. This would open a portal between two worlds and allow entities to enter. It could have been opened elsewhere in Rome earlier in the year. Therefore, the beast (aka the Antichrist—1 John 2:18–22; 4:3; 2 John 7; 2 Thessalonians 2:1–12) was already in the world of that time and went to the temple as prophesied.

Revelation was written before the portal opened because it was prophesied about his coming. John and Thessalonians were written a little later, speaking of how he was already present in the first century and not in our current century. The eighth beast from the pit could have entered the temple as an unseen presence. Eagles and images of the emperor (ensigns) were carried in front of the armies and considered divine honors, which would be considered abominations. No one would see him because hauntings are usually unseen with gradual manifestations of a presence. He could only be seen with eyes of the Spirit by the Spirit.

Hauntings are not seen with eyes of the flesh. This speaks of why idolatry with sacrifices is spoken against in the Lord's commandments; it opens portals or doors to the other side, which allows evil spirits of all kinds to enter. Yeshua's sacrifice is very powerful because it opens a door of another kind to the Father.

Yeshua is the portal or door to go through for salvation. At His death, there were many signs: saints rose from the dead, earthquakes occurred, the sun was blocked by clouds, and the veil of the temple was torn in two. We should still partake of the body and blood—even if the saints of that time are now physically with Him in the kingdom and do not need to partake of it. I think we should until He is revealed to us too by the Spirit and we enter to be with Him.

10. Titus (later deified; AD 79–81)

Mount Vesuvius erupted in AD 79 and killed many people on land and sea. The city of Pompeii was destroyed and buried. Day turned to night. "The second angel sounded, and something like a great mountain burning with fire was thrown into the sea" (Revelation 8:8).

It was recorded that during the eruption, and some regarded it as fiction, that some people had witnessed "men of gigantic stature ... traversing the earth, and circling in the air, by day and by night" (*The History of the Roman Emperors*, volume 2, 4219).

Could they have seen the holy angels? Others may have doubted their testimony because they did not witness it themselves. It sounds like people today who say it didn't really happen if they didn't see it too.

11. Domitian (claimed to be God; AD 81–96)

Daniel's little horn from the kingdom rose after the ten horns. He persecuted the saints. He was not one of the ten horns, but he came after the ten. Daniel's prophecy of the beastly kingdoms ended with the end of the Flavian dynasty. He claimed to be God. The Messiah came sometime around AD 70–96, but there was either an extended stay or another return in order for the Crusades to occur.

Feasts

From the time of the birth of Christ until about AD 96, the fulfillment of the feasts occurred:

All of these were fulfilled within the first century and continue today: "His mercy extends to every generation ... Call on the name of the Lord, and you shall be saved."

- Passover (Yeshua celebrates and His crucifixion)
- Unleavened bread (death for three days)
- Firstfruits (His resurrection)
- Pentecost (harvest, Holy Spirit, baptism of Joel)
- Gap of forty years (earthly) and not two thousand years as many believe. Why five times longer than Hebrews slavery in Egypt? Why five times longer than Israel without a prophet? Why the long limbo? What is this long gap for between the feasts?

Feast of Tabernacles or Booths:

- Trumpets—defeat enemies and Second Coming
- Day of Atonement—purifying the bride of Yeshua, resurrection of saints
- Tabernacles—feast and reign with the King, hence a reign that continues on a new earth

The Order in Revelation

Revelation 19:11–21 (circa 70–96)

The Messiah's return was in the first century as early as AD 70 and as late as AD 96, according to Daniel with the little horn (Daniel 7:9–14). He came "in the days of these ten kings" or Roman emperors (horns), and there was war with the beast, probably from AD 70–96. Yeshua was here unseen fighting and setting up a kingdom.

Caiaphas, the high priest, was more likely a very old man, and some disciples could have still been alive. Yeshua knew the generation he'd come in but not the day or hour. The beast and false prophet were judged by Yeshua. Yeshua is like a thief in the night. He comes while people are unaware and are sleeping spiritually.

Revelation 20:1–10 (circa 70/96– AD 1080/1096)

- millennial reign in heaven and/or unseen dimension of earth
- resurrection of saints only and Satan bound
- His kingdom unseen yet present in the world still

Revelation 20:7–10 (aligns with circa AD 1095–1291)

- Crusades or Gog and Magog (Ezekiel 38–39)

The war continued with Yeshua in the earth. Certain people saw Yeshua at this time (Ezekiel 39:29). Gog and Magog were the nations called from the ends of the earth at that time to surround the holy city—not the Russians of this era. Some teach that Gog and Magog is Russia, but Russians today don't fight with swords, horses, charioteers, or bows and arrows. The Crusaders fought with horses, swords, and charioteers, and bows and arrows.

Israel was restored after Crusades and not before. Matthew 25:31–33 could have occurred as or after they died.

- Harvest of the tares with wheat or the resurrection of the dead with saints until the end
- Satan loosed

Daniel 11:40; Ezekiel 38:4, 5, 8, 15; 39:3, 9, 20 and Revelation 20:7–10 speak of the same event (the Crusades). Do we war with swords, bows and arrows, shields, horses, and chariots today? No, but the nations that were deceived and tried to seize the city Jerusalem, the camp of the saints (Jews), during the eleventh and twelfth centuries did. The Crusaders were deceived by Satan, so it makes sense that the Jews and Jerusalem of that era were targeted and attacked. Satan had something to do with the delusion, deception, persecution, and slaughter of the Jews at that time. This is discussed in a little more detail in chapter 9.

Revelation 20:11–15 (The Day of Terror and Judgment)

- Signs of this are seen even now.
- Heavens and earth pass away or extinction. Fire and intense heat burn earth.
- Possible mega, super massive black hole which could be the portal to the lake of fire, the Second Death, into which the unholy and defiled, the natural and spirit realms, the old order is cast (thrown) into or pulled into. This is powerful and large enough to move the stars and constellations and also have Death and Hades cast into it. Just as no one can leave the lake of fire, nothing can leave a black hole once the event horizon, or gateway, is crossed.

CHAPTER 4

The Tribulation

Matthew 24:23–28 and Luke 17:20–37 includes a proverb: "Wherever the corpse is, there the vultures will gather." This is mentioned by Yeshua. It doesn't mean that His Second Coming would be so obvious. How could that be the meaning if Luke wrote that the kingdom doesn't come with signs to be observed—and the apostles will not see it with their natural eyes? How is it then obvious with the natural eye? If so, one verse shortly after contradicts the other verse in the same passage.

It could be that He was making two points with one proverb. The first point is in Matthew. One interpretation could be that the false messiahs and false prophets were to be the corpse, and the vultures were the gullible, naïve, and deceived people who followed them and gathered around the false one whose insides were like a corpse.

The disciples were warned by Him to not follow them, for it would be like following or going to a walking corpse and possibly getting trapped (deceived). Instead of feeding off the living bread of heaven, they would feed off of a corpse (trusting and obeying the deceiver) and die. False prophets and messiahs were a part of the times to come in the first century, but that does not encompass the described passage.

There is another literal and symbolic interpretation of the verses in Matthew could allude to the coming attack, fall, and desolation of Jerusalem in AD 70. This proverb Yeshua used could symbolically mean that *the Jews in that city were the corpse, and the vultures were the Roman armies: "Where the corpse is, there the vultures will gather."* He uses a proverb to describe the sign the believers would see before they had to flee for their lives. He is describing how it will be just before His return. He is describing *death. He is also describing quite literally how birds of prey will come and eat the corpses of the Jewish inhabitants of Jerusalem.*

Matthew 24:29 says that immediately after the tribulation of those days. The tribulation He is referring to is the destruction of the city and the temple—not a future tribulation in modern times. The latter interpretation is better applied to the verses considering the context of the passage. If this interpretation is offensive to a Jew, it's the truth that was spoken by the Messiah Yeshua Himself. History supports the fulfillment of this proverb in this interpretation.

In Luke, the proverb becomes literal. The bodies of those "taken" will be consumed by the vultures where the proverb becomes literal. Some interpret the phrase "One will be taken, and the other left" meant those "taken" are the raptured believers. "They did not understand until the flood came and took them all away" (Matthew 24:39). Those the flood took were destroyed.

It also says,

> There will be two men in the field, one will be taken and one will be left. Two women will be grinding at the mill; one will be taken and one will be left.

The words "took" and "taken" imply a destruction and death of the individuals. In Luke, it is the same. The disciples asked, "Where, Lord?" They did not ask where they were left, which is obvious—the field, the mill, in bed—but where are they taken.

Using the proverb literally, Yeshua said, "Wherever the body is, there also the vultures will be gathered." That is where they are "taken." This is not about the Rapture. Lot's wife was "taken" with destruction. When they tried to save their lives, they were "taken" to or with destruction. *When believers saw the "vultures" (literally and figuratively) coming and surrounding Jerusalem, it meant there was a smell of death. They were warned to get out quickly and flee to the hills of Judea—or they too could be taken with this tide of death.*

In the story of Achan (Joshua 7:16-18, 25-26), it describes how the tribe, families, and the men "were taken". They were chosen, probably by lot, to come forward for judgment. Achan's sin was found out and he and his family were stoned for it. Not a good end for someone "taken".

How can this proverb be applied to generations of today within the context it was spoken? Some believe it is about the rapture. It is a strange interpretation and comparison to think that "corpse" could represent Yeshua. Could the "vultures" represent the saints of a future generation to describe the Rapture? Why would Yeshua compare the Rapture to a corpse and vultures? Why use a dark and death analogy to represent something glorious and full of life, such as the first resurrection? This can't be what Yeshua meant.

> For just as the lightning comes from the east and flashes even to the west, so will the coming of the Son of Man be in His day. (Luke 17:24)

This verse can't contradict Luke 17:20–21: "The kingdom doesn't come with signs to be observed. People will not say, 'Look, here it is!' or 'There it is!'" These verses can't mean His arrival will be obvious to everyone with the natural eye but at the same time not obvious or seen with the natural eye. Just as lightning is visible across the sky in that region and the Spirit is poured out upon those around Jerusalem and the tribes that live near the city, so will the eyes of their spirit be opened as the Son of Man arrives. Lightning flashing in skies across Los Angeles is not seen by those in Houston or New York; only those who live in Los Angeles see it across the sky. Lightning flashes are not a global event. If the Spirit is poured out on the inhabitants of Jerusalem, according to Zechariah 12, it is not written that He also poured out on the inhabitants of Egypt too. "Every eye" is the eyes of the spirit opened by the Holy Spirit to see into the unseen dimension.

> But immediately after the tribulation of those days the sun will be darkened, and the moon will not give its light, and the stars will fall from the sky, and the powers of the heavens will be shaken. (Matthew 24:29)

The "powers of the heavens will be shaken" could be entities and principalities that reside there. There have been heavenly signs before that are recorded in scripture. The sun stopped moving for Joshua while in battle (actually the earth stopped spinning); the wise men followed the star to Bethlehem. It could have been a UFO, but the men did know what else to call it. It looked like a star, but stars don't travel within our atmosphere and hover over cities. It became very dark when Yeshua was dying on the cross. What could Yeshua be speaking about? It could have been solar and lunar eclipses and meteor showers, which look like falling stars.

The NASA websites, eclipse.gsfc.nasa.gov/SEhistory.html and eclipse.gsfc.nasa.gov/LEhistory/LEhistory.html list the history of eclipses that have occurred. I find it interesting that solar eclipses occurred around AD 29 (as the Messiah's ministry began), AD 33 (around the crucifixion of the Messiah), AD 59, and AD 71 (shortly after the temple destruction). Some could have been unrecorded, but they did occur. Lunar eclipses occurred AD 33 (around the Crucifixion of the Messiah) and AD 71 (shortly after the temple destruction). Pliny wrote about two eclipses in fifteen days in AD 71:

> For the eclipse of both sun and moon within 15 days of each other has occurred even in our time, in the year of the third consulship of the elder Emperor Vespasian and the second consulship of the younger. (*The Natural History*, Pliny the Elder)

Eclipses could cause the sun to grow dark as sackcloth and the moon not to give light or turn red. Meteor showers appear as stars falling from the sky. How else would people in the first century know they weren't stars but meteors falling through or across the sky? This is why we still see stars in the night sky today.

Both Matthew 27:45 and Luke 23:44 records a solar eclipse as Yeshua died,

> Now from the sixth hour darkness fell upon all the land until the ninth hour.

> It was now about the sixth hour and darkness fell over the whole land until the ninth hour,

Luke continues in verse 45,

> Because the sun was obscured;

Another way to put it, "the sun failing".

This was two solar eclipses, witnessed and recorded by Pliny and

Yeshua's apostles, one in AD 33 and another in AD 71. Eclipses can signify important events. How did these eclipses play a part in Scripture?

The eclipse of AD 33 was most likely at the time Yeshua died on the cross as recorded by Matthew and Luke. When Luke wrote that "The sun was obscured", it was by the moon.

We have solar and lunar eclipses in our present age but we can't ignore that both solar and lunar eclipses occurred in the first century shortly after the AD 70 temple destruction and desolation.

The first part of Matthew 24:29 reads, "But immediately after the tribulation of those days". What tribulation? The destruction of the temple and the desolation of Jerusalem was the tribulation. Both eclipses occurred in AD 71 shortly after that tribulation. This is not a coincidence, but fulfillment of prophecy and Yeshua's words. Why set this information aside, ignore it, and continue to look for a tribulation followed by two eclipses? Many don't put the pieces of the puzzle together. They miss this footprint.

> And then the sign of the Son of Man will appear in the sky, and then all the tribes of the earth will mourn, and they will see the Son of Man coming on the clouds of the sky with power and great glory, and He will send forth His angels with a great trumpet and they will gather together His elect from the four winds, from one end of the sky to the other. (Matthew 24:30, 31)

The mourning of the tribes of Israel must have lasted for some time after the temple was destroyed. The mourning of the tribes which began with the temple destruction could have continued well after its destruction. Could it be they mourned once in AD 70 as a result of both the destruction and revelation of Yeshua? Could it be they mourned two separate times in the course of the year for the temple and the second time at the revelation of Yeshua? The Jews would not get over that event so quickly. The temple was rooted into their lives and it was very traumatic to them to have it removed so violently.

Did Yeshua return in AD 71 instead of AD 70 or was there a sign in AD 71 that indicated that He had already arrived and was present as a thief in the night in an extended stay, or Parousia? Futurists still look for a coming tribulation that fulfills this prophecy. Since both a solar and lunar eclipse occurred in AD 71 immediately after the tribulation of AD 70 according to Yeshua's words, then Matthew 24:29 was fulfilled.

In God's sense of time, several months or one year later is immediately after. This is not a coincidence, but fulfillment of prophecy. Many don't put the pieces of the puzzle together. They miss this footprint, evidence of someone's presence.

Again, how do we know a first resurrection took place after the temple's destruction and the tribulation that came with it? From the verses in Matthew above, Yeshua said it would happen after the tribulation. But it was also spoken to Daniel,

> Many of those who sleep in the dust of the ground will awake, these to everlasting life, but the others to disgrace and everlasting contempt. But as for you, go your way to the end; then you will enter into rest and rise again for your allotted portion at the end of the age. (Daniel 12:2–3)

Again, "go your way to the end" means the end of the temple sacrifices and offerings. The "end of the age" is the Jewish age with the temple at the center of their lives. It was at this end that a resurrection would take place.

Some preterists interpret the sun, moon, and stars to mean the religious authorities of Jerusalem who were lights of the people being turned off as they were killed in AD 70. This can't be true since many of them were like "white-washed sepulchers with dead men's bones and everything unclean." Yeshua called their teachings "leaven" or evil. John the Baptist called them "Brood of vipers." Yeshua called them "sons of their father the devil."

How can these authorities and leaders be considered a light when Yeshua said they were like blind men leading the blind and a den of thieves? Or ones who refuse to enter the kingdom of heaven and keep others from entering? They are in no way a light to their communities. They don't shine in the land if, when Yeshua was born, it was written that in a land of darkness, there shone a light. How is the land dark if they are also light? The Jewish leaders were in the dark as well.

CHAPTER 5

The Two Reigns of the Saints or the Continuance of One

While the kingdom of God can be in the midst of its citizens while they dwell here on earth, Yeshua said His kingdom was not of this world (John 18:36). It will never be a part of this natural, evil world. He did not want to establish a visible kingdom here on this earth. He refused to take over Rome when they tried to make Him king (John 6:15). When He was tempted by the devil to receive the kingdoms of the earth if He worshipped him, Yeshua refused to worship Satan (Matthew 4:8–10).

The earthly reign is on the new earth, where Revelation 22:5 specifically says, "They will reign forever and ever." First, in Luke 17:20–30, Yeshua says His kingdom is not physical form as we understand this dimension. It doesn't come with observation, and people will not say, "Go here, look there." How can it be visible and physical on this present old earth if it is not seen with human sight as Yeshua suggested here?

Second, Yeshua said in John 3 that the kingdom of heaven cannot be seen except by the Spirit. One has to be born of the Spirit to see and enter it. He suggests that His kingdom is a spiritual kingdom and not a natural, earthly one. So, again, how can the kingdom be natural?

Third, even though it is written in Revelation, "Every eye will see," one has to consider if it is the eye of the spirit when man is filled with the Spirit or the eye of the human flesh that we are most familiar with. Yet many who are supposed to have faith, which is the substance of things *not seen*, say, "No one has seen and written about it being physically here in the natural realm, so when was it fulfilled?" They always revert back to what is seen in the natural when teaching about the kingdom. Their understanding doesn't stay in the Spirit. I don't understand why anyone would argue that His kingdom is only natural and not spiritual.

The reign of the saints is mentioned in the book of Revelation twice: first in chapter 20 during an old earth and then during and on the new earth in Revelation 22.

The first mention is one of an *unseen* kingdom for a *limited* time of one thousand years with the Messiah during the old *present* earth, but it is not necessarily on the natural earth. In Revelation 20:4, 6, the words "earth," "in the world" and "visible kingdom" is not written. This is adding to Revelation. There are those who were raised first and were from the Roman age. They did not receive the mark of the beast or worship his image. They were not from the modern ages, and they probably judged the tribes if Israel before the Diaspora. *The millennial reign is during the time of the first, old earth, but it is not necessarily in it.*

It's not eternal if it's only a thousand years. Verses 5 and 7 specifically say, "When the thousand years are finished" and "when the thousand years have expired." This part apparently is not forever and ever. The thousand years are not symbolic of eternity.

Is *the reign* only a thousand years? Is that *only the time the old creation has left* before the battle and judgment with the second death, which is only a thousand years? According to Revelation 22:5, their reign continues in the new earth. Did the saints' reign ever really end? Was it the time of the saints' reign left during the existence of an old earth? What actually ends is *the time this old earth and order has* until the battle, judgment, and little more time until the passing and destruction. During this finite time, the first-century saints reigned and judged the tribes of Israel, which were tribes before they were scattered, and knowledge of which tribe they belonged to was lost. Yeshua told the twelve (really eleven) apostles in Matthew 19:27–29, not us, that they would sit on twelve thrones judging the twelve tribes of Israel. This most likely was during this millennial reign. The new earth would be considered "the regeneration."

The reign of the saints should be thought of in stages. The end of the first stage of this reign, during the existence of the old heaven and earth, ends with the battle and judgment of Satan and the armies in the natural and spirit realms. This is a transition stage from old to new. The end of this reign does not necessarily cease altogether, but it continues as the second and final stage into the new creation forever and ever. The saints are to reign perpetually. The saints will still reign with Him as His trusted, chosen people or "bride" or "queen." We can't say we are no longer His "queen" or wife because the thousand years are over. A "queen's" role in the kingdom of heaven will not end. The reign of the saints seems to be the continuance of one reign alongside her King.

I wonder if the saints remaining in the earth in latter generations are still only a bride or also now a queen or in the least a "queen in waiting." We are a kind of bride-queen just by relation to the saints who have reigned and are with Him now. Being of that same olive tree, vine, the seed of Abraham, we are not only a bride still in this natural realm but a queen of sorts in relationship to the others with Him in heaven. We are a bride in knowing the reality of fulfillment, but we are not fully queens in the fullness of it, not being in the same dimension as He is in with the other saints. We are about to enter the fullness. For us, the countdown to fullness and entrance into His world has begun.

The saints were beheaded and resurrected, and most likely, some holy ones before them reigned in the unseen space of earth. "They surrounded the camp of the saints" (Revelation 20:9). The saints are either the Jews or the resurrected saints who were beheaded in the Roman Empire—not us or those in the natural realm of that time and era. They were reigning with Him. There are limitations we have that they don't have because of this natural flesh, and they were judged and rewarded already. We in the natural have not been yet. For them, it was not just a reality; they saw the fullness. Believers today only experience the reality as the first-century believers did. We will not know the fullness until we are resurrected and rewarded as they were. However, there should be less resistance because the head of the enemy has been crushed and judged. There will be persecution, but the saints today should prevail over their enemies.

Satan wanted back the keys of death and Hades for the power that was taken from him. He also wanted back what Yeshua returned to them—the rule and authority in His name in the unseen realm of earth and the air—which is why he surrounded their camp with the nations he deceived and ruled over. Satan was willing to battle for it, but he was defeated. He and the powers, principalities, and rulers in the dark realm who were with him were defeated.

If humanity rules the natural, then why does Yeshua give back what we already have? The saints reign in the natural world but more so upon the new earth.

The kingdom is seen with eyes of the Spirit by the Spirit (John 3:3, 5, 7). How is one to "see the kingdom" without the Spirit and/or with eyes of flesh? Why do so many believe His kingdom is physically seen on earth with eyes of flesh, yet when Yeshua said that to see His kingdom one must be born of the Spirit to see it—implying it is unseen, but only seen by the Spirit—they don't believe that? They do not have faith to accept this. The spiritual can be physical and very real, but His kingdom is not earthy, fleshy physical. It is not of this world, and it will never be. *If flesh and blood cannot inherit the kingdom of heaven, then how do we see the kingdom of heaven with eyes of flesh and blood?*

The millennial reign of saints is the reign in the realm that was once Satan's, but he pirated it. The Messiah returned it to humanity (the saints) in the thousand-year reign. This realm is within the earth and the air of the first heaven of the unseen dimension. Persecution dwindles, and the kingdom of darkness crumbles. The saints should be martyred less and less often since there is none to overpower them on earth. The authority and power are the same as in the first century, but there is expansion and furtherance of His kingdom. David heard an army marching on top of the trees, but they did not see. The prophet asked God to open the eyes of the king, and what was revealed was a great heavenly army. His kingdom is not seen with eyes of flesh and blood. "Faith is the evidence of things not seen", so we must have faith in matters of a spiritual kingdom.

What was a sign in the natural realm that a millennial reign happened in the spirit realm? What might be the footprint?

Lynn Louise Schuldt wrote,

> The main Roman religion changed from the worship of old pagan deities to Christianity. The Emperor Constantine in the fourth century made the illegal minority sect of Christianity the religion of the Empire. He, along with some 250 bishops, assembled at Nicaea for the first ecumenical council and formed the Nicene Creed who believed in one God, the Father Almighty, maker of heaven and earth. The Byzantine Empire was known as "the kingdom of heaven on earth."
>
> In 1095, one thousand years later, the Crusades began. The nations were deceived and they marched across the breadth of the earth and surrounded Jerusalem. Jerusalem had been the camp of the saints and the beloved city. Although only the first and sixth of the eight Crusades to take the Holy Land succeeded, the Crusades ended in

defeat in 1291 with the Moslems in Possession of Palestine. The fire from heaven which destroyed the Crusading armies may have been the Lord Himself.

Many Jews were killed by Crusaders on their way to and within Jerusalem, which means the popes and Christians of that time were deceived by the devil. They had become anti-Semitic and supported the persecution and killing of Jews. Satan had his hand in it. This was fulfillment of the prophecy of Gog and Magog.

The spread of the Gospel across the earth today and the increase of Christians and Messianic Jews is a sign in the natural world of a kingdom that has come in the Spirit. What started out so small has become worldwide. More and more people are being set free from the bondages of darkness and coming into the light.

Where many see a harvest, and it is a large one, I also see a coming kingdom that has defeated and is taking over the darkness. Its light is prevailing as it spreads. It is subduing darkness underneath it. I see a conquering King who is taking charge over the powers, territories, and possessions of his enemy. All in the kingdom of darkness are now captives of Yeshua to submit, be changed, and be saved or destroyed. It is in His hands to do as He wishes what God has placed in His hands and possession. Everything has become the property of the King. Even if it is evil, He will destroy with fire whatever is unholy, displeasing, and useless to Him. Either one surrenders and begs the mercy of the King or is destroyed. His enemies do not have an option to their woes.

What is another sign that His kingdom has come? The fact the Roman Empire fell and is no more is a sign. The fact that the kingdoms spoken of in Daniel are no longer here says something stronger and more powerful moved them out of the way. In the absence of one, there is the presence of another as a thief in the night. The statue doesn't fall, crumble, and blow away all on its own, and many centuries later, the kingdom of God begins to show up.

There is no mysterious 1,500-year gap between the statue and the Rock that comes and crushes it. Something great moved it out of existence. Something toppled all the other kingdoms and crushed them to dust. Something is here now, and it is God's kingdom. His kingdom is not of this world, and it is spiritual. Many know the Roman Empire is no more, but they do not make the connection that it is a sign of a visitation of someone great—a very great and mighty King, renowned in the heavens.

What's another sign of the presence of a kingdom? The terrors, troubles, and woes the Crusaders went through were a judgment from God. His wrath was upon them in the form of hunger, thirst, disease, confusion, loss, panic, and other judgments. Many of them died on the way to or at Jerusalem. Many returned home in defeat. They weren't successful. Someone was against them as they battled at Jerusalem, someone they couldn't naturally see. The battle of Gog and Magog or the Crusades used horses, swords, and arrows, which no nation today fights with on earth. So how could Gog and Magog be of our era and time?

The increasing and continual spread of the gospel across earth beyond the borders of the now fallen Roman Empire, the absence of the four worldly kingdoms and their judgment by an unseen force, the judgment upon the nations during the Crusades are signs that there is an unseen presence of someone, and the collapse and increased disorder in the world and countries to indicate a fall of dark powers in spiritual places. It takes faith to believe this.

In the second mention, the reign on the new earth is an eternal reign. It is the second stage or continuance of a reign that began during the existence of an old earth (Revelation 22:5; Daniel 7:18, 27; Isaiah 65:17–25; Isaiah 11; Ezekiel 40–48; Revelation 21–22; and Revelation 15:5–16:1). The temple is in heaven, and the city has no temple but the Lord. During this earth, the throne of David is established in Jerusalem.

The kingdom of God is in a dimension that our earthly bodies are unable to detect. One can only see it by the Holy Spirit. On the new earth, our new bodies will be able to detect the reality of His kingdom easily, with little effort, what is now unseen by our flesh. It is like the monarch butterfly that comes out of its cocoon. Though it was "reborn" from a caterpillar in North America, it is able to—as a butterfly—instinctively home its way to where the other butterflies gather in Mexico even though it has never in its life been there or seen it. It can detect and sense, it knows its way, and it has the capability to fly. It could not do all these things as a caterpillar. It was never taught or instructed how or where. It flies alone; no one leads it. It had to be born again or resurrected in a sense.

This reminds me of a large, dark colored butterfly in the month of October 2019 that arose up from near the garage door inside my garage as the door closed. It flew up high toward me as the garage closed. It landed on a shelf above my head. Its signal was cut off and it seemed to ask for help by landing near me. When I opened the garage door halfway, it knew it was open and immediately flew straight toward the opening and left. It had an ability to sense something I couldn't understand. It had a unique tracking ability. I didn't have to help it. It just knew where to go on its own. Most bugs flitter about the light or just land on something and buzz around trying to locate an opening.

It is the same with us. Inside of us, we are changing like a caterpillar. Though we are limited, there are gifts we have now that help us. As we are made new and go into our cocoons (being reborn in this body of flesh by the Spirit and/or resurrection from the dead), we emerge as a new creation with new abilities and powers. The saints are like butterflies who just know where home is, they know the way. They are free. It becomes instinctive. While the unsaved are like the other insects trying to search for the opening to the door or the way to freedom.

We have the ability to know the way to the New Jerusalem and to our Father in heaven even though we have never been there before or seen it. We are able to easily and instinctively do things we were incapable of before. We will instinctively home our way to the New Jerusalem where our King is. We will have this knowing just as the butterfly does. We as nations will gather—just as the monarch butterflies in Mexico do—in the New Jerusalem. It will come naturally, just as it does for the monarch. This knowing is innate in every believer. It takes faith to believe in the truth of a very real kingdom made up of a different substance, which our flesh cannot reach, attain to, or sense with the senses we are most familiar with and rely on. This is why Yeshua said we must be born again of the Spirit. Though we do not understand fully now, it is there inside us by the Holy Spirit.

Think of a cocoon. The creature is not dead, but it is still and silent. It changes. Though dead, we are not dead. We sleep—still and silent. We change. For the saint (actually anyone), death is not the end; it is a change. It is a gateway to newness. For some of the wicked, it is a change to a beast or an evil form for destruction. For the saint, the umbilical cord for life is the Holy Spirit. He keeps you while you sleep.

We already have authority in the natural realm of earth—but not the spiritual realm. The saints have been limited in the natural realm. The Prince of the power of the air dominated in the first century (Ephesians 2:2). Upon His return, the saints meet the Lord in the air. This was written in the future time of His arrival to Paul's generation (1 Thessalonians 4:17).

This verse indicates a displacement in the air of a prince of darkness by a conquering King, Yeshua. Yeshua dismantles and destroys the kingdom of darkness.

In the unseen realm of first heaven (the air) and earth:

- Satan fell from heaven as lightning, but where did he fall to? To earth, but in the natural realm, we don't see this dragon physically. We never saw him fall like lightning to earth as Yeshua. No one recorded it. So, where else could he have been? In a realm we can't see that is still considered of earth. This is a space that Satan fell to and from where he ruled humans on his throne.
- Adam and Eve were banished from this realm where the tree of life was. It could be that their bodies had an ability to traverse this space before the fall, and death entered.
- Yeshua traversed this space after His resurrection and before ascension to the Father.
- This was from where the saints reigned for a thousand years.
- Humans (specifically the saints) will be given authority and rule back in the spirit along with the natural realm.
- It is where God's army ports when He went before His people, Israel, in battle.
- It is where Moses and Elijah met with Yeshua on the mount.
- It is where Yeshua returned in clouds of heaven with angels.
- It is where He fought evil powers and entities of the dark kingdom who are assigned over the nations, including the beast, the false prophet, and Satan.

If we understand that it is from this unseen realm that the saints reigned with the Messiah (and He does have His throne in heaven beside the Father too), then why do we think that Yeshua wins back for us the rule and authority in a reign of just the natural realm and not the spiritual? Doesn't what is of the spirit come first and before the natural? The Messiah's kingdom is not of this world, which is in the natural realm.

As believers, the rule doesn't necessarily end with the thousand-year reign; it continues into the new earth. The thousand-year reign of Revelation marked the time of a spiritual reign during the existence of an old earth—not necessarily visible on this present earth—until the time of battle, but the reign of His saints doesn't stop. As believers in Yeshua, if we truly believe that the authority that was given away through deception to the devil was returned to us by Yeshua, what are we doing with that authority for earth's sake? Should it be only used for the spiritual realm and not the natural one? Creation waits for the revelation of the sons and daughters of God. This spiritual reign will continue on the new earth. If the saints have already reigned with Him, what does this mean for believers today? We shall reign on the new earth.

For believers, spreading the Gospel of the kingdom was one aspect of our calling, but there was another one: ruling earth. Should we have practiced the former while neglecting the latter?

According to His will, we serve Him in the transition and changing of the old to new order, according to our faith and abilities. He rules over creation and over darkness, and in Him, so do the believers. One said, "We plunder the powers of darkness and establish the rule of Jesus wherever we go by preaching the King's domain." The authority the saints have does not change from the first century on, but what changes as time progresses is the region into which God's kingdom expands and experiences less and less resistance as He takes over the enemies' kingdom and does with it as He wishes.

Yeshua becomes our resource for everything we need to live here when the earth is unable to produce resources anymore and is only able to produce because of His Living Word. God is the glory of the temple—His people. Surely the righteous shall inherit the earth. May His name be lifted up and praised now and forever. Amen.

CHAPTER 6
Kingdom Takeover/Day of the Lord

This is about a great and renowned One who conquered and judges. This is about One who has conquered and is changing and removing an old order and bringing in a new one. At this moment, He is making massive changes to the world and to the kingdom of darkness for they have become His possession to do as He wishes in accordance with the will of the heavenly Father.

Satan is judged. The idea that Satan was bound and is judged now is not contradicting Peter and Paul's statements in 1 Peter 5:8 or Ephesians 2:2. Satan is not omnipresent, being on earth and in the lake of fire too. The lake of fire is not a place one can enter and exit at will, whenever they choose, not even angels. The lake of fire is not the same as Hades which contains fire too. Hades is the first death; the lake of fire is the second death.

In Hades, the abode of the dead where Lazarus was, an entity can enter and exit at will. Fallen angels do not have special rights, privileges, benefits, or passes to enter and exit the lake of fire at will. Once in, they are locked in. He has servants and children who have their evil nature, but they go the way of their master. It would be difficult convincing them otherwise during their generation in the first century.

Yeshua has fulfilled much now. *It is no longer about dry and arid places in the earth evil spirits go to, now is the time of torment.* Nations are in the dark today because they must be born again to enter and see the kingdom. They are bound by fleshly lusts. Remnants of Satan's kingdom still influence.

We are at the culmination of the Day of the Lord. Where does the fire of the Day of the Lord come from? Is it from only one or multiple sources? Is it a combination of sources? Is it Hades where Lazarus was? Or is it the sun, a supernova, or a possible super massive, mega black hole which is eerily similar to the lake of fire? It seems they bear a likeness to each other. It reads in 2 Peter 3 that the heavens (plural) and earth would pass away and be dissolved by fire. Words from different translations like *destroyed, pass away, disintegrate, disappear, dissolved,* and *everything* mean nothing remains. This does not lend itself to only a purging of earth where something is left behind as some teach but to destruction or "dissolving" as described in 2 Peter 3 where it is no more. It is gone. There is nothing left to remind us that it ever existed. It does not mean fire cannot come from multiple sources, natural and supernatural, seen and unseen. Let's run through the reasoning:

Hades or Gehenna (Lazarus and The Rich Man)

This story takes place during the old heaven and earth because the rich man asked if his brothers, who were still living on earth, could be warned about this place. Yeshua couldn't be projecting forward into the future with this story when Hades was thrown into the lake of fire here (Revelation 20:14) because the heavens and earth pass away before or as Hades is thrown into the lake.

How could the rich man ask Abraham to send Lazarus to go warn his brothers who are on an existing earth about the place he was in? This fiery, dark place is deep within the earth, but it is too small to destroy both the heavens (plural) and earth. There were two parts in Hades for the saints: where Lazarus was and where the wicked were. There is heat and flame that can affect the spirit there—but to a lesser degree than the lake of fire because Lazarus's spirit thirsted. This seems to be part 1 of death. Hades is thrown into a place that is *so much bigger* than itself. Hades does not swallow itself; it cannot be thrown into itself. Hades is cast into something else massive. Here is the place of different levels of punishment. This would not move the stars out of their places. It is not written that earth alone passes away, but both the heavens and earth pass away. The fire within earth is not enough to destroy the heavens (plural). The lesser cannot consume the greater. If the lake of fire is within the earth, how do the heavens get destroyed too? This place cannot be the lake of fire mentioned in Revelation.

The Sun

This can destroy the first heaven and earth and the solar system and swallow up Hades, but it does not move the stars out of their places and the other heavens, including space. This fire is made for the natural realm. The makeup of this fire is different because it would probably burn the natural only but not what is spirit. One star alone probably would have little effect on the spirit. It shines and burns only in the natural realm.

The sun most likely does not shine in the spirit realm. A light dawned on those sitting in the land and shadow of death (Matthew 4:15, 16; Isaiah 9:1–2; 60:1–3). If the land was dark, the natural light of the sun could not shine on in the spiritual dimension of earth. Natural light does not reach there. The sun is not sufficient enough to burn what is of the spirit. It burns what is in the natural. Perhaps the fire of millions or billions of stars could do more damage to the natural and spiritual realms.

Supernova Explosion

This could destroy several systems nearby, including the first heaven and earth. It could not destroy space or the heavenly bodies (plural). Again, this may have little effect on what is spirit. This fire is made for the natural realm.

Meteors/Fireballs

They burn what is in the natural. They could damage and destroy earth, but do not destroy the heavens. Meteors, probably considered stars in the first century, may have been witnessed falling toward earth shortly after the AD 70 destruction of the temple after an eclipse of the sun and moon. In a cyclical pattern of prophecy, more sightings of meteors and fireballs striking earth are being witnessed in recent years. Although these do not change and destroy the heavens, their increasing appearance could be a sign of something changing in the heavens and a warning to the inhabitants of the earth of impending judgment and doom. A meteor strike on the level of that brought the dinosaurs to extinction can increase the temperature on earth.

Super Volcanoes

They burn what is in the natural. They can do damage and destroy earth, but do not destroy the heavens or move the stars out of their places.

Lake of Fire or a Super Massive Black Hole

I believe this is the fire that John the Baptist is referring to in Matthew 3:8-12. In verses 10 and 12, he says fruitless trees and chaff would be burned with unquenchable fire. This is a place we cannot see yet. This fire consumes the spirit and body. It was made for the devil and his angels who have spirit bodies/flesh. The flame was created to easily destroy their spirit bodies—not just what is of the spirit but also what is of the natural. It does not have a limit to what can burn. It is created for the mind, soul, and body.

The flood of Noah's time destroyed the natural world, but this fire will destroy what is natural and supernatural, what is above and below. The flood only killed the world of that time leaving the heavens untouched and earth to remain, the coming fire destroys the heavens and earth and all within them. The fire is worse than the flood. I think that the fire is from the same source—burning the heavens and earth, but also the dead in Hades.

It is common for believers to speak of the lake of fire as one kind of flame for the dead during the judgment and the fire reserved for the heavens and earth is another kind of fire, but the source of this fire could be one and the same and it is an actual physical place. Believers today tend to think that the fire will only destroy earth leaving the heavens untouched. They also tend to think it is just like the flood where the earth is not destroyed, but remains. They don't consider how massive, destructive, and terrifying this will be encompassing everything natural and supernatural in its path.

So when 2 Peter 2:10–13; 2 Peter 3:10, Isaiah 13:6–10, and Isaiah 34:4 are read, how many believers think that this could be the second death, the lake of fire? The same fire that destroys the dead also destroys the heavens and earth. The same fire that destroys the heavens and earth also destroys the dead. The source is the same for the most part. This is where the beast, false prophet, and Satan are. The fire in the Day of the Lord that consumes the heavens and the earth could very well be the same as the second death coming upon the heavens and earth and all that is on and under the earth.

The place is massive and easily swallows up Hades and death when these are cast into it. This is not the Hades in earth where Lazarus was. This is a part 2 of what he experienced in part 1. If Hades was terrible enough in part 1, then how much worse is it going to be in part 2 with the second death. This would go from an unseen realm to one that is natural. It is huge and massive enough to swallow Hades, death, the heavens (plural), and earth, and it can move the stars from their places or cause them to disappear. Astronomers have noticed expansion or spreading out of the stars and millions of black holes in space.

If the heavenly bodies above burn, melt, and dissolve, then all that is in and under them will as well, including earth. The greater consumes the lesser. How is it that the earth is only purged and left if the heavenly bodies above and around it burn, melt, and dissolve too? The beast and false prophet are already there. They were thrown alive into this place (Revelation 19:20). Nero went into the abyss (which may have been another type of black hole) upon death and as the beast, a spiritual entity, was cast alive into this place (Revelation 17:8). He came out of the abyss and went to his destruction. Revelation says the serpent was thrown into the lake of fire where they were—not into Hades.

Could this be a mega, super massive black hole in space? Whose intense heat and fire consists of many stars? With the weight of gravity so dense and massive to burn and tear apart what is not only natural, but spirit too? It has a weight of gravity so dense that all that crosses its gates is torn apart to its base. Natural light cannot escape from black holes. Their pull is very strong. It could easily swallow up the earth, death, and the fiery Hades under the earth. It could swallow up planets, stars, asteroids, light, and much of what is in the heavens. A black hole could make the stars above disappear or move and give the appearance of fleeing. It can move the stars out of their places or cause them to vanish as the earth grows old and dies off as it was written in Scripture:

> Lift up your eyes to the heavens, and look on the earth beneath, for the heavens will vanish away like smoke, the earth will grow old like a garment, and those who dwell in it will die in like manner (Isaiah 51:6; see also Isaiah 66:22–24)

> From whose face the earth and the heaven fled away. (Revelation 20:11)
>
> And if anyone's name was not found written in the book of life, he was thrown into the lake of fire. (Revelation 20:15)

The above scriptures indicate two disasters, not one. If the first disaster doesn't kill humankind, the second certainly will with the exception of the saints who inherit the new earth. It occurs either at about the same time or one right after the other one. It is not just earth's extinction below, but also its fleeing along with the heavens or both being pulled into a fiery abyss. I don't understand anyone who says the earth cannot or will not be destroyed with black holes of varying sizes lurking everywhere in space. They downplay the severity of how it will be. The creator is capable of destroying.

The lake of fire existed during the first century. John would not call it a "super massive black hole". No one could see this coming unless they were sensitive to the signs. The fire in the Day of the Lord that "burns like a furnace" seems to be this. The super volcanoes and other forms of natural fire are also reserved for the Day of Judgment. It is here the tormenter of the fiery, dark Hades becomes the tormented. It is here that he joins the beast and false prophet.

> Wail for the day of the Lord is near! It will come as destruction from the Almighty. Therefore all hands will fall limp, and every man's heart will melt. They will be terrified, pains and anguish will take hold of them; they will writhe like a woman in labor, they will look at one another in astonishment, their faces aflame. Behold, the day of the Lord is coming, cruel, with fury and burning anger, to make the land a desolation; and He will exterminate its sinners from it. For the stars of heaven and their constellations will not flash forth their light; the sun will be dark when it rises and the moon will not shed its light. Thus I will punish the world for its evil and the wicked for their iniquity; I will also put an end to the arrogance of the proud and abase the haughtiness of the ruthless. I will make mortal man scarcer than pure gold and mankind than the gold of Ophir. Therefore I will

> make the heavens tremble, and the earth will be shaken from its place at the fury of the Lord of hosts in the day of His burning anger. (Isaiah 13:6-13)

Isaiah 13:6-13 describes the Day of the Lord which extends across millennia. In this description it describes making man "scarce" and "exterminating its sinners" which has the same meaning as *extinction*. It describes fire with the phrase "faces aflame". It describes "the heavens and earth shaken from its place" (see also Hebrews 12:26-28). It describes "the stars of heaven and their constellations not flashing forth their light". What is massive enough to cause stars to not shine anymore and actually cause trembling and shaking in the heavens? Hades within the earth where the dead are, a Super volcano, meteors, and the Sun cannot do this. This could be describing a mega black hole lurking unnoticed.

One thing to keep in mind, there are probably different types of black holes. As creator, He can design one to fulfill His words of a destruction of the heavens we see along with this earth. Scientists speculate what is on the other side of a black hole. Could it be a path to an alternate universe where if one makes it across they can never return or a place that destroys altogether breaking everything down to subatomic material? Could one be the bottomless abyss described in Revelation and another one a lake a fire? Could they be all of these as He purposed them, each one having their own function and purpose?

In 2 Peter 3:10, it reads the heavens pass away with *a great noise* or *roar*. A black hole could perhaps produce that much sound as it engulfs the heavens. Maybe even the explosions of supernovas as stars are being destroyed.

The words "cast", "thrown", and "fled" could also be pictured as a black hole pulling in heaven, earth, and people inside of it. First century minds did not understand the concept of the force of gravity. They would not describe the vision of the lake of fire, as in Revelation, as something that pulls, swallows, and draws things inside. Someone seeing a vision of this in the first century has a picture of being cast, thrown, and fleeing, but to a modern mind observing what black holes do, the picture is the same except we understand it as pulling away. It's like standing at the top of a building or tree and observing an object drop from a great height. To a first century mind, it is falling, but also it is thrown and cast away. To a modern mind, it is falling or being pulled away from you. We are more familiar with the force of gravity. It is also like a ship sinking into the depths of the ocean that is pulled down by gravity. Likewise, with a black hole, anything that comes too close sinks into it because of gravity. Both perspectives are not wrong, the picture is the same, but it's described differently.

Heaven and earth fled from His presence (Revelation 20:11; Revelation 21:1) could be a picture of being on the inside of a black hole (containing fiery sides and bottom) that is pulling many stars, planets, asteroids, gases, and light inside *away from His presence and away from this present universe* they all used to exist in. Seeing this from within a black hole gives the picture of fleeing *from Him* as it is pulled into a black hole. If something is pulled into something by gravity, it has the motion of fleeing from something.

> All the host of heaven will wear away and the sky will rolled up like a scroll; all their hosts will also wither away as a leaf withers from the vine, or as one withers from the fig tree. (Isaiah 34:4 NASB)

> All the host of heaven shall be dissolved, and the heavens shall be rolled up like a scroll; all their host shall fall down as the leaf falls from the vine, and as fruit falling from a fig tree. (Isaiah 34:4 NKJV)

Revelation speaks of a solar and lunar eclipse to occur before great panic and terror falls on the nations of the world and possibly during the time of the second resurrection where there will be wheat and tares. These do not have to be the same eclipses as the ones in AD 70 after the temple destruction.

With prophecy being cyclical, this could be a dual fulfillment where the first fulfillment was in AD 70 around the time of the first resurrection, and the other fulfillment in the near future at a second resurrection. The first fulfillment where "stars" are actually meteors and fireballs and that generation would not call them meteors. The second fulfillment is actually stars being moved by a great unseen force during the continuing visitation or another visitation of the Lord.

> I looked when He broke the sixth seal, and there was a great earthquake; and the sun became black as sackcloth made of hair, and the whole moon became like blood; and

the stars of the sky fell to the earth, as a fig tree casts its unripe figs when shaken by a great wind. The sky was split apart like a scroll when it is rolled up, and every mountain and island were moved out of their places. Then the kings of the earth and the great men and the commanders and the rich and the strong and every slave and free man hid themselves in the caves and among the rocks of the mountains; and the y said to the mountains and to the rocks, 'Fall on us and hide us from the presence of Him who sits on the throne and from the wrath of the Lamb; for the great day of their wrath has come, and who is able to stand?' (Revelation 6:12-17; Matthew 24:29-31; Mark 13:24-27; Hebrews 1:12)

But the day of the Lord will come like a thief, in which the heavens will pass away with a roar and the elements will be destroyed with intense heat, and the earth and its works will be burned up ... looking for and hastening the coming of the day of God, because of which the heavens will be destroyed by burning, and the elements will melt with intense heat! (2 Peter 2:10, 12)

A massive black hole could cause shaking and trembling as it moves the stars and earth out of the places. It could cause constellations to change and not give their light anymore. This would be a huge sign to pay attention to.

To be "cast" or "thrown into the lake of fire" can be synonymous with being pulled into a black hole with hot, fiery stars. Once anything passes the point of the event horizon, which is like a gateway, nothing can leave. Nothing exits a black hole. Nothing exits the lake of fire either, not even Satan. If we look at some pictures of black holes, there is a fire surrounding a black sphere. That fire looks like a twisting and turning fiery lake around a black center dragging everything around and inside without anything escaping free from its massively powerful grip. I can see how a black hole can be the second death spoken of in Revelation. How many make the connection and believe it?

In 2016, a group of scientists discovered gravitational waves (an invisible and very fast ripple) in space using sound waves with a specially made device and technology. Gravitational waves were predicted by Albert Einstein a hundred years earlier. They think that this could be either a supernova explosion or two black holes colliding. It was heard as a short chirp.

In 2017 and April of 2019, astronomers picked up on gravitational waves. Yasemin Saplakoglu in *Space.com*:

> Astronomers detected such gravitational waves from a neutron star collision in 2017 and from one in April of 2019 . . . But gravitational waves from collisions of such massive objects typically last longer and manifest in the data as a series of waves that change in frequency over time as the two orbiting objects move closer to each other.

As recent as January 14, 2020, astronomers detected more gravitational waves. Yasemin writes:

> A mysterious cosmic event might have ever-so-slightly stretched and squeezed our planet last week. On January 14, astronomers detected a split-second burst of gravitational waves, distortions in space-time . . . but researchers don't know where this burst came from.
>
> One more likely possibility is that this short-lived burst of gravitational waves comes from a more transient event, such as a supernova explosion, the catastrophic ending to a star's life.

They do not know what could be the source of these waves. It could have been Betelgeuse star going supernova or two merging black holes.

Perhaps this could mean more than they think. Perhaps this ripple in space is a sign of the heavens being shaken and something is coming our way. It is to be revealed what it is. According to scripture it isn't really a good thing. It is not a coincidence that as earth dies, a collision or explosion is heard from deep space (heavens tremble), yet scripture describes disaster occurring on earth, but also the heavens too around the same time. Scientists are excited about this, but this could be signaling something terrifying.

Scientists suspect that the giant star, Betelgeuse, already exploded. It was seen dimming. We wouldn't see the explosion yet in our sky now, since the light of the explosion hasn't reached us yet. What we see is an intact giant star still as though we look at what it used to be, not what it actually is now. Could this be one way how "the stars of heaven and their constellations will not flash forth their light"? Another way is the loss of their mass upon entering a black hole due to tidal forces?

Black holes are capable of tearing objects down to its basic unit. It obliterates everything. The temperature near and within is extremely hot with the many stars it swallows up. Black holes could "dissolve" the elements of the heavens and earth, which also means they disintegrate or disappear. All of which is taken out of existence.

Black holes could cause "the sky to be rolled up like a scroll" and actually "move mountains and islands out of their places". A black hole could split the sky apart. It can give the picture of stars being cast away like leaves off of a fig tree or "withering". The word "withering" or "rot" could be the dimming of their light or disappearance of stars, which a black hole could cause.

It is my guess that with all the black holes spotted in the heavens with the fire that comes from billions of stars, there is one black hole or gateway reserved for our solar system or galaxy. With every black hole, He is judging and destroying angels and entities, His enemies in the heavens. Perhaps all the black holes are entry ways to the one place, the lake of fire. *When we see a black hole, we could be looking at second death itself. We could be looking at the gate or portal to the second death.*

They are eerily the same or similar to each other. It is not a coincidence that they each have characteristics that are the same or similar. It is not a coincidence that astronomers are discovering more black holes in recent years as much prophecy has been fulfilled too. Earth has been very fortunate to avoid many catastrophes from space, but according to His word, this fortune will soon run out. This goes along with the saying *if it looks like a duck, quacks like a duck, walks like a duck, it's probably a duck.* Likewise, if the lake of fire, or second death, does the same thing as a black hole as described in Isaiah and Revelation, then it is most likely a type of black hole.

If men are already terrified with the signs of earth dying now, what will they be when they begin to see this and there is nothing anyone can do to save them? It is out of their reach. Saying this can't happen will not keep it from happening just as much saying the apple won't fall to the ground. Gravity is going to cause the apple to fall to the ground just as much as God's word is going to come to fruition.

We now see earth passing away and growing old with the birth pangs that began in the first century, but what is lurking in the heavens that no man can quite understand or see that could destroy and swallow up earth, death, and Hades and every natural creature and spiritual entity in its path? What is it that approaches us or pulls us toward it without us knowing it? Even if we could save the earth, which can't happen contrary to Yeshua's word, there still remains something huge that changes not just the earth, but the heavens we see at night causing it to change, move, flee, and vanish.

Who can escape the wrath of God? Who has the authority and power to override and make void His word? We are all at His mercy. How can anyone downplay what is written in Scripture and say the world is never going to end or earth can't be destroyed? How can they say this as though it is not serious and they say anyone who says otherwise is an idiot? We must be careful that we don't have the same attitude, disregard, and unbelief that the people of Noah's time had and were destroyed by water.

I think the state of the planet now is a sign of what is to come in the heavens. The Scripture speaks of both of these occurring at about the same time. At a time when earth is growing old and is dying, the heavens begin to vanish. According to Isaiah, this is what we or younger generations will begin to witness too. If some people are already terrified at what is currently happening to earth, what will they do when they see what is happening in the heavens? God has timed this well. This is why there has to be an exodus of a different kind. We have to get out of here. We should watch the heavens very closely.

With this, how can one teach that the fire that will burn the earth, will only be a purging therefore earth will remain? How can this earth remain if the stars are moved out of their places and disappear, vanish, or fall away? Is He not able to destroy what He also created? "He destroys those who destroy the earth", but how can humans destroy earth, but He is somehow incapable of destroying it? Is He not able to create a brand new earth untouched by evil, sin, and death?

What about Israel? His people will inherit not just a city, but a new earth. They will have a heavenly city upon the new earth as an inheritance free from evil and death. No one will ever try to take their land and city away again.

Spontaneous Combustion

Spontaneous combustion is when objects suddenly burst into flames without a natural source to cause it.

There are stories of streets melting, traffic lights melting, and the bumpers of some cars melting in the East (see video under Spontaneous Combustion).

In all these things addressed above, including climate change, what are the inhabitants of earth doing? They do the same things that those of Noah's, Lot's day did, and also those in the generation of the AD 70 destruction and desolation: eating, drinking, marrying, buying, selling, and building. It is everyday business as usual until destruction comes and takes them.

I ponder three questions:

1.) How is it that many have seen Satan in the lake of fire by vision, dream, or death experience and also in the world visiting his servants with missions to do? Does he have special privileges, rights, passes, or benefits that he uses to leave the lake of fire? Is it the fiery Hades or the lake of fire? He is not omnipresent, so how is he in two places at once? No one considers this as they listen to the testimonies of witnesses who have visited hell and have supposedly sat down in person with him. It makes sense if it is the underworld of fiery Hades they refer to, but it doesn't make sense if it is the lake of fire.

2.) How is it that nine hundred years after the Crusades, Satan is still roaming the earth when it was written in the book of Revelation that he was thrown into the lake of fire? Again, how is he in the lake of fire and on the earth at the same time? Perhaps it is the fiery Hades he goes to and fro from, not the lake of fire. With the fulfillment of Gog and Magog as the Crusades, this could strongly indicate the imminency of his casting into the lake of fire along with the death and Hades. According to Revelation, he is cast into it before the heavens and earth is destroyed and flees from Yeshua's presence.

3.) How is it that people have visions, dreams, and death experiences of Satan in the lake of fire, but they still expect the beast and false prophet to come in the near future in the earth? How is Satan in the lake of fire before the other two? Revelation 20:10 says, "He was thrown into the lake *where the beast and false prophet are also.*" This indicates that they were already there ahead of him.

There is already a contradiction between what futurists experience and testify about and what they believe and teach. You can't teach that the beast is to be revealed after the temple is rebuilt, yet have visions of Satan already in the lake of fire well ahead of the beast and the false prophet. People are mistaken and contrary to the book of Revelation. *The serpent is not found in the lake of fire before the beast is even known to give the mark out on the earth. This is an error. This is a sign that if the devil is in the lake of fire now, then surely the beast and false prophet came already.*

Either the serpent is in Hades with a way to go back and forth between the two places or he is in the lake of fire with the beast and false prophet where they can never leave and go in and out of. If he is in Hades, which will imminently be cast into the lake of fire, it makes sense how he can traverse to and fro.

Also, "tormented day and night forever" (Revelation 20:10), suggests that earth exists when he is cast into the lake. It suggests that he is cast into a lake of fire before or while earth passes away. He may not even realize it is being done, like a frog in heating water. He is already being cast without knowing it.

So how is Satan in the lake of fire and also roaming the earth? The lake of fire is a place and has a location. It is in the spiritual realm. He can't do both. The answer seems that he is not omnipresent or able to leave hell.

He either:

- Traverses between Hades and earth, which in the near future will be cast into the lake of fire or,
- The earth, with Hades inside, is now beginning to be cast into the fire. They are becoming one.

The lake of fire is manifesting into the natural realm. Revelation 20:11–21:1 is a picture of the passing away or extinction. It is also a picture of fire burning everything in both dimensions of heaven and earth.

"The sea gave up the dead who were in it" (Revelation 20:13). The picture here is one of evaporation and drying up due to the heat and fire to reveal the dead. There is no longer any sea; there is no sea anymore because the heat and fire caused it to dry up (Revelation 21:1). "Death and Hades thrown into the lake of fire" is fulfilled while or after heaven and earth burn up. Could this be the climate change we are seeing? Are the catastrophes, disasters, and heating of earth signs of this beginning to happen?

Peter writes that heaven and earth will burn with fire and everything will melt with intense heat (2 Peter 3–15). Psalms and Isaiah say heaven and earth will pass away, which is the same as extinction, and scientists are already seeing this happen.

No one sees deeper than or beyond that of climate change or the Second Coming of the Messiah. These birth pangs don't end with Yeshua's second coming in the first century. They continue. No one sees the bigger picture. Everyone stops short of what is really happening on an even larger and frightening scale and scope.

Scientists explain the natural aspect of what is happening, but what is the spiritual aspect? Global warming and climate change could be one of the signs of the manifestation of the lake of fire. The second death was not meant to stay put in only the spirit realm; it is to manifest into this natural reality. It is not something that just stays over there in one location. Many don't think of the lake of fire doing this. Many think people go to it, but it comes to the unsaved too. It approaches the ungodly like a flood. It moves. It looms over and overshadows the wicked and faithless. It burns through and will spread like a wildfire. Is it a black hole?

The old heavens and earth seem to be becoming one with the lake of fire. What is occurring in the spirit realm is showing signs of manifesting in the natural realm. Perhaps the greater is beginning to swallow up the lesser.

Part 2 is looming over the heavens and earth. If you think part 1 is bad enough, and that's a prequel, there is a part 2 that is hard for the mind to fathom. The fire from this lake is different than the fire in Hades. It seems Hades's flame does not torment evil entities, but the lake of fire's flame will. Satan, demons, and the nations of the earth, dead and alive, don't understand the magnitude of what is going to unfold. It is a terrible thing to fall into the hands of an angry God.

Even in space, with how light travels, we will not see it coming before it's too late. If light from a distant star or galaxy reaches us thousands or millions of years after it left that location, then what we see in the sky is a past from that long ago. We do not see what is now occurring. The galaxies and stars are either moved or missing. They might have already been destroyed with fire, but how would the inhabitants of the earth know it? The night sky gives the false illusion that all is at peace when behind "the veil of the past," the heavens are actually in chaos in the deep. We, on earth, can't see it yet. Perhaps UFOs have become more noticeable in our time because they sense it from space. If Satan's kingdom has ties in space, if the Lord's enemies have ties there, then Yeshua must destroy them too as conquering kings do.

Just as the tongue (a natural part) is a fire that sets the course of one's life on fire, and this comes from hell, hell sets on fire the heavens and earth through the works of humans (a natural part), which could be in the way humans sin, transgress His commands, and destroy earth. As the tongue is set on fire by hell, so too will the heavens and earth be set on fire by hell. Where there is sin and death, it will find that person and surround them like floodwaters.

Scientists say that climate change is man-made, perhaps in part it is, but God's Word shall stand: "He will destroy those who destroy the earth." Climate change could be the natural sign of what is coming from the unseen spirit realm. Heaven and earth are sinking or being cast into a lake of fire. The kingdom of darkness is sinking into it as well. It is like a sinking ship just beginning to go down. We have to see the big picture, which is the natural and spiritual realm together. What is occurring in the natural realm is a sign of what is occurring in the spirit realm. We have to put the pieces of the puzzle together. The lake of fire is here and is beginning to manifest into the natural realm. Fire coming from the spiritual realm happened before.

When fire fell from heaven upon Sodom and Gomorrah, upon Elijah's sacrifice, and as it did upon Gog and Magog, it manifested from the spirit realm of heaven into the natural realm of earth. There is a sea of flames that the heavens and earth we see, feel, and sense, and also the kingdom of darkness are sinking into it.

The Day of the Lord is here and burning like a furnace. Read Isaiah 13:1–13; Joel 1:14–20. The Day of the Lord, which began in the first century and continues today, comes burning like a furnace, ending with what scientists call climate change. It describes the battle with the nations (Crusades). It also describes food, resources, and trees being burned and water drying up. It says the animals pant from thirst.

Hades is releasing her dead with "ghost sightings," "hauntings," or even people with physical bodies are seen. All these things we are seeing now. Where are we going to go? Where are we going to hide? Ghosts, demons, fallen angels, evil powers, and entities cannot hide from His wrath. Heaven and earth are going under.

The saints know how to hide in the Lord, and the fire cannot touch them because of the blood of Yeshua. The Word of the Lord shall stand. Heaven and earth are now passing away and shall be consumed in fire as it is written in the Bible. This is very serious and surreal. The people of the world do not understand that the eternal fire, God's wrath, is at the door and coming in. It is coming to an earth near you.

Another sign of something fearful coming: listen to the testimonies of people who have encountered ghosts, demons. Watch how the evil spirits behave. It is like they are fleeing or hiding. Why are some found under beds, in attics, in the walls, in the dark corners of basements, in abandoned buildings, in bunkers, and in the woods? It isn't just because there could be a portal. They seem to hang out there, and it's their go-to spot. How many holy angels have you read or heard about doing this? The only reason why a holy one would do that is to fight against an evil entity or set as a guard on a portal, but they wouldn't hang out there.

How many holy angels have you heard walking around attics for many years? What would it look like if Gabriel was hiding in Mary's closet to tell her the news of her being chosen? I think it's weird, unusual, and something is up. This is something fugitives do. What are they fleeing from? Who are they hiding from? Why are some eager to get into the natural realm and escape the wicked world they come from?

Think of Noah and the ark. The ark is the cross/altar/covering in Yeshua. The floodwater, which represents baptism and saves the believer, can also be a metaphor for the lake of fire. Eight were saved from destruction as they were covered. The world of that era wasn't covered. The world of that time experienced destruction by water, but current and future generations will experience a destruction of fire.

The door to the ark is closing, and the door to salvation is closing. The Gospel will not be spread anymore. Are you in the ark? Will you be inside before the door closes? Are you covered by the blood? How many can you get on the ark or in the lifeboat? How many souls are on earth and will be doomed? There is nothing the inhabitants of earth can do to save earth. The Word of the Lord—spoken through Isaiah, Psalms, and Peter—shall stand. The heavens and earth shall die, and who can override what the Lord has spoken? Who can reverse His decree? How can this just be a purging when the heavens above, under which earth exists, are destroyed too?

Think of Lot and his family. The angels removed the saints from the doomed cities under the cover of salvation by order of the King. The fire that fell from heaven began in the spirit realm, manifested into the natural world, and consumed everything in the doomed cities. This represents the lake of fire.

This world is under visitation. The world is facing extinction and destruction in fire. People focus on the signs in the natural and earthly realm, but they don't consider that it precedes something even more terrifying from the spirit realm. It will get worse before it gets better, it is only better for the saints, and it will only get worse for this world. This world is in grave trouble.

It is frightening enough to think earth is going into extinction because of human destruction. It is even more horribly terrifying to think everything is sinking into a lake of fire that is beginning to manifest into the natural. The lake of fire or hell is not just a place people go; it is a place that approaches like a black hole in space. The lake of fire or hell doesn't just destroy the spirit; it destroys the natural too.

Where futurists see an imminent Second Coming, I see death and fire in the presence of a King. I see a King already taking over, changing, and destroying what belonged to the devil. It is burning through even as the natural fires burn. Spontaneous combustion could be one of the signs.

Many Christians expect a Second Coming, but what comes is fire in the presence of or before the face of the King. The kingdom of darkness, the dead, and this modern world are facing an impending and imminent judgment.

The kingdom of darkness is without a head. It comes to an end quickly, and Yeshua is in control of it—not Satan. He has the keys of death and Hades, and He made the lake of fire. When a king is captured or killed—the heart of an army and the head of an empire—the massive force with him will most certainly collapse. The empire collapses. The conqueror takes over, disassembles, and destroys the possessions of the conquered and they become his.

The kingdom of darkness is in His possession now. There is great fear, confusion, anxiety, and an unraveling of the nations and the world. If the demons were afraid and trembled while their master roamed the earth in the first century, during and after Yeshua's incarnation, they tremble much more now that the time of torment has arrived. There is still opposition, fight, enmity, and hostility against the holy, but they are not given into anyone's hand unless God wills it.

There is no one to overcome or prevail against the saints anymore. There is so much more submission and less resistance to the victorious

King who has mastered them. It should be easy to shift atmospheres with a King present with His holy angels stationed at the doors and beside of saints to protect His sheep and His armies in a place like the Ark of the Covenant was among Israel.

Yeshua is not stuck in the highest heaven ; *He carries the heavenly government with Him wherever He goes.* Just as the idol was thrown down in its own temple, in its own territory, on its own turf, when the Ark was taken by the Gentiles—it fell twice and had its hands broken—the dark entities are thrown down and broken and bow to the name of the Holy One who goes wherever He pleases in a territory that He takes over and destroys.

The earth is old, aged, torn, worn, and broken. There is abuse and destruction of His footstool. He destroys those who destroy the earth. As a conquering king takes over and destroys the people and possessions of the conquered and they become his, God's kingdom comes and takes possession and destroys what is defiled and belonging to the devil. The devil's own servants and children are evicted in the resurrection from earth and judged as having no way to pay the debt of their sins.

There is a takeover of one kingdom over another, and a new order of the kingdom of heaven is established. The passing away of heaven and earth is not an isolated event to mark only an end and beginning. It is a sign of a kingdom taking over another—in the unseen and seen dimensions in heaven and on earth. The King of heaven is making changes to the woe of many and to the blessing of others.

What about the land of Israel? Everything shall burn, but what the saints today should look for is a city, a New Jerusalem in heaven, that will come in the new order of God's kingdom. What is unseen and from heaven is greater and everlasting, and we should look for this. What He has to give is not just a small piece of land, but also a whole planet with a city from heaven for His people. Believers, both Jew and gentile, will inherit this. No foreign nation or people will ever take this from us. We will not ever have to fight over what God has given His bride. The world doesn't have another planet, His people do. How awesome is that?!

Ranked from high to low, there are first rulers over the darkness of this world (cosmic powers), powers (authorities), and then principalities (rulers). Cosmic powers hold authority over nations and regions of the earth as did the prince of Persia in Daniel. We can see what is happening to these powers as Satan's kingdom is being overtaken and dismantled by the kingdom of heaven by looking at what is happening to the peoples and nations of the earth today. It is a major sign. Many in spiritual warfare say that demons fight over territory and take over certain regions of earth, but it is a vain thing they do. All these regions will be destroyed with fire. "The territory gained by the enemy" becomes irrelevant at this point. It is stupid to fight over territory that is now the property of King Yeshua and one He deems to be doomed according to His righteous judgment.

Think of the Crusades when the nations of Gog and Magog went to Jerusalem to surround it. God said,

> Princes of Rosh, Meshach, and Tubal (who could be a reference to spiritual powers), not just merely man, I will put hooks in your jaws and I will bring you out. (Ezekiel 38:1–4)

Many read Ezekiel and Revelation and think the Lord is only against the nations (flesh and blood), but He was also against the spiritual forces and principalities over them. He warred against Satan. He warred against the nations and judged them, but how does He war against them and judge them and not their spiritual rulers too? Why does a conquering king war against the people of a land but bypass the leaders, rulers, and kings in the spirit? Why would Yeshua do the same?

Yeshua cuts at the head and also the feet. He condemns the bottom, but he also brings condemnation to the top. We must know that the signs shown in the natural among the nations reveal what is happening in the spirit with the powers and rulers. Are these saints who have already reigned still fighting the kingdom of darkness? Since they have reigned in Him, they have prevailed over Satan and his kingdom.

Many nations today are in unrest. Due to civil wars, corrupt governments, climate change, lack of food and water, filthy water, disease, and increasing heat, there is mass migration. When the Babylonian king and Rome came against Jerusalem, they surrounded the city and cut off a major resource—water. The people began to run out of water and eventually food. They became weaker and began to cannibalize each other as their city burned. In part, this is what is happening to earth.

You could say Yeshua is cutting off the water supply and burning the cities of His enemies. He is evicting and destroying them. Water is being cut off. In certain places, the sky is bronze, there are severe droughts, and food is becoming scarcer. Seas, rivers, and lakes are drying up or are polluted (Zechariah 14:10). The inhabitants are becoming weaker and are migrating. The earth is heating up (and it is prophesied in Peter's epistle) and will burn. Fear is overtaking the people of the earth, and sleep begins to withdraw from them.

If the principalities in the dark realms had it together, why are the nations they are in charge over so distressed? Why is there fear, unrest, and panic among the nations they rule over? Sounds similar to what was done to the Crusaders when they went against Jerusalem. What does this say of the rulers and powers over the nations in the spirit realm? It is unraveling and becoming unpinned more and more as they are without their king, and Yeshua changes the order that we know and takes over everything that belonged to the enemy.

The earth heats up in fulfillment of Peter's words:

> But by His word the present heavens and earth are being reserved for fire, kept for the Day of Judgment and destruction of ungodly men … But the day of the Lord will come like a thief, in which the heavens will pass away with a roar and the elements will be destroyed with intense heat, and the earth and its works will be burned up. (2 Peter 3:7, 10)

The last sentence sounds like spontaneous combustion or a type of black hole.

The peoples of earth are being displaced from their regions. There are few places for them to go. The Holy One is taking apart the heavens and earth, which will perish, and the kingdom of darkness is in an upheaval and collapsing. These powers are being displaced as well. The birth pangs of wars, famines, and earthquakes began in the first century with His arrival, but for the world, it continues to this day. Because He has come, they continue in His visitation.

The Day of the Lord spans millennia. These are the signs of His visitation and the collapse of the kingdom of darkness. The King will show intent of what He will do and the reality of what will occur for every individual with unpaid sin debt and their tie to the kingdom of darkness, which He has now as His captives. They are His. They are bound in chains of darkness, yet He will judge them as conquering kings do. One's chain of bondage (sin) to this evil kingdom is a tie to the domain He will destroy. He shows His intent not just when humans die but while they live. The door is closing. Citizens in the kingdom of darkness have no rights over what is now the King's possession to do with what He pleases, according to God's will.

There are more sightings of UFOs, which could be a mix of holy and unholy powers. The rulers, powers, and principalities are in terror of the Holy One, the one God. There is nowhere for them to go to hide from God and His anointed, Yeshua. If you want to know what is happening in the spiritual realm, look at what is happening with the nations. Also, there are testimonies of people who have seen and heard of the dead rising with physical bodies, and these are not ghosts. It seems Hades is already releasing her dead. Yeshua said these things would happen.

So, even though His kingdom is not of this world, by faith, it can and will have an influence on what happens in it. As a conquering King, He is taking over. This takeover began with the saints' millennial reign from heaven and in the unseen realm around AD 96–1096.

Without faith, one can miss His kingdom for it is seen, known, and felt with eyes of the Spirit—not the eyes of flesh. Many expect to see with eyes of flesh. Where is the faith that His kingdom is now present unseen, not to come in the future? Instead of asking "Where is He?" in times of tragedy, ask "Where is my faith?"

We are now under a visitation. The sea to be ventured and walked upon is not just the earthly seas; it is the sea of faith in this takeover of His heavenly kingdom over kingdoms, powers, principalities, rule, authority, dominions, and every name under heaven. There is so much more we could ask Him for and don't. If saints know and understand the truth, they have faith accordingly and are saved and glorify God. There is power, authority, victory, and triumph. If one doesn't know, there is no faith. If there is no faith, one doesn't believe. If one doesn't believe, one doesn't ask. If one doesn't ask, there are no miracles, signs, or wonders. Perhaps if one is of the world or does not have faith accordingly, they are subject to its persecutions and are overcome. Resurrection of wheat and tares is now. There are still enemies, but they are doomed.

Believers today must understand the kingdom citizenship and the reality and fulfillment of a victorious and present kingdom of God or visitation of a great One. There is an unseen reality. Many believers today have a first-century mind-set. It is like having a messenger sent to others to say the war has been over for some time.

Some signs of this reality are the absence of the four worldly kingdoms for millennia; the collapse and increased disorder of the world and countries in different ways; and the flourishing and increasing power and presence in the midst of believers who know the truth and have faith. What should be detected is the advancement of an unseen, yet very much present otherworldly kingdom. It is almost like having a Holy haunting. The active and peaceful presence or force of another world accompanies the people of the living God.

Is Satan still the prince of the air? Dr. Myles Monroe explained:

- "Whenever one king grew strong enough to invade another king's property, he could extend his holdings."
- "The glory of a kingdom is determined by the size of the king's territory."
- "No king can have dominion unless he can claim ownership over territory."
- "The ruler of the kingdom of light created the physical place called the earth in order to extend the kingdom of heaven."
- "Heaven is a real place, and that it is the first real country, the original one, and that all other kingdoms since the beginning of time have been mere shadows of the kingdom."

If Satan has been judged, he has lost this dominion and territory to reign in. It now belongs to God, and He gives it to whoever He wishes. Where His presence and name is, that is where His dominion is, and it is under His authority. Its residents are His captives.

Ephesians 2:2 and 1 Thessalonians 4:17 suggest a displacement in the air of a prince of darkness by a conquering King, Yeshua, upon his arrival and during His visitation. Yeshua throws down and casts away His enemy, the devil. Yeshua dismantles and destroys the kingdom of darkness.

Mr. Munroe also writes, "They (many religious, unregenerate Christians) can only rise to the level of jurisdiction under which they live."

Jurisdiction is the limits within which an authority or control may operate or the territory under a given authority or control:

- This can be Christians who do not have kingdom thinking, but are religious without relationship to the King. Their primary thought is their earthly country's government—not God's government. The kingdom is not first or even in any of their thoughts.
- This can apply to the authority a believer has over certain hierarchies of fallen angels/demons, according to one's faith.

- It can also apply as jurisdiction of knowledge or the limits a believer has according to the keys or knowledge they have and the faith they possess in it. When one's knowledge and belief in it are limited, so are the works that can be accomplished for the kingdom. Also, according to what one knows and believes, so it is. According to one's faith, so it is. Faith comes from hearing the Word.

Think about miracles, signs, and wonders. Some don't believe they occur today; for them, nothing happens. Their knowledge jurisdiction is contained. When they know it and grab hold of it, manifestations of the Spirit begin to happen according to the level of faith they have. Healing manifests, the dead are raised and strengthened, and addictions are broken. Their jurisdiction has progressed, but it may still be limited.

Those only baptized in John's baptism did not know Yeshua was the Messiah in fulfillment of the prophecy (Acts 18:24–28; 19:1–7). They had knowledge of truth, but they weren't updated in that knowledge. Their faith could only match up with what they knew. Their scope, boundary, and knowledge were limited. Their mind-sets and methods of teaching scripture were not quite accurate or up-to-date.

They were like Windows 98 on PCs today. They are outdated and don't function with correct updated software. They weren't false teachers. They were like the man in the woods, thinking the world outside was one way for many years, but so much has happened since then. Many believers are here today. They have a first-century mind-set and refuse to open up to what has been fulfilled by faith. They don't believe many things already happened in the spirit realm. When they accept the knowledge and apply faith, more manifestations of the Spirit occur than they have already experienced.

They, in effect, draw even closer to God than they already are. They draw nearer to Him, become more mature, and eat more solid food. According to the updated and accurate knowledge of truth, their faith propels them to another level of jurisdiction. It is not adding to or subtracting from the Word of the King; it is keeping pace and walking with Him as He takes out the old and creates and brings in the new order of things. We should progress with Him.

While He stays the same in truth, justice, mercy, and character, we progress with whatever changes and newness He brings. The old order was never false or wrong, but it can't be used the same way in the kind of world He is bringing into existence. The world shall become different, so the laws must be different. It is game over for the kingdom of darkness. Believers fight darkness differently because they operate with a current truth and deeper, higher level of faith where they see the conquered kingdom from another perspective than how believers in the first century and today do. It is like viewing an event, a game, or battle on ground level and up close or on a high hill or mountain. One gets a better picture of what is happening on a high hill because more is witnessed and one sees a broader scope of things. This person may see a different way to fight due to a noted weakness in the opponent. A person on ground level sees those things close up and have a limited view.

The experience of spiritual warfare should change when one is convinced of God's judgment of Satan and his kingdom after the Crusades and his eternal fiery torment. Yeshua has not only triumphed and conquered disarming Satan; it has taken over and destroyed the kingdom of darkness. All that belonged to the enemy is now property of the conquering King to do as He pleases—even if He sets it on fire. What territory does he now own if he has been overthrown? It is in the Yeshua's hands to do with the enemy's possession what He will.

If miracles, signs, wonders, and the kingdom of God were powerful and yet distant during the days of the previous worldly empires, how much more is it now after they have passed away and God's kingdom has drawn nearer and arrived? How much more effectual and powerful with little to no hindrance? Again, it takes faith.

Yours is this kingdom, Lord God, which has crushed to dust the kingdoms of the world from the Egyptian to the Roman empires and even to the kingdom of the devil/darkness. You have conquered them, and they are in Your hands now as they are in fear of Your dominion, power, might, and just judgment. The time of their torment has arrived.

CHAPTER 7
The Recognized Comings and Visitations of God

Yeshua is king renowned in the heavens. As king, he had a throne during the time of the Old Testament. As king, He went back and forth between His throne in heaven and the earth below. He made many visitations unbeknownst to the world, and only known to some of His servants. Below is a list of these past visitations.

(Note: * equals the most recognized by the church as comings of God.)

Note how God came only known to a few of His own people, not to the entire world:

1. The Flood: Genesis 6 describes evil was in the land (vv. 1–13), then God visits earth unknown to the world (v. 5). Noah, the prophet, was sent and preached to them (2 Peter 2:5). Salvation through water for those who believed (Genesis 7), the earth and unbelievers were destroyed by water (7:21–23). The earth is renewed (chapter 9).
2. Tower of Babel: Genesis 11— there is evil in the land (11:4), God visits earth unknown to world (v. 5). Language causes division and a destruction of plans (vv. 8, 9).
3. Sodom and Gomorrah: Genesis 18, 19 describe evil in the land (vv. 18:20–21). God visits earth unknown to world (vv. 18:2–17, 21). A prophet was sent to warn (19:14). The holy are saved (19:17). The destruction comes (19:24–26).
4. Genesis 32:24–32: God visited earth. Jacob wrestled with God unknown to the world.

5. Exodus from Egypt: There was evil in the land with the idolatry and the slavery (chapter 1, 12:12). God visits unknown to the world within the burning bush (3:1–9). The firstborn are struck and die as judgment (12:12, 13). The prophet Moses was sent to Pharaoh (chapters 3–4). Judgment comes upon the Egyptians in many forms (chapters 7–11). The Hebrews are delivered and saved after crossing through water (chapters 14:13–22). Destruction comes to the army of Pharaoh (14:23–31). There is a new beginning and renewal for the Hebrews (chapter 15). Moses saw His form and He spoke to him face-to-face (34:28–35; Numbers 12:4–9).
6. Amos 2, 4, 5, 9: This describes the evil in the land (2:4, 5). A prophet sent to the people (2:11, 12). There were judgments (4:6–13). God visits unknown to world (5:17). There is renewal (9:11–15).
7. Zechariah 14: He possibly visited in either BC and/or in AD times on the Mount Olives.
8. * Yeshua's incarnate coming in first century AD as a human, the Gospel is preached, evil was in the land, signs and warnings given, prophets and Yeshua sent, He visits in the flesh unknown and unrecognized to the Roman and global world. He is popular in Israel, though not accepted by all. There is healing, deliverance, salvation for believers. The destruction of the holy temple (Yeshua's body in AD 33 and temple of stone in AD 70). This coming was without condemnation and judgment of people, only salvation through faith in the Messiah as the Lamb.
9. * The glorified, spiritual coming of kingdom of heaven in the first century from AD 70–96. Paul's letters and Revelation are written. There is evil in land. There are signs, warnings, judgments, prophets sent, and the Messiah comes in glory unknown to the world (visitation like a thief in the night which is unexpected and while people were asleep/unaware of the thief), but seen among the tribes of Israel at that time and they mourned as they saw the pierced One. The Spirit of God opened their eyes. Resurrection and first reign of saints with Messiah in unseen kingdom. The apostles judged the tribes of Israel on thrones in the millennial reign. The time of judgment against the beast and the false prophet. Satan is bound and released to deceive the nations of the eleventh and twelfth centuries.
10. Gog and Magog and judgment on those nations (The Crusades

from AD 1095–1291). Yeshua visits unknown to the world of that era to fight and judge the deceived nations. They did not recognize it was He who struck them. He had to be present in the earth to do this. Ezekiel 38, 39; Zechariah 14; Matthew 25:31, 32; Revelation 20:7–9.

11. Extinction or the passing away (dying) and destruction of heaven and earth with fire (2 Peter 3:1–13; 1 Thessalonians 5:1–11; Revelation 20:11–21:1). Evil is currently present in earth. Yeshua could be now visiting individuals, but visitations/appearances concerning this imminent destruction could be coming to individuals, home groups, churches, and synagogues in the Spirit. His visitation (or coming) is or will be unknown to the world. Visits will be unknown to the world or at least not believed in if heard of. His prophets are sent to His people, judgments are on world and salvation for believers (changes, translations, movement, and resurrections/removal). Destruction with fire comes in different ways. There will be renewal with a new heaven and earth and New Jerusalem.

CHAPTER 8

Every Eye Will See Him
(Zechariah 12 and Revelation)

Zechariah 12 and Revelation

Zechariah is not sequential in the events. He jumps from the Second Coming and outpouring of the Spirit (chapter 12) to Yeshua's death (chapter 13) to the battle with nations in the distant future (chapter 14). While chapter 12 is a coming in AD 70 with resurrection of saints on Mount Zion (Revelation 14), chapter 14 is another possible coming upon Mount Olives before the crusades begin. This is why His coming can be more than one return as He traverses or an extended stay, or Parousia, across the millennia. Zechariah 12 reads:

> I will pour out on the house of David and on the inhabitants of Jerusalem, the Spirit of grace and of supplication, so that they will look on Me whom they have pierced; and they will mourn for Him, as on mourns for an only son, and they will weep bitterly over Him like the bitter weeping over a firstborn. In that day there will be great mourning in Jerusalem, like the mourning of Hadadrimmon in the plain of Megiddo. The land will mourn, every family by itself; the family of the house of David by itself and their wives by themselves; the family of the house of Nathan by itself and their wives by themselves; the family of the house of Levi by itself and their wives by themselves; the family of the Shimeites by itself and their wives by

> themselves; all the families that remain, every family by itself and their wives by themselves. (Zechariah 12:10–14)

Yeshua is referencing this scripture when He speaks to the daughters of Jerusalem, who are to become "the wives who mourn by themselves."

> Daughters of Jerusalem, stop weeping for Me, but weep for yourselves and for your children, For behold, the days are coming when they will say, "Blessed are the barren, and the wombs that never bore, and the breast that never nursed." Then they will begin to say to the mountains, "Fall on us," and to the hills, "cover us." For if they do these things when the tree is green, what will happen when it is dry? (Luke 23:28–31)

The last sentence means if they do these things while Yeshua was present with them and done to Yeshua Himself, what will happen to them when He's gone? It will be terrible for them.

> Behold, He is coming with the clouds, and every eye will see Him, even those who pierced Him; and all the tribes of the earth will mourn over Him. So it is to be. Amen. (Revelation 1:7)

> And then the sign of the Son of Man will appear in the sky, and then all the tribes of the earth will mourn, and they will see the Son of Man coming on the cloud of the sky with power and great glory. And He will send forth his angels with a great trumpet and they will gather together His elect from the four winds, form one end of the sky to the other. (Matthew 24:30, 31)

> "They shall look on Him whom they pierced." (John 19:37)

> "Every eye will see Him" (Revelation 1:7)

Many ask where was it in history that everyone saw him come. If no one has seen Him, then He hasn't come yet since it is written that "every eye will see Him".

One must go back to Zechariah 12 and read carefully:

> I will pour on the house of David and on the inhabitants of Jerusalem the Spirit of grace and supplication; then they will look upon Me whom they pierced.

Then it goes on to name the families of Nathan (prophet), the royal families, and the house of Levi (priests) that would mourn along with or as the inhabitants of Jerusalem who were specifically chosen to "see the one whom they pierced."

Just as the Jewish rebellion against Rome was beginning (the one seven of Daniel), there were eyewitness accounts in AD 66 of armies of holy ones in the heavens around Jerusalem from Iyyar, Josephus, and Tacitus. The preterist website, Revelation Revolution, makes note of that: http://revelationrevolution.org/jesus-the-son-of-man-was-seen-in-the-clouds-in-a-d-66/.

Luke 10:18 and Revelation 12:7–12 speak of Satan's fall to earth. This was not before the creation of the world as some teach. He is not going to be kicked out, fall to the earth, and enter heaven again during Job—only to be cast out again. This was apparently while humans existed: "Who deceives the whole world, accuser of the brethren who accused them, Woe to the inhabitants of the earth."

Satan fell from heaven like lightning. Why didn't nations talk about this and write this down for future generations? Why didn't everyone see this spectacular and unusual event? The world was blind to it. This was seen with the eyes of the spirit. Yeshua saw in the Spirit.

Dual Fulfillment of Zechariah 12

1. John 19:34–37. First fulfilled at His death (John 19:37; 20:27). The single fulfillment was *His piercing*, but *people looked on Him* (every eye in Jerusalem saw). Jewish people around *Jerusalem* and of *their tribes would mourn* Him will be fulfilled again according to John.
2. Revelation 1:7. John again writes, "Every eye will see Him; even they who pierced Him ... all the tribes of the earth will mourn." This was fulfilled again at His Second Coming. The first-century generation pierced Him. If Zechariah 12 was only fulfilled at His death, then why would John mention it again in

Revelation years after Yeshua's death and resurrection? So, there may be a dual fulfillment here—not of the piercing, but of the people looking at Him and tribes in Jerusalem mourning Him. Here it is cyclical.

Consider also possible dual fulfillment of "Out of Egypt I called my son" (Hosea 11:1; Matthew 2:15; Hebrews 13). The Great Commission also suggests a dual fulfillment of those verses too.

The twelve tribes of Israel, in and around Jerusalem, mourned. In their humbled state, without food (a kind of forced fast), and being close to death, the eyes of their spirit would have opened. While it was recorded by an historian that they mourned for the temple, they mourned too for the One they saw and had pierced. This is what is written in Scripture by the prophet Zechariah. The mourning could be heard all over that area.

> The Jews who were in the temple uttered a piercing cry of horror, when they first beheld the fire issuing from that sanctuary, which they esteemed the most august and most holy place upon earth, in which all their feelings of veneration and piety were concentred, and with the preservation of which they had lately associated their strongest hopes of deliverance from the arms of their heathen invaders. The terrified spectators in the city returned the lamentation when they saw the holy mountain enveloped in flames; and many, whose strength and power of utterance had been almost destroyed by the famine, opened their lips once more in shrieks of uncontrollable anguish. The hills around Jerusalem echoed the dreadful tumult, which was made by the noise of the irresistible flames, the crash of falling buildings, the shouts of the infuriated legions, and the groans of those who sank into the conflagrations, or were transfixed by the sword. (*The History of the Roman Emperors*)

What else or who else was it that they saw as the Spirit was poured out? The Jews are the tribes of the earth that mourned. They would have been making supplications for deliverance and salvation from the Romans, which never came.

One sign was seen in the heavens for a year:

> The superstition of the Jews did not permit them to expiate these prodigies ... A comet had been seen for a whole year; and, although modern philosophy has taught us to regard such phenomenon with indifference, yet it was always viewed by the ancients as the harbinger of some fearful occurrence. (*The History of the Roman Emperors*)

In the Law, every matter must be established by the testimony of two or three witnesses. Josephus, Tacitus, and Sepher Yosippon (who came later) wrote about what many people at that time observed on more than one occasion between AD 66 and AD 70.

Josephus wrote about another sign seen in the heavens, which supports Yeshua's words of the clouds of heaven and the holy angels:

> A more extraordinary appearance was exhibited in the heavens, when, before sunset, chariots and bodies of armed men were seen traversing the clouds, and besieging cities. (*The History of the Roman Emperors; The Works of Josephus*)

These men traversing the clouds were His holy angels. Yeshua had to be visiting too. He must have arrived with His army. In the spiritual realm, where dark principalities and powers are, much was going on. This account from a historian during that era is not a symbolic or metaphorical account; it is literal. If there was an army, there must have been a King somewhere.

This is an account from Josephus, who had the Spirit poured out upon him so that he saw in Spirit and wrote about this. This would make sense since he was in Jerusalem at the time and was a descendant of the high priest Jonathan. He was also the son of Matthias, an ethnic Jewish priest. According to Zechariah 12, His Spirit was poured out upon the Jewish tribes around Jerusalem. Most likely, Caiaphas, the high priest, must have seen him too according to His words spoken during His trial (Matthew 26:64). Yeshua's words did not fail to come to pass with Caiphas.

Tacitus, a first-century historian, wrote,

> In the sky appeared a vision of armies in conflict, of glittering armour. (Tacitus, *The Histories*)

KING YESHUA'S VISITATION

In later days, Sepher Yosippon wrote,

> Moreover, in those days were seen chariots of fire and horsemen, a great force flying across the sky near to the ground coming against Jerusalem and all the land of Judah, all of them horses of fire and riders of fire. (*A Medieval History of Ancient Israel*)

> The temple was disturbed by nocturnal miracles. At a late hour of the night, the altar and the Holy house were illumined with a great luster, which for the space of half an hour equaled the brightness of daylight. (*A Medieval History of Ancient Israel*)

Wasn't the beast that was in the temple as the abomination destroyed by the brightness of His coming? Josephus described it:

> And at the ninth hour of the night, so great a light shone round the altar and the holy house that it appeared to be bright day-time; which light lasted for half an hour ... on another night, the eastern gate of the temple, which was made of brass, and was so heavy that it required the strength of twenty men to shut it, appeared to open of its own accord, and the captain of the guard was summoned to witness the prodigy, and to see the gate closed again. At the feast of Pentecost, as the priests were going to perform their sacred functions in the temple at night, they were terrified by a mysterious agitation and tumult, and afterwards heard the voice, as of a multitude, saying, "Let us depart hence." They felt a quaking, and heard a great noise, and after that they heard a sound as of a great multitude, saying, "Let us remove hence."

Concerning the gate opening and closing on its own, Josephus writes,

> But the men of learning understood it, that the security of their holy house was dissolved of its own accord, and that the gate was opened for the advantage of their enemies.

> So these publicly declared, that this signal forshewed the desolation that was coming upon them.

From this supernatural sign, the priests understood the desolation was coming. They knew from the book of Daniel. They were not only speaking about their earthly enemies, the Romans, but I believe they picked up on the fact that something was wrong spiritually too. Paul writes,

> And you know what restrains him now, so that in his time he will be revealed. For the mystery of lawlessness is already at work; only he who now restrains will do so until he is taken out of the way. (2 Thessalonians 2:6, 7)

This gate opened for enemies in both the natural and spirit realms so that whoever it was restraining the beast back, now left the temple (hence the voice saying, "Let us depart hence"). This holy one departed for not only the Romans to come in, but the beast too. God Himself, or a holy angel, was no longer restraining him.

The priests knew and understood these signs, they read the signs well, and then publicly announced that the desolation foretold long ago was coming to Jerusalem. Who brings the desolation? The abomination brings it. Who is the abomination? The beast is the abomination. This is the beast, or second abomination, mentioned in Daniel's one seven, who is not Antiochus Epiphanes. This is the beast, or second abomination, mentioned by Yeshua in Matthew 24:15, who was to come after He was cut off or died.

According to Revelation, it is an evil king who died of a fatal head wound, claimed to be god, "once was (was alive as a king), now is not (now dead as John writes), and is about to come out of the abyss and go to his destruction" (Revelation 17:8). Note the phrase, "is about to come out". This was soon to happen and was not in a far distant future.

Nero never entered the holy temple while he lived, but died in AD 68. According to Scripture, he went to the abyss, and came out of it a spiritual entity. The beast was coming to the temple through the unclean sacrifices and idolatry of the Roman army as they trampled the temple grounds. Sacrifice opens the door to the spirit realm. He would be attached to their ensign or idol. Sacrifice and offering ends in the holy house and the altar is destroyed. During or shortly after this, Yeshua comes to destroy him with the brightness of His coming and the breath of His mouth.

With the beast is the false prophet who performs signs and wonders. The false prophet is not just with one head, Nero, but with all the heads of the beast. There were many false prophets before and during the temple's destruction:

> Also it will come about in that day that the prophets will each be ashamed of his vision when he prophesies, and they will not put on a hairy robe in order to deceive. (Zechariah 12:4).

> And a great multitude had assembled in it this very day, trusting to the declaration of an impostor or enthusiast, who had promised them, that they should receive some extraordinary tokens of deliverance. The impious rulers had suborned many false prophets, for the sake of reviving the hopes and supporting the courage of the people; and now the end of their delusions had arrived. (*The History of the Roman Emperors*).

Concerning false prophets and imposters, Josephus (and Acts 21:38) records,

> And now these impostors and deceivers persuaded the multitude to follow them into the wilderness, and pretended that they would exhibit manifest wonders and signs, that should be performed by the providence of God … Moreover, there came out of Egypt about this time to Jerusalem, one that said he was a prophet, and advised the multitude of the common people to go along with him to the mount of Olives, as it was called, which lay over against the city, and at the distance of five furlongs. He said further, that he would shew them from hence, how, at his command, the walls of Jerusalem would fall down; and he promised them that he would procure them an entrance into the city through those walls, when they were fallen down. (*The Works of Josephus, Antiquities of the Jews*, volume III, 6)

Was Yeshua warning the disciples of this man in Matthew 24:26?

There are three things to point out in this one Old Testament passage of Zechariah 12:

First Point

Many believe that *every earthly eye of flesh* will see. The Spirit was poured out upon those mentioned in Zechariah. *The Spirit opened their spiritual eyes, but it is not the physical, fleshly ones that need opening.* Everyone has eyes and ears of the spirit. All are blind and deaf unless God opens them to see and hear. There is natural sight and there is spiritual sight.

"They have eyes, but do not see; ears, but do not hear (see Deuteronomy 29:4; Ezekiel 12:2; Isaiah 6:9, 10).

Revelation 2 and 3 talks about "He who has ears to hear, let him hear what the Spirit says." That suggests we have spiritual ears, but not all hear. Yeshua said in the Gospels, "He who has ears to hear." This is speaking of spiritual blindness and deafness, not physical.

The Second Coming was an actual, literal spiritual event. What is spiritual is not less real than the physical just because no one can see with their physical earthly eyes. These people would see Him with eyes that were opened by the Spirit. What they saw in the Spirit, the rest of the world—those who weren't of the tribes of Israel specified in Zechariah—would not see.

The Second Coming was a spiritual event only revealed by the Spirit poured out upon the people of Jerusalem. "We walk by faith, *not by sight*" (2 Corinthians 5:7).

"Faith is the substance of things hoped for, the conviction of things *not seen*" (Hebrews 11:1). Here is where faith is required; the eyes and ears of the spirit were opened by the Spirit. No one can enter or see the kingdom unless they are born of Spirit.

Yeshua asked, "Will the Son of Man find faith when He returns?" *Faith is kingdom reality, though unseen to many. His kingdom is known by the Spirit and faith.* Faith must be based on truth. If there is no knowledge of the truth and no Spirit, there is no power.

If Yeshua came already, then why is the Holy Spirit still given? He should leave when Yeshua comes. According to Zechariah, He will pour out His Spirit upon the house of Israel (believer and unbeliever) at the Second Coming. They will look upon the One they have pierced. They will see His return because of the Spirit, so the Spirit can't leave if this is how they were to have their eyes opened. We need the Spirit to see Yeshua or the kingdom of heaven. His Spirit won't leave us.

> "I will not hide My face from them any longer, for I will have poured out My Spirit on the house of Israel," declares the Lord God. (Ezekiel 39:29)

His face is seen by the Spirit of God. Ezekiel 29:25–29 speaks of Israel being gathered back from the lands of their enemies, and then they will begin to see Him. It has been centuries since the Crusades. Right now, Israel is being gathered back to the land in fulfillment of this prophecy. Soon, yet before the passing away, He will be unveiled to Israel. They will see His face. He will forgive and sanctify them again, pour out His Spirit on them soon, and teach them His name again. Is this a kind of dual fulfillment?

According to John 3:3, 5, 7 one must have the Spirit to "see" the kingdom. Luke 17:20–30 explains that the kingdom is in the midst and within us, not seen with physical and natural, fleshly eyes. The Son of man was revealed by the Spirit. Yeshua said, "It does not come with observation, nor will they say, 'See here' or 'See there.'"

It is not a physical, earthly kingdom in this world to be looked at. How is it not public, but yet still public? So, how can He say this and at the same time say, "Every eye will see Him"? Are people going to see him or not? This is a contradiction no one addresses—unless He means it is seen with the eyes of the spirit, by the Spirit, and not with physical eyes to observe. Many people miss this (see also Matthew 24: 26–31 and Luke 21:23–28). This was to be a huge sign to the disciples that this was a false Christ if it was with physical eyes of this flesh.

The Messiah will not be found in the upper room or in the wilderness. This also supports how Yeshua came as a thief in the night while people slept. He came in the Spirit. How do we whole heartedly accept, without question, John 3 for what it says, yet when it is said the Messiah's return was spiritual, it is doubted and questioned? *Does one really believe Yeshua when He stated in John 3:3–7 that the kingdom of heaven can only be seen by the Spirit? If one doubts a spiritual coming, then how can one truly accept His words about seeing the kingdom by the Spirit? How does anyone believe one without the other when they actually go together?*

A couple of other places in scripture speak of people seeing the unseen. Ezekiel 1 speaks of the prophet Ezekiel seeing the throne of God and describing it. No one else was seeing this but him. In 2 Kings 6:13–23 speaks of the armies of heavenly hosts being seen with spiritual eyes *only after* the prophet prayed. No one else was seeing this but these two men.

If the armies of heavenly host were not seen at first with the eyes of the body, does this mean it is not literal? Is it only allegorical, symbolic, make-believe, and not real—just as futurists accuse preterists of making the Second Coming of the Messiah? They say preterists make the spiritual coming of the Messiah one that is allegorical, symbolic, make-believe, and not real instead of literal. In Ezekiel 1 and 2 Kings 6:13-23, I see *what is spiritual can also be literal*. No one would argue this, but why do they argue against a spiritual second coming?

In Acts 13:1–12, during Saul's first missionary journey, *he was filled with the Spirit and fixed his gaze* upon Bar-Jesus, a magician, a pronounced a blindness overcoming him. I believe Paul was seeing something as his gaze was fixed on him that he would not be able to see with his natural eyes. He could only see and speak what was happening as he was filled with the Spirit. Paul was filled with the Spirit, and it was revealed to him what was occurring in the spirit realm with the eyes of his spirit and in a short time manifested into the natural realm. As Saul spoke these words, no one else present saw what he was seeing in the Spirit (because the Spirit did not fill them only Saul) until it manifested quickly into the natural world where their eyes of flesh actually could see the fulfillment of his words. The phrase "fixed his gaze upon him" could indicate that Saul was seeing something first before anyone else did and only through the Spirit. Who would argue against this, but why do they argue against a spiritual second coming?

There was another time in the Bible when spiritual ears were opened when they heard horses or an army marching above the trees. Just because no one else could see or hear with natural eyes does not mean it was less real or did not occur.

In Acts 7:54–56, the Spirit opened the spiritual eyes of Stephen. Only Stephen saw Yeshua and God in heaven's throne room. None of the religious leaders in the same room with him saw Yeshua. They remained blind spiritually because it is the Holy Spirit who opens spiritual eyes to see spiritual things related to His kingdom. This wasn't a vision he had.

Yeshua even spoke about how He only does what He sees His Father do. He saw His Father with eyes of the Spirit; He saw things no one else was seeing. Just because no one else saw the Father doesn't make what Yeshua was seeing and hearing less real or nonexistent. In Mark 1:10,

Yeshua "saw" the dove with the eyes of the spirit (not with natural eyes). The Spirit hovered over the waters, similar to Genesis, when He was baptized and was empowered immediately for service.

The mark of the beast upon the idolaters and the holy name on the foreheads of saints was spiritual. This mark could have been implemented unnoticed/unseen to the fleshy eye. Many believe the mark is a physical mark on our flesh or a chip in the body; they don't think it very well could have been one on the spirit/soul. Believers today say they have His name on their foreheads, but no one sees it. Believers have faith that the blood of the Lamb washes their sins away, but no one sees it. However, there may be evidence of it in the form of miracles, signs, and wonders (MSW).

Remember Balaam and the Lord and the story of Balaam, the donkey, and the angel in Numbers 22–25. He saw the Lord with eyes of the Spirit through sorcery at one point and by the Spirit of God later (Numbers 24:1–19).

Also, in 2 Kings 2:8–14, Elijah told his servant Elisha that if he saw him being taken away into heaven (with eyes of the spirit), he would have his mantle, but if he did not see him, then he would not have it. Elisha saw Elijah taken on a chariot of fire by the Spirit. Without the Holy Spirit, Elijah's transport would not have been witnessed by Elisha. Elisha needed the Spirit of God in him to witness a spiritual event related to the kingdom. If he did not witness his departure, the Spirit of God wasn't with him.

Elisha could not see this spiritual event with natural eyes alone. His eyes had to be opened to the spirit realm of the kingdom of heaven by the Holy Spirit. Do we say that because this was a spiritual event that it was metaphorical, allegorical, or symbolic? Does it mean it wasn't literal because it was spiritual? Most would agree that this was a spiritual event and was literal. Why can't the witnessing of the Second Coming of the Messiah be understood in the same way?

In Ezekiel 39:29 it reads, "I will not hide My face from them any longer, for I will have poured out My Spirit on the house of Israel" which indicates we see His face by the Spirit, not with flesh. Isaiah 54:8, 9 reads, "I hid My face from you for a moment". In Acts 7:55–56, Stephen saw into the throne room of heaven, which is in the highest heaven *only by the Holy Spirit*. Revelation 1:1; 1:10–18 has the phrases: "In the Spirit," "I saw," "Placed His right hand on me." These phrases suggest Yeshua was physical at the time of His revelation to John and not in fulfillment of a Second Coming but to advise the churches. This was not a vision; it was an appearance in the Spirit.

- John 20:12. Mary saw angels.
- John 20:14–16. The eyes of flesh were not opened.
- John 14:19. The world will no longer see, but the disciples will see Him at the resurrection. The Spirit was permitting them to see Him.
- Luke 24:16 and 24:31. Their eyes prevented them from recognizing Him, and then their eyes were opened to recognize Yeshua. The spirit world is even more real than this earthly realm we dwell in.

There are two types of sight and two types of hearing (2 Corinthians 5:7; 4:13–18; Hebrews 11: 27, seeing Him who is unseen, Hebrews 11:6–7). The kingdom of God is a spiritual one and not a natural earthly one. The Second Coming was a spiritual event with spiritual eyes and ears as the Spirit was poured out; it was unseen with the physical eye of flesh. We cannot rely on the flesh to see and hear things of the Spirit. "Flesh and blood cannot inherit the kingdom of heaven." Why do we expect to see the kingdom of heaven with flesh and blood, our natural eyes?

So in any of the above incidents, do we conclude that because no one else saw it with natural eyes, except those upon who the Spirit permitted, none of these things really happened? Since they did not see the dinosaur, but only the footprints, therefore it really did not occur? Do we disregard the footprints, evidence, testimonies, or even the manifestations that followed?

In John 14:16–21, the world will no longer see Him because they cannot receive His Spirit. The disciples will see Him upon His resurrection and also upon His return because they have the Spirit with and in them. It will eventually fill their bodies (the temple). His ascension and return were by the Spirit. It is the Spirit that reveals Him.

In the parable of the ten virgins, one must ask, "Is this how people miss the coming, which is like a thief in the night and see themselves shut out or missing it?" (Matthew 24).

Those filled with the Spirit "see" Him with the eyes of the Spirit and become like Him. Others are not filled with the Holy Spirit, go away, and are preoccupied with life's concerns. They miss the moment of His arrival or the time of His visitation. They are neither ready nor filled to see the kingdom and so enter into it. They have scripture (lamps), but they don't understand it (in the dark). They have lamps without understanding from the Spirit. One must have lamps (scripture) and an understanding of it by the Sprit and be filled as well so they know to be ready to enter.

Many Christians today have scripture, but there is no light of understanding. "Thy word is a lamp to my feet." When it comes with the Spirit, He is "a light unto my path." The Spirit is the oil and flame that gives light to understanding of scripture—and light for eyes of spiritual individuals to see Yeshua and the kingdom. If you wait to see with natural eyes without scripture or an understanding, you have no lamp therefore no light. You'll miss it. You are asleep. If you have scripture and wait to see in the natural without the Spirit, you have a lamp that is not lit, there is no light.

Without light, one reads in the dark or with a darkened mind. The rabbis, Pharisees, Sadducees, scribes, elders, and priests in Yeshua's day read scripture with darkened minds or in the dark. This is how scripture is added to and subtracted from, distorted, and misinterpreted so badly that it leads people away from God in disobedience and rebellion, keeping them out of the kingdom of God.

This is similar to those who see spirits, ghosts, and demons that others can't see in the same room or building with everyone, but no one else sees it. There are those who are able to communicate with beings of the spirit realm. Those who can't see most times will doubt the one who sees these beings and think they are crazy or lying. They doubt them until they begin to experience, see, and hear the paranormal themselves. It is like what futurists do to the preterists who believe this is how the Second Coming happened as a spiritual event. They won't believe until the see the dinosaur, either there aren't any footprints or the footprints are not enough for them. So, like doubting Thomas, if they don't see it with the natural eye themselves, then it is not true. Those born with gifts to see and communicate with the spirit realm cannot see the kingdom or Yeshua. They must be born again to see it and enter. They may see angels, but they do not see the kingdom.

Second Point

"They will look upon Me whom they pierced." *This is a clue from the Old Testament and Yeshua's own words that He would come back to the very generation that killed him.* Yeshua was crucified in the first century by the generation of that time. Those who would see Him were of that first-century generation because it was during that time, in that area, from that specific group of people who pierced Him. Yeshua returned to the generation He died in. He did not die in any other generation, including ours. No other generation after this one would see Him come in fulfillment of Zechariah 12 because they did not pierce Him.

We, of this age, would not see this prophecy fulfilled because no one of this age and generation pierced Him. No one of the second, tenth, or seventeenth centuries would see this prophecy fulfilled because no one from those ages or generations pierced Him.

Some might say, "We all pierced Him and put Him on the cross." If so, He should come back in *every* generation many more times to fulfill this. We will all look upon Him at judgment, but we all understand Matthew 24 talks about His Second Coming. This passage means believers and unbelievers in and around Jerusalem.

Now His coming could be perpetual in that once He returns, He comes and goes at will between the realms and crosses dimensions. He traverses and visits as he did during the BC era. We are in the Day of the Lord, which could last thousands of years since a day is like a thousand years. He remains as a thief in the night (1 Thessalonians 5:2), unrevealed to the eyes of our spirits. We are in a day of visitation.

What Yeshua says at different times in the Gospels is supported by Zechariah 12. The following verses speak of people of the first-century generation who would see:

- "This (the one near, not far away) generation will not pass away until" (Matthew 24:34–35)
- "There are some standing here (His disciples) who will not taste death until they see the Son of Man coming / see the kingdom" (Matthew 16:27, 28; Mark 8:38–9:1; Luke 9:26–27)

Yeshua spoke these words six to eight days before the transfiguration to more than three or even twelve disciples. When these verses are backed up by 2 Peter 1:16–18, it gives the impression that the coming Peter was referring to was on the mountain. His transfiguration on the holy mountain was not a "coming in His kingdom." The transfiguration was only to confirm His majesty as a king who has a kingdom.

Peter wrote that he was a witness to his majesty—not to His coming. He and the other apostles taught about the imminent return of the Messiah in His kingdom, which was confirmed by the testimony of witnesses who saw His majesty. Yeshua speaks in these verses of His Second Coming with the angels of God. There were people who stood where he was at the time who would see His coming in their lifetime. The words "some standing here," which are synonymous with "this generation," refer to the people of Yeshua's generation, not ours. How can "some standing here" mean a distant future generation? Yeshua was not mistaken. Yeshua meant what He said and said what He meant. Many people teach that these passages refer to the transfiguration, but they do not.

Some futurists say preterists are not literal in their interpretation of scripture, but the interpretation they give for this is not literal. It is not the same. First of all, there was no army or multitude of angels (only Moses and Elijah). Secondly, there was no rewarding of people. Third, there was no "coming" in a kingdom or "clouds of heaven" in the transfiguration on the mountain. There was a cloud that came over the disciples like a tabernacle.

Last of all, I believe the "some" refers to more people than Peter, James, and John. The Lord meant His Second Coming and not the transfiguration. Some of them will see the coming and the kingdom. The eyes of the spirit are opened by the Spirit at His coming. According to John 3:3, 5–7, no one can see the kingdom of God unless He has been born of the Spirit.

- "You (the disciples) will not finish going through the cities of Israel when the Son of Man comes" (Matthew 10:23). This is a first-century return. Read the chapter on "The Great Commission."
- "When (not "if," which gives certainty that some of the disciples will be expected to see these things, not another generation) you (the disciples) see these things, look up, your (the disciples) redemption draws nigh" (Luke 21:28). This is a first-century return.
- John 21:22, 23. "If I want him (John) to remain until I come, what is that to you? You follow Me!" If the Lord willed, John could have remained alive at His coming. This is a hint that though John may or may not have been alive at His coming, Yeshua knew He would return in John's generation. It could be that John would not taste death when He returned. The word "if" gives an uncertainty. What was uncertain in this statement was if John would be alive; what is certain is that Yeshua would return to his generation.

And the words spoken to Nathaniel (John 1:51), who was a disciple, either saw a vision like Jacob's marking Yeshua as the chosen one. It could also refer to the Second Coming he would witness.

The high priest Caiaphas (Matthew 26:64), who was of the priesthood (see Zechariah 12 again—they will look upon Me who they pierced), was of the house of Levi and played a crucial role in having Him killed (pierced), and they are both of the first-century generation. Even though Caiaphas did not believe (as many who mourned around Jerusalem at that time), Joel says "I will pour out my Spirit upon all flesh."

Regarding Caiaphas, some say, "Oh, he would see Yeshua at the resurrection." Why tell Caiaphas he would see Him "coming in the clouds of heaven"? There are many who would not see. Yeshua made several statements about coming in that generation that pierced Him *before* it passed away; it suggests Caiaphas would see Him by the Spirit *before* he died (as Nathaniel would among others of that time).

I think it is possible to see Him in our era by the Spirit. There are people who have spoken of encounters with who they believe to be Him in hospitals and other places. How can they have these encounters with the Son of God if He hasn't returned yet—unless He returned again? Are we ready to open the door to Yeshua the King? This confirms what Yeshua meant by "this generation."

Matthew 24:29–31; Revelation 6:12–17; Luke 23:27–31

All three above passages speak of the same event: the Second Coming of Yeshua. Most of us understand and can agree that this is the Second Coming of the Messiah. Revelation 6 contains both descriptions in Matthew 24 and Luke 23. These descriptions happen at the same time: during the generation of those women in the first century. It wasn't just during the time of the temple's destruction—but His coming too.

It is important to note that in the last passage (Luke 23), Yeshua is speaking specifically to the "Daughters of Jerusalem" who were following and lamenting Him. To them, He says, "Weep for yourselves and for your children." This is not directed to women in the far, distant future millennia away, but to women in Jerusalem in Yeshua's first-century generation. They weren't told to lament for the women and children of a distant, future generation.

Let's tie it together:

- "Turning to them," "Daughters of Jerusalem," and "yourselves and your children"—Yeshua's first-century generation.
- "Then they will begin to say to the mountains and rocks, 'Fall on us ... Cover us.'" This is written in two of the passages and linked to the Second Coming.
- "From the face of Him (presence) who sits on the throne and the wrath of the Lamb!" This is His Second Coming.

All three occur at the Second Coming during the first century. This was fulfilled during the days of those "Daughters of Jerusalem." He specifically addressed them and not a future generation.

They do not "begin to say, 'Fall on us'" hundreds or thousands of years later. There is no mysterious, long gap between Luke 23:29 and 23:30. All three passages are tied and linked together; they are not separate. The description of the changes with the earth and heavens, what is said by terrified people, the Second Coming, and women of the first century are all linked to one event. These passages are connected, and they link people of the first century to the Second Coming. This confirms what Yeshua meant by "this generation."

> You taught in our streets, we ate and drank in Your presence ... master rises up and shuts the door." (Luke 13:22, 27)

This alludes to the Second Coming or a judgment that begins shortly after. This does not mean that people of our current and future generation can't be shut out too. If we don't repent, we can be shut out too. This speaks of people in the first century—and not a future one. Yeshua didn't teach in the streets of latter generations, and no one from later generations ate or drank in His presence. The first-century generation did. This confirms what He means by "this generation."

They saw Him with eyes of the spirit by the Spirit. The above verses are all supported by the Old Testament passage in Zechariah 12 of which generation he would return to: the one that killed (pierced) Him.

- Daniel 2:44. "And in the days of these kings (Roman emperors), God will set up a kingdom." This suggests God's kingdom

- Daniel 7:21–22. "The little horn (Domitian) made war against ... them, until the Ancient of Days came." This suggests that Yeshua returned in the first century.

Scriptures with Yeshua's own words confirm which generation He meant He returns to. There are no Old Testament scriptures or quotes from Yeshua in the four Gospels to support the interpretation that our current/latter generation, millennia away, is the one to "see these things." This refers to fulfilling the Messiah's Second Coming, the initiation of the Day of the Lord, and the day of visitation.

This Day of the Lord seems to begin with them and end soon with us or a near future generation. The Day of the Lord seems to span many of our years (millennia). "With the Lord, a day is like a thousand years, and a thousand years are like a day." A day to Him is different than a day to us because He is eternal. A futurist cannot explain their interpretation with Old Testament scriptures or Yeshua's words. However, Zechariah 12:10–12; Daniel 2:44; 7:21–22 and Yeshua's own words strongly suggest it is a first-century generation—not ours or a future one.

The fact that the interpretation of a first-century generation has support and backing from the Old Testament confirms the true meaning of what Yeshua meant by "this generation." For the phrases "last days," see chapter 14.

Third Point

This is a reference to the twelve tribes of Israel back when Jews knew the tribes they were in before the Diaspora. These were the same twelve tribes Yeshua told His disciples they would judge (Matthew 19:28; Luke 22:30). This is not the Jews of today in this generation since most don't know the tribe they're from. Some may know they are Kohen or Levitical. Neither do the tribes of the earth include the tribes of Africa, tribes of the unknown/unfounded Americas, or the tribes of Europe and Australia. The scripture specifically says the tribes of the earth, *which are from David and in Jerusalem. Zechariah is very specific as to which tribes/families of the first century would see Him come.* It doesn't even say all Israel of that time would see Him. It mentions only the area around Jerusalem. This was for a people of a certain time, place, generation, age, empire, and tribe—not us. It does not say the entire global earth would see Him.

Yeshua returned to a Jewish Jerusalem during the first century, during the time when there would be all twelve Jewish tribes, unlike the Jerusalem of today. How does the Jewish Messiah return to an earthly Jewish Jerusalem without its Jewish tribes in existence?

Zechariah tells us who "every eye" is—as well as where, how, and when "every eye" will see Him come in fulfillment of these prophecies.

Many believe Zechariah 12:10–14 and Ezekiel 39:29 will be fulfilled at the same event and at the same time: the future Second Coming of the Messiah. Zechariah 12 was fulfilled during the Second Coming of the Messiah in the first century, and Ezekiel 39 is to be fulfilled during our current times with the return of the Jews to Israel during His visitation or Day.

The Jews, both in the first century and present day, will have the Holy Spirit poured out on them, and each time, they will see Him by the Spirit. God poured out his Spirit during Pentecost in Acts. He poured it out with the return of the Messiah, and He has and will pour His Spirit out again in these days.

He is not finished with Israel. He has not replaced them, but He will reveal Himself to His brothers just as Joseph revealed himself to his brothers. I believe He will do this by the Holy Spirit before the extinction of the heavens and the earth.

CHAPTER 9

Zechariah 14: The Day of the Lord and the Nations of the Crusades

Futurists don't read Ezekiel 38–39 sequentially or literally. They teach that these chapters are an imminent future event of Armageddon despite Ezekiel's description of the types of weaponry and gear used to fight the war (they symbolize this).

When they get to the end of the chapters 39:25–29, when the Jews return to their own land, it is prophecy that is currently being fulfilled in our time. The events are taught out of order to support their interpretation. This interpretation best fits their understanding, but it makes better sense if these were concerning the Crusades of the past, and today's Jews are returning to their own land in fulfillment. The sequential order is kept, and the Crusaders and the nations all fought with the type of weaponry and gear described.

The Day of the Lord is one that spans centuries and millennia either from about AD 70 through the Crusades to Jerusalem or AD 96 to now. It is a day that, like many things in prophecy, occurs over a broad span of time. "With the Lord, a thousand years are like a day, and a day is like a thousand years" (2 Peter 3:8; Psalm 90:4).

The Crusades are what humans saw in the natural realm, but He was present in battle and judgment unseen to human eyes. By the Spirit, one could see Him and what He was doing here on earth in the Spirit. It is interesting that in verses 23–24, it reads that He hid His face from them. No one would see Him in Spirit for it is by the Spirit He is revealed. The Crusades were prophesied in Ezekiel 38 and 39. They were prophesied in Zechariah 14 and in Revelation. These chapters go into detail about what the Crusades would be like. Everything mentioned in these chapters happened to Jerusalem at some point during the Crusades. The Lord still considered Israel a nation during the Crusades, even if the nations did not. Israel was a nation in the ninth to eleventh centuries. Read chapters 38 and 39, and then actually read what happened during the Crusades. It describes the Crusades fully. Jerusalem was the center of the world during the Crusades of AD 1095–1291 (Ezekiel 38:12).

Some futurists say that preterists are not literal but symbolic and allegorical about the Second Coming of the Messiah. The futurists will read in Ezekiel concerning Gog and Magog:

> All your army, horses and horsemen, all of them splendidly attired, a great company with buckler and shield, all of them wielding swords … all of them with shield and helmet. (38:4, 5)

> Then those who inhabit the cities of Israel will go out and make fires with the weapons and burn them, both shields and bucklers, bows and arrows, war clubs and spears. (39:9)

> You will be glutted at My table with horses and charioteers, with mighty men and all the men of war. (39:20)

The Romans and later the nations during the Crusades fought with horses and all of these types of weapons. No modern, developed nation fights with these anymore. Yet futurists want to symbolize these to be tanks, guns, missiles, planes, bombs, bullets, and gas. They say that, in the near future, the nations of the world will gather together around Jerusalem for Armageddon or World War III. Who is being symbolic and allegorical in their interpretation? They don't take Ezekiel literally. No modern, developed nation is going to go back to fighting with those kinds of weapons. It has to have been fulfilled in the past, but when? During the Roman Empire and the Crusades, they all literally fought with horses, charioteers, chariots, bows and arrows, swords, war clubs, shields, helmets, bucklers, and spears, and they surrounded Jerusalem in battle during AD 70 and AD 1096–1291.

Also, when do presidents and prime ministers take the place of kings who actually go out to war with their armies? Sitting presidents usually don't go out to war to fight with the troops like most kings did. Kings don't visit the troops; most times they are encamped with them and go out to battle with them (2 Samuel 11:1). Only one American president actually went out to fight with the troops, and that was James Madison in the War of 1812. Kings were on the battlefield in some way, leading them or watching the battle and making decisions. Though there are kings who rule countries in our time today, there are some countries that have never had kings or don't have kings anymore. How can Gog and Magog be fulfilled in our time and on this first earth without kings from the north and east? How are futurists literal in this when they symbolize it?

The name Gog and Magog seem to be a person, a spiritual entity. In Ezekiel 38:21–22 and 39:11, it says "him" and "his troops" and "his horde." Gog and Magog many times are understood as the nations with earthly kings and armies, but these words seem to infer that these are spiritual entities or principalities over nations of the world. Yeshua did not fight directly against the nations. He fights against the powers, authorities, principalities, and entities over them. Since what is done in heaven is done on earth, or what is unseen reveals itself in the natural realm, this is the sign that manifested the Crusades to Jerusalem.

Zechariah 14:1–5; Matthew 24:15–16; and Acts 1:10–12 speak of the Second Coming of the Messiah in the first century and the Crusades with the nations to Jerusalem in AD 1095–1291. When Yeshua mentioned that some of the disciples ("when you see," not "if you see") would see the abomination of desolation standing in the holy place and then said "those who are in Judea must flee to the mountains," He could be referencing Zechariah 14:4,5 for this in AD 70. Zechariah 14 could have happened around the time of the crusades instead of AD 70.

Many still expect the Mount of Olives to split open. Somehow in the past, the Mount of Olives split to allow for this escape out of Judea. Again, I don't see this as difficult to explain if we remember the story of Korah's rebellion and how these men perished from the land of the living in Numbers 16:30–34:

> But if the Lord brings about an entirely new thing and the ground opens its mouth and swallows them up with all that is theirs, and they descend alive into Sheol, then you will understand that these men have spurned the Lord. As he finished speaking all these words, the ground that was under them split open; and the earth opened its mouth and swallowed them up, and the their households, and all

the men who belonged to Korah with their possessions. So they and all that belonged to them went down alive to Sheol; and the earth closed over them, and they perished from the midst of the assembly. All Israel who were around them fled at the outcry, for they said, "The earth may swallow us up!"

The earth splitting in Zechariah was not as deep as the account in Numbers. The split in Zechariah was wide enough to allow people to walk from one side of the mount to the other side through a valley without closing in around them, but the opening was not a deep split that swallowed things and took them down into the earth. The opening in Numbers was so deep that it took people down within it. Just as the earth closed back up in Numbers, it is possible the earth closed back up in Zechariah to prevent others from following those who were fleeing to the mountains during Yeshua's visitation. If people are fleeing, then the mount had to be shut again and the valley removed to allow escape and prevent capture from their enemies. It is a possibility that as the people were fleeing, their enemies ran after them through the valley (just as the Red Sea closed in over the Egyptians swallowing them up), Mount of Olives did the same, closing up around the enemies so that they remain buried within the Mount of Olives. The fact there is a fault underneath Mount Olives shows it is possible for a fault to open the earth on Mount of Olives and close it again. Perhaps one proof could be in the skeletons buried in unusual and unnatural positions discovered within the mount itself. Perhaps this is an undiscovered mystery that He left hidden and unknown to humans waiting to be unveiled at this time. Maybe this is an undiscovered footprint.

Another scripture that describes earth opening up is Revelation 12:15, 16:

> And the serpent poured water like a river out of his mouth after the woman, so that he might cause her to be swept away with the flood. But the earth helped the woman, and the earth opened its mouth and drank up the river which the dragon poured out of his mouth.

In an article by *Geology Page*, "earthquakes can make thrust faults open violently and snap shut". The men of Korah's rebellion fell into a thrust fault. The fault underneath the Mount of Olives could be a thrust fault. It also reads:

> Experiments reveal a new mechanism that could explain the source of a destructive feature of the 2011 Tohoku earthquake.
>
> The work, appearing in the journal *Nature* on May 1, shows how the earth can split open – and then quickly close back up – during earthquakes along thrust faults.
>
> A team of engineers and scientists from Caltech and Ecole normale superieure (ENS) in Paris have discovered that fast ruptures propagating up toward the earth's surface along a thrust fault can cause one side of a fault to twist away from the other, opening up a gap of up to a few meters that then snaps shut.
>
> Thrust fault earthquakes generally occur when two slabs of rock press against one another, and pressure overcomes the frictions holding them in place. It has long been assumed that, at shallow depths the plates would just slide against one another for a short distance, without opening.
>
> However, researchers investigating the Tohoku earthquake found that not only did the fault slip at shallow depths; it did so by up to 50 meters in some places. That huge motion, which occurred just offshore, triggered a tsunami that caused damage to facilities along the coast of Japan, including at the Fukushima Daiichi Nuclear Power Plant.
>
> That opening of the fault was supposed to be impossible.
>
> The team was surprised to see that, as the rupture hit the surface, the fault twisted open and then snapped shut. Subsequent computer simulations – with models that were modified to remove the artificial rules against the fault opening – confirmed what the team observed experimentally: one slab can twist violently away from the

other. This can happen both on land and on underwater thrust faults, meaning that this mechanism has the potential to change our understanding of how tsunamis are generated.

This tells me that what was prophesied millennia ago and written down confirms that this is possible even in our day and age and scientists are only catching up to scripture. It is possible that the valley that formed along a fault under Mount of Olives centuries ago in fulfillment of scripture to save the people back then had closed back up again.

Just because the natural aspect of these things are explained scientifically doesn't negate the fact God had anything to do with it and it doesn't prove that there is no God. Scripture speaks of these things before scientists found the explanation of it. They do not understand the spiritual aspect of it.

Another explanation is that the mountain split in spirit. Just as Philip was transported by the Spirit through space and dimensions (Acts 8:39–40), so too it is possible God caused the mount to split to allow escape in the Spirit. How do you believe Philip's transport in the Spirit but not a possibility of the mount splitting in the Spirit?

Now, how did the crusades to Jerusalem begin? It begins with a people from the north (Europe) coming down to Jerusalem as foretold in Ezekiel 39:2–7:

> And I will turn you around, drive you on, take you up from the remotest parts of the north and bring you against the mountains of Israel. I will strike your bow from your left hand and dash down your arrows from your right hand. You will fall on the mountains of Israel, you and all your troops and the peoples who are with you; I will give you as food to every kind of predatory bird and beast of the field. You will fall on the open field; for it is I who have spoken,' declares the Lord. My holy name I will make known in the midst of My people Israel; and I will not let My holy name be profaned anymore. And the nations will know that I am the Lord, the Holy One in Israel.

It reads, "I will turn you around" which indicates that these nations would return to Jerusalem. The Crusaders did return as prophesied. God turned them around nine times. There were about nine crusades to Jerusalem that ended with the children's crusade. The Crusades began to collapse around the fifth one. Many of these hordes were buried on the way to or in Israel (Ezekiel 39:9–24).

It was a deceived pope who encouraged these European "Christians" or Catholics to go to Jerusalem. It was the people of these centuries whose hands were stained with blood. It is contrary for believers today to believe that these Christians' hands were stained with blood for the killing of Jews during this time, but yet this had nothing to do with fulfillment of the Gog and Magog prophecy in which the devil deceived them to do this evil thing against the Jews. We cannot believe one idea without the other. As a preterist believer, I cannot separate these two ideas–they logically connect. As a preterist believer, I cannot believe we go back to fighting with bows and arrows. A futurist separates these and fails to make the connection. They do not see how this was Satan deceiving the nations from the north and this must be the prophecy of Gog and Magog. This is fulfillment of prophecy in which these so-called Christians, who were actually sinners and wolves in sheep's clothing, were deceived with these evil thoughts which led to their hands being stained with blood. The Crusaders were deceived by the devil, which is described in Ezekiel:

> Thoughts will come into your mind and you will devise an evil plan (this was Satan deceiving them), and you will say, "I will go up against the land of unwalled villages, I will go against those who are at rest, that live securely, all of them living without walls and having no bars or gates, to capture spoil and to seize plunder, to turn your hand against the waste places which are now inhabited, and against the people who are gathered from the nations who have acquired cattle and goods, who live at the center (or navel) of the world (which is Jerusalem) ... Have you come to capture spoil? Have you assembled your company to seize plunder, to carry away silver and gold, to take away cattle and goods, to capture great spoil?" (Revelation 20:7–10; Revelation 16:13–16; Ezekiel 38:10–13).

In Ezekiel 38:14–16, God describes how the people of the north in Europe would come against His people Israel who are living securely:

> On that day when My people Israel are living securely,

> will you not know it? You will come from your place out of the remote parts of the north, you and many peoples with you, all of them riding on horses, a great assembly and a mighty army; and you will come up against My people Israel like a cloud to cover the land.
>
> And they came up on the broad plain of the earth and surrounded the camp of the saints and the beloved city, and fire came down from heaven and devoured them. (Revelation 20:9)

The fire of Revelation 20:9 is mentioned in Ezekiel 38:22 and 39:6. This fire came with the hail that fell to earth.

> Pope Urban II initiates the Crusades in 1095, and the Crusaders capture Jerusalem in 1099.
>
> The Crusades fail to win the Holy Land because of Crusader rivalry and greed; men begin to question medieval concern with the future life.
>
> Between the 11th and 14th centuries, the powers of Europe launched a series of Crusades to liberate the Holy Land from Islam, after Pope Urban II had demanded a "Holy War" against the infidels. In 1099 the Crusaders captured Jerusalem from Seljuk Turks, and went on to set up a chain of Christian kingdoms in Palestine. These kingdoms were soon minced by a revival of Turkish power, and further Crusades had to be launched to relieve them. ... In 1291 the port of Acre, the last Christian stronghold in Palestine, fell, and with the rise of the Ottoman impregnable throughout Middle East.
>
> What should have been a great Christian adventure proved to be a story of greed and ambition, and ended in disillusion. (*The Last Two Million Years*, 220–223)

Read James 3:13–18. This was a deception from Satan over the nations—the nations were disillusioned.

> The sixth angel poured out his bowl on the great river, the Euphrates and its water was dried up, so that the way would be prepared for the kings from the east. (Revelation 16:12)

When was this fulfilled? Who was from the east that crossed the Euphrates River during the Crusades and was in Israel? Muslim Arab kings with their armies who lived in the east near India would cross the Euphrates to fight.

Those as far as China came.

It was written about Genghis Khan of the Mongols and his army:

> In 1206 he set out to conquer the world and very nearly did; he took northern China, including Peking, during 1211–1212. Their empire was built on the efforts of ruthless and courageous nomadic warriors who did not surrender or take any prisoners. The Mongols seem to have had unlimited mounted warriors who could tirelessly travel for days across the steppes of central Asia, each man carrying "two or three bows, three large quivers full of arrows and an axe and ropes for hauling siege engines of war." These tough nomads, according to the Pope's envoy, observed a strict moral code and dealt abruptly with thieves and adulterers by putting them to death. On a long campaign the troops to be slaughtered and eaten. "When they are going to make war, they send ahead an advance guard ... they are going to make war ... They seize no plunder, burn no houses and slaughter no animals; they only wound and kill men." The well-disciplined military machine provided a following wave of troops to take care of the plunder. ... in all their tasks they are very swift and energetic. All the women wear breeches and some shoot like the men. These people of the central Asian steppes were for the most part pagan but there was an influential minority of Nestorian Christians—a heretical sect which broke from the early church and expanded eastwards in the fifth century ... In January 1256 *the Mongol army began to move west*; it crossed the River Oxus under the command of Mongka's brother, Hulagu. ... The cities of upper Mesopotamia were the next to be overrun, and *in*

> the autumn of 1259 the Mongol army crossed the Euphrates and was soon at the gates of Aleppo. The Great Khan, Mongka, died while campaigning in China in August 1259. (*The Crusades*, 167–169)

Were they ever in the Israel?

> The leader of the Mongol embassy which *arrived in Cairo* to demand the Sultan's submission was executed and an army led by the Mamluk Sultan Qutuz prepared to march against the Mongols in Syria. Qutuz crossed the border on 26 July 1260 and took the small Mongol garrison at Gaza ... news was received that *the Mongol army had crossed the Jordan and entered Galilee.*

To arrive in Cairo, which is in Egypt, from the east at that time, they had to go through Israel. Keep in mind that the Crusades ended in 1291, the Mongol army from the east crossed the Euphrates River and were in Israel in 1259–1260 before the Crusades to Jerusalem was ended. An embassy and an ambassador would represent their king.

The Crusaders (Gog and Magog) were drawn out and challenged to war by God:

> I will turn you about and put hooks into your jaws and I will bring you out, and all your army, horses and horsemen, all of them splendidly attired, a great company with buckler and shield, all of them wielding swords; ... After many days you will be summoned ... It shall come about in the last days that I will bring you against My land, so that the nations may know Me when I am sanctified through you before their eyes, O Gog. (Ezekiel 38:4–9, 16)

It says they were "splendidly attired" which means they were clothed in full armor. The Crusaders were dressed in armor and carried swords. Who dresses in armor and carries swords today when going to battle? Will modern day or future generations revert back to armor and swords? The Crusaders, along with many other nations, were also a "great company" that went to Jerusalem.

The "Christian" Crusaders were not true believers in Yeshua. They practiced sin and lawlessness. There was sin among the Crusaders, which brought on the plagues:

Killing and pillaging occurred:

> Large numbers of Muslims retreated to the temple area and were caught and cut down by pursuing Crusaders; Jews, who ran to their synagogue, were burnt alive when the building was put to the torch and almost everyone the Christian troops came across in their house-to-house search for loot was killed. When Raymond of Aguilers walked through the city he saw "piles of heads, hands and feet ... in the houses and streets, and indeed there was a running to and fro of men and knights over the corpses." No one knows how many lost their lives in the massacre but scholars these days point out that the city had been largely emptied of its civilian population before the siege began." (*The Crusades*, 66).

Concerning the Turks,

> Bohemond's anonymous chronicler was among the victorious knights: "We pursued them, killing them for a whole day, and we took much booty, gold, silver, horses, asses, camels, oxen, sheep and many other things about which we do not know." (*The Crusades*, 40)

> The long march of the Crusaders was marked by carnage, pillage, and destruction: the massacre of the Jews in the Rhineland; thieving and slaughter in Hungary and the Byzantine Empire. (*The Crusades*, 37)

> For two days the Crusaders did nothing but kill and pillage. The few surviving Jews were sold into slavery. (*The Crusades, 52)*

Fornication was practiced:

> The chroniclers consistently blamed military reverses on the lust and fornication of the Crusaders, and at Nicaea

all the camp brothels were closed down. But by the time they reached Antioch the bordellos were back in business. *(The Crusades, 48)*

Even before the Crusades began, rival popes were caught up in a lot of sin, which was perfect ground for Satan to thrive in when he was released before or around AD 1096:

> In Rome, rival popes imprisoned, starved, mutilated, castrated, blinded, and assassinated each other. (*AD 1000: Living on the Brink of Apocalypse*, 5)

The people were also sinning:

> Sons murdered fathers, husbands killed wives, sisters fought brothers for possession of a castle or manor. As early as 909 ... archbishop of Rheims, lamented, "The cities lie in ruins, the monasteries are burned or destroyed, the earth, men live without law and fear of punishment, abandoning themselves to their passions. Everyone does as he pleases, defying the laws divine and human, as well as the orders of their bishops. The strong oppress the weak. Everywhere there is violence against the poor who are helpless to resist—equally helpless the churches and cloisters who cannot defend what is theirs." (*AD 1000, Living on the Brink of Apocalypse*, 5)

The plague mentioned in Zechariah 14:12–15 is more likely the one that happened to the Crusaders, Gog and Magog, as they came against Jerusalem. It also came on the animals:

> So also like this plague will be the plague on the horse, the mule, the camel, the donkey and all the cattle that will be in those camps. (Zechariah 14:15)

The following account mentions the army and horses affected by a plague. Hmmm, could this be Yeshua? Concerning disease and plague, it is recorded,

> Many lives *and horses* were lost but disease was the Christians' greatest enemy, according to James of Vitry. It was, "*a contagious disease with no natural causes, divinely sent down on a great part of our army* either to cleanse us from our sins or so that we should be more deserving of the crown. For the thighs and legs first swelled up and then festered; *also superfluous flesh grew in the mouth.*" Between one fifth and one sixth of the army were said to have died in the epidemic but, in spite of its depleted strength, the Crusader army was gradually wearing down the resolve of the garrison at Damietta. (*The Crusades,* 145).

> But Damietta's garrison had also suffered from disease and starvation and, when a Christian sentry spotted an empty tower, the Crusaders brought up scaling ladders and climbed into the town to discover that almost all the Muslim troops were ill and that the civilian population, drastically reduced by disease, amounted to only 3000 people. (*The Crusades*, 145)

What does Zechariah say about this plague?

> Now this will be the plague with which the Lord will strike all the peoples who have gone to war against Jerusalem; their flesh will rot while they stand on their feet, and their eyes will rot in their sockets, and their tongue will rot in their mouth.

The book, *The Crusades*, describes that

> Hunger and disease dogged the Christian army all the way back along the bank of the Nile.

It also reads,

> The sickness that had stricken the army now began to increase to such an alarming extent, *surgeons had to remove the gangrenous flesh before they could either chew their food or swallow it.* It was pitiful to hear around the camp the

cries of those whose dead flesh was being cut away; it was just like the cry of a woman in labour. During the retreat, Louis was suffering so badly from dysentery that a hole was cut in his drawers." (*The Crusades*, 163).

This is gangrene, the rotting of flesh spoken of in Zechariah 14. The Christian Crusaders even had it in their mouths and on their tongues. It increased because it was the Lord who struck them.

It is not a coincidence that Zechariah writes concerning those who went to war against Jerusalem, "their flesh will rot while they stand on their feet, and their eyes will rot in their sockets, and their tongue will rot in their mouth" and there is an actual historical account of these Crusader armies who went to war against Jerusalem suffering from rotting flesh so much so, *"surgeons had to remove the gangrenous flesh before they could either chew their food or swallow it"*. I believe they had gangrene on their eyes and everywhere else too for it was a plague among them.

Here, history supports the fulfillment of prophecy. This is an obvious footprint of an unseen dinosaur. How many futurists will accept or ignore this fulfillment of prophecy too? How many will disregard this footprint because they just have to see the one who made the footprint? If they don't see Him, then it just isn't true. The dinosaur then was never really present here on earth. So where is faith?

Yeshua visited the Crusaders. He left a footprint. There was a visitation no one recognized. The Crusaders were struck by Yeshua. Yeshua was present at this time to battle and judge these nations coming against His people, the camp of the saints. He was present to fight against the evil entities coming against those who were reigning with Him. This is a sign that Yeshua was still present, still visiting earth, an extended stay since the first century or even traversing between heaven and earth throughout the millennia. "A thousand years are like a day, a day like a thousand years."

We must recognize the signs of His visitation. In battle, no one at that time and even when latter generations, who read these historical accounts, recognized it was Him who struck the Crusaders in battle. Hence the phrase "thief in the night." No one during the temple's destruction in AD 70, no one during the Crusades, no one today as earth dies reads the signs correctly. They expect to see with eyes of flesh, but it is the eyes of the spirit, by the Spirit, that we see. In the very least, learn to read the signs of fulfillment that occur in the natural accurately.

In July, a strange plague spreads throughout Antioch. The diseased show strange black swellings about the size of eggs in their armpits and groins. The swellings ooze blood and pus and are followed by boils and blood blotches on the skin. The sick suffer severe intestinal pain and begin to cough up clots of blood. Everything that issues from their bodies-breath, sweat, bloody urine, and blood-blackened excrement-smells rancid. After five days of agony, they finally die. (*The Complete Idiots' Guide to the Crusades*, 75–76)

Again, this is a sign of Yeshua's judgment against the Crusaders who were against Jerusalem and His people. The Jews didn't understand that He was fighting for them.

According to Zechariah 14:13,

It will come about in that day that a great panic from the Lord will fall on them; and they will seize one another's hand, and the hand of one will be lifted against the hand of another.

It was written there was confusion among the Crusaders:

Amid the panic and misery there was an attempt to evacuate the sick by galley. (*The Crusades*, 163)

Now concerning them turning on each other,

Dissension among the princes is reflected in a breakdown of law and order between all factions within the Crusade. Knights engage in bloody battles with other knights; vassals with other vassals; peasants are murdered in their sleep; serfs steal from serfs; women are sexually violated in the streets. Now famine again besets the Crusaders. Princes and knights begin to forage the local countryside. Hunger becomes so acute that incidents of cannibalism occur. When Raymond and Bohemond raid Ma'arrat-an-Nu'man, the soldiers "cut pieces from the buttocks of dead Saracens, which they cooked, but when it was not yet roasted enough by the fire they devoured it with savage mouths." (*The Complete Idiots' Guide to the Crusades*, 76)

They roused the Christian population and their help opened the gates to the waiting army. *There was uproar and mayhem*—the Crusaders poured into the city killing all the Turks they came across, and *in the confusion many Christians as well*. (*The Crusades*, 50)

In Matthew 24:29–31, when Yeshua speaks of His return to Jerusalem, He was referencing Zechariah 9:14–17. Zechariah14:5b seems to suggest another return before the crusades begin. The Lord was present here, though no one saw Him with eyes of flesh. The signs of His presence were apparent. He struck the nations with His rod. They were uprooted from the earth as they battled. He judged the nations (Matthew 25:31, 32). He will continue to judge the nations. If they did not see Him by the Spirit, more likely they saw him upon death as their judge and the One who struck them. The blood on His garments from this battle was the blood that flowed during this time from men who were killed from among these nations. It was like a winepress.

Overall, the crusades against Jerusalem weren't a great success. They returned back to their countries defeated. They were humiliated and there was great loss. It seems Yeshua wasn't finished with those nations yet. About a generation later, He visited them on their turf, in their territories and slew many by the millions almost wiping them off the planet. He struck them severely just like He did with the Philistines when the ark was captured and they were struck with tumors in their own land (1 Samuel 4–6). It was also just like He did with ancient Egypt striking them with ten plagues in their own land (Exodus 7–11). Did either the Philistines or Egyptians see Him walking throughout their territories? No one saw Him. He was like a thief in the night among them. Not even Israel saw Him. Only Moses saw Him. They were blind to Him. What am I talking about?

It is interesting to note that as the crusades to Jerusalem was coming to an end the deadly outbreak of bubonic plague occurred in China and spread west to Europe in the 1300's. This plague almost took out all of Europe. It struck China in the early 1330's. This plague was also known as the Black Death. This plague struck the eastern and northern nations that came up to war against Jerusalem from 1095 to 1291. Religion didn't protect the religious, for even the friars and nuns were struck with it.

One might say: *Bubonic plague, or Black Death, was spread because Europe began trading with Asia and the rats with fleas came into the countries and spread it, so it wasn't God. The Crusaders did not bring it from the Holy Land.* If we remember the ten plagues of Egypt, there was probably a natural explanation for those plagues to occur where one plague led to another. The first plague probably began due to a change in climate drying up the Nile River or an increase in red algae or bacterium. The frogs came out of the increasingly red water. When they die, insects such as lice, gnats, and flies came to feed off of them. The frogs are not there to eat the gnats and flies which increased. The insects, maybe the flea, carried disease causing boils. It could be that the boils in Egypt could be the same disease as bubonic plague. Strange weather phenomena, a volcanic eruption, or maybe an eclipse probably occurred to cause darkness. Hail and locusts came after this. An increase in a fungus contaminated the grain killing the firstborn who may have had double portions of it according to an Egyptian custom.

So even though there can be a scientific explanation into how one plague led to another plague through natural causes does not mean it wasn't God, nor does it mean He didn't cause it or allow it to happen. He uses the laws of nature, creation, customs, climate, weather, and even life forms unseen to the human eye to accomplish His purpose.

Even though bubonic plague was caused by the flea, I believe this was God's hand against the very nations who fought against Him at Jerusalem, even as far east as China. Did it come with the Crusaders returning from the Holy Land? Most likely it did not, but it doesn't mean God did not use this against them just as He used other things against the Egyptians. In his anger, He struck the Europeans by the millions. He used the tiny flea against the nations. It is written in the book of Exodus, He used the frog, locusts, gnats, lice plagues in ancient Egypt.

Was the bubonic plague a vengeful visitation from an angry God of Israel? Considering the rapid spread and harsh severity of it, that it happened shortly after the crusades (about a generation later) to the very nations who came against the holy city, and seemed to end suddenly, I tend to believe so. This could be another footprint indicating He was here. He was angry with them for going to war against Jerusalem and killing Jews. A curse fell upon the nations who fought against Him and His city. A generation after the crusades may be decades to us, but it is like minutes to Him. Not much time passed between these two events.

It seems to this day, He is angry at the nations and the descendants that came against Jerusalem centuries ago for not coming to His feast. In judgment, He sends severe droughts all over the globe. This is discussed in the following chapter.

He used the natural progression of one plague leading into the next one against the Egyptians. He probably used an Egyptian custom against the firstborn. He used the bacteria to make Miriam leprous. He used the black ravens to feed Elijah for a certain time. He used Nebuchadnezzar to bring judgment upon Israel when they rebelled against Him. He caused the brook to quench Elijah's thirst until it was time for it to dry up. He used a worm to eat the plant that gave shade and relief to Jonah. He used a fish to swallow Jonah. He used a fish to catch a coin so that the disciples' tax could be paid. He used a Roman census in Israel to bring about the birth of Messiah in Bethlehem at the right time. He used the star to lead the wise men to Bethlehem at the right time. I believe He used the nations of United States of America, United Kingdom, Soviet Union, and China to help end the Holocaust. He called them against Germany as judgment. Just as He used the trade between Europe and Asia to bring about bubonic plague, could it be that He is also, in the last century, using our excessive use of fossil fuels against the world today which is causing the climate to change for the worse? I believe it is possible. He allows fossil fuels to be permissible for us to use, but not beneficial in the long run to accomplish His purpose. This is the wisdom of God. God uses supernatural and natural things to bring about His purpose in fulfillment.

If some Christians can believe that a change in climate began a series of plagues in Egypt by God's hand, why is it hard for them to believe that a change in climate today in the planet could begin many troubles now by our use of fossil fuels, which can be by His hand? They did not witness the plagues or climate change in Egypt, but still believe it happened, yet they witness the climate change and troubles today, and they doubt, question, and laugh at it. *Consider that just as a possible climate change in Egypt led to a series of devastating and terrifying plagues, a change in climate today could lead to something similar or worse.* Believers must recognize that history in a different way is repeating itself, but on a much larger scale. Take care that your heart is not unbelieving as the people of Noah's day who laughed and mocked him. One has to be blind or hardened not to see the earth vanishing and dying right before them.

One can scientifically explain the natural circumstances and conditions that brought about the plagues of Egypt or the Bubonic plague and conclude it wasn't God. They fail to recognize the spiritual side of it. Others say *how can He do such a thing? He is merciful, kind, loving, gracious, and patient.* They forget that He is also just, holy, and righteous. They forget that vengeance is His. They forget that it was foretold before it happened and at His word and with humble obedience to Him, He relents and it stops.

Many believers would say the plagues among the Crusaders, the Black Death, or plagues in recent centuries are all from the devil. We must not be quick to credit that which is from God's own hand (whether spiritual gifts, mercy, or judgment) to the devil lest we blaspheme His Spirit, which is not forgivable. Yeshua has the keys of Death and Hades and judges the nations with a rod of iron. He wounds and He heals, He kills and brings to life (Deuteronomy 32:39–43; Revelation 1:18; 19:15). We must wisely discern the hand of God even in our century.

Here, in His extended stay or visitation over a thousand years later, He showed Himself King of kings. History supports the fulfillment of this prophecy in this interpretation. Here are clues, the footprints of a dinosaur that was present at this time.

CHAPTER 10

The Prophecy of the Plague of Worldwide Drought Is Now Fulfilled

The morning of April 14, 2019, six days before Passover, I had just woken up, but I closed my eyes again for a few minutes. I had a vision with my eyes closed:

> I am standing beside and slightly behind Yeshua sitting on His throne observing what is happening. I see only the back of Yeshua's head, but He is wearing a crown and dressed like a king. There is a table set up before Him with plates, cups, food, and bread. His throne is facing the end of the guests' table. The table sits about twenty or thirty people. I don't know who is coming. It is few guests for a king to have. No one is there yet. He is preparing for their arrival. The dining area is covered, and high above, there is a beautiful outside scenery and open for fresh air to come in. There is a beautiful sky and nature outside. There seems to be a body of water below. A servant boy of about eight or ten years old comes up to Him and asks where he should put the unleavened bread he had in his hand. It looked like he was carrying a basket of bread and asking Yeshua where every piece he held up should go. Yeshua is moving His hand and pointing to where He wants the boy to place it and talking to him. The servant boy is setting up the table according to His specific directions.

I opened my eyes. I closed my eyes again and had another vision unrelated to this one.

> Then it will come about that any who are left of all the nations that went against Jerusalem will go up from year to year to worship the King, the Lord of hosts, and to celebrate the Feast of Booths. And it will be that whichever of the families of the earth does not go up to Jerusalem to worship the King, the Lord of hosts, there will be no rain on them. If the family of Egypt does not go up or enter, then no rain will fall on them; it will be the plague with which the Lord smites the nations who do not go up to celebrate the Feast of Booths. (Zechariah 14:16–19)

"Families" could also mean the nations. Either this means the nations that survived the Crusades were advised to go to the earthly Jerusalem to celebrate or in repentance, humility, and in spirit worship King Yeshua who is in the heavenly Jerusalem. God seeks those who worship Him in spirit and truth.

Throughout the millennia, even since His return and through his extended stay, He has been sending out invitations to many to come to His feast of booths. Many have rejected it. The following passages refer to the feast of booths.

> The kingdom of heaven may be compared to a king who gave a wedding feast for his son. And he sent out his slaves to call those who had been invited (the Jews of His generation) to the wedding feast, and they were unwilling to come. Again he sent out other slaves saying, "Tell those who have been invited (the Jews of His generation), 'Behold, I have prepared my dinner; my oxen and my fattened livestock are all butchered and everything is ready; come to the wedding feast.' But they paid no attention and went their way, one to his own farm, another to his business, and the rest seized his slaves and mistreated them and killed them. But the king was enraged, and he sent his armies and destroyed those murderers and set their city on fire (the temple's destruction in AD 70). Then he said to his slaves, 'The wedding is ready, but

those who were invited were not worthy. Go therefore to the main highways, and as many as you find there, invite to the wedding feast.' Those slaves went out into the streets and gathered together all they found, both evil and good; and the wedding hall was filled with dinner guests (every resurrected person out of both resurrections and every global nation who believes in Him even to this present day). But when the king came in to look over the dinner guests, he saw a man there who was not dressed in wedding clothes, and he said to him, 'Friend, how did you come in here without wedding clothes?' And the man was speechless (either because he did not know what to say or he was dead to Him—a tare). Then the king said to the servants, 'Bind him hand and foot, and throw him into the outer darkness, in that place there will be weeping and gnashing of teeth.'" For many are called, but few are chosen. (Matthew 22:2–14)

Be dressed in readiness, and keep your lamps lit. Be like men who are waiting for their master when he returns from the wedding feast, so that they may immediately open the door to him when he comes and knocks. Blessed are those slaves whom the master will find on the alert when he comes; truly I say to you, that he will gird himself to serve, and have them recline at the table, and will come up and wait on them. Whether he comes in the second watch, or even in the third, and finds them so, blessed are those slaves. But be sure of this, that if the head of the house had known at what hour the thief was coming, he would not have allowed his house to be broken into. You too, be ready; for the Son of Man is coming at an hour that you do not expect. (Luke 12:35–40)

What is happening now with the earth and to the nations that dwell in it is much bigger than we realize. He has crushed the head of His enemy and won the fight with principalities over the nations. Now He cuts them off at the feet, the bottom where it will hurt the nations of the world the most. Water has now become a very precious commodity. Civil strife is occurring due to declining drinkable supply of water. When the nations can no longer live where they have dwelt for centuries because of drought and famine and mass migration occurs, He affects the princes who are over these nations. Where do these entities hide from His presence? It is akin to a king who surrounds a city and cuts off its water supply and other resources to starve the inhabitants to surrender or die. He has surrounded this world and has cut off water to many nations.

Which nations are affected by lack of rain, water, and drought? Central and South Asia, Afghanistan, India, Iran, Pakistan, and Tajikistan, Mongolia, northern and western China, Iraq, Uzbekistan, Syria, Jordan, many regions of Africa, Australia, and parts of the United States, including California and Texas.

Have the nations gone up to Jerusalem? No, for most have been struck with drought. Drought has been occurring globally in this passing away or extinction of heaven and earth. This plague has struck many nations of the world. Egypt has experienced severe droughts over the years. In an article from *Egyptian Streets* it is written:

> Egypt's standing is below the level of water poverty and the country is suffering from water scarcity stated Egypt's Minister of Agriculture and Land Reclamation Ezz Eddin Abo Setit ... For the last couple of years, Egypt has been the focus of climate various reports which have adamantly secured Egypt's placement as a country in high-risk of water problems in the near future due to water scarcity. According to the Guardian, the UN predicts that Egypt will be approaching a state of "absolute water crisis" by 2025 and that the nation is already below the United Nations' water poverty threshold.

According to the *New Humanitarian* report on rural Pakistan:

> Water shortages and crop failure caused by record-low rainfalls in Pakistan are forcing some farming families to abandon their land, fleeing what officials say is the worst drought to hit the country in years, while others are selling their last breeding animals or seed stocks to survive.

What about the droughts in Europe of those nations that went to Jerusalem?

According to a journal in Europeandroughtcentre.com, the droughts are expected to worsen:

> 400 million people in Europe could be affected by more severe droughts if global temperatures rise by 3 degrees Celsius, according to a team of international scientists. The team warned that droughts will become more frequent and last longer if global warming exceeds the 1.5 degree Celsius limit set by the Paris Agreement, with potentially severe impacts on agriculture and the economy.
>
> The projected environmental changes are also expected to negatively impact water content in European soils. If temperatures rise by three degrees, each square kilometer of land would lose 35,000 cubic metres of available water, according to Thober ... "This will have great implications for agriculture, forestry, water supply and tourism."

Dr. Samaniego told the *Daily Mail*,

> "If the models are right, we should start thinking about how to adapt and mitigate these changes. The time to act is now".

The website, edo.jrc.ec.europa.eu/edov2/php/index.php?id=1052, maps the current droughts of Europe.

According to *Business Insider*, Europe experienced one of the worst droughts in decades which devastate South Europe crops:

> Drought in southern Europe threatens to reduce cereal production in Italy and parts of Spain to its lowest level in at least 20 years, and hit other regional crops including olives and almonds. Castile and Leon, the largest cereal growing region in Spain, has been particularly badly affected, with crop losses estimated at around sixty to 70 percent. This year was not bad, it was catastrophic. "I can't remember a year like this since 1992 when I was a little child," said Joaquin Antonio Pino, cereal farmer in

> Sinlabajos, Avilo." Olives are affected; drought is the latest headache for olive growers already plagued by insects and a bacterial disease in recent years.

What about the droughts in China whose ancestors crossed the Euphrates during the Crusades? The New York Times reports:

> Officials governing a large area of northern China say their region is suffering from the worst drought on record, leading to crops wilting and farmers and herders growing desperate to get water to farmlands, grasslands, animals and their households. The drought is affecting the northeastern and eastern areas of the Inner Mongolian Autonomous Region, which is near Beijing. In recent years, Chinese scientists have attributed extreme weather patterns in China, and especially in northern China, to climate change. The region of Inner Mongolia and its residents have been hit especially hard by wide fluctuations in the weather.

Drought has been occurring globally for a couple of decades. After the extinction, the destruction of earth with intense heat and fire, and the judgment of the dead according to 2 Peter 3:7–13 and Revelation 20:11–21:1, on the new earth the nations will eventually learn and go up to Jerusalem to celebrate the feast of booths (Zechariah 14:16). They will bring their glory into the city (Revelation 21:22–27). Yeshua will appoint kings in the new earth to lead the nations and do so according to the will of the Lord.

CHAPTER 11
Blessed Is He Who Comes in the Name of the Lord

Some have asked, "When is He returning?" Futurists believe there are two things that need to happen in order for Messiah to return: the proclamation of the Gospel to the ends of the earth and for Jerusalem to proclaim, "Blessed is He who comes in the name of the Lord." They believe Matthew 23:36–39 and Luke 13:35 as something to be fulfilled in the future during our modern days, two thousand years after Yeshua spoke those words. They believe He will not come again until modern-day Jerusalem proclaims, "Blessed is He who comes in the name of the Lord!" According to them, it is then that the Lord will appear to a modern-day or a future earthly Jerusalem.

Some also believe that though His generation in the first century saw the temple destroyed and the tribes were scattered, they did not call upon Him. Therefore, to them, His Second Coming and the temple's destruction were not the same event. This means the shout of praise, "Blessed is He who comes in the name of the Lord!" must be spoken by those of a distant generation.

If we read Matthew 21:1–11 and Matthew 23:37–39 and then read Luke 13:31–35 and Luke 19:28–44, there is a difference in the order it is written. No one notices there is a difference between how Matthew and Luke write it. No one speaks to this difference. The triumphal entry and Yeshua's prophecy are in reversed order in these two Gospels. Futurists tend to use the Gospel of Matthew to support their view, which has the triumphal entry first, and then use the prophecy next, therefore implying a future fulfillment to usher in the return of the Messiah. A comparison with the Gospel of Luke shows the prophecy first and the triumphal entry a week later, supporting a fulfillment of Yeshua's prophecy in that first-century generation and not a future one. Futurists aren't going to address this difference, refer to the Gospel of Luke, or believe this is fulfilled in the triumphal entry into Jerusalem. As a preterist, I tend to lean on the Gospel of Luke, but I am not going to ignore the Gospel of Matthew.

We can't say that He said this twice: before and after His triumphal entry. We can't say He meant two different things: Matthew meant one thing and Luke meant another. They both speak of the same thing. Let's look at Mark 11:1–10 and John 12:12–19, which also mention His entry into Jerusalem, but there is no mention about the prophecy Yeshua made. So, which Gospel is accurate? Should we ignore or remove the one that does not support our view and only recognize the other one which does? Should we tear a Gospel out of our Bibles? Which Gospel and which verse would give the best support to which view comes closest to accuracy of what actually happened?

Does this have a relation to a first-century coming of the Messiah and not a Second Coming in the future of our time? Even in the Gospel of Matthew, which is used by futurists, despite placing the prophecy after His triumphal entry, it can be argued that Yeshua said this to the generation that He was pierced by *which is the first-century generation* (Matthew 23:36—"this generation"). Both verses read: "From now on you (to the crowds and His disciples, Matthew 23:1) will not see Me until you (the crowds and disciples being addressed) say, 'Blessed is He who comes in the name of the Lord!'"

Note how this is in the same chapter as the prophecy. In the phrase "this generation," many understand this verse to be speaking about the generation being addressed at that time. The words here speak of the same generation that rejected Yeshua in the next chapter of Matthew 24:34.

In the Gospel of Matthew, the prophecy comes *after* the triumphal entry into Jerusalem, and it could likely have fulfillment in His return with clouds of glory *in the first century*, not today. Futurists might say, "They did not say, 'Blessed is He who comes in the name of the Lord,'" but how do you know they did not say it? "Because they did not repent." The phrase is not one of repentance, but praise. I can't prove they did say it around AD 70, but you can't prove they didn't say it either.

The Gospel of Luke is written proof that the people said it *in the first century* upon His triumphal entry into Jerusalem as He rode on a donkey. *Either way, whether Matthew or Luke is read, the phrase was to be spoken to that generation in the first century.* We can't dismiss this as mere coincidence and continue to await Jerusalem today to fulfill these words as though they were never fulfilled. This wasn't a coincidence that they said these exact words during His entry, it was fulfillment. Many don't put the pieces of the puzzle together. They miss this footprint.

These words do not mean that all of Jerusalem repents (perhaps many do anyway), but they will literally say this phrase of praise to Yeshua. These words were fulfilled about a week after Yeshua prophesied this according to the Gospel of Luke. He returned to Jerusalem riding on a donkey, and *a multitude* said, "Blessed is He who comes in the name of the Lord" (Luke 19:37, 38).

This is also in fulfillment of Zechariah 9:9:

> Rejoice greatly, O daughter of Zion! Shout in triumph, O daughter of Jerusalem! Behold, your king is coming to you; He is just and endowed with salvation, humble, and mounted on a donkey, even on a colt, the foal of a donkey.

Yeshua was coming to them on a donkey, and the multitudes in Jerusalem saw Him.

Now are we to believe this is interpreted as the Second Coming of Yeshua just because it says, "Blessed is He who *comes*" and "Your king is *coming* to you"? Whether a futurist or a preterist, this has little to nothing to do with His Second Coming in the clouds of heaven with the holy angels. It has fulfillment in His return to Jerusalem a week later.

About a week after the crowds of Jerusalem praised Him greatly, He was rejected by the multitudes and crucified. No, this wasn't repentance. Yeshua never said specifically that they would repent when He said this. So, from the time of Yeshua prophesying this until his death is about two weeks. How quickly His Word was fulfilled—not in two thousand years but only in one week! According to Matthew, this was spoken to that generation and not a future one. According to the order of Luke, this had nothing to do with a Second Coming.

Could these words be cyclical in a dual fulfillment and happen again? Yes, it could be, and it wouldn't necessarily be wrong or out of line if Jews in Jerusalem said this today. So, let it be said, "Let everything that have breath praise the Lord!"

Peter speaks to the Jewish brethren of that generation:

> Therefore, repent and return, so that your sins may be wiped away, in order that times of refreshing may come from the presence of the Lord; and that He may send Jesus,

> the Christ appointed for you, *whom heaven must receive until the period of restoration of all things* about which God spoke by the mouth of His holy prophets from ancient time. (Acts 3:19–21)

Doesn't Elijah, who came as John the Baptist, restore all things (Matthew 17:11; Mark 9:12)? Does he at least usher in the beginning of these things? What is the period or time of restoration? Was it not during the time of the Rock in Daniel when the kingdom comes and destroys the kingdoms of the world and all opposed to it? What is the sign for this? The absence of those kingdoms and their nonexistence for many centuries is a sign. This can't be ignored. Another sign is the trembling, quaking, and removal of all things temporal during our day with the calamities and devastations happening worldwide. The eternal kingdom shakes all that is temporal.

> And likewise, all the prophets who have spoken, from Samuel and his successors onward, also announced these days. It is you who are the sons of the prophets and of the covenant which God made with your fathers. (Acts 3:24–25)

"These days" refers to the days since Yeshua's first coming, and "you" refers to the Jewish men of that generation.

CHAPTER 12

The Time was Shortened—Not Lengthened

"Where is the promise of His coming? … For all continues as just as it was from the beginning of creation" (2 Peter 3:3–10). This was said back in the first century—and even today by some. This statement says that many think He hasn't returned yet, but it later suggests that the Second Coming or Day of the Lord is not visible or noticeable to the world, those in the natural realm, or else they wouldn't have asked this.

Yeshua told His disciples that most of them would not see it with observation, hence, the phrase used was "thief in the night." What will be obvious to the world in the natural are the signs in Matthew 24: the passing away and destruction with fire. The Second Coming was seen with eyes of the Spirit by the Spirit of God. No one can see or enter the kingdom of God unless they are born of the Spirit because the kingdom is Spirit (John 3:3–5). The Father seeks those who worship in spirit and in truth (John 4:24). We must set our hearts on the things above for He is from above (John 8:23).

Why do futurists say He tarries for two thousand years? "The Lord is not slow about His promise, as some count slowness, but is patient." He tarried for a short time, as it is written in Matthew 25:5, "Now while the bridegroom was delaying," but not for two thousand years, putting His Word on hold for fulfillment. He does not tarry for long—even though it may seem that way.

In the time frame that He has allotted and predetermined for all things to be fulfilled, He has allowed people time in between to repent and be saved. In other words, it's not that His Word was supposed to be fulfilled at a particular time, but He changed His mind, the date, and era and decided to wait and push pause.

From the beginning, He set a certain amount of time where every word shall be fulfilled, but He left room in that preset time frame for people in every generation to repent and be saved as His Word comes to pass. "For yet in a very little while, He who is coming will come and will not delay" (Hebrews 10:37). "And heed the things which are written in it; for the time is near" (Revelation 1:3).

It was near to their time when this was written and not ours:

> Not forsaking our own (those being addressed) assembling together, as is (present tense in the author's time, not ours) the habit of some, but encouraging one another; and all the more as you (the one being addressed) see the day drawing near. (Hebrews 10:25)

Yeshua, speaking of the tribulation during the time of the temple, even mentioned that the days were shortened (Matthew 24:22). Paul, in 1 Corinthians 7:29, stated the time has been shortened. If time was shortened, how can we say He waits and tarries for almost two thousand years? If He "shortens the time," then how does He also tarry and wait before He even begins to fulfill His Word? *If we say He tarries, He has lengthened the time, not shortened it.* If we say He tarries, we say He has no zeal.

If Paul is suggesting in 1 Corinthians 7:29–31 that those men in his generation (not ours) who have wives should be as though they had none, this speaks to the imminence of a tribulation and Messiah's coming in the first century or maybe even the second century—but not in our current century.

There is a contradiction. Many acknowledge that He shortens the time and waits until many come to repentance only because it is written in the Bible, but their teaching or explanation contradicts the Bible. There are no gaps between the worldly kingdoms in Daniel. It is not written that God pauses and places kingdoms on hold. They run consecutively. Only humans create gaps where there should not be any to fit our own understanding.

CHAPTER 13
The Visitation

> However, when the Son of Man comes, will He find faith on the earth?
>
> —Luke 18:8

This speaks about faith for supplications and petitions in prayer, but it could also be applied in recognizing the time of His extended visitation. Is there enough faith on the earth from the first century until this current century, which is the span of the Day of the Lord, to recognize the signs of His presence, His visitation?

Yeshua is not limited, bound, imprisoned, or attached to only one place, space, or time. He is a free spirit, free to go to the third heaven and anywhere in this universe and beyond or to anywhere on/within this planet. God has not stopped speaking, working, loving, or living. His Spirit is active. His coming is either ongoing in an extended stay or He traverses so there is more than one coming. It started in the first century and continues today. He is present. His presence is a sign of a visitation(s).

If we look at clues in the Bible, it will suggest to us where Yeshua has been for the past two millennia as a thief in the night as people sleep. He has been here on an extended stay. He has been everywhere—but mainly right next door to us on earth. He is on the other side of the gate, veil, wall, or door. He is in this realm in another dimension that our bodies can't detect. Scriptures suggest He visits the old earth between His Second Coming and its passing away. The length of time that passes between seems to be a Day of the Lord, which spans thousands of years:

- Coming. Feet on Mount Zion, battle with the beast and false prophet on earth, tribes of the earth seeing Him after the Spirit was poured out on them.
- Battle. His fight with the nations (Gog and Magog), Valley of Jehoshaphat (judgment), His garment stained with blood during battle. Blood is on earth—and it cannot inherit the kingdom of heaven. For there to be man's blood on His garment, He had to have been here on earth somehow crossing into our natural dimension as He battled the nations on earth and the powers over them.
- Judgment/Passing Away. Heaven and earth pass away as they flee from His face/presence, the dead released from sea and Death and Hades. This is already beginning to happen.

These passages suggest the King has been or is on earth—but in a realm unseen and this for two millennia. He is in another realm, dimension, and space near to us on earth. His coming could be compared to a haunting, though He doesn't haunt. But just like a haunting, there is a mostly unseen presence with manifestations and signs. There is activity of some sort. Sounds can be heard, and there may even be physical appearances of the Spirit. It is like what preachers and evangelists do at meetings. They are in the anointing, and the Spirit opens their ears and eyes to things no one else is seeing or hearing. They prophesy and see visions; they see spirits, demons, angels, and the Spirit of God. Everyone at the meetings accepts it as true and praises God. There are signs and manifestations of His presence. This suggests a crossing over from one realm to the next without many noticing Him.

Another kind of visitation is from what has become seen by many. UFOs are being seen more often in this day and age and are a sign of a visitation. They could be from both holy and unholy angels and entities. The star that was seen by the wise men could have been a star, but it could have been a UFO because it moved slowly across the sky as the wise men followed it. The wise men would not know another name for such an object. It did not stay in one spot as stars typically do. Planets and stars would not purposely move over a specific region or area of earth to be followed and then suddenly stop and hover over a city. The planets and stars would move in a faraway space—not over and within the atmosphere of earth. Planets and stars do not behave this way, but an alien object would.

There was an intelligent mind behind the movement of this star or white, bright, glowing orb that the wise men saw within the atmosphere of earth. It watched them, patiently waited for them as they traveled, stopped, and hovered. It led them exactly over the region where the Messiah was in Bethlehem. The term UFO would not be used back then, and star would be the only word to describe it. Here I can see here how not all UFOs are demonic, but some could be holy.

The "Phoenix Lights" looked like stars too and are similar, but there were several lights that moved—not one. Both of these events are signs of a kind of foreign visitation. Yeshua was visiting as an alien, or a foreigner, to this world as a baby. Mary's pregnancy as a virgin with God's Son as the Spirit came upon her. No man impregnated her; the Spirit of God did. Someone from another world, from heaven, could impregnate a virgin. I am not suggesting Mary was abducted; God does not need to abduct anyone. Yeshua wouldn't need to be taken; He was to remain here for several decades. He had a mission here.

Think of the Nephilim back then. Some of these Nephilim were titans, much taller than giants, whose fathers were sons of god who went into the daughters of men, who are aliens or foreigners to this world. There are women in this modern century who testify of alien abduction and become pregnant. During the first or second trimester, the fetus is removed and taken to another place. If true, these abductions seem to be happening with more frequency.

The difference between what could be happening now and what happened in Noah's day is the offspring are not just on the planet earth, as the giants were—they are in the heavens too. These offspring are more spread out and harder to find. They are like scattered seeds. Also, they may look more human, and it can be difficult to discern a true human from a hybrid. If it is true that hybrids are being created between humans and other types of beings, as it was during Noah's day, perhaps this is why the heavens, and not just the earth, will burn with fire for this would not be the will of God.

Some teach the earth is just purged with fire, yet it remains, but how can it remain if the heavens above "dissolve" all around it? How can God burn earth but leave the heavens that contain forbidden offspring? It is a frightful notion that humans with their evil and sinful natures are being bred with very highly intelligent beings. Combining a sinful and depraved nature with high intelligence is a monstrous combination. It will be just as bad as or even worse than in Noah's day. If Christians believe the account of Noah in Genesis concerning who fathered the giants of his day, why would it be erroneous to think this is also a possibility in this day and age? Did the people of Noah's day think he was a lunatic for believing that sons of God, or angels, bred and had children with women, and these became Nephilim? Didn't they refuse to believe and mock him as he built the ark?

Another view is that these are not sons of God; they are a distant terrestrial creation and were never heavenly. They were never cast out from the third heaven of God's throne as the angels were; they were a mysterious creation of God that we had never heard of. They were kept from us. God does have mysteries, and there are many things we do not know. It would be arrogant to think we are the only creation in this vast universe of His.

Perhaps their world was destroyed, and they are seeking a spiritual side that we seem to possess, which they don't have. They were far removed from it with the destruction of their terrestrial planets. Their atmosphere was ripped away, and their terrestrial planets became uninhabitable to them. Perhaps, in that sense, they were cast out. When we think of creation, we think of heavens and earth without thinking that there are other life forms in other parts of the universe. When the scripture reads that creation moans and groans waiting for the revelation of the sons of God, perhaps it is not just earth and all that is in it. Perhaps it is also the heavens and all that is in them that seek the revelation of the sons of God. Perhaps human rule through Yeshua is not just of earth but of the space heavens as God portions it. When it says in the Bible that all in the heavens on earth and below the earth will bow and say Yeshua is Adonai, perhaps these are counted too. They, in their own ways, seek a connection with God. It says, "Preach the Gospel to all creation." They, another distant foreign creation, seek a kingdom in their own way.

Earth is being visited. Notice how all this is lining up in this visitation:

- Biblical/spiritual view: Arrival of kingdom (the Rock), Crusades/judgment of Satan, passing away of heavens and earth, wheat/tares, destruction with fire, and lake of fire.
- Earthly/space view: Arrival of UFOs more noticeable during the twentieth century, climate change, imminent extinction, earth heating up, more fire.

Note how their visitation here coincides with an imminent extinction upon the earth; they run parallel. Some of these could be holy, and some could be unholy. Some of them could be His servants sent to save

His people from a doomed planet. Perhaps this is how those who are alive and remain are caught into the air to be with the Lord forever. Perhaps this is the mystery of the Rapture revealed. UFOs could be involved in this.

It is prophesied that heaven and earth will pass away and be destroyed with fire just like the world was destroyed with water during the time of Noah. If this earth is destroyed and there is a new earth, this could be a way He could decide to take us there. Is this how the King makes provision for the peoples' exodus or mass migration off this planet? He once said, "Will the Son of Man find faith when He returns?"

One must approach the kingdom like a child. His kingdom is not of this world. Believers are aliens, citizens of another world, and we don't belong here. There could be other ways too that He could remove us from a doomed planet. God is not limited. We need to open our minds to what His kingdom holds. Some of them could very well be His enemies fleeing the destruction of their own worlds, which are already on fire. They could be trying to hide from His presence and have nowhere to go. A combination of both could be happening now.

There was a show with a description of an abduction. There was a conference where there was communication—either lectures or images—between aliens and captives. In that communication, they indicate a warning or time of tribulation is at hand and a promise to help. Then there is a charge or purpose of the captive. The captive doesn't understand the mission until the time comes. I wonder if this warning is about climate change, the increased birth pangs the earth is facing now, and extinction or passing that is already begun to happen.

Just because one cannot see or hear with a physical eye or ear doesn't mean it is not real or that it is make-believe, fiction, fake, nonexistent, figurative, allegorical, symbolic, or not physical. To believe this makes one a skeptic and a doubter, and they don't have faith like they think they do. Spiritual things can be very physical in their own ways. Spiritual beings can appear, disappear, eat, dance, ascend, descend, go through walls, talk, sing, laugh, attack, and hug.

Yeshua said that the coming of the kingdom would not be with observation so people wouldn't say, "Look here, see there, come in here, and go out there" (Luke 17:22–24). His return would be spiritual, not as someone in flesh and blood. His return is not seen with the human eyes for the world cannot see Him again.

It is written in John 14:19, 20:

> After a little while the world will no longer see Me, but you will see Me; because I live, you will live also. In that day you will know that I am in My Father and you in Me, and I in you.

When someone proclaimed the Messiah was in an inner room, most likely it was a man as a false messiah in flesh and blood. Yeshua would not come that way again. The only way to see Him is by the Spirit because we are in Him and Him in us. The world will miss Him. The disciples saw Him again at His resurrection. Later this would be true for believers in the first century who see Him across the sky. Because He dwells in the temple of our bodies and we are under the shadow of His wings, we are in Him and Him in us. We have His Spirit, so according to His time, we see Him by the Spirit. The world cannot see Him again because they do not have His Spirit. The only exception of unbelievers seeing Him is according to Zechariah 12 when the tribes of Israel in Jerusalem, believer and unbeliever, would see Him. The tribes of the earth (tribes of Israel in Jerusalem) would see Him coming with the eyes of the spirit as the Spirit is poured out.

He can be seen by many at the same time in the Spirit just as lightning that flashes across the sky from east to west is seen by many but not by everyone in the world. There are unbelievers in the tribes who would see Him too (including Caiaphas). This is something false Messiahs cannot do. Many Christians quote "every eye will see Him" to mean "look here, see there" with our physical eyes, which is not how Yeshua taught how the kingdom would come. They do not understand or make the connection that it is with spiritual eyes. Yeshua also said no one can see or enter the kingdom unless they are born of water and the Spirit (John 3:3–8).

The eyes of believers seem to be opening up more and more. He seems to be making physical appearances to some. There are reports of sightings of Yeshua. More people are seeing Him. A couple of Jews walked on a path and wondered if it was Yeshua they saw walking ahead of them. He physically visited another person in the hospital and healed them. A messianic rabbi told his congregation about a Muslim woman who was visiting another congregation and felt, in her spirit, a King pass and walk by her. The rabbi's congregation praised God about this testimony.

I personally have sensed Him come up to me and stop as I praised Him.

He was walking from my left and stopped in front as if He was inspecting me. His presence left, but I never saw Him. My eyes were not open to see Him there, but He was there. I have seen Him in my peripheral vision. I catch glimpses of Him as though there is a veil over my eyes. How are these sightings happening if He has not returned? It seems He has, but no one is making the connection between this and the fulfillment of the prophecy. These sightings and impressions are not visions or dreams. This goes back to Ezekiel 39:29:

> "I will not hide My face from them any longer, for I will have poured out My Spirit on the house of Israel," declares the Lord God.

This means He reveals His face to His people through the Spirit or His people see Him as his Spirit is poured out upon them.

The absence of all the other kingdoms attests to the fact the something or someone is here unseen and has been here for two millennia. The Rock of Daniel is here. There have been changes in the sun, moon, and stars; waves of sea terrifying man; islands vanishing and being moved. "I will change earth like a garment" suggests He is present, still here, unseen to the prophets, seers, psychics, and clairvoyants. He is a thief in the night.

It was not recorded that anyone saw Him fighting against the Crusaders, no one witnessed it. Perhaps no Crusader saw or heard Him as the battles raged, because it wasn't His Spirit poured out upon those nations, but His judgment and wrath was poured out upon them. The world of that age would not see Him because they did not have His Spirit, they were not born again. He is hidden from their sight and could never see His face.

His people should be able to pick up on the signs of His presence or detect His footprints even if they don't see Him. We should be able to look at the clues in history, the footprints, and say, "Someone great has been here, someone great has been among us again". Should we conclude that because the world of Noah's day did not see God with their natural eyes that God did not visit the world at that time? Should we conclude that because the Egyptians and the Hebrews didn't see God as Moses did or that the Egyptians don't have a written record of this story, that He did not deliver the Hebrews miraculously with signs and wonders or that He didn't visit the earth? Should we say the same with Lot's deliverance and Sodom and Gomorrah's destruction? We can't say because the world has not seen Him in the past, He has not visited earth. "What is born of the flesh is flesh, what is born of the Spirit is spirit" (John 3:6).

From the first century AD until now, people will be in the Day without "seeing" it (2 Peter 3:4, 8–9). They will wonder, "Where is it?" The Day is present; they are in it because it is like a thief in the night. They don't know it because they are asleep. The eyes of their spirit are blind, and their ears are deaf. We must wake up for we are in the day of visitation. A thief in the daytime comes suddenly when people are awake and aware, but a thief in the night comes suddenly when people are not aware or awake—and they don't recognize there is a visitation happening and a thief is in their house. The coming is unannounced because life continues as normal until destruction happens (like Noah and Lot). The one who is of the light and is awake recognizes the day of God's visitation, accepts it, and opens the door to Him (Isaiah 10:3; Hosea 9:7; Micah 7:4; Luke 19:44; 1 Peter 2:12).

If He visited when the earth was pristine, yet evil and violence were only in certain parts of earth. Why wouldn't He reveal Himself when the earth is old and dying and there is extinction in progress? Why wouldn't He visit with violence and evil now covering the globe? It is only going to get worse. It will culminate in the fulfillment of His words, "Heaven and earth will pass away, but my words will by no means pass away" (Matthew 24:35).

CHAPTER 14
The Temple as the Center of Jewish Life (The End)

The temple was the center of Jewish life before its end in AD 70. The temple is the key to understanding and interpreting prophecy and certain verses in the Bible. "The end" refers to the temple and its sacrifices and tithes to the Levite priests—not the end of other things. The end of the temple marked the end of an age or Jewish temple culture, but it was not quite the end of the Roman Empire or the end of the earth. The temple was a major landmark of prophecy.

Prophecy revolves around Yeshua, but the temple also has a major place in fulfillment. Its presence and absence were major signs of when a prophecy was being fulfilled:

1. Daniel 9:26; 12:4, 7, 9, 11–13. "The end" is specifically referring to the end of animal sacrifice and the temple. "Power of the holy people comes to an end … all these things … finished" refers to the temple. The temple is in context.
2. Matthew 28:16–20 and Mark 16:15. The end of the age here is referring to the temple and not the end of time and the world. The temple is in context since the disciples were just asking Yeshua about its end (Matthew 24:1–3).
3. Joel 3:1–5; Acts 2:17–21. The "last days" in the early first century were the last days of the temple before its destruction. The disciples received the Holy Spirit in fulfillment of Joel before the temple's destruction. The spirit was again poured out to people to see the coming of Yeshua in the Spirit. Yet the outpouring does not stop; it continues through the Day of the Lord, which spans thousands of years to our day. His mercy extends to every generation, and

He saves all who call upon His name. The power of the blood and the gift of the Spirit don't end. There is still healing and forgiveness of sins.

4. Revelation 22:10. "Time is near" is a reference to the end of the temple and the coming of Yeshua. This letter was written about AD 69—not AD 95. To measure the temple, a temple has to be present. To foretell that the court has been given to the nations (Roman Gentiles) in Revelation 11:1, 2, there has to be a temple present. For the Antichrist to set himself up as god in the temple as Paul wrote, there has to be a temple present. It will not be rebuilt a third time.

5. 2 Thessalonians 2:1–12; 2 Timothy 17–18. To declare and teach a fulfillment to the Day and the resurrection happened when a temple was still present and the Antichrist wasn't revealed yet by the Spirit was false and erroneous at the time Paul wrote this. This does not necessarily apply today, but many futurists still use it against preterists.

CHAPTER 15

The Great Commission Then and Now (Matthew 28:16–20; Mark 16:15)

The disciples had fulfilled their duty in their time and era. Should the Gospel not be spread anymore? No, everyone must fulfill the duty God has commissioned him or her to do even in this day: "preached among the nations, was believed on in the world" (1Timothy 3:16). This was fulfilled. It is not written, "It will be preached, will be believed."

Many read "Go into all the earth" to mean the planet. Earth to a first century person is different than how a person in the twenty-first century understands earth.

It "has been proclaimed to every creature under heaven" (Colossians 1:6; 1:23b). This is past tense, so it was fulfilled. Paul believed he accomplished his mission.

Let's look at some Scripture that speak of "earth" or "world" and see if the meaning could be the same between the span of centuries.

It was prophesied, "Then another third kingdom of bronze, which will rule over *all the earth.* " (Daniel 2:39). Are we to believe this means just the territories Alexander the Great conquered or *the entire planet earth*? Does this mean this prophecy is for a future generation because Alexander did not accomplish this literally in his lifetime? We know he didn't conquer the global earth reaching as far as Western Hemisphere crossing the Atlantic Ocean and the Far East where the Mongolians dwelt, the continent now known as Australia, or the indigenous tribes deep in the Amazon jungle or other unknown places back then. So here, "earth" does not mean every continent or the unknown countries and tribes that we know of today. "Earth" means the territories, countries, and regions conquered by Alexander, therefore the Greek empire.

In Luke 2:1, the "world" or "inhabited earth" is the Roman Empire, not the entire global earth. Did the Barbarian, Germanic, Celtic nations have to be registered? Did the natives of the Western Hemisphere in the undiscovered Americas have to go be registered? Did India and other Asian nations come to be registered too? Were these all a part of the Roman Empire? No, no, no, and no. There is an understanding that "world" or "inhabited earth" means the Roman Empire.

In Acts 11:28, a great famine was coming "all over the world," or the inhabited earth during the reign of Emperor Claudius. Was the entire global earth, even the undiscovered continents (unknown to and unconquered by the Roman emperors at that time), across the Atlantic, Pacific, and Indian oceans affected by this great famine too? No, we read this and understand that "all over the world" or "inhabited earth" meant the territory, countries, and regions under the reign and rule of the Romans.

Matthew 24:14 is fulfilled if Yeshua meant "world" as the Roman world and "end" as the end of the temple. Since Yeshua had just finished speaking of the end/destruction of the temple, this is the end He is referring to (Daniel 12:11–13). Daniel writes about an "end" to the temple. This verse also mentions a resurrection of saints happening around the first century:

> Then at the end of days (1,335 days of the temple and its sacrifices, not the end of time or the world) you will arise (resurrection of saints) to receive your portion.

Luke 21:1–9 talks about the temple and the coming end of the temple. This goes with 1 Corinthians 15:23–28 ("those who are Christ's at His coming," which includes Daniel). This is more likely, especially with Paul claiming that the disciples have fulfilled their calling to spread the Gospel.

Many interpret "end" in this verse to refer to the end of time and all worlds, which includes every generation that will enter the world from then until the modern time. "End" is the end of the old heaven and earth. Paul is not incorrect in what he wrote to Timothy and the Colossians. Nature also witnesses and testifies (Psalm 19:1–4; Romans 10:18; 1:8; and 1 Thessalonians 1:8). Romans 16:26 is not an exaggeration; it is a fulfillment: "Has been made known to all the nations."

The past tense in Paul's time of writing meant fulfilled, and it went into "all" the earth, not some of it. *The words "earth" and "world" meant something different to a first-century believer than it does to us today. We can't apply our modern understanding of what "earth" and "world" mean to first-century writing. Our scope of understanding is much broader than their understanding.*

Yeshua also said, "You (the disciples) will not finish going through the cities of Israel when the Son of Man comes" (Matthew 10:23). The disciples wouldn't finish preaching the good news in Israel before Yeshua returned again in glory because many Jews rejected it—and the Messiah's return was imminent. It doesn't mean they wouldn't finish in the entire global earth, which would include the unknown, undiscovered, and distant parts of earth that we now know exist. If they were to go into the world that was known to them, it is possible that the Gospel was spread in the known world and empire of that time, and Paul says that it was—though not in Israel as Yeshua stated.

Someone might say, "Yeshua meant that the disciples wouldn't finish going through Israel during that initial send-off two by two, He did not mean later after He ascended." Let's reread the previous verses. In Matthew 10:5–15, it is clear that Yeshua is speaking of what the disciples should do in the next few days since they are just being sent out to Israel, not to the Gentiles.

In Matthew 10:16–19, Yeshua is speaking of a time in the future about the disciples preaching in Israel after Yeshua ascends. Verses 17–18 are key here and make the distinction between the times because none of the eleven disciples were delivered up to councils and scourged in synagogues before Yeshua died on the cross. They were not brought before governors and kings before Yeshua even died on the cross. This obviously was speaking of a time after His ascension before He would return in glory again. Yeshua told the disciples, not us today, that they would not finish going to all the cities in Israel before He came back to that generation because the Jews rejected Yeshua and the Gospel.

That is how soon Yeshua returned to that generation. He did not tarry. If they did not finish going to the cities of Israel, the days were shortened as Yeshua stated. In Romans 16:26, "has been" is past tense and therefore fulfilled. The word "all" means it went into all the inhabited earth. The same inhabited earth as in Luke 2:1. The same world as Acts 11:28.

His mercy extends to every generation, and He saves those who call on the name of the Lord. The door is not shut on latter generations. The four corners of the earth here are the known inhabited earth, not the global planet (Revelations 20:8). The signs in the book of Matthew that Yeshua said would happen and the Great Commission do not stop when fulfilled; they continue even after.

CHAPTER 16
The Imminence of His Coming in the First Century

What is imminent is not His coming, but heaven and earth passing in His presence and destruction. The nearness of the end-times was taken literally (Matthew 24:33, 34; 1 Corinthians 7:29; Philippians 4:5). These are the days of His kingdom. His coming marked the beginning, the dawn, of the Day of the Lord, which ends after thousands of years, including a millennial reign unseen to a fleshy eye. He comes at the beginning of birth pangs, the beginning being during the Roman Empire, yet continuing to our generation. The birth pangs don't stop until the end of the first heaven and earth.

- Luke 21:32. Some say, "It does not mean Jesus had a mistaken notion He was going to return immediately." Yeshua wasn't mistaken! In Matthew 24:29–31, Yeshua says, *"Immediately after* the tribulation in those days … they will see the Son of Man coming." The word "after" is noted because it is not before or during the tribulation of AD 70. "Immediately" speaks of how soon after.
- Romans 13:11, 12. "It is already the hour for you to awaken from sleep; for now salvation is nearer to us than when we believed. The night is almost gone, and the day is at hand." The words "is already", "now", "is almost gone", and "is at hand" are occurring during Paul's generation, not ours. When Paul wrote this, it was for the believers of that age and generation. Present generations should also awaken from sleep. Salvation is also nearer to us.
- 2 Thessalonians 2:1, 2. "Now we request you, brethren, with

- regard to the coming of our Lord Jesus Christ, our gathering together to Him."
- Hebrews 1:1, 2. "God ... in these last days has spoken to us in His Son." It is the last days of the temple.
- James 5:7–9. "The coming of the Lord is at hand. ... the Judge is standing right at the door." Yeshua was ready to enter through during the time of this writing. James speaks to believers of that generation, not us. We did not exist yet.
- Peter to those who resided as aliens. "According to His great mercy has caused us ... who are protected by the power of God through faith for a salvation ready to be revealed in the last time" (1 Peter 1:5).
- 1 Peter 1:6, 7. "You ... may be found to result in praise and glory and honor at the revelation of Jesus Christ." "Grace to be brought to you (written directly to believers to whom it is addressed) at the revelation of Jesus Christ" (4:17). The word "you" is to the people the letter is written to. "The end of all things is at hand" (4:7). "The end of all things" is the end of the temple sacrifices as foretold in Daniel, not the end of time and earth. The phrase, "at hand" is imminent to that first century generation, not ours. "For it is time for judgment to begin with the household of God" (4:17). "It is time" is present at the time of this writing, not in the future. The judgment to begin with the household of God is the AD 70 destruction and desolation of Jerusalem and judgment of believers and unbelievers in that generation. Peter is not writing to his generation about something far off in the future to them that was to occur in a future generation. What would be the point in using present tense or using words that express a short amount of time for something in the distant future?
- 1 John 2:17. "And the world is passing away" (the world/age of his time).
- 1 John 2:18. "Children, it is the last hour ... from this we know that it is the last hour." "It is" is present during that generation, not ours.
- 1 John 3:2. "We know that when He appears, we shall be like Him because we shall see Him just as He is." "We" refers to the believers then, not us today. Our generation today cannot be part of a "we" if we didn't exist yet.

- Revelation 1:1. "The Revelation of Jesus Christ, which God gave Him to show to his bond-servants, the things which must shortly take place." *Shortly* in the dictionary means: In a short time; soon. "Soon" cannot be more than two thousand years after this was written.
- Revelation 1:3; 22:10. "For the time is near." "Do not seal up the words of the prophecy of this book, for the time is near." It was near to his time, not ours.
- Revelation 3:11; 22:7, 12, 20. "I am coming quickly." Quick equals moving or acting rapidly; speedy. Occurring or achieved in a brief space of time. This definition explains how imminent His return would be. Two thousand years later is not quickly.
- Mark 14:41–43; Matthew 26:45–47. "Is at hand" equals "immediately" or "while He was still speaking."
- 2 Thessalonians 2:8. Fulfilled.
- Luke 21:22. "These days" are the early first century. "All things which are written will be fulfilled," including the Second Coming.
- Luke 12:35–48 (and verse 22). "To us" equals the twelve. "Everyone else" is outside groups or another generation. Verse 22 is "to the disciples."
- Matthew 25:1–13. "Now the bridegroom was late." He was delayed in the first century for several decades or a generation, not for two thousand years.
- Hebrews 10:25. "Not forsaking our own (those being addressed) assembling together, as is (present tense in the author's time, not ours) the habit of some, but encouraging one another; and all the more as you (the one being addressed) see the day drawing near." The day was drawing near to that generation, not ours.
- Hebrews 10:37. "For yet in a very little while, He who is coming will come and will not delay." The words, "in a very little while" can't mean two thousand years. In Habakkuk 2:3, the Lord's Day was not to be delayed, and He would not tarry. According to a futurist view, two thousand years is a huge delay, and He tarries for a long time, which doesn't show much zeal for Zion and fulfilling His Word. If we are already in the Day of the Lord, then He did not tarry or delay

- at all. He fulfilled His Word as promised. His Word has not passed away.
- Yeshua (Matthew 24:22) was speaking of the tribulation during the time of the temple. He even mentioned that the days were shortened.
- Paul, in 1 Corinthians 7:29 stated the time had been shortened. If time was shortened, how can we say He waits and tarries for almost two thousand years? If He "shortens the time," then how does He also tarry and wait before He even begins to fulfill His Word? If we say He tarries, He has lengthened the time, not shortened it. If we say He tarries, we say He has no zeal to fulfill His Word. If Paul is suggesting in 1 Corinthians 7:29–31 that those men in his generation (not ours) who have wives should be as though they had none, this speaks to the imminence of a tribulation and coming in the first century or even maybe until the second century, but not our current century.

It seems there is a "man in the woods" syndrome. They aren't lied to, but it's a mind-set—a lack of an update. Their faith is limited to the truth they know or believe. Truth sets you free, and one's faith increases with it. With knowledge of untainted truth comes freedom, faith, and power.

Like Apollos with John's baptism, or believers who are taught there are no miracles, signs, or wonders or in earthly terms—some people don't use technology, drive vehicles, use outdated fashion, and by live by outdated knowledge. In prophecy, there is no progression or growth. They are stuck in the woods because of old truths, old errors, and old realities when there is fulfillment and another reality. Knowledge of the truth increases faith, which can unlock hidden doors. Myles Munroe wrote: "They (many religious, unregenerate Christians) can only rise to the level of jurisdiction under which they live." According to what one knows and believes, so it is. According to one's faith, so it is. They lack the keys of knowledge to progress.

A different level of jurisdiction in knowledge happens when one gains, matures, and excels in the revelation of truth. Faith is built on this and grows, and the mind is renewed and changed. Faith comes by hearing the Word of God. We are given the keys of the kingdom or knowledge of the kingdom. The battlefield begins in the mind.

If there are things one believer knows, that another is not aware of yet, they can better prepare, practice, teach, and fight because their faith is strengthened and practiced. One sees the kingdoms from the mountain; the other sees them from the valley. One sees it from the inside; the other sees from the outside. However, both are on the same team, and though they fight or take over in the name and by the Holy Spirit, they attack differently with different skills, gifts, or greater level of faith.

Apollos could do so much more for the kingdom when he was updated about Yeshua. With the revelation of the truth, he was propelled to another jurisdiction that he could never have known unless he was told and taught because his faith was smaller—because the knowledge he had of Yeshua was small. It is like America in World War II before nuclear weapons. No other nation knew about this possibility until one man, Einstein, spoke of it and taught about it. The nations then fought with missiles, but who knew about nuclear bombs? Until a revelation of truth about atomic fission was introduced, humanity was limited in how it could fight.

Fighting with swords, spears, chariots, and javelins transitioned to guns, missiles, tanks, and cannons. It changed because of the revelation of a truth. Look at how many nations have nuclear weapons now. Look also at how much technology has grown since the seventies and eighties. The same is true spiritually. This is why I believe understanding the accurate fulfillment of prophecy is important to one's faith.

Salvation is twofold for those of this era, primarily from eternal damnation apart from God, but also from the peril the earth is in with super volcanoes, climate change, severe droughts, wildfires, spontaneous combustion, lightning, human neglect, earlier migration, extreme weather, strong storms, tornadoes, dust storms, heat waves, coral reefs dying, food prices increasing, deforestation due to man and beetles, ice caps melting, flooding, islands sinking/vanishing, higher demand for energy, animal extinction, and an unknown galactic change with the stars. The galactic change moves the stars. There are impending and unfolding disasters.

The nations of the world only see a plan A (gas and oil use—greedy; careless) and plan B (alternative energy—perceive there's a hole in the ship, and it's sinking). Water comes in faster than can be pumped out. They have no plan C (Yeshua, faith, awake). The world sees no other ship. Believers have a plan C. In fact, it is their only plan because the King has spoken: "Heaven and earth shall pass away" (Psalm 102:26, Isaiah 51:6). They shall pass away no matter what the nations do.

Yeshua is our only plan. He is the plan. He is plan A, B, and C. This ship called *Earth* is sinking. We have to move away from disasters or get off of this planet or perish. God is righteous and just. He will not condemn the righteous and cause them to undergo wrath and judgment. May He be glorified in their midst. Spaceship (ways of transportation: John 6:21; Acts 8:39, 40; Noah); chariots of Fire (Elijah); walking into another dimension (Enoch).

When there are calamities and woes unfolding in the earth, this is not a call for panic or fear. We should be ready to act. We trust in the Lord, but we know that trust is twofold: passive, which is waiting on Him, and active, which is doing exactly what He would command us to do when it is time to act. We trust that what He says will work, and we obey equal acts.

What does this mean for Israel? It is by no means over for them. They will still have His promise of a land. Either on this earth renewed after a fire or a literal new one in another location in space. He will create a new one. Perhaps through them comes salvation—a word from the Lord—from the disasters and crises currently unfolding on the earth. Perhaps to them and believing Gentiles, there will soon be an imminent revelation, or unveiling, of the King to His brothers who are here and have been here all along for two millennia in this Day of the Lord. It is not so much a coming (which is fulfilled) as it is a revelation of a thief in the night. His coming and His Day have both been like a thief in the night. Many have slept and have not discerned the Day of the Lord. Perhaps those who make Aliyah to Israel will be taken en masse from there before the destruction.

This view of preterism does not diminish the hope of a believer. There is the hope of salvation from the destruction of this heaven and earth and eternal fire. I believe in celebrating the Communion service "to show the Lord's death until He comes" (1 Corinthians 11:26) or is revealed by the Spirit in this day of His visitation.

The blood of Yeshua has power to this present day, and I proclaim its eternal power in the act of Communion until my body is changed and like He is. The first-century believers probably don't need to do Communion because they dwell with Him in the same dimension that His kingdom is in. Believers can have a confident expectation about the future: salvation. The church should bring the kingdom by waking up and opening the door to the King. He has not left us; we still can have divine intervention during these final days of earth. It does not deny Israel of her future. It does not deny the power of the Messiah because He is present in another dimension unseen to our eyes of flesh.

Is there to be a mass migration of a different kind? Are we ready to open the door to the King? Are we ready for the Spirit to open our blind spirit's eyes and ears to see the unseen? Are we ready to see His mighty salvation? Perhaps this is how all Israel will come to Him with this revelation. The nations will look to him for justice and salvation (Isaiah 51:4–6). He is the hope. There could be more interaction with Him with hearing Him as a corporate body or a Shekinah.

There should be many prayers offered concerning the crisis the earth is in, but little is offered as a corporate body of believers. Some say, "Jesus is coming" and "Trust in God," but few people call on Him with these catastrophes unfolding with more intensity and frequency like birth pangs.

King David, Daniel, and Shadrach/Meshach/Abednego called on His name in times of peril and persecution. If any believer was in a plane about to crash, a tall building on fire, or a ship about to sink, none would just say, "I'm just going to trust God," sit back, and not pray to Him about the serious situation that was occurring around them or not pray for members of His fold who live in and are undergoing troubles in the unstable and perilous regions of the earth. Believers would call on His name and cry out to Him in any of these situations.

We need His wisdom, encouragement, comfort, salvation, and deliverance. As long as we are here on this perishing and vanishing earth, we should seek His face. We need His grace upon us in this time of weakness and despair for the world. He is surely our hope and salvation. They pray about issues in their personal lives that trouble them, and they should never stop because He does care about His people, but the passing away of heaven and earth dominates over everything else except hell. The spreading of the Gospel should continue because the door is quickly closing. No one can repent or be saved once everything is extinct and destroyed. This should continue to be the priority, and then we should hear from the King as to what we are to do in this terrifying and truly frightening dying of earth from which no one can escape except through Yeshua.

The Complacency of the Church

- As a body, there is little to nothing done as far as stewardship for the damaged earth that is redeemed through the obedience of the second Adam, Yeshua. They believe they are stewards and creation is redeemed, but little is done to show it as a group. There is little prayer offered for it. Perhaps earth's redemption through Yeshua is seen and fulfilled in the new heaven and earth, not necessarily this one.

- They don't make the connection between history and the fulfillment of the Lord's words in prophecy.
- They recognize the signs in heaven and earth as a sign of an imminent return of Christ, but not as evidence of a passing of heaven and earth/coming destruction in the presence of a returned King who is like a thief in the night. Are they awake as the watchman who should be watchful of their master's return? Are they alert enough to open the door to Him? If one is sleeping, he is not going to be aware and alert enough to know the master was here.

Shepherds say that sheep are dumb. They need someone to watch after them. They can easily be led astray. How is it that an unbeliever can recognize the danger before God's own sheep do? How do unbelievers think of ways to be stewards of earth, which is a gift, and think of ways to save it, but believers in Yeshua are not thinking they are the righteous ones to inherit the earth?

All the more, we need to have faith in this time. During this time in which hope is fleeting and deep darkness is upon this world, He is our light, hope, and salvation. No matter what ideas about alternative sources of energy and preservation they come up with (which is stewardship), the Word of the Lord shall be fulfilled: "Heaven and earth shall pass away, but my words will never pass away." What is implied by this statement is that humans are too late and too complacent in repairing the damage and destruction they have done.

God has said, "I will destroy those who destroy the earth." Humankind destroys and doesn't properly steward the earth that we are put in charge over, so humankind will suffer from the destruction we have caused, and then fire will fall from God out of heaven. Everything will melt with intense heat (global warming/climate change) as Paul and Peter wrote. It is inevitable what is happening to heaven and earth because the King's Living Word has gone forth. There really is nothing we can do at this point to preserve and save earth from its doom. God is creating an upgrade. Scientists are confirming with their findings of climate change what the Lord spoke of millennia ago. Even if humankind changes our habits of using fossil fuels in time, heaven and earth will still pass away according to the Word of the Lord. The climate could go way beyond tipping point and run away—fast!

If one doesn't believe this preterist interpretation of prophecy alone, consider the signs the earth is showing now. One must understand the signs of heaven and earth. One must look at the reality of climate change and how it fits with the fulfillment of heaven and earth's passing away. Yes, Yeshua said many of these signs were birth pangs, but He didn't say they would stop. I don't think they stop with His Second Coming; they stop when earth is dead and the resurrection is fulfilled to the last generation. One has to set aside former understanding of prophecy and reconcile what is occurring globally with the world now and with what God said would happen. We have maybe a little less than a century, how much less a millennium.

Questions to Ponder

Futurists ask preterists, "If the Lord came in the first century, when was the visible thousand-year reign on this earth?" Well, I have to ask them, considering the rapid deterioration of and massive die-offs occurring upon earth, how does Yeshua initially come after extinction? Also, how do the saints return to this old earth for a thousand-year reign if it won't be here for any living thing to inhabit it?

It appears the earth's end is approaching quickly with greater intensity, and knowing this, when will there be time to fulfill everything futurists expect to happen in prophecy, especially with an earthly, visible millennial reign? The math doesn't work. There's no time for a thousand-year reign. What kind of reign is it with a planet that is destroyed and dead? The earth is only getting worse, not better.

There must have been a fulfillment. One has to rethink how and when the thousand-year reign occurred. When will there be time for a temple to be rebuilt in Jerusalem with a functioning sacrificial system? When will there be time for a reign of a coming beast/Antichrist? When will there be time for a battle of Gog and Magog and a judgment in the Valley of Jehoshaphat? When in the very short time left for earth do all the prophecies that the futurists still believe to come to pass will be fulfilled? Again, there is really no time left for this.

With extinction in progress now, what animals will be left to sacrifice in the third temple to come? What will humans "rule" over as God intended in this old earth for thousand years? Why would the saints return to rule a desolate, burnt, dead earth? How is the beast going to cause tribulation in the world if everyone is dead? Who are we and Christ to battle if nothing is left? How does Gog and Magog happen in an extinct earth?

Those who say, "Don't believe it" are like those in Noah's day who would not believe him even though there were probably signs of an impending flood. They laughed at him and denied it. Lot's sons-in-law did not believe him either. Do you see where I am going? The signs occurring now with earth do not line up to the prophecies the futurists believe are yet to come.

We must read the signs, not ignore them or deny them. The churches teach this in error. Earth is dying. The fact that earth is passing away before our very eyes should tell us where we are in the prophecy. There is no room for everything the futurists expect to happen.

The Lord has fulfilled so much since the first century. If humankind's existence in this order is coming to an end soon and will be history, then there must have been fulfillment of the Lord's Word that many people in the church have missed.

To the full preterist, I have to ask some questions: How can this be the new heaven and earth when it is obvious that it is dying? Why would God call this the new heaven and earth as everything within only two thousand years is perishing quickly? Why would God create a new heaven and earth to only be destroyed within two thousand years when the first one is considered millions of years old (to others six thousand years)? That doesn't make sense.

Earth's dying is "the landmark" of prophecy that shows everyone where we are in the fulfillment of prophecy. This is one event that is blatantly visible and felt by everyone on the planet. Everything may appear normal in certain parts of the world, but if we look closely, things are not normal.

With climate change, it only gets hotter and hotter. This seems to confirm what was written by Apostle Peter (2 Peter 3:10–13): "The elements will melt with intense heat; both the earth and the works that are in it will be burned up." He goes on to say that "because of the Day of God, the heavens will be dissolved being on fire, and the elements will melt with fervent heat."

Scientists have said that earth could become as hot as Venus. Apostle Paul issues a warning about being alert and sober as the Day of the Lord approaches (2 Thessalonians 5:1–11). If we are in the Day of the Lord, we have to be ready.

People make aliyah to Israel, but even Israel is not immune to climate change. The Dead Sea and the Sea of Galilee and the fish that swim in it are disappearing. They have developed ways to desalinate water as the farmlands dry up. Yet God's Word shall stand: "Heaven and earth will pass away."

Both views should rethink where this generation is in the fulfillment of prophecy with earth passing away swiftly.

CHAPTER 17
An Explanation of 2 Thessalonians 2 and 2 Timothy 2

Some use these verses against preterists regard them as false teachers and heretics. A preterist in Paul's day would be considered a false teacher and a heretic. Paul wrote this in the decades before the temple's destruction in AD 70. At the time Paul wrote this letter, it was false to say the resurrection and the Day of the Lord had come to pass. It was not based on or in line with the truth of fulfillment. Certain things needed to happen first to confirm this fulfillment.

In 2 Timothy, Paul said that these two men overthrew the faith of some, which means they took them off the path of truth. People's faith was no longer based on truth. Some people probably began to sin and disobey God's commandments, thinking it was too late for them. When one's faith is based on the truth of God's Word, God will confirm it. One's faith will grow; the power and glory of God will be displayed. God will oppose falsehood, and the doctrine will not grow or have much root. It will do little to vanquish sin and cause repentance unto God. One can lose salvation for believing lies and deceptions.

I think in their understanding of prophecy, that if those of that generation did not make it in the first resurrection, they were left for the second which is doom for them.

In 2 Thessalonians, Paul writes that a "falling away comes first, the man of sin is revealed, the son of perdition, who opposes and exalts himself above all that is called God or that is worshiped, so that he sits as God in the temple of God, showing himself that he is God." Yeshua said in Matthew 24 that false Christs and prophets would rise up to deceive, and if the days were not shortened, the elect would not be saved. This says there were many to fall away during this time just before the temple's destruction.

Who is this lawless one? I believe it was Nero. According to Revelation, he died of a head wound before the temple's destruction and then rose from the pit as a beast (an entity) to enter the temple of God in AD 70. He was destroyed by Christ's glorious presence. The beast and Yeshua were revealed by the pouring out of the Spirit to people in Jerusalem. They were seen in the spirit by the Holy Spirit.

In verse 7, Paul wrote that "the mystery of lawlessness is already at work," which meant it was already present in early AD at the time of his writing. It is written that Antichrist was already in the world (1 John 2:18; 4:3), which meant the Antichrist was present in the early first century. The world of that era was passing away, and the Roman world did pass away (1 John 2:17).

People read these verses with a first-century mind-set. It is like they are in some sort of mental time warp. They think that something that was present in the first century, in that era, is also present in our current time—two thousand years later—without any fulfillment.

Anyone who comes saying in this present day and age (the twenty-first century) that the resurrection is past and Christ came, as a preterist, would be considered false if:

- The temple still existed in Jerusalem today in the twenty-first century untouched by war.
- The armies never came to surround Jerusalem.
- There was never a desolation of the holy city.
- Animal sacrifices were still offered in the temple to this very day uninterrupted.
- The office of the Levitical priesthood was never disturbed and ended.
- There was no person to fit the criteria for the beast and Antichrist (as Nero did).

There were certain very important things, which did not occur, had to come to pass first. However, these things did occur and came to pass in the first century. Also, a full preterist could be considered false because not everything has been fulfilled yet. They run ahead of everything and fall out of line. Some people want to use these two passages to claim the preterist view is heretical, despite the fact that the signs Paul wrote about must happen first did come to pass a few decades after he wrote about it. Anyone in Paul's day who said things came to pass when obviously it didn't, especially with a temple present, was a false teacher. They weren't in line with the book of Daniel, which is the book of prophecy that early believers were going by. Daniel wrote about both the temple destruction and two resurrections that followed. So to talk about a resurrection fulfilled without a temple destruction would not be in line with the truth of Scripture. It was false and erroneous.

To say the Word of the Lord has been and is being fulfilled at the present time is not erroneous if it is based on the truth. If it is the truth, God will cause it to grow powerfully. To say many things are fulfilled today is not a falsehood if they truly came to pass. What Paul wrote was true and accurate at that time, but it wouldn't apply now. Time and history have changed. One can't ignore events in history or the signs that support fulfillment, such as the destruction and absence of the temple. One can't say that because these passages are in the Bible, that to ever say at any time anything is fulfilled is false.

To accuse and condemn an obedient believer of heresy is erroneous, especially without taking into careful consideration that maybe we should test, pray about, and study this more. Perhaps we are in the presence of a King who came as a thief in the night; before Him, heaven and earth pass away as nations sleep unaware. Perhaps this is the wake-up call.

CHAPTER 18

Was the Resurrection Fulfilled? (Luke 24:39–43; 2 Timothy 2:15–21; Revelation 20)

The key words in 2 Timothy are "ungodliness," "upset the faith of some," "abstain from wickedness," "some to dishonor," and "cleanses himself from these things." This suggests that it was not only wicked to teach the word of truth inaccurately, but this distortion of the truth causes people to forsake and sin against God.

The resurrection of first-century saints, those beheaded because they refused to worship the beast and even Daniel among others were raised up to be with the Lord. This is fulfilled. The latter resurrection of the wheat and tares is occurring now and in the near future. The harvest is here and ready.

If one listens to the testimonial accounts of people who have seen someone who has died and then physically appears to them, it is a sign of a fulfillment. The world takes all ghost stories and classifies them as ghost stories. Yeshua's resurrection would be classified as a ghost story today, but it isn't a ghost story. His is a resurrection story. Yet many hear ghost stories or stories of angels and demons, but some are actually resurrection stories.

Yeshua made the distinction between a ghost and one who rises from the dead (Luke 24:39): "A ghost does not have flesh and bone, as you see that I have." We should make the distinction too. Yeshua did not say, "A ghost is actually a demon" or "A demon does not have flesh and bone", He said the word "spirit" or "ghost". Yeshua doesn't refer to ghosts as demons.

There are actually ghosts, the spirits of deceased individuals. Yeshua didn't deny the existence of ghosts, where there are people today who would say they are actually demons posing as ghosts. They will quote Hebrews 9:27 and say there are no ghosts.

> And inasmuch as it is appointed for men to die once and after this comes judgment. (Hebrews 9:27)

I believe that there are spirits in Hades below and upon the earth where they are in a haunt, or type of prison, for the Day of Judgment. I understand these haunted places to be a lesser judgment where others suffer a greater judgment of going beneath earth and suffering the fire below. All of these spirits who remain in the earth as it passes away will be cast into the lake of fire, the second death. They are judged, but are put on reserve for the Day of Judgment by fire. They have no escape.

It is like when someone who is guilty of murder in the worldly courts is pronounced guilty by a judge and jury, they go to prison, and then wait in a prison cell for their execution, they are on death row. They have already been judged, but are waiting the punishment. When a person dies, there is a judgment. They are assigned a place on top (lesser judgment) or underneath earth (greater judgment of Hades fire) like a prison cell, a haunt if you will. When the day of execution arrives (second death), they die eternally in fire. Remember that Hades is not second death for the second death swallows up Hades. They are two different things. One is bigger and greater than the other one. One is small, the other is massive. The tares are thrown into the fire of second death. This interpretation does not go contrary to Hebrews 9:27 or Luke 24:39.

Now can a demon disguise itself as a deceased individual? If they have that power, yes, but I would not put everything in one basket and say all ghosts are demons.

There are people rising from their graves and doing what Yeshua did. They have physical flesh-and-bone bodies, they talk sometimes, they eat, they appear out of nowhere and disappear out of closed spaces, and they dance. Churches today are not discerning this fulfillment of the Lord's Word. They avoid such stories so they do not pick up on the fulfillment of what is spoken of in Daniel 12:2 and John 5:27, 28. They know of saints being with the Lord after death from testimonies given or visions seen, and some have visions or have actually visited hell.

We should be shrewd—yet innocent and holy. We should not be ignorant—but know. We should be wise and understand, but how are we wise and shrewd when we don't have knowledge? How does one's faith increase if knowledge doesn't? You can't ask, speak, or act according to a faith because you don't know. How does one believe Yeshua is Adonai or ask for healing or obey commandments if they don't know? One may not see, but one must know. How does a believer in these days ask, speak, and act according to an increased faith if they don't know of the fulfillment of prophecies? They remain in a faith of first-century believers and don't progress and grow. They don't build on top of the faith they already have.

Hades and death are releasing their dead. Who are these cursed and condemned? Those who are not born again, the energy feeders, the tormenters, the beasts, the ones who lure children away to their deaths, those who attack maliciously, those from whom darkness pours forth, and those who never leave their haunts, which have become prisons until the time of judgment. Some have their appearance remain the same, but for others, it transforms into something else like Nero's did. He later came up out of the pit, probably after an unclean sacrifice was made by the Romans, to defile the holy temple sometime after his death. Many Christians miss that part.

The resurrection of the wheat and tares has been occurring and continues until after the passing away of the earth. This is the resurrection of the good and evil where they are separated as the parable of Yeshua describes. If there are no believers at the second resurrection, then how does Yeshua's parable fit in the fulfillment if one event is only of the good and the second is only of the wicked?

Also, the Lamb's book of life will be opened. Why have the book of life present if God knows no one will make it into the kingdom? It says too, "If anyone's name was not found." It doesn't say, "No one's name at this resurrection was found." The following verses support the fact that there is a resurrection of the good and evil together: Luke 3:16; John 5:25–29; Daniel 12:2, 3; Matthew 3:12; Matthew 13:24–30. The harvest here is the second resurrection. As grain comes out of the ground, so do people come out of the ground. This is not talking about people accepting the Gospel as it's preached.

There is a judgment already in progress. Listen to the testimonies of those who died and rose again back into their earthly bodies. Also, it makes no sense for the devil to be roaming as a roaring lion in this age, but at the same time, he has been judged and seen in hell too. He is not omnipresent. He does not go in and out at will whenever he chooses. Once in, he is locked in. There can't be an escape or exit. During the time of Paul, this was true, but so much has happened since then. Satan has been judged already, so what does this say about the kingdom of darkness? They will go the same way as their master. Evil is prevalent in the spiritual realm, but their master and king is crushed and judged. These are not the days of going to dry and arid places; these are the days of judgment with fire.

There is still a kingdom of darkness, but it is more real to the sinner because he's in it; it's a part of him. The things he experiences are different than a saint. In a battle, what happens to the army of a king who has been captured and killed? It's not good. Doom awaits them. So, what happens to the kingdom of darkness whose master has been judged? How does he have a throne in hell, but Ezekiel says he's in the lowest part of the pit?

If all this is true, the signs and the power of God will follow to support this truth. Is this a teaching to lead people astray from the truth of the Lord? If this is the Day of the Lord, how much more sober and alert should we be and how much more should we "be diligent to be found by Him in peace, spotless, and blameless"? How much more faith should we have in His presence?

The day of visitation is upon us; it is here. He is truly here as a thief in the night who comes while people sleep. They are unaware of what is happening. The sons of light understand this and receive it. Though there seems to be a resurrection that has begun, many of the wicked from BC and AD times will rise from their graves to a dead, extinct earth on the last day. The judgment continues.

CHAPTER 19

The Passing Away, Destruction, and Hell

> By the word of God the heavens existed long ago and the earth was formed out of water and by water, through which the world at that time was destroyed, being flooded with water. But by His word, the present heavens and earth are being reserved for fire, kept for the Day of Judgment and destruction of ungodly men. (2 Peter 3:5–7)

It was the world that was destroyed during Noah's time, not the heavens and the earth. The heavens and earth remained. Peter makes it clear that it is not just the world that will be destroyed with fire; it will also be the first heaven and earth and all that's in them, including humans. The destruction of Sodom and Gomorrah with fire from heaven left nothing of the two cities, the inhabitants, or their works. Sodom and Gomorrah can't be found. Sodom and Gomorrah were exposed, and their works were laid bare. Everything was worthy of the flame. Any remnants of the city are hard to find. There is a lot of dirt and salt.

The destruction is viewed by some believers as far off—thousands or hundreds of years away. It is downplayed because the heavens and earth can't be destroyed. Some believe—both futurists and preterist—that earth is not going anywhere and believers aren't going anywhere. It is almost like they are saying, "Noah and Lot needed salvation from those disasters, not us. Salvation today is from hell, not catastrophes that come upon the earth. Even though Peter says the heavens and earth will be destroyed by fire this time, it really won't. That is not what he meant."

There is a tone of unbelief in what they profess and teach. They don't take it seriously. They see the coming fiery destruction as one just like the watery deluge of Noah's day (or even Moses and the Hebrews through the Red Sea). They believe that only the people and works are destroyed, but earth remains; the only difference is fire takes water's place.

I understand Peter to mean it will be so much worse than it is possible to believe. Earth and space will become unlivable and incapable of supporting life of any kind. There is no place where anyone can hide from His presence or wrath. If one is not covered under the shadow of the Messiah's wings, they will be destroyed:

> But the day of the Lord will come like a thief, in which the heavens will pass away with a roar and the elements will be destroyed with intense heat, and the earth and its works will be burned up. Since all these things are to be destroyed in this way, what sort of people ought you to be in holy conduct and godliness looking for and hastening the coming of the day of God, because of which the heavens will be destroyed by burning, and the elements will melt with intense heat! But according to his promise we are looking for new heavens and a new earth, in which righteousness dwells. (2 Peter 3:10–13).

It reads, "the earth and it works", not just "it works". The English Standard Version translates verse 10 "and the works that are done on it will be exposed," which many take to mean that the earth will not be destroyed. To understand verse 10, look at the following verse: "All these things are to be destroyed in this way." The word "all" includes the earth.

Addressing his letter to believers in his generation of that era, Peter writes "what sort of people ought you to be in holy conduct and godliness looking for and hastening the coming of the day of God". What's the point of this reminder or warning if they couldn't be caught up in His wrath? How can they be judged by fire if this is an event so far off from them in a distant future and not during or shortly after the time of their generation? If anyone of them backslid and forsook the Lord, they would not rise in the first resurrection (hence "Blessed and holy is the one who has a part in the first resurrection" –Revelation 20:6), but rather they would be reserved for the coming destruction with fire. They were sleeping and did not watch for the master. They are doomed in the resurrection of holy and unholy, wheat and tares, sheep and goats where they are condemned.

There is no second chance for people of that generation. This is why

Paul said that those who proclaimed the resurrection is past had destroyed their faith, because this meant there was no second chance for them, they were to be doomed to destruction in the distant future. For them to rise up in the first resurrection means they are blessed and holy. It means they would reign with Him. For one from that generation to rise up in the second resurrection meant eternal damnation.

What about us of latter generations? Are we doomed to destruction since it has past? No. Where the second resurrection meant doom for a backslider in the first century, there is hope for us. The second resurrection is the wheat and tares, the sheep and goats, the holy and unholy, the righteous and the wicked. The presence of a book of Life indicates that there will be people saved whose names are written in it from latter generations, though "few are saved".

If God can create an earth, He is also capable of destroying it. If He created the heavens, He is also capable of destroying them. If He can bring it into existence out of nothing, He can take it out of existence. He is their Creator. It is possible for Him to do this. He can also create a new one as it is written that there will be a "new" heavens and earth.

Merriam-Webster defines "new" as "not old, recently discovered, recognized, or learned about, not formerly known or experienced, unfamiliar, refreshed, regenerated." How is the earth new if we recognize it as the same one or if it was formerly known? How is it new if it is familiar to us? After the destruction, the heavens and earth will either be purged by the fire and changed into a very new, upgraded earth—or the new earth will be a whole different planet untouched by sin, curse, evil, and death.

Astronomers have discovered several earthlike planets in space. One of them is Kepler-186f:

> NASA's Kepler Space Telescope discovered an Earth-like planet circling a nearby star within the Goldilocks zone of our galaxy. Kepler-186f is around 500 light-years from Earth in the Cygnus constellation. The habitable zone, also identified as the Goldilocks zone, is the area around a star within which planetary-mass objects with enough atmospheric pressure can sustain liquid water at their surfaces. (*The Science News Reporter*, 2018)

The heavens will be destroyed by burning, and the elements will melt with intense heat. This does not mean that only the temple, Jerusalem, and the old elements and order of the Old Covenant are done away with. In the phrase "the earth and its works will be burned up" both are destroyed:

> Each man's work will become evident; for the day will show it because it is to be revealed with fire, and the fire itself will test the quality of each man's work. If any man's work which he has built on it remains, he will receive a reward. If any man's work is burned up, he will suffer loss; but he himself will be saved, yet so as through fire. (1 Corinthians 3:13–15)

"The day" is the same day in both verses: "the day of the Lord." The fire is to test, show, reveal, or expose *the quality* of every human's work on the earth: believers and unbelievers. It will expose whether or not the work is holy or unholy, of light or darkness, eternal or temporal, of the earth or of heaven, according to the will of humans or the will of God, pure or impure, carnal or spiritual, fruitful or fruitless, or done out of humility or out of pride. Will the work survive through the catastrophic temperatures? It will be "evident" (or "exposed") whether or not his work was built on gold, silver, and precious stones—or wood, hay, straw.

If the heavens are destroyed with intense heat and burning, so will the earth for how can earth escape from under the heavens? This is a very terrifying thought, but "it is a terrifying thing to fall into the hands of the living God" (Hebrews 10:31). When the works are "exposed," barely anything will survive the flames and heat. The earth and its works will be laid bare and will not hold any weight in the presence of His glory. They will flee from Him. This means it is no more.

How does one refuse to believe that Yeshua the King judges anyone while accepting that in any war or battle on earth past or present, many kings either take captives as slaves or kill those on the opposing side? Is this not God's right if He owns what He has created to begin with or if He takes captive the devil's possessions? Is it not His right to destroy what is defiled, corrupt, and abominable?

If you have a fruit tree that bears horrible fruit, deadly fruit, or no fruit, is it not your right to have it removed and destroyed from what is your property and domain? What good is it to you? Would you have a corpse that does not respond to you? It neither feels, sees, nor hears you. It will rot and corrupt the inside of your home and property? Only a cruel, murderous, unloving, unmerciful person throws dead plants, flowers, trees, and corpses out of their house or property, right?

What kind of person are you? How inhospitable and unkind you are to refuse a person, known to be very evil, entry into your home to influence your household, cause harm, steal and destroy, and change the rules and procedures of your household? Why don't you invite everyone who is a stranger in the neighborhood and in your town to your parties and gatherings? It doesn't matter that you don't know them and they don't know you.

You don't think this of yourself or anyone else for good reason, but you think this way toward God who is holy? Likewise, what good is a person to God who bears evil fruit, who never has been born again, who refuses to be, who is an enemy, and who is a servant and/or child of the devil whether they believe it or not? Why would He keep such a one as a servant/slave? This evil slave would disobey in some way or defile what is holy? He is useless to Him.

How do you have this right to rid yourself of evil things, but God does not? He will not destroy what or who is evil because "He's such a merciful, kind, and good God." He is also a holy God. He will too have them removed and destroyed from His property and domain. The dead soul, which is eternal, will be destroyed in an eternal flame.

The flame matches the eternal soul's existence. Humans have pyres for rotten corpses, and the flame expires with the existence of the body. The souls of humans are rotting; there is a stench one cannot sense. Since the soul is forever, the flame is forever too. It is an eternal funeral pyre.

Kingdom Takeover

The conqueror kills and destroys all. He takes no POWs, captives, or slaves. Massive changes are taking place in heaven and on earth. The dead are not in His book. They are the losers in the war between kingdoms. They can't pay their debts for their sins, they are "evicted," and they are thrown into the lake of fire. The passing away of the heaven and earth is a sign of a kingdom overtaking everything in heaven and on earth. A time of judgment is occurring.

In the video, *Medieval Dead*, Tim Sutherland, an archaeologist, described the transition that happens when a nation or kingdom wins or loses a battle or war, such as at Visby:

> If you win or lose a battle, it is a momentous occasion for either the victors or the losers. And when this happens on a national scale, it means massive changes take place across a whole country and maybe even over the whole continent ... And these people in the grave are presumably most of them—are the losers. The fact that the Gotlanders lost and the Danes won means there's now a seat change across whole of that island. The Gotlanders, who were phenomenally wealthy people, suddenly are ruled by somebody from an external country.

It is the same between the kingdom of darkness and the kingdom of God, and there are massive changes taking place in heaven and on earth. With Yeshua's win and the devil's defeat, massive changes are taking place. The kingdoms of the world and the darkness that naturally were wealthy suddenly are ruled by the Anointed One, Yeshua, from an external country or world so to speak. The dead are the losers.

The world, the dead, the princes, and the rulers in the unseen realm suddenly find themselves ruled and judged by Him who has come from the highest heaven. Everything the enemy had possession of in the land, water, and sky becomes the property of the conquering King. It is in the King's hand to do what He wishes with what used to belong to His enemy in the kingdom of darkness: to keep, to change, or to destroy. This first heaven and earth must pass away and burn with fire according to the Word of God. All must be judged and pass away, and Yeshua brings in a new order of the kingdom of heaven.

Worldly systems are shaken, broken down, and collapsing under the weight of glory of the present kingdom. His eternal kingdom shakes all that is temporal. According to the 2019 UK Report,

> In the extreme, environmental breakdown could trigger catastrophic breakdown of human systems, driving a rapid process of "runaway collapse" in which economic, social and political shocks cascade through the globally linked system.

Humankind is a destructive species, but this is also a sign of the presence of an eternal kingdom shaking all that is temporal.

CHAPTER 20

Addressing Futurist Arguments against the Preterist View

Some futurists use the following points against a preterist view. I speak to these arguments or reasoning the best I can.

Time Texts

The time texts in Matthew and Revelation such as "this generation" and "I am coming quickly" are only a couple of many other verses that give reasonable meaning to the fulfillment of prophecy in the first century. There are many other verses that give clues of Yeshua's coming in the first century, not just these two (refer to chapter 16).

When Revelation Was Written by Apostle John

Many futurists believe Revelation to be written around AD 95 and rely and put their faith in only the historical support. A preterist goes by the historical support given in the clues within the book itself and history. As a preterist, I do not base the date of the book based on my theological position, but by the clues given in the book of Revelation itself. By understanding those clues (discussed in chapter 3 of this book) that suggest the time the book was originally written, a preterist can find *the biblical support* for their theological position they hold, align to, and maintain.

    A futurist does not pay attention to those clues or ignores them; therefore, in their interpretation, the timing of the writing and fulfillment is offset to the future. A futurist does not rely on biblical support from within the book itself, but from humans. If they rely on that historical support from humans, they date the book to be written to fit their interpretation without regard for what the angel spoke. What the holy angel speaks trumps anything a human, who can err, would speak for the angels stand in the presence of God.

There are a few things within the book of Revelation that are past and current events within the first century (John 12:1–13:10). Many people can agree that the war in heaven, Satan's fall, the birth of the Child (Yeshua), His ascension, and the rise of the beast of the sea (the Roman Empire) occurred before or as this book was written. It is possible that this book was written after and during some of the visions that were already past and current when he wrote it.

The primary support for a date of Revelation is within the book itself. Biblical support from John and the holy angel who stands in the presence of God is the primary support before any other person's word who did not directly receive the visions as John did. A human's word from history cannot take precedence over an angel that stands in the presence of God. This takes precedence before anything else. Revelation had to be written before AD 70 based on a few clues within the book itself.

To ignore, symbolize, or consider the clues after anything historical is backward to me. Clues within the book should come first. The reader should first consider and give attention to these clues in the book and in Daniel—and then see where in history's time line this fits in the puzzle. Based on these clues written in the book of Revelation and the words Yeshua spoke in the Gospels, there is *biblical support* for a date of Revelation before AD 70. How the clues fit into the history of the Roman emperors in the first century gives the *historical support*.

To date a book based on Irenaeus and Polycarp, who are men who can err and have fault, and not the clues found within the book itself and the history of the first-century Roman emperors is redating the book. It is impossible to be a futurist with respect to Revelation if the angel and John are right. It is impossible to be a futurist if we see how the clues fit into the history of the Roman emperors.

History supports the fulfillment of this prophecy in this interpretation. Many of the prophecies were fulfilled after the book was written. There could have been copies of the original book written and circulating the empire around AD 95. I believe the original book of Revelation was written before AD 70. Yeshua returned in the first century before or during AD 70, and He does an extended stay or a traversing in the Day of the Lord.

Putting your faith in humankind, who is fatally flawed, is dangerous.

We should put our faith in the scripture given by the Holy Spirit. The Holy Spirit, Yeshua, and the angel did not lie. The clues in the book of Revelation point to this book being written before AD 70. Put no faith in the flesh.

Not One Stone of the Temple

Matthew 24:2 says that not one stone of the temple would be left standing, one upon another. Some futurists believe that because the Wailing Wall, several rows high, still stands that it wasn't fulfilled yet. Yeshua said, "Not one stone of the temple." My understanding of the Wailing Wall is that it is a wall that surrounded the temple, but it was not part of the actual temple or its foundation. It is holy because it is on the Temple Mount. It is not the side or wall of the actual temple. The temple was destroyed as He prophesied. He did not say the walls surrounding the temple would be destroyed too.

The Great Commission Fulfilled, yet Continued

> This Gospel of the kingdom shall be preached in the whole world (or inhabited earth) as a testimony to all the nations, and then the end will come. (Matthew 24:14)

What is this end? What exactly is it the end of? Daniel 12 and Matthew 28:20 speak of "the end of the age," which is more a Jewish age that ends with the sacrifices in the temple. The context of Daniel and Matthew suggests this is what they are talking about. Things change drastically for the Jewish people with the end of sacrifices and the temple system. This was the center of their lives; it was a big part of their world and customs. As a people, they would have to figure out a way to live without it. This was a huge adjustment and adaptation for them to make after having practiced this for centuries. It was an end of a Jewish age.

Their "age" is not the same as the world's "age." Their day is not the same as the world's day, their year is not the same as the world's year, and their feasts and festivals are not the same as the world's feasts and festivals. These are a people set apart in many ways from the world. As a people, they had their own systems apart from the world around them. Yet when Gentile Christians come teaching what "age" means, not being familiar with the temple and never having it as a part of our heritage, they misinterpret it. "Age" comes to mean something different.

This is also what Gentile Christians do when interpreting what the word "food" means when Yeshua, who was speaking to His Jewish brethren, declared "all foods clean." What is food for Gentiles is not food for Jews too. Even their "food" is not the same the world's "food."

When Gentile Christians come with their Gentile customs (and what they are used to eating) teaching what "food" means here—not familiar with, ignoring, setting aside, or avoiding what is written in Jewish law about clean and unclean food—they misinterpret it and think it is now proper to eat unclean meat. Gentiles must understand that Yeshua was having a family discussion with His fellow Jews.

Gentiles had no part in this discussion about food. Why do we think He was also referring to the unclean food Gentiles eat? Gentiles forget that this is Jewish and their faith stems from a Jewish faith in a Jewish King. This is the arrogance that Gentiles have. Gentile believers want to "do what Jesus did," but they don't even consider that the Master they serve never—even to this day—eats unclean food. Gentiles don't want to be like Him in this way; this is the exception.

The Jews of that generation would also understand the Gospel of the kingdom of heaven coming preached by John the Baptist and Yeshua to be tied to the prophecy in the book of Daniel with the Rock that knocks over and crushes the other kingdoms. They would better relate to what John and Yeshua meant than us. These current generations, being born later, are far removed from this, and therefore view the Rock in Daniel's prophecy as something future, not past and present.

According to Paul, the Gospel was preached in the world of his time, and then the end of the temple came in AD 70. Paul wasn't exaggerating (Acts 17:6; 1 Timothy 3:16; Colossians 1:6, 23).

The "world" Yeshua refers to is the Roman Empire, the known world, and surrounding areas. The "inhabited earth" or "world" is the Roman Empire (Luke 2:1 NASB). Now are we to believe that this census taken here includes those in the Americas, Asia, Africa, and Australia too? Weren't those places inhabited too? No, we simply understand that "world or inhabited earth" here means the Roman Empire or the known world of that age. So, why don't we apply this simple understanding to the Great Commission?

The disciples had a witness and the commission spoken directly to them to preach the Gospel was fulfilled in the Roman Empire of that era. At the same time, the Great Commission does not end. It continues today. Those who come to believe through their message have a witness too and share it with others. They fulfilled their duty, and the Gospel was spread in the empire. In this sense, it was fulfilled until the end of the temple, yet it should continue until the end of life on earth.

The power of the blood and Holy Spirit, victory and triumph, defeat of enemies, purification, and visitation is for today, and the Great Commission and mercy continue to every generation today—and way beyond the Roman Empire where many nations visited or lived:

- Mark 16:15. The "world" here is the Roman Empire or the known world of that time.
- Matthew 28:19. Many nations were within the Roman Empire.
- Acts 2:5–11. "From every nation under heaven." People from all over the known world, which is the Roman Empire, were in Jerusalem. This was not an exaggeration.
- Matthew 24:14. Yeshua meant "world" as the Roman world and "end" as the end of the temple.
- Daniel 12:11–13. Since Yeshua just finished speaking of the end/destruction of the temple, I believe this is the end He is referring to. Daniel writes about an "end" to the temple. This verse also mentions a resurrection of saints happening around the first century: "Then at the end of days (1,335 days of the temple and its sacrifices, not the end of time or the world) you will arise (resurrection of saints) to receive your portion."
- 1 Corinthians 15:23–28. "Those who are Christ's at His coming." This includes the prophet Daniel. This is more likely, especially with Paul claiming that the disciples have fulfilled their calling to spread the Gospel. Many interpret "end" in this verse to refer to the end of time and all worlds, which include every generation that will enter the world from then until the modern time and "end" as the end of the old heaven and earth. Paul is not incorrect in what he wrote to Timothy and the Colossians (see also Psalm 19:1–4; Romans 10:18; 1:8; 1 Thessalonians 1:8). Nature also witnesses and testifies.
- Romans 16:26. This is not an exaggeration, but a fulfillment. "Has been made known to all the nations." In Paul's time, "has been" in the past tense equaled fulfilled. It "all" went into all the earth, not some of it.
- Matthew 10:23. "You (the disciples) will not finish going through the cities of Israel when the Son of Man Comes."

If the disciples wouldn't finish preaching the good news in Israel before Yeshua returned in glory, then how could they technically finish in the entire global earth, which would include the unknown, undiscovered, and distant parts of earth too? It is possible that the Gospel was spread in the known world and empire of that time, and Paul says that it was, though not in Israel as Yeshua stated.

- Matthew 10:5–15. Yeshua is speaking about what they should do in the next few days as they are just being sent out to Israel—not to the Gentiles.
- Matthew 10:16–19. Yeshua is speaking of a time in the future about the disciples preaching in Israel.

None of the eleven disciples were delivered up to councils, scourged in synagogues, or brought before governors and kings before Yeshua died on the cross. This obviously was speaking of a time after His ascension before He would return to them.

Yeshua told the disciples, not us, they would not finish going to all the cities in Israel before He came back to that generation. That is how soon Yeshua returned. He did not tarry. If they did not finish going to the cities of Israel due to their rejection of the Messiah, the days were shortened as Yeshua stated.

The AD 70 Tribulation Was the Worst for That Generation

The interpretation of the tribulation must be kept within the proper scope (Matthew 24:21; Daniel 12:1). Note how the conversation began with a question about the temple and how it will end. The end of the temple marked the end of an age, not quite the end of the Roman Empire.

The horrors of the extermination camps of Hitler, the destruction of Israel and most of Judah by the Assyrians, Nebuchadnezzar's destruction of Jerusalem, the Khmer Rouge, the Rwandan horror, and the horrors of World War II, including the saturation bombing of German cities, and the dropping of the atomic bombs on Japan are tragedies of a much broader time frame and in other generations in a different world and also of mostly unbelievers, Jews, and Gentiles.

Yeshua is speaking of His particular generation during a certain period of time in that part of the world (Roman) before the temple's destruction. It involves the temple of God (abomination and destruction) and also believers in Yeshua, not necessarily only the Jews. The "world" referenced in Matthew is since the Roman world began, and 2 Timothy 4:10 and 1 John 2:17 speak of the present world of Paul and John's time. Remember that the tribulation Yeshua refers to is one involving Jerusalem and the Jewish people, not the inhabitants of the world or the global planet. Jerusalem and the Jews are at the center of the tribulation just as they were at the center of the Crusades or Gog and Magog. In each case, they are the focus, not the world.

We can learn from them, take lessons, and apply them to our world. Josephus described his generation in the first century, and it was awful. He records that during the years of the siege, 1,100,000 people perished, most by pestilence and famine, and 97,000 were taken captive. As long as the temple existed, for those generations in the first century in the Roman world, it was as bad as it was going to get.

The tribulation has to be related to opposition to the kingdom of God during the time of an earthly temple, not necessarily to unbelieving Jews and Gentiles after the destruction of the temple as in the Bar Kokhba rebellion or the Holocaust. The Great Tribulation was of a certain generation, of a certain world (Roman), and of a certain group of people (the elect and Jews, not Gentile unbelievers) during the short time the temple had left to stand. Within the world of that time, there would not be a worse tribulation of believers and Jews before the end of the temple.

Anything else horrible that happened in the world elsewhere in another time and place after the temple desolation does not count here. If it's unbelievers, it does not count. The Holocaust does not count toward the fulfillment of this verse.

This does not mean believers are never persecuted again. Believers were greatly persecuted in the first century—even through Nero's and Domitian's reigns. It extended to Trajan's reign (AD 108) and there was more persecution around AD 303, which was the greatest and the last during the Roman Empire. Believers still are martyred today in certain countries, but the temple of stone is gone.

One has to compare within the time frame and location of the temple and the Roman Empire, which is a beast, not within the time frame of humankind on the earth from Adam until the present day. The time frame for Matthew 24:21 is from 27 BC–AD 70, which is from when the Roman Empire began until the abomination came and the temple was destroyed.

Was there a worse tribulation within the Roman Empire for the Jews and believers? There wasn't a worse tribulation; Yeshua's words are true and not confusing. Those tragedies before the Roman world and after the temple desolation were terrible, catastrophic, and evil, but Yeshua wasn't talking about Gentile unbelievers or those outside the Roman Empire in location or time or Jews born after the temple's destruction.

Keep the words within their proper scope and context. The temple is the key to understanding this verse. In this understanding, what Yeshua said in Matthew is literally true and has been fulfilled. *When such a broad perspective is taken in the interpretation, you miss what Yeshua really meant and end up way off target.*

The Tribes of the Earth Seeing the Son of Man

Refer to chapter 8 for more information. "Gathered" means resurrected. The elect are believers—not just Jews as a people. Unbelievers (Jew and Gentile) are not gathered, but they would be scattered. If they are gathered for anything, it would be for judgment like the tares in the parable of Yeshua. Tribes of the earth are the tribes of Israel.

I believe the Spirit of God opened the eyes and ears of the hearts (spirit) of the people (and believers—the awake) to see and hear. The Bible says, "They have eyes, but do not see; ears, but do not hear" and "Seeing, they do not see; they hear, but do not hear."

Yeshua said He would come as a thief in the night. A thief in the day comes suddenly when everyone is awake. A thief in the night comes suddenly when people sleep and are not aware of him. Paul warned not to be of those who sleep but of those who are awake.

"Every eye will see" could be spiritual sight with eyes of the spirit, not physical eyes. What is of the unseen realm is not less real than the physical realm where we are. What is seen in the Spirit is not less true or real; it is even more real than our world. It is not metaphorical.

The entire earth would probably not see this—only the tribes and believers of the first century who were chosen to see as the Spirit was poured out upon them.

This Generation

Futurists accuse preterists of taking only this phrase literally and nothing else. Everything else is symbolic. About the only "generation" verse futurists seem to misinterpret and not take literally is this one. "This generation" means the same in these verses: Matthew 11:16; 12:38–41; 16:4; 24:34;

Mark 8:12, 38; 9:19; Luke 11:29–32, 50, 51; 17:25; 21:32; Acts 2:40; 1 Peter 2:9; and Matthew 12:39–45. If you understand the phrase "this generation" in these verses, why not in the other verses about the Second Coming unless you want to see what you want to see?

When these verses are read, they understand them to be the generation of the disciples' time, not ours or any other generation. They don't have a problem with these verses. They take these literally, but they don't take the one on the Second Coming literally. The only verse in the New Testament they interpret for "another generation" is the one about the Second Coming. If Yeshua did say "your generation," futurists would not interpret it to mean the disciples' generation. They would believe it was talking about their generation.

If Yeshua meant a future generation would see these things, why didn't he say it? Why not say "that generation" or "another generation" or "those not yet born"? Why say "this generation"? Yeshua didn't even say "the generation that sees these things." He said "this generation."

Look up the word "this" in a dictionary: "The person or thing present, or nearby, or just mentioned; the one that is nearer than another; the present occasion or time." Look up the word "that": "Being the one farther away or more remote." Don't these simple words convey the true interpretation? Just by the word "this," the word "generation" He refers to is the one present at His time and the disciples' time when He spoke these words, not one far away and in the future. Yeshua meant the generation He was in, not another.

Note: In Luke 21:20–22, it is written that in the days of Jerusalem's desolation that all things written would be fulfilled. The generation during the time of the temple is the one Yeshua is referring to, not ours. "All things" include the return of Messiah to Jerusalem.

Second note: "Generation" can't be taken to mean "race" because it would not make sense in any of the verses above where generation is written. It almost seems anti-Semitic to interpret it as race. Hitler would have loved that because then it would have supported his cause: "The Jews will not pass away until all these things are fulfilled." So once these things come to pass, the Jews go extinct and are extinguished as a people. This can't be the meaning.

Some use a broad base of reasoning to explain that just because a scripture says "you" or "this generation" or "we" that it speaks to all generations. A distinction must be made based on the context between a verse that is about wisdom, commandments, direction, and teaching and instruction, counsel, warning, judgment, or prophecy. The former can be received and practiced by every generation. Every generation can benefit from learning from examples of previous generations even though it wasn't addressed to them.

The latter is different because it has a time, season, day, hour, or a generation of fulfillment. There is a time in which it must come to pass, and there is a rare possibility of a dual fulfillment. The prophecy of Yeshua's death and resurrection will not occur again in another generation. It was a once and for all act that occurred in one generation, but all who believe Him benefit.

His Second Coming occurs within one generation in the first century, and as One not bound to one place and traverses to fulfill the will of the Father, He can return as many times as needed to accomplish this. I believe that with the prophecy of Gog and Magog, the Crusades from about 1095–1291 were either another or the same visitation of Yeshua who fights and judges the nations, principalities, and powers that gather around Jerusalem with chariots, horses, swords, bows and arrows, and spears. We don't battle and war with these things anymore. It is outdated.

There are examples of where "generation" is used, but we have to keep in mind too that we of latter generations can learn from the example of others or the warnings to others even though the verses were originally spoken to people of long ago. By heeding the warnings or obeying the commandments as they did, we can only benefit as they had. By ignoring His Word, we suffer and are judged too as they did even generations later (Deuteronomy 32:5, 32:20, Psalms 24:6, 112:2; Luke 9:41; Matthew 16:4; Mark 8:12; Luke 17:25).

Later generations can learn from Scriptures where others are being addressed directly (Galatians 3:26–27; 4:6–7; Ephesians 2:19; 1 John 2:12–14; Matthew 5:20; 8:11; 19:28–29; 26:29; John 3:3; Ephesians 2:8–9; Romans 5:8; John 3:3; and Mark 13:35–37). While many things written in scripture can be applied to our lives today, a futurist's reasoning is very broad, which in some ways makes them miss the mark when it comes to prophecy.

> But I say to you, I will not drink of this fruit of the vine from now on until that day when I drink it new with you in My Father's kingdom. (Matthew 26:29)

Yeshua drank wine with the disciples and most likely drinks wine with them today. This was a word or prophecy for them, not us today. Not that we will join them and drink wine with Him too. Some people conclude, "Yeshua is not drinking wine with us on earth so this is not fulfilled." Yeshua specifically stated that He would drink it with the disciples *in His Father's kingdom, not necessarily on the earth. The Father's kingdom is not of this world or this old earth and is unseen by us.* It can be in the midst of believers because they are citizens of His kingdom.

"What I say to you, I say to all, 'Be on the alert'" (Mark 13:35–37). The futurists believe it is all generations, not just one generation. I believe it is all within His generation who believe (the world is never alert), but also even after His coming, believers today should wake up to His visitation as a thief in the night.

Signs in that first-century generation include Matthew 24:3–4; Luke 11:30–31; Matthew 16:4; and Mark 8:12. Some futurists argue that Yeshua said to his generation (or "this generation," which again futurists understand to mean the generation He came to live among, not a latter generation) that no sign would be given to them except the sign of the prophet Jonah, which is the resurrection of Yeshua.

They ask, "If this was the only sign given, then how are all the signs in Matthew 24 fulfilled in AD 70?" The context is important for understanding what He meant here. We must read Matthew 16:1 and Mark 8:11 to understand what He meant by no sign being given to them.

By ignoring the context, futurists fail to make the distinction between the different kinds of signs. There are earthly, worldly signs and there are heavenly, spiritual signs. They fail to see that the signs the Pharisees and Sadducees wanted to see were signs from heaven. Yeshua, the Bread of heaven, was to be the only sign from heaven in His resurrection from the dead. There was another part to the sign of Jonah from heaven to be given to that generation according to Zechariah 12. His return as the Holy Spirit is poured out upon Jerusalem, and the twelve tribes mourn Him who is pierced.

"The sign of the Son of Man will appear in the sky" (Matthew 24:30). Again, the Bread of heaven is the only sign for them to see if the Spirit came upon them. They see that the One who they pierced has truly risen from the dead and is in glory with the holy angels. This could still be under the sign of Jonah. His resurrection and His return as the Bread of heaven are both under the sign of Jonah—the only sign given to that first-century generation.

The sign of Jonah isn't just Yeshua in the heart of the earth since Jonah was in the belly of the fish. The men of Nineveh were rising up (resurrection) with that generation at His coming and condemning them for unbelief in the Bread of heaven. This is done as the tribes of that generation mourned. The men of that generation will see the sign of the men of Nineveh standing up and condemning them before the King who has returned. It is too the sign of Jonah.

To paraphrase Yeshua: "I am the sign from heaven. There is no other sign you need from heaven." What other sign from heaven can be greater than Him? If He did perform another sign from heaven, they still would not believe Him because they are hardened and wicked. They reject him; therefore, anything He does they'd consider it of the devil. "He casts out demons by Beelzebub" (Matthew 12:24; Luke 11:15).

The signs in Matthew 24 were earthly and worldly signs. The Pharisees did not ask to see earthly and worldly signs, and Yeshua did not restrict these kinds of signs, but He did restrict any from heaven. Again, the Bread of heaven is the only sign for them to see if the Spirit came upon them. The signs in Matthew 24 were fulfilled beginning in AD 70 and continue to this day. These earthly signs don't necessarily end when He comes again; they increase until the heavens and earth pass away in His presence. These earthly and worldly signs are not necessarily just for His generation or just for ours. They are progressive and grow worse throughout history—and through the remaining generations—until everything passes away and goes extinct.

Speaking of metaphors and symbolism, when the Ezekiel passage on Gog and Magog is read, futurists symbolize the weapons and horses to represent modern-day weapons and not literal horses, swords, and chariots, which were used in the Crusades but not in modern wars.

Also, to some of them, the millennial reign is not one thousand years literally; it is eternity. How does a finite number represent eternity? It is written that they would be finished and expire, but some futurists do not take it literally.

Take the phrase "some standing here" (Mark 9:1; Matthew 16:28; and Luke 9:27). They say fulfillment is literal and accurate, but when interpreting these verses, they say it was the transfiguration. It is not the same. They teach that these passages refer to the transfiguration, but they do not. Futurist say preterists are not literal in their interpretations of scripture, but the interpretations they give for this is not literal; they are not the same. First of all, there was no army or multitude of angels (only Moses and Elijah). Secondly, there was no rewarding of people. Third, there was no "coming" in a kingdom or "clouds of heaven" in the transfiguration on the mountain. There was a cloud that came over the disciples like a tabernacle. Last of all, I believe the "some" refers to more people other than Peter, James, and John. The Lord meant His Second Coming, not the transfiguration.

While Yeshua and Peter say that baptism saves, they will not take them literally and say, "They didn't mean it saves, but it symbolizes what happens when you accept Christ." They don't understand the power of water's testimony, the spiritual part it plays in salvation, or how many witnesses are needed to establish a matter.

How can they say scripture must be taken literally and accurately, yet they symbolize, use metaphors and symbolism and allegories, and that is okay for them, but not for a preterist?

When You See

Some futurists believe the "you see" refers to a coming people, not the apostles since they did not see these things. "When you see the abomination of desolation which was spoken of through Daniel the prophet, standing in the holy place (the holy temple)" (Matthew 24:15). The "you" refers to some of the disciples. "You" is not the reader; it is the person or people being addressed:

- John 1:51 (possible return or a vision like Jacob's)
- Matthew 10:23; 21:20 ("When you see Jerusalem surrounded by armies")
- John 21:22, 23
- Matthew 16:27, 28
- Mark 8:38–9:1
- Luke 9:26–27

Some of the twelve apostles could have been dead and never saw these things unless they were counted in the first resurrection. According to His words in these verses, some of them, which could have been more than twelve disciples present when Yeshua spoke these words and even younger than the twelve apostles, would see Him come and not taste death.

The phrase "this generation" could still be His disciples—He had many others and not just twelve—to be alive and see these things. How do you know that His other disciples did not see the signs Yeshua spoke of? How do you know that all of the other ones outside His inner circle were killed too? Therefore, these followers, the young disciples when Yeshua spoke this, are the remnant generation that is still alive to see it. If there were more disciples, some of whom were younger than the twelve apostles, present there when He said this, it is possible they saw these things. Therefore, He is speaking to most of them. Many futurists just assume the twelve are the only ones there listening to Him.

Luke 10:1 says He appointed seventy disciples to preach the Gospel. Luke 19:37 says He had a whole crowd of disciples praising Him during His triumphal entry. Acts 1:15 says that Peter stood in the midst of about 120 disciples. Paul writes in 1 Corinthians 15:6 that "He appeared to more than five hundred brethren at one time, most of whom remain until now, but some have fallen asleep." Did you catch that? Most of the five hundred disciples remained, and only some died. Probably some more died by the time AD 70 rolled around. Most of the twelve apostles fell asleep, but there were disciples alive when He returned.

Yeshua even appeared to Paul after His ascension (1 Corinthians 15:8). That's interesting—I thought He wouldn't appear until Jerusalem cried out the praise or the beast was in the temple. Interesting how Yeshua traversed in the Spirit appearing to Paul before His official Second Coming, but this seems to go over our heads.

John was in the Spirit, and He appeared to John while writing Revelation 1:10–16. He again appeared before His official coming. Again, this goes over our heads. Seeing Yeshua wasn't a vision; He actually appeared to John. Note that to see the Lord, John had to be in the Spirit first, just like it was written in Zechariah 12. This is how Jerusalem saw Yeshua come.

Were Paul and John seeing a figment of their imaginations, a symbol, or something literal? Again, this goes over our heads. How do we accept Paul and John seeing Yeshua as the Spirit came upon them with the eyes of the spirit, but when a preterist says His coming is a spiritual coming, we don't believe or accept it? Could this explain how—even in our day today—He has appeared to some and how some have felt His presence by the Spirit even after His return?

Even Caiaphas (possibly a middle-aged Levite at this point) would see Him come again (Matthew 26:64). Yeshua told him he would. Caiaphas could have seen Him in the spirit before He died as the Spirit was poured out upon the tribes. This supports the verse "this generation will not pass away until." Caiaphas, who was of the first century generation, did not die until these things happened while he lived. Caiaphas was of the house of Levi, which is one of the tribes the Spirit would be poured out upon in Jerusalem.

Note that it is "when you" and not "if you." A Christian who reads "When you pray" (Matthew 6:5–7) or "Whenever you fast" (Matthew 6:16–17) understands that it is a command, not an option. It is speaking to the apostles specifically, but we learn and practice what He taught them about. It is an expectation of the apostles to practice this. In this case, "when" gives certainty/faith that the disciples would see the beast. "When" is telling the disciples to expect it in their lifetimes. "If" would make it uncertain for them but certain for another generation. "If" is not used here. People will misinterpret a word within a context to suit their understanding or theology, but they won't do it with the same word in another context.

Another clue that it is in the generation of His disciples is it says an abomination would be standing in the holy place, which is the temple of their generation, not another one. Some of them would see this in the Spirit as He is poured out (Zechariah 12).

There are no Old Testament scriptures to support the interpretation that the current /latter generation is the one to "see these things." However, Zechariah 12:10–12 and Daniel 2:44; 7:21–22 strongly suggest it is a first-century generation, not ours or a future one. The fact that this interpretation has a support and a backing from the Old Testament confirms the true meaning of what Yeshua meant by "this generation" (see chapters 8 and 9).

Nero the Antichrist

How does Nero, who died in AD 68 of suicide, sit in the temple of God claiming to be God and be destroyed by the brightness of His coming without ever setting foot in Jerusalem (2 Thessalonians 2:4–8)? Revelation 13:3; 17:8, 11 speak of the Beast (Nero, Antichrist) dying of a fatal head wound (which Nero did) and rising from the bottomless pit. Nero is the one described in "who was, now is not, and is to come". When John wrote "who was", Nero was once alive and reigned. When John wrote "now is not", Nero was dead at the time of the writing. When John wrote "is to come", Nero was to come up out of the bottomless pit as a spiritual entity described as a beast. Who is to come (rise again from the dead)? His fatal wound was healed. All of this is a clue to a rising from the pit. He came up again as a beast.

Yeshua rose from the grave, and His disciples saw Him, not the world. The beast rose again, and some saw him—but not the whole world. Spiritually, though unseen with physical eyes, people were marked by him just as believers in Yeshua had His name on their foreheads. Spiritually, he could have entered the temple of God and defiled it with his unseen, evil beastly presence.

What is spiritual is even more real than the world we are in now. And it could have been fulfilled that way. Nero was in the temple—not when he was an emperor before AD 70—but more likely after he rose from the pit to defile it as a literal beast circa AD 68–70. It was prophesied in Daniel and Revelation that a king or an emperor would be a beast. He was in the flesh and morphed into one after rising. Nero was the eighth head in the spirit after he died.

One has to think that a portal from the spirit world was opened, and something similar to a haunting was going to happen. It would look fierce and horrifying. This also suggests that some people keep their human appearance after death, but there are others who morph into monsters or hideous beings sometime after death (see chapter 3).

Isaiah 13:6

This verse, written around 740–686 BC but not fulfilled until 539 BC, seems to indicate a fulfillment that is in the far future. The phrase "at hand" or "near" used in this verse gives a sense of immediacy as seen in Mark 14:42, 43. If we say this verse in Isaiah was written circa 700 BC and Babylon fell 539 BC, then that is about 161 years, which is more at hand and nearer to fulfillment than two thousand years! In the preterist view, the apostles' same use of the words from AD 35 to AD 69 is about thirty-four years. The time from AD 35 to AD 95 is about sixty years. Both are still better than two thousand years. Thirty-four or sixty years are more "at hand" than either 161 or two thousand years.

But God stands outside of time so that thirty or two hundred years are like minutes or hours to Him. To Him, this is "at hand." He would see fulfillment approaching quicker than humans would. Eventual fulfillment that is a long way off to humans is literally "at hand" to Him. A thousand years are like a day, and a day is like a thousand years. So "at hand" could be decades or up to a couple of centuries, but not close to two millennia. This shows imminence of a bringing to pass His Word shortly after it left His lips.

The "at hand" can occur within or shortly after a generation's life ends. So, what Isaiah prophesied in the eighth century BC was to God "at hand" or "near" in 539 BC when Babylon fell to the Persians. To Him, it's about to happen. So, when the coming of Yeshua is "near" or the end is "at hand" or "the kingdom of heaven is at hand," to Him, it is about to happen, which could be within or shortly after a generation's life ends. It's from His perspective, not a human perspective, and two millennia is not considered "at hand" or "near" or about to happen.

With two thousand years, where is the Lord's zeal to even begin to bring His Word to pass? Where is the Lord's zeal for Zion? The day was not to be delayed, and He would not tarry (Hebrews 10:25, 37; Habakkuk 2:3). According to a futurist view, two thousand years is a huge delay, and He tarries for a long time, which doesn't show much zeal for Zion or to fulfill His Word.

According to a futurist view, His Word did pass away, but they won't admit that's what is implied by their interpretations. If we are already in the Day of the Lord, then He did not tarry or delay at all; He fulfilled His Word as promised. His Word has not passed away.

Matthew 23:34–36

The "this generation" was not referring to those who actually murdered Zechariah, the son of Berechiah four hundred years ago (2 Chronicles 24:20, 21). Yeshua is not saying the generation from four hundred years ago will bear the guilt of the prophets' murders. He is saying His current generation will bear it, hence "this generation," those living at the time He spoke these words.

Matthew's use of the term "this generation" is referring to the generation Yeshua is in. He addresses this to the scribes and Pharisees (verse 29). In verse 32, Yeshua said they would *bear the guilt of their fathers* who were murderers from many generations or centuries ago. Yeshua is speaking to certain men of His current generation, calling them a brood of vipers, and asking how they will escape condemnation. The men of His current generation were to take the full measure of judgment of their forefathers; it was to fall on them because someone great was present in their midst. The generation four hundred years ago, their fathers, did not have God in their midst. Yeshua's generation really did not have an excuse with God physically in their midst.

Luke 10:8–16 condemns the cities of that generation. Previous generations did not have it as bad as they would because God was in their midst. "This generation" does not mean race; it means a group of people living at the time Yeshua spoke those words.

Jeremiah 29:1, 10

He is addressing elders and "all the people Nebuchadnezzar had carried off captive from Jerusalem to Babylon." "All the people" includes those younger so that they would be the ones God "would bring back to this place" after seventy years. After seventy years, the young when this was first spoken would become the elders. In this case, one who was a child or teenager who became an elder after seventy years saw this fulfilled. Someone who was carried away at ten years old would be eighty years old when it was fulfilled.

"You" is the people of Israel (even four hundred years later) and not an individual (Malachi 3:23). "You" is used in Genesis 50:25, but Joseph prophetically speaks to Israel about the seed. He made Israel's sons—his brothers' equal tribes—take an oath.

Judgment of Humankind during and after the King's Arrival

The story of the rich man and Lazarus (Luke 16:19–31) indicates a separation between these two men, a sheep, a goat, wheat, and a tare even while the first earth existed: "Send him to my father's house for I have five brothers—in order that he may warn them." To send Lazarus to his father's house indicates the first earth is still present.

There was already a judgment issued for or against these two men. Some say this was a true story and not just a parable. This could be prophecy of something to come true at Yeshua's Second Coming, or Parousia, as a king and judge in the first century while the first earth existed. Separation and harvest happen in the presence of the Judge of human souls. First-century saints ruled and have judged. Modern-day saints still could have a part to play in the judgment.

There are many interesting accounts of people in modern day generations having visions or experiencing heaven and/or hell (or Hades). I believe these accounts are in line with prophecies written in the books of Daniel and Revelation regarding the judgment before the throne of God. Some have witnessed people in hell (or Hades) or in heaven as though the souls have already been harvested, judged, and rewarded.

Similar to the rich man and Lazarus, it seems that judgment is happening before the passing away of heaven and earth, yet death and Hades have not been cast into the lake of fire. There is in part a harvesting and judgment that happens when humans die. They are either assigned a place in Hades or enter into the kingdom of heaven. "It is appointed for men to die once and after this comes judgment" (Hebrews 9:27). This is part 1; part 2 involves the lake of fire.

In their visions or experiences of heaven and hell, some people testify that Yeshua even tells some of them He is coming very soon. How does harvesting and judgment happen before Yeshua's Second Coming when Matthew describes it happening after or during a coming? I understand part 1 of the harvesting and judgment to happen during His Parousia.

> But when the Son of Man comes in His glory, and all the angels with Him, then He will sit on His glorious throne. All the nations will be gathered before Him; and He will separate them from one another, as the shepherd separates the sheep from the goats. (Matthew 25:31)

This is like the rich man and Lazarus. It does not read "But *before* the Son of Man comes in His glory with the angels and sit on His glorious throne." It reads, "But *when* the Son of Man comes". This separation, or harvest, begins at His coming, so for some time now, and according to the experiences and visions some believers have had, He has been doing this.

Even as the old earth existed, people have been assigned a place after death. After the Crusades or Gog/Magog, according to Revelation 20:11–15, there is part 2 of judgment in which they are cast into the lake of fire. This is coming very soon during or after the heavens and earth goes extinct.

In a futurists view, it seems judgment occurs before He even comes. According to Scripture, judgment happens during or after His coming. The fact many are having actual experiences of heaven and hell and observing souls being judged indicate He had come already. If it is true that He is saying He will come again, perhaps it is for deliverance of His holy people in the natural body, who have not slept or died yet, out of destruction upon the earth. Those who are asleep or dead are already under judgment or salvation. So the mystery remains even today that not all will sleep, but all will be changed.

The first resurrection of Revelation 20:4–6, says they were "those who had not worshiped the beast (Roman emperors) or his image, and had not received the mark on their forehead and on their hand," which means this occurred in the first century or maybe in the second century. These are the saints of that time: maybe even Daniel and the holy ones of the house of Israel.

The second resurrection I don't interpret to be just the wicked, but the wicked and the holy in succeeding generations. We could say the judgment in Matthew 25:31 continues here after the passing away of earth. What began at the Second Coming, "when the Son of man comes in His glory," as the first earth existed continues after it is gone. This also aligns to Yeshua's parable in Matthew 13:24–30 and 13:36–43 of the wheat and tares and also Matthew 25:31, 32 of the sheep and goats.

If the second resurrection was only of the wicked, why have a book of life present at all if He knows no one will enter it? "And if anyone's name was not found written in the book of life, he was thrown into the lake of fire." The word "if" suggests that there will be people's names found in the book of life; even people of later generations can still enter into the kingdom of heaven. If the second resurrection was only of the wicked, then where do Yeshua's parables fit into a judgment of sheep and goats or wheat and tares gathered together before Him and then separated? His mercy extends to every generation (Luke 1:50).

Do we negate the testimonies and historical writings of people who lived during the first century or during the Crusades who record what was prophesied in scripture? Do the current testimonies override or have more precedence than historical accounts that match up to the prophecies? I believe He traverses between worlds in the unseen realm even upon this earth. He was here during the Crusades. *Perhaps the mystery is not a coming in fulfillment of Zechariah 12 but an appearance, or revelation, to deliver us out of a dying earth,* just as the Hebrews were delivered out of Egypt, Noah's family was saved from a watery destruction, or Lot escaped a fiery destruction. In each case, there was a type of exodus from a doomed place or people. This should be an encouragement to us, not confusing.

We could either perish in the extinction—or He could deliver us out of it. Why are His people starved when He said that the Father knows we need food, drink, and clothing? If earth is failing, dying, and broken, according to the Word of the Lord, how do we stay? Where else do we go? Why do the saints stay on a planet that is heating up if the elements will melt with intense heat? Why do we stay on a planet on fire? We who are awake and alive need a Deliverer.

Revelation 20

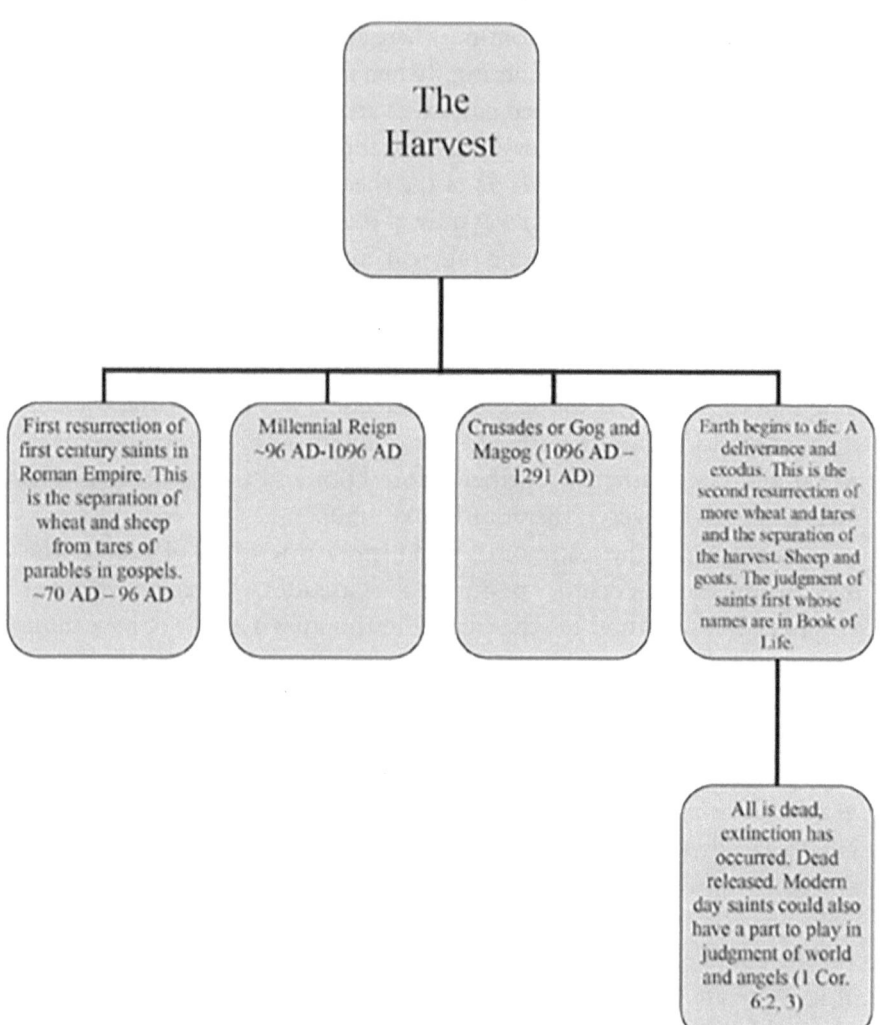

Time Line of Harvest and Judgment

We must not forget that as these accounts of the spiritual worlds of heaven and hell and judgment are being shared and told to us. In the natural world, there is a "passing away" or extinction that is underway. They are occurring almost together, realigning with what was written in Revelation 20:11, 12. There is a passing away of heaven and earth, but during and even after this, there is judgment of all humankind, holy and wicked.

Other Points

- Acts 17:31. "Set a day in which to judge the world." The word "day" could mean Day of the Lord, which spans thousands of years or at the extinction.
- The millennial reign is one that occurs during the time of the old earth, not necessarily in the natural realm of earth. The reign continues in the new earth. The millennial reign is not forty years long (AD 33–70).
- 1 Corinthians 15:26; Revelation 21:4. In part, it is abolished with the rising and transformation of the saints in the first resurrection and to come. Total abolishment of death is coming. It will be thrown in the lake of fire. This is imminent.
- Acts 1:9–11. His ascension was physical and visible. His return was physical, not a vision. What is spiritual can be very much physical, but of a different substance. His return was visible—but by the Spirit of God. No one can "see" the kingdom without the Spirit of God. Spiritual sight is involved here.
- Some ask, "Do we fast and take Communion still?" Yes, we do because we are not in the unseen space the resurrected saints can be in. They don't have to anymore, but we should. They see and hear Him constantly, but we don't. We are still in that space of the natural realm that passes away, but they have crossed and have reigned.
- Matthew 24:29; Mark 13:25. Some futurists would ask a preterist if there are stars in the sky. If a preterist said yes, then preterism must be false and heretical because the stars have to fall out of the sky in the end-times. Therefore, since we all see that they still remain, preterism is defeated. As said in a previous chapter, eclipses could cause the sun to grow dark as sackcloth and the moon not to give light. Meteor showers and shooting stars appear as stars falling from the sky. The

first-century generation would not call it "meteors," but stars. How would they know they weren't literal stars but meteors falling through the sky? This is why we still see stars in our night sky.

Did the people in BC or early AD generations understand that the sun is a star? They never called it a star. We understand it is a star, but did they? I don't think so. One thing to consider is the three wise men at Yeshua's birth could have been observing and following something other than a star, it just looked like a star. Stars don't behave the way they do in the Gospels: traveling within our atmosphere and hovering over a city.

If our own sun doesn't do this without killing all life, how does a star farther out of our solar system do this? The sun would swallow earth with a burp. What stars since then move and hover over cities? What else would the prophets, seeing this in a vision, or the wise men, seeing the fulfillment, call it? The only thing to come up with is a star.

Did these people know that the moon doesn't emit its own light and reflects the light of the sun? They did not understand this. Did they understand that the earth revolves around the sun? No, they did not understand that. They believed the sun moved and revolved around the earth. Did they understand that "the star" they saw in the east rise, also known as, "the bright and morning star" (referencing Yeshua) was actually a planet, later to be called Venus, reflecting the light of the sun? Did they understand that earth wasn't flat with edges, but spherical? But we accept their writings anyway, though they are not scientifically accurate. So, do you think they would understand that stars falling from the sky are not stars, but meteors or shooting stars? No, they would not understand this either. Yet we of modern generations, who know what stars are, tend to interpret the scripture with a modern understanding of what actually is. You can't apply modern thinking to a first-century or BC writing. Their idea of certain things was not fully developed. This does not make their writings unholy or false or deceptive. The scriptures are still the written Word of God.

Consider the scientific concept of light years was not understood yet. In space, with how light travels, we will not see it coming before it's too late. If light from a distant star or galaxy reaches us thousands or millions of years after it left that location, then what we see in the sky is from long ago. We do not see what is now occurring in the night sky. The galaxies and stars are either moving or missing. They might have already been destroyed with fire, but how would the inhabitants of the earth know it?

One thing to keep in mind is that the night sky gives the false illusion that all is at peace, but behind "the veil of the past," the heavens could very well be in chaos all around us in the deep. We on earth just can't see it yet. So, are the stars even still there? Have they moved? Are the constellations still in place? It is easy to look up and say yes. How would anyone know when we stare at a distant past and not at how it actually is now?

The stars deep in space are not where they seem to be. The light we see coming from those galaxies and stars left thousands or millions of years ago. With the passing away, it might soon be revealed, and frighteningly so, the swift changes in the heavens that have already or are currently taking place. We just don't see behind "the veil of the past." Again, people rely too much on their natural eyes and not faith.

Another consideration is a dual fulfillment of a solar and lunar eclipse just before the revelation of the designated black hole to change the view of the heavens that causes them to "split apart like a scroll when it is rolled up, and every mountain and island were moved out of their places". In this case, it is not meteors, but stars that move in the heavens caused by the great force of a mega, super massive black hole.

CHAPTER 21
The Two Hands

Consider for a moment that if the Word of God up to this point has come to pass, then we are at the passing away of heaven and earth. It is already underway. What is to come is judgment. The door to salvation is quickly closing. No more millennia, no more centuries, only decades are left. The effort of environmentalists and organizations to save the earth is then futile and in vain. The Lord has spoken, and there is extinction underway with perhaps a remnant of people and animals left.

Who can turn back His Word? Who can change His mind? Who can make His Word void and empty? There is no time left for everything that futurists teach to happen: the millennial reign, rebuilding the temple with a beast to come in, a tribulation followed by both a solar and lunar eclipse in Jerusalem, Gog and Magog coming against Israel, or Armageddon. This surely is not the new heaven and earth as full preterists believes. Many are asleep in regard to those things fulfilled prophetically and those things in the earth in the natural that are quickly deteriorating.

There are two ways to look at this and question or argue about this crisis we are in as it worsens over the coming decades.

The One Hand

On one hand, as stewards and as children who will inherit the new earth, some Christian churches are saying that the body of Christ should be doing more to save earth and the life on it. Why are so many other churches opposed to and critical of the cause of environmentalists? Why is little to nothing said against the poachers, black markets, abusers, and those who kill for sport and profit? What about the pollution and destruction humans have caused? God saved animals through Noah. God remembers them in the fourth and tenth commandments by protecting them and giving them rest.

There's a priority of humanity over creation and understood since we have more value than animals do. But does this priority come at the exclusion and indifference for creation? Christians believe we are stewards of those things He has given us, and Yeshua gave back the dominion that Satan stole from us. The righteous and the meek shall inherit the earth, and creation is redeemed through Yeshua too, but little to nothing is done to help creation. We worship, adore, and praise the Creator, but we show little to no love for His creation, which is in great peril right now. How does one love a Creator but show little concern over earth, His footstool? How does one love a Creator but have little to no regard for creation that is groaning in pain and faces extinction?

How can He condemn and "destroy those who destroy the earth" if His very own people on this earth have contributed to and use—either directly or indirectly—forms of fossil fuels, landfills, and sewer systems. He has answered, granted, and honored the prayers and petitions of His people who in some way, directly or indirectly, to one degree or another, involve fossil fuels. How can He judge us for using it when there is no commandment or warning not to? Where there is no law, there is no sin. He doesn't send prophets or angels to warn against it. No ideas or wisdom was given shortly after the industrial age began on how to prevent this, but would we have listened to Him anyway? He knew this was going to happen. For example, what happens when one must drive a car or ride in a plane to preach the Gospel in another city or country?

Are fossil fuels one of those things that "are permissible, but not beneficial" or "all things are lawful, but not all things are profitable or edify" because He is silent on the issue, and there are no kingdom laws against its use (1 Corinthians 6:12; 10:23)? The impression is that it is permissible for a certain time of a certain era, but it is not preferable or beneficial in the long run.

Paul wrote, "Let no one seek his own good, but that of his neighbor" (1 Corinthians 10:24). Some Christians who want to change our source of energy would ask, "How have those richer countries sought the good of the poorer countries? How can we, as believers, say, 'I want gas in my car!' at the peril and condemnation of other countries that are in the middle of the climate crisis? Aren't we seeking our own good and not that of our neighbor?"

Some Christians say, "Humans are of more value than animals," and another group of Christians says, "Think of your fellow poor brother or poor neighbor who suffers and cries as the wolf is at his door because you want gas in your car. Where is the concern, the love, for the neighbor you are commanded by God to love? If not for creation, think of the misfortune of your neighbor. Love your brother afar off for whom Christ died for and neighbor and brother who is nearby. We help after disaster strikes, but should we also help as a steward to lessen the blow?"

Yeshua said in so many words that more will be given to he who is faithful with little than he who is faithful with much (Matthew 13:12; 25:28, 29; Mark 4:25; Luke 19:26). If we can show Him that we are faithful with the little that is left with the little time that is left, He can entrust us with the new earth.

There is a new earth, but if we can't care and act for this one (with the little that remains on it and with the short time left of it) what responsibility, power, authority will God give us over the new one? If we show Him that we take this one for granted with little regard for our poor brothers who we are commanded to love, how can He entrust us with much more? How do we inherit a new one when we participate in the destruction of the present one with unbelievers? We shouldn't be counted as one whom God will destroy or in the least (since we are saved by grace) given little on the new earth because of what we are doing or fail to do now.

If we don't do anything for creation or for our neighbor or our brothers in the Messiah, then do it because this is His footstool. He worked six days to create this for humankind, and we, as His children, should not take His gifts for granted.

If there is any good deed done (visit His people in prison, visit His people who are sick, cook food, clean and wash, run a business, spread the Gospel, and do so many things in His name), there are fossil fuels involved to some degree. He prospers many who use them. I heard one man write about how there are automobiles in His very own storehouse! There is also trash produced by the body of Christ. Sin is one thing, but pollution is another. How can He spare one group for using fossil fuels and condemn another who uses them too? At the same time, He will not destroy the righteous with the wicked. If one person does something small, and everybody is doing something to help (however small it is), it really helps in the big picture.

Should God's people argue among themselves about this? Should we be divided?

On The Other Hand

On the other hand, is it God's will to prevent the passing away and save the earth? Or is it to fulfill His Word and let it go into extinction? Are we to oppose the Word of the King and say He's wrong or line up to His will and say it will happen? If the decree or Word of the King has gone forth, who can stop it? Who can nullify what God has spoken and make it void? Any act of opposition to His Word is futile and vain.

With the little time the earth has left, what can the body of the Messiah do since the King spoke in Psalms, Isaiah, and the Gospels that heaven and earth would pass away? Would it be in vain? It is inevitable; the climate of heaven and earth is going to run away and humans won't be able to bring it back to stable, safe, clean, and livable conditions for all life. Since He has spoken and the Word of the King has gone out, it is going to happen. The implication in Yeshua's words, "Heaven and earth will pass away," says that He knew that humankind would understand it too late. Humankind will not believe, and some of them will even mock it. The crisis is now.

What scientists are discovering just confirms what God spoke ages ago. Anyone who does not believe the truth doesn't believe His Word that everything will perish. God is not subject and bound by the laws He created for nature, including the laws of physics and gravity. He is above and outside these laws that scientists are beginning to understand. If people don't believe this, they will never understand how God does miracles, signs, or wonders. They will think the events in the Bible are fiction and fables.

We pray about personal matters in our own lives that are important to Him. We pray for salvation and deliverance from all kinds of bondage and death. We pray for salvation from hell. We don't pray about this matter, and we need salvation and deliverance in this too. This is the eight hundred-pound gorilla in the room. No one really takes a look at it in the body of Christ. We trust God and pray about it, but we don't think about the other matters that affect and concern us.

If believers were in a sinking ship or burning building from which there was no way out, would His name be called on in prayer, His face sought, and His wisdom/direction requested—or would they just trust God and sit back and do nothing? If one loses their job, they don't just sit back and not pray or do nothing and trust God. They pray, they seek, they knock, they go forth, they inquire, they follow God's guidance, and they act. The truth of God is confirmed with His power. If one is a true believer in Yeshua, they will recognize the truth and the hand of God.

So, no matter what hand, in the least, prayer should be made to God—even if there is nothing we can actually do today. God can preserve His people, those who have faith and trust in Him. Whatever He tells us to do, we should be careful to follow it. We should act according to His Word. We must be ready to act in faith to whatever He commands or directs us to do for the remaining time here—in preparation to leave earth (migrate) or help others—be they people or creation. We need to get ready; the tide is coming in quickly. Don't set your hearts on possessions or money. Where there are no resources, money is useless and becomes worthless because there is nothing to sell or buy. Billions of dollars can be worthless where there is nothing to buy or sell that is necessary for life. God has to become the focus more and more as the natural begins to be stripped away. He is salvation for us today.

What do we pray?

- His salvation and deliverance from this,
- wisdom to get prepared,
- that our eyes and ears be opened by the Holy Spirit so we can see God's kingdom,
- His provision of necessary resources that the earth is too weak or unable to provide for His sheep to live here for as long as He wills us to live here until He decides to remove us,
- not to allow the righteous to suffer and be destroyed with this,
- that His holy name be glorified and be renowned in the world among His people because they notice a mighty presence in the midst of the people who cares for them and provides,
- that redemption from this place will happen because there is really no place to migrate to,
- that He would reveal Himself to the Jews and Christians because we need Him now,
- His comfort and encouragement.

As the world despairs, God is becoming more and more present for His people, and with the outpouring of His Spirit, we will see His face. We will see His salvation. Something great is occurring now: a visitation of a great King.

CHAPTER 22
A Warning from Two Signs

How do you prepare for the unthinkable? As journalist Matthew Todd put it, "We face a reality so terrible no one can comprehend it." We must understand the present reality of how His Word has found its place in fulfillment.

> The field is ruined, the land mourns; for the grain is ruined, the new wine dries up, fresh oil fails. Be ashamed, O farmers, wail, O vinedresser, for the wheat and the barley; because the harvest of the field is destroyed. The vine dries up and fig tree fails; the pomegranate, the palm also, and the apple tree, all the trees of the field dry up. Indeed, rejoicing dries up from the sons of men. (Joel 1:10–12 NAS)

Should we humble ourselves even as the priests did of long ago, but in the fear of the Lord's presence?

> Gird yourselves with sackcloth and lament, O priest; Wail, O ministers of the altar! Come, spend the night in sackcloth O ministers of my God, for the grain offering and the drink offering are withheld from the house of your God. (Joel 1:13)

But with the smile of His countenance and the sound of His voice, rejoice for the bridegroom has come! We can also draw encouragement from Joel 1:14–20:

> When I heard, my whole body trembled, my lips shook at the sound; weakness overcame my limbs, but I wait calmly for the day of trouble, when it comes upon our assailants. For even if the fig tree doesn't blossom, and no fruit is on the vines, even if the olive tree fails to produce, even if the sheep vanish from the sheep pen, and there are no cows in the stall; still, I will rejoice in ADONAI, I will take joy in the God of my salvation. ELOHIM Adonai is my strength! He makes me swift and sure-footed as a deer and enables me to stride over my high places (Habakkuk 3:16–19 Complete Jewish Bible)

An event or true story can be a sign for a person, group of people, nation, or the world. Jonah and the fish was a sign and a warning of things to come for the nation of Israel. Three days and nights in the belly of the fish was a sign to Yeshua's generation of His imminent death and resurrection:

> But he answered and said to them, an evil and adulterous generation craves for a sign; and yet no sign will be given to it but the sign of Jonah the prophet; for just as Jonah was three days and three nights in the belly of the sea monster, so will the Son of Man be three days and three nights in the heart of the earth. The men of Nineveh will stand up with this generation at the judgment, and will condemn it because they repented at the preaching of Jonah; and behold, something greater than Jonah is here. (Matthew 12:39–41)

Yeshua is seen in the stories of a few men of the Bible. Joseph, Moses, and even Samson, though men with fault, represent Yeshua in their life stories. Many see Joseph and Moses as a type of deliverer, but not many speak of Samson too.

Joseph, an unfamiliar brother to his Hebrew brothers due to his Egyptian dress and language, was jailed and in prison for something he didn't do. He also dressed as a Gentile and a deliverer from starvation across the land.

Moses, at one time in his life dressed as an Egyptian, and he was a deliverer of the Hebrews through the Red Sea. Moses and Samson delivered the Hebrews during a time of oppression under Gentile rule. Yeshua came to His people during the people's oppression under Roman rule.

Samson was a judge and deliverer of his people from the Philistines. He was captured and jailed, and he died taking many Philistines with him. The way Samson fought off the Philistines on his own represents how Yeshua fought off the spiritual enemies on His own with the power of the Holy Spirit. Samson killed a thousand Philistines with the jawbone of a donkey, and Yeshua cast out a legion of demons with only a word.

Samson's blindness could represent the curse Yeshua took upon Himself for our sake, and it also represents His separation from His Father in heaven. The way Samson took down his enemy by being in the enemy's camp is how Yeshua did it. Yeshua's death put Him in the enemy's camp to take the keys of death and Hades.

Samson's death in the Philistines' territory brought down the Philistine walls with a great crash, and Yeshua's death brought down the enemy's walls with great shaking and a crash. An earthquake occurred the moment He died. Samson's weakness represents Yeshua's weakness when He took upon Himself the sins of the world, becoming a curse for us. It marked Him and put Him in death's path.

If you know you can deliver yourself out of a situation and refuse in order to save others, it is a type of suicide. Where there is sin, there is death. Samson's suicide is like Yeshua's "suicide." He willingly laid down His life, but if He wanted to, He could take it up again. He refused to. The Jews of His generation had Him jailed and killed, but He also laid down His life so others could live. He could have easily saved Himself.

All three Hebrew men married Gentile women, and Yeshua made a covenant with Gentiles and included them in His flock of Jews. Yeshua was in the story of these men of God. Yeshua is also in *Titanic* and *Schindler's List* in different ways.

The coming judgment and the crisis that is currently underway all over the earth runs parallel to two events that occurred in the last century. There are similarities of these two events with the judgment in the Bible. One is *Titanic* and the other is *Schindler's List*. Adonai is telling us something through these two tragic events. The signs earth is giving and these two events are a warning from Him: no more millennia, no more centuries, only a few decades at best, which are merely minutes to Adonai.

The inhabitants of earth have merely minutes in His time before they are called to account before His throne. Humans challenge nature and God and wind up losing. Nature is in the hands of God. According to the prophecy of the passing away, there is a death sentence for heaven and earth. The neck is in the noose.

Titanic

Planet earth and the world are like *Titanic*. The few lifeboats are Yeshua—a humble lifeboat—and the other ship, *Carpathia,* or America , are the kingdom of heaven. The life jackets are the Gospel of His kingdom, and either people receive the life jacket or reject it. As the lifeboats hang on the ship almost unnoticed by the passengers who live their lives until there is great peril, so too the inhabitants of the earth fail to recognize a visitation of Yeshua until their lives are in danger. There were signs of the presence of icebergs in the ocean—the smell and the calmness of the waters—yet no icebergs were seen nearby. Though unseen, they were in the area like a thief in the night just like Yeshua.

Even when I think about the Crusaders who in the pride of their hearts came against Jerusalem and the Jews, and Gog and Magog came against Yeshua, the Rock who wasn't far from them. They went straight toward Him, and without regard for the signs of a presence, they hit the Rock and had great peril and trouble because of it. In the end, many of them died in an ocean of battle around Jerusalem. They were unaware they had hit a type of iceberg, Yeshua, and they went down in the first and second death for it. Yeshua did not move or go anywhere, but they did. He brought them down for allowing deceit, sin, and pride to go up against the apple of His eye.

What was it that earth or humankind hit? They are hit with a type of rock, an iceberg, which some see as fossil fuels—but it can be seen as Yeshua as well. He isn't moving, but He breaks those who fall on Him and crushes those upon who it falls.

While the iceberg is the death of people in one generation at the beginning of the industrial age, it is life for a limited time to another latter generation with the towing of the remaining icebergs to supply fresh water to the people of several countries that face water scarcity. *Wasn't Yeshua the rock in the wilderness who pours out water for the people to drink as the iceberg does? Isn't He like an iceberg that can bring a lofty ship down to the bottom and can also give life? He wounds, but He heals too. Yeshua doesn't move, as the iceberg hardly moves, but He has been there a long time.* Is it that He is in the way or that the world goes full speed ahead not paying attention or correctly reading the signs of His presence or the time in the prophecy we are in. Many are listening to teachers who are in error, telling them what they want to hear and not the truth that is at the door.

The pride of humans goes against God and nature, bringing them down to the deep in the end. The servants and officers on the ship are the watchman sent by God who see the danger and begin waking passengers up and get on their life jackets. They try to get people ready to get off the ship. It's time to leave someway, somehow, but there are only a few lifeboats.

Many reject the life jacket or Gospel because they believe they don't need it. It is nonsense to them—or it is not fashionable and out of date. They don't realize how serious it is; they don't believe the ship can sink and people are overreacting. Many don't believe the earth can be destroyed and think it can recover someway and somehow. They don't understand the damage that has been done to the ship. It cannot recover from the water, or CO_2, pouring into it. They even try to use buckets to get the water out, but it is too late.

Those on the bottom of the ship are the poor, undeveloped countries. They have no cushion and feel the devastation first and the most. They are in despair and begin to flee to the higher parts of the ship, away from the danger, hence the mass migration occurring in Africa, the Middle East, and South/Central America.

Those on the top of the ship have a cushion; they are the rich, developed countries. The rich don't feel it as much. There is very little shaking and rumbling, but they resume their daily activities, parties, dinners, work, and shopping as though nothing is happening. They scoff and say, "Not even God can sink this ship!" or "This earth is indestructible!" As the poor try to go to safety, the rich try to keep them out of their areas and out of their lifeboats, condemning them to peril and destruction.

Just as the airtight doors of *Titanic* were closed shut, we must enter through the door, Yeshua, or we will be left outside knocking and asking to come up from the bottom of the ship. Once the door is shut, it won't be opened again—or He can't be reached.

Who is the captain? The leaders of the world are already—or will be—at a loss about what to do, just as Captain E. J. Smith was upon realizing the enormity and severity of what was going to happen in a very short time. For refusing the King's invitation and rejecting the life jacket, they will go down with the ship. Leaders will become indecisive, confused, and fearful of what to do. Just as this was the captain's first catastrophe of this great scale, it will be the world's first great catastrophe. Unlike the captain though, by the time they realize they need to come to a full stop, it is too late. The catastrophes will force them to stop everything.

As many refuse the life jackets and fail to get on the lifeboats (Yeshua), many perish for not accepting the Gospel and being covered by Yeshua, the lifeboat. There are no more lifeboats. Just as there are few lifeboats, few will be saved and many will perish—just as Yeshua said in the Gospels. Those who perish, just as it was in Noah's day and in Lot's day, will understand too late. The door has been shut on them. There is no more salvation; they do not have oil in their lamps. They did not believe; therefore, they did not prepare.

Earth's fate is sealed as it was written in the prophecies. They try to reverse the ship, shut the dampers, and use no coal to avoid crashing. Just as they tried to save *Titanic* from sinking, some try to save the earth as parts of it—islands and coastlands—go underwater as sea levels rise. Just as they tried to delay the sinking, some will try to delay the inevitable.

Just when we think we are doing great with alternative forms of energy (or the use of steam on the *Titanic* as the alternative to using coal, a fossil fuel) there is a realization. The pressure and stress of seawater entering *Titanic* is like the stress we have put on the earth finally bringing it to a breaking point—the point of no return.

The birth pangs are just unbearable now. And just as *Titanic* moaned and groaned under the pressure of incoming seawater, so the earth too moans and groans. Something has to give. And just as the bulkhead of compartment 6 collapsed in *Titanic*, everything in heaven and earth, in the presence of Adonai, will collapse. This is when the panic from the world sets in.

There will be some who turn back to destruction against the Word of the Lord even after hearing the Gospel, thus the dead with life jackets. These say, "Lord, Lord," but they are lawless or fall back without ever really getting on the lifeboat. Could it be that the grids across the globe go down just as the grid did on *Titanic,* turning off all power?

This world has plunged into great darkness of a natural and spiritual kind. The people fleeing from one end of the ship to the other end as *Titanic* tilts and slips into the ocean could represent mass migration to safety, far from the disaster at the opposite end of the ship, which we see as mass migration today. People are fleeing their home countries where there are catastrophes and disasters and are trying to reach safety. They flee by the thousands even as those of *Titanic* fled. Eventually, just as the ocean swallowed the entire ship, so too the threat of death will fall upon all the rich and poor, the young and old, male and female, and every Jew and Gentile from every nation as earth fails.

The ocean is either a type of baptism or a type of lake of fire. Many people, just like in Noah's time, won't make it because they do not believe and will act too late.

Yeshua shines the light out upon the expanse of the deep waters and shouts, "Hello, is anyone out there? Can anybody hear me?"

The people are dead; they do not see His light or hear His voice. There was no faith in the truth. They will call and cry out to Him for help, but they refuse to give up their sins, which weigh them down and keep them from getting into the lifeboat even after hearing the Gospel.

The weight of sin gives death right over them. The door is shut. He will not answer to those who weren't ready, who refused to go to His feast. Just as *Titanic* disappeared into the sea, the earth disappears into the heat and fire as it was written by Peter. As *Titanic* was a tiny speck in the middle of a vast ocean, so earth is a mote of dust in outer space with no help coming.

The humble lifeboat is Noah's ark; the humble cross is Yeshua. Do we despise the humble lifeboat (Yeshua, the sacrifice) who is so near to us and is able to get us to safety? Just as the lifeboats were the only way for people on Titanic to be saved, Yeshua is the only way to be saved. Cling to the cross, your lifeboat, the ark, the Messiah. Many will seek what the Gospels said about Him, and perhaps in panic, chaos, and with violence, they will try to enter the kingdom.

The lifeboats were only halfway filled for almost the same reasons people reject the Gospel of the kingdom of God. They prefer to stay on something they know that is strong and well-built. Why leave the ship to go on a rinky-dink, humble lifeboat? Why leave the world they know for something that is unseen and practically a fairy tale. Yeshua is a crutch. They don't want to leave their husbands or wives or families. Their families are worth more to them than the kingdom, or they love their families more than the kingdom. They were told it was no emergency and that it was not really bad. They did not get on the lifeboats because they didn't understand or believe the urgency was real. The same people don't take Yeshua seriously; they procrastinate because everything in life is going well for them. Their family members may influence their decisions or put pressure on them not to believe the Gospel of the kingdom. If they take it seriously, they are fanatics or are going overboard.

The people on the lifeboats had bread to eat. Could this represent the bread of heaven we eat? Those of us who are saved in the lifeboat, are we to quickly rejoice while witnessing disaster and the death of many? Did Noah rejoice hearing all the cries and screams of those dying in the ocean? Will we be held in awe at the sight? Silence will dominate and be profound, not rejoicing.

Many will drown and perish in the sinking ship or the ocean, being pulled down with the suction the ship causes. Upon reaching *Carpathia* or American soil, many will inquire of the names on the list or the Lamb's book of life—whether their loved ones made it in or not. Those on the list are those who were saved through the water (like Noah's family) and saved through Yeshua. They will find out that their other loved ones' names were not found in the Lamb's book of life. It will be a time of rejoicing and sorrow, bittersweet and traumatizing. Yet unlike *Titanic*, the survivors' fate is one of blessed future for believing—not one of shame and regret.

The storyline James Cameron wrote into the movie, what he made up, represents part of what is true. Just as Jack, a character with fault, was poor, falsely accused, and jailed for having something of great value, Yeshua—a man who had nothing to lay His head on—was falsely accused of several things and jailed for claiming something of great value. He was King of the Jews and had a kingdom. Just as Jack died so that Rose could live and get into the boat, so Yeshua died for us sinners so that *we could live and get into the boat and be saved in Him. He died so that we could live through water.* Just as Rose called out almost too late, and the boat almost passed her by, if we take the whistle and cry out while there is still time, He will turn around and save us if it is not too late. Time is running out quickly.

Another way to see what it could also represent is just as *Titanic* sank into the depths of the Atlantic Ocean, so too much of the heavens and the earth could sink into the depths of a super massive black hole with its many fiery stars if this is how destruction with fire is to happen.

This is a reminder of Noah's ark and how the same water that killed the world only saved a few. It is another sign of baptism. I believe that in the story of *Titanic*, He is reminding and warning us. Yeshua and we are in the story, the true events of *Titanic*. Yeshua is the iceberg and the lifeboat. *Titanic* is earth, the ocean is a black hole. *Titanic* is our story.

Schindler's List

The Holocaust was an evil time—a curse across the land for Jews and Gentiles. Both the victims and the persecutor were cursed. Those who cursed the Jew were cursed themselves. The tide of death swept across the land, and Hades opened wide its mouth. An evil tree took root and spread its poison across the land. Egyptian and Hebrew slavery, persecution under the four kingdoms of Daniel, the Crusades, and the Holocaust are evil trees. They entangled everyone they came across, ensnaring many, and with no deliverer, they perished. Death comes as a tide and no one can keep it from coming. If you are in its path, you perish. Without knowledge (and even faith), the people perish.

The Holocaust is a sign to us. People mainly talk about what happened from a historical standpoint, focusing on the natural side of it, but there is a spiritual meaning to and warning from the Holocaust. I believe God allowed it to happen to warn us of what is to come after this life. The deceived will perish, those without a shepherd will perish, and those who did not pay attention to the signs will perish without hope and a deliverer. This is true for both the Jew and the Gentile. We should be horrified and angered about what happened historically, but we should also be horrified and angered about it spiritually. The Holocaust represents hell—except hell is greatly magnified and eternal.

In the Holocaust, who did Hitler and the Nazis represent? They could represent Satan, demons, fallen angels, other entities, death, curse, and a "living" fear who are delusional in their loyalty to their evil, wicked leader. Hitler's suicide with a bullet to the head could represent Yeshua's crushing Satan's skull with His foot or even the sword of the Spirit.

Their speeches were lies and deceit to lure and trap humans in the pit of gas and fire. The gas chambers and crematoriums were hell or Hades. As it was in the Holocaust, so it was in hell/Hades. There is hunger, starvation, disease, worms, unquenchable thirst, darkness, hopelessness, tears, fear, no air, a terrible stench, strange clinging insects, nakedness, great weakness, screaming, and weeping. In their weakness, there was little to no rest.

Just as it was done to many people in the Holocaust, all material goods are taken away from humans when they die. No one can take possessions when they go to heaven or hell. Possessions are destroyed or stolen, never to be touched or seen by the person again. All memories associated with those possessions disappear. God is not there to deliver anyone. There is separation from God and all the good gifts He gives.

There is a question that was asked during the Holocaust and the temple's destruction in AD 70: "Where is God? Why doesn't He save and help me?" Many believers and Jews today don't talk about Holocaust this way because they don't see it as a sign or warning from God. There is shortsightedness, a failure to not make the connection between them.

Schindler was known as a thief. Yeshua comes like a thief in the night. Schindler was a gentile, but wasn't Joseph and Moses thought to be a gentile at first by the Hebrews? Schindler's paying of money to save more than a thousand Jewish people during World War II from certain death during the Holocaust is like Yeshua's payment with His blood to redeem us from death and have our names written in His book. Those who pleaded for the salvation of their loved ones by bringing their names up to Schindler are those who have prayed and petitioned King Yeshua for other's salvation. Schindler gave water to Jews suffering from heat in the trains; Yeshua gives living water to whomever thirsts and asks Him.

The names of the few Jews who were called and chosen out of death to work in his factory for a price represent those who were called, have come to believe in Him, and are chosen out from death to live under the shadow of His wings and live in His kingdom with the price of His blood. There is hope, relief, and joy as the saved Jews walk through the factory's gates just as the called and chosen will walk through the gates of His kingdom. How grateful and appreciative are those who enter His kingdom. Those of us who are safe in the factory, are we to quickly rejoice while witnessing many being led away to death with fire? Did Lot rejoice hearing all the cries and screams of the cities being consumed in flame? Will we be held in awe at the sight? What silence will pervade in the midst of us?

The factory was a haven where no one died, and no one dies who enters His kingdom; it is a haven and a refuge. It is known that Yeshua is good. Schindler gave his entire fortune as a sacrifice to purchase Jews from certain death, and Yeshua gave his life with blood as a sacrifice to purchase all who believe from certain death.

Schindler's list was "an absolute good and was life," and Yeshua's book of names is "an absolute good and is life." As the lists of the names of traumatized and shocked survivors were bittersweet, so the Lamb's book of life is bittersweet. His book is the book of those who survived through Him to live. If one's name was not found in the book, that person didn't make it or wasn't chosen just as those who did not make it or weren't chosen by Schindler. He wished he could have saved more, but he couldn't.

The lists are sobering, sad, and joyous—and the Lamb's book is bittersweet. The Holocaust is the curse spoken of in Deuteronomy 28:15–68 coming to fulfillment, but it is also a sign to the generations to come after it. We should look at Holocaust differently. *It is God's voice speaking through the tragedy to us of salvation out of great darkness and death. He is in the story of the Holocaust. Yeshua is a type of Schindler. It is Yeshua's story. It is our story too. It is His sign and warning to all the inhabitants of the earth—not just for the Jews but for the Gentiles too.*

Yeshua rejoices over those who have come to His feast, but He is sorrowful over those who won't make it. He longs for more to come if they only believed and were faithful to the end. I can imagine it is bittersweet even for Him. As Schindler longed for more names on his list, Yeshua wants His hall and table filled. He must think, *How many are in My book? Could just one more come in and sit at My table with Me? No, I must fill my table!*

The Comparison

The stories of Joseph, Moses, and Samson as Hebrews among Gentiles represent Yeshua. Schindler was like Him in the story. Both of these tragic events depict the saved and the doomed. Both have a list of names of the few saved. Tragedy came to the rich, poor, young, old, male, female, Jew, and Gentile. People were living their lives until the dark hour. Their world stopped and grew dark. Desperation, despair, hopelessness, fear, confusion, panic, and uncertainty surrounded them like a cloud. They were without comfort or encouragement, not understanding what awaited them.

Many were forced to leave all they had and knew; all their worldly possessions were gone. Everyone was reduced to the same level in the face of death. In each case, the men were separated from the women and children. Death in one event came in the form of water and freezing cold; in the other, German soldiers had bullets, gas, torture, and burning ovens.

Death comes to the inhabitants of the earth in the form of hunger and thirst, drowning, burning, murder, exposure to elements, heat stroke, and disease. The collapse of order on the *Titanic* and in the ghettos as Jews were led out resembles the collapse of the environment, climate, governments, and economies in coming years.

In each of these stories, groups of survivors were relocated out of the area in which death had occurred to one where they could live. *These two events, along with the present deterioration of earth, are not a coincidence.* They are signs of what is to come and coincide with prophecy. God is warning us, but do we hear Him? Are we listening? Under whose shadow do we dwell? If one is found in sin, he is under the shadow of death. Without the covering of the blood of the Lamb, what will become of him? When He casts death into the lake of fire—and one is in death and not in Yeshua—what will become of him? Being in death, he is cast into the lake too. If one is in Yeshua and Yeshua is in Him, the fire cannot touch him. There is a spiritual and dimensional law at work here. Both represent what is happening and will continue to unfold in the coming decades as surely as God's Word is true.

In both stories, few people were saved. The *Titanic* not having enough lifeboats for everyone goes along the lines of "many are called, but few are chosen" (Matthew 22:14). Many on *Titanic* had a lifejacket, just as many through the millennia have heard the gospel, but many still drowned with their lifejackets on. So too, many perish having heard the gospel because they do not get into the lifeboat, they are not in Yeshua and Yeshua is not in them.

Just like Noah's arc, if we are not in the lifeboat, which could represent Yeshua, the water will kill. It is only when we are in Yeshua, who is like the arc and the lifeboat that water saves. This is what Peter meant in his letter that just as the arc brought the eight people, who were few, through the water, Yeshua brings us to God. Yeshua is the arc and lifeboat. He writes, "Baptism now saves you" (1 Peter 3:18–22).

Just as the Hebrews walked between the waters of the Red Sea and were saved, we are saved too. The same water that killed the Egyptians who pursued them saved the Hebrews. The Egyptians who followed them were destroyed by the same water. In the story of Noah and Moses, water was a witness *for the good* of the people who believed and obeyed. It was a witness *against those* who did not believe and were God's enemies. The Hebrews were in Him, or protected, by the Passover they recently partook of.

Out of water creation came into existence at the word of God; water gives life, but in and of itself does not save. Water apart from Him cannot save. In Him, water and fire cannot harm, they save. The same water that kills them saves us. The difference is Yeshua. He uses water for His purpose. The holy name of the Father, the Son, and the Holy Spirit is the difference. Apart from His Spirit and Name is destruction in water and fire. These elements must submit under Him and if we are found in Him, they cannot harm us, but He makes them work for our good. Water then is a witness for our good, but only because of His holy name which they are bound to submit to. It is Yeshua who causes fire and water to make the distinction between the holy and the wicked. To those who are His and those who are not. He places His holy name upon us so we are recognized and not harmed in the day of destruction. The flame and water does not recognize His enemies and destroys them. The flame and water recognize its Creator, and if we are in Him, it recognizes us.

It is true that apart from Him, water does not save. To say, contrary to Peter, that despite being in Him it does not save, is like saying He wouldn't do the same for us that He did for Noah, the Hebrews, Lot, or Daniel's friends. It is like saying He wouldn't cause the water and fire to make the distinction and therefore abstain from harming us. It will destroy us who believe in the day of destruction just like it did all His enemies. It is like saying that He will forsake us in the day of disaster, woe, and calamity. It is like saying water and fire will swallow us up and consume us despite our faith or despite His holy name upon us.

Remember the story of Shadrach, Meshach, and Abednego in Daniel 3:19–30? The same fire that saved them also destroyed those valiant warriors who increased the heat of the furnace and threw them inside. The only difference was Yeshua. Those three holy men were in Him and He caused them to be untouched by the flame in every way. The fire submitted to Yeshua, and therefore to the three holy men. That fire was a type of baptism and a witness for their good. Also, perhaps they prayed together and where three or more are gathered in His name, He was there with them to protect them and cause the fire to make the distinction before King Nebuchadnezzar that they are His servants and not to be destroyed. The fire testified on their behalf, but did not testify for the one's who threw them in the fiery pit. It was against them and killed them. It did not recognize them as belonging to God.

The lions in the den made the distinction with Daniel. As hungry as they were, they did not open their mouths against His servant. They submitted to the Creator's authority. However, the false accusers who sought Daniel's death, along with families, were torn apart and consumed by the lions. The lions did not recognize to spare God's enemies. The holy servants of God have a spiritual mark that sets them apart and nature recognizes it.

What does the story of the three holy men saved through the fire have to do with us? Current and latter generations are facing a destruction of heavens and earth with fire. We must have Yeshua's covering over us as a shield, a hedge of protection around us. The fire knows Him. He will cause the fire to speak for you to your benefit. The fire of His Spirit causes the fire of destruction to submit to Him and make the distinction between the holy and unholy.

I don't know about you, but I want water and fire to make the distinction with me in Yeshua and speak as a witness for my good, not for my destruction. I want them both to respond to me the same way it responded to His other holy servants who were saved from them by Yeshua. I don't want water and fire to just be powerless symbols to represent a meaning. In the day of destruction this is not what any believer should want or expect. There must be a powerful response by them to His name.

So let it be true the following Scriptures which to me suggest the power and witness of baptism:

- Isaiah 43: 1, 2, 16. "But now, thus says the Lord, your Creator, O Jacob, and He who formed you, O Israel, Do not fear, for I have redeemed you; I have called you by name; you are Mine! When you pass through the waters, I will be with you; And through the rivers, they will not overflow you, When you walk through the fire, you will not be scorched, nor will the flame burn you, For I am the Lord your God, the Holy One of Israel, your Savior."
- Psalm 66:12. "We went through fire and through water; Yet You brought us out into a place of abundance."
- Psalm 77:19, 20. "Your way was in the sea and Your paths in the mighty waters, and Your footprints may not be known. You led Your people like a flock by the hand of Moses and Aaron." Does he not do this today spiritually?
- Isaiah 51:10, 11. "Was it not You who dried up the sea, the waters of the great deep; who made the depths of the sea a pathway for the redeemed to cross over? The ransomed of the Lord will return and come with joyful shouting to Zion, and everlasting joy will be on their heads. They will obtain gladness and joy, and sorrow and sighing will flee away."

So am I saved by my works? No I am saved by His work. It is He who brings me through the water and fire causing them to submit under Him. You have to ask yourself if you can make the same statement Peter did, "Baptism now saves you", and leave it at that.

Sometimes there is an exception to dying in fire with martyrdom. Christians in the first century were burned alive at the order from the beast, Nero.

The same with *Schindler's List* where there was a limit to how many Schindler could add into his list to save—"many are called, but few are chosen". Likewise, from every generation, few will be saved, many will perish. These are Yeshua's words, how can we contradict Him?

In both stories, the men were separated from the women and children. Could this mean that many men will perish before the women and children do? In India, there are many women with children who are without husbands or fathers because many farmers are committing suicide. In Africa, it is mainly the men who leave to go to Europe or some other country to try to make a living, leaving the women and children behind. Sometimes, the men don't return and are assumed dead. The sign of the separation has already begun.

If God wills believers remain here to see the passing away, many believers may be traumatized by the worsening of events on this planet and saddened that many people they thought would make it into the kingdom perished. Just as the story of Noah and Sodom and Gomorrah tells us what is to come during a time when everyone is preoccupied with their own lives, these two stories tell us what is to come in the last few decades of this old earth.

There is a lesson that God wants us to learn from and prepare for. It is a warning to us of what is imminent. There are many who don't give a thought to the iceberg ahead or care if we even hit it. There are many who don't give a thought to the fiery ovens and hellish chambers they will be cast into. There are many who don't give a thought to their eternity because building, marrying, making money, buying, and selling are all they care about. This life is more important. All things carry on as usual. Nothing can stop or change what they want or plan to do. To those who don't know Yeshua, there is no lifeboat or escape. There is no other earth. He will cause the meek to inherit the earth.

This could be a time of testing and faith to purge and prune off the dead branches. Don't complain, don't forsake Him, and don't be like Israel in the wilderness. Look to him as a resource to provide your resources and obey Him. The time of humbling is at hand, and we are at His mercy. If you forsake Him, you will die and never see His promise. This extinction and destruction are the closing of the door for the preaching of the Gospel. Once closed, no more can be saved. It's done, finished.

Do you think the people during Noah's, Lot's, and Moses's days, when they were warned of impending danger, believed the flood or fire from heaven could ever happen? Did they believe God would part the sea before He actually did? The Jews of AD 70 could not believe the temple of God would be ransacked or that God would intervene and they would overcome the Romans. Their unbelief of the impending destruction of the city and temple was worsened by the false prophets who told them what they wanted to hear—that they would be victorious over the Romans. Instead of fleeing the city, they stayed, fought, and perished in the onslaught that ensued.

Some people on *Titanic* did not believe the ship could sink. There were like some Jews at the beginning of the Holocaust who could not believe the Germans were committing atrocities against their people. Could a people be so evil and malicious? Did they take the signs seriously? In all these events was found unbelief in a present reality that was hard to face.

God's time is not our time. A thousand years are like a day, a hundred like an hour, but what about decades? They could be like mere minutes to Him. While it took more than two hours for *Titanic* to take on water, the last one to three minutes of Titanic's sinking happened very rapidly. In these last few decades or minutes left of earth, collapse will occur rapidly. To Him, it is no time at all.

The time of an exodus is at hand from this dying land where believers in Yeshua were once slaves. The time is at hand of an exodus from a planet from which all life came out of the water. As Moses and the Hebrews walked through the waters as it parted and so God delivered them, so too we must leave this planet through the water of the air by God's hand. As Noah and his family drifted upon the waters and escaped death, so too we must get in the ark, in the cross, in the lifeboat to be saved. We must leave the cradle of human civilization—earth. We leave to go to a new land flowing with milk and honey—a promise land—the New Jerusalem upon a new earth in a new heavens. Upon this Zion, Jerusalem will never be surrounded and attacked by enemies again.

There is to be an exodus of a different kind. There is to come a harvest of His people, both sleep and awake. For such a time as this, He has been fulfilling the prophecy of the Jews return to Israel gathering them for a great and awesome deliverance just as He has done before in their history. He gathers them to save from impending destruction of both the planet and the heavens in which earth is contained. Will He cause the water and fire to recognize them once again as His holy people, to be unaffected, unmoved, and unharmed in any way? He will bring this about for the glory of His name. Nature, creation, the elements, and the laws that govern them will be lifted and once again they shall come to recognize all those who are His servants in every country who bear a great and holy name. For this great salvation of both Jew and gentile, He shall be made known and feared among the nations of our current world.

False prophets (like those of AD 70), super-positivity, warm fuzzies, feel-good messages, downplaying the severity of what is happening, and super optimism are not going to stand in the face of reality. Downplaying the severity of the Word of God will not stand or save us. This will not overwhelm this impending environmental destruction of our biosphere. This did not save farmers from losing their crops and flooding their fields. It did not save people from Harvey or the wildfires. This does not save people from climate catastrophes. This will not save from other various unforeseen disasters to come one after another to wipe out the world. We have to align ourselves with reality and with prophecy. Not doing so gets people in trouble as seen in the past. However, it is good to have faith and hope in God. It is good to seek His face and be encouraged by His Spirit.

Part II

A Visitation of a Different Kind

CHAPTER 23

The Witnesses: Body, Blood, and Spirit

In this part of the book, I share things that I think will be useful to know as the body of the Messiah. I hope these things will be edifying for the holy body during these days and years of global crisis, devastation, and extinction according to the will and Word of God. The following chapters speak of three witnesses of earth: blood, water, and the Spirit (the Word of God).

There's a visitation of a different kind that happens through a spirit's attachment to objects. It opens a portal to the spirit realm or heaven. Knowledge of the blood and body of Yeshua (Communion) and how it works by faith is the key that gives access into the presence of God, His kingdom, and the resources and provisions there.: "We have confidence (boldness) to enter the holy place by the blood of Yeshua" (Hebrews 10:19). Read also Ephesians 1:3; 2:6–9, 13–16. "And seated us with Him in the heavenly places in Christ Jesus" (see also Ephesians 3:10; 6:12).

Points of Contact or Bridges between Two Dimensions

The unspoken but understood dimensional law of points of contact in the Bible was practiced. The practice was never given a name or considered a supernatural law at work. *A point of contact is a link, a connection, a door, or a portal to the unseen dimension that the flesh cannot attain to.* It is a bridge between two dimensions. It is how spirits infiltrate this natural world and advance. It can be almost any object that turns "into a bridge to otherworldly realms." It allows change or transfer to happen between two realms or the atmosphere.

Our flesh limits us in this. In our case, it is a connection to the kingdom of heaven or the Father. It is like having a phone number. In many miracles, signs, and wonders, items were created out of nothing or multiplied. In many of the miracles, there was a small or certain amount of an item that multiplied or changed. It's almost as if the transfer from an unseen storehouse or a change could not happen unless there was an earthly contact—a way or a conduit to transfer or make something happen. It seems to be a law at work to allow exchange between two dimensions. It is a law that even God uses.

Many understand that Ouija boards, voodoo dolls, tarot cards, pagan shrines and altars with their unclean sacrifices, tea leaves, broken mirrors, and masks are evil and can permit spirits or entities to enter their dimension to attack and disrupt their environment. The story of the Jewish dybbuk box is another one. These unholy items are to the unsaved what God-established, holy contacts are to us. When people experiment and practice these things, they also have intent, an open mind, and an expectation.

When Achan took of the spoil after battle against the commandment of God and was found out, he was killed (Joshua 7). God knew there was a curse in the congregation—perhaps there was an unclean spirit attached to those objects he stole. He took "a beautiful mantle from Shinar and two hundred shekels of silver and a bar of gold fifty shekels in weight". These items could have been used in worship at an idol's temple. As Elijah's mantle had the power of Spirit on it, as Yeshua's hem had the power of Spirit on it, the apostle's garment or shadow had the power of Spirit on it, so too could this mantle have an evil power on it. Achan probably did not notice or detect it, but God saw this evil thing in the camp which could explain Israel's defeat and His anger. It was not only Achan's greed and disobedience that angered God, but his greed and disobedience could have opened the door to something evil entering into the camp of Israel and troubling it. Not many teachers see past the greed and disobedience. They don't make the connection of how disobedience can open doors to evil spirits and curses. Remember Adam and Eve's disobedience by eating the forbidden fruit opened the door for death to enter.

Points of contact can be open doors or have entities attached to them. They know these are dangerous to play with. They warn others to stay away from these. These are also points of contact because they open doors, gateways, or portals for entry and communication between dimensions. Somehow, this meaning for holy contacts was lost throughout the centuries in the church. Faith is stumped by others. Many believe with two hearts, not one.

Even God uses objects, but they are not images of His creation in heaven or earth. They are not chosen by humankind. The holy objects were not to be worshipped. They represent Him, and it is according to how He established it—not according to humans. Why would God be jealous over an object unless there was an entity attached to it? Why was one of the commandments against making an image to worship? It's so easy for humans to lose sight of this because we are sensual creatures. We seek the object—but not God's presence. He is behind the veil that caused the miracles, signs, and wonders to happen. There was much power in this point of contact between heaven and earth. God established these as a model of heaven above and also points of contact.

Through Yeshua (in the communal body and blood), there are things that currently take place as one takes it. It's not just something in the past. His body is a cleft in the rock and a refuge we hide in spiritually. His wings cover us, and we are in His shadow. This is how we are "in Him." When the Father sees us, He sees Yeshua—or He sees Him with us.

> Pleading the blood releases a spiritual cover that protects and delivers us ... However far your sphere of authority or blessing extends, apply the blood. No matter what, don't leave the protection (covering) the blood provides ... Don't ever walk away from the blood line. (*The Hidden Power of the Blood of Jesus*)

There are holy and unholy points of contact with the unseen world (John 6:32–35, 44–58; 10:9; 14:4–6; Luke 24:30–31). In Communion, the bread and wine are so much more than merely symbols that memorialize an important event, and we partake out of obedience. There is more meaning to this—a very powerful one. It is a major point of contact.

Throughout the Bible, there are several other points of contact. These include the altars built and their sacrifices (they were built after an appearance of the Lord; to petition the Lord; fire fell from heaven onto Elijah's altar at Mount Carmel), the widow and her small amount of oil, the loaves and fishes, anointing oil for healing, the water to make wine, the rock that spewed forth water from a rock, the burning bush, Aaron's rod, Samson's long hair, Elijah's mantle, the hem of Yeshua's garment, the high priest's ephod, the manna that appeared in the desert, the Passover lamb and blood on doorframes before leaving Egypt, when Yeshua was incarnate on earth, the Ark of the Covenant that struck men with cancer or dead if they came too close or blessed them greatly, and the water baptism into the name.

In Genesis 14:18, Melchizedek, the high priest of God Most High, brought out bread and wine. He brought out the presence. These were not just a meal to show friendship and hospitality, but as a king and priest too, he knew what these represented. In this one sentence, it says he brought out bread and wine and was a priest of God. *A priest should understand the unseen and the spiritual significance of the natural, hence faith.* There is a spiritual significance to what he was doing. It was deeper than a mere meal of hospitality and friendship or a symbol. We, as priesthood today, should also understand the spiritual significance of the natural. There is a power behind what is done by faith and in wisdom.

The Ark of the Covenant caused the idol to fall prostrate before it twice, breaking the hands off. At its arrival, the Jordan River parted, and the walls to the city of Jericho were weakened and fell down. A holy priest fell dead when he touched it. Usually people think of the Ark of the Covenant as detached from His world and one that had gold and symbolic items in it, but His Spirit was attached to it. The Ark was a conduit of sorts. The glory of God rested on it. It went into battle with them. The Israelites believed God walked among them when they saw it.

The ark alone would have no power unless His Spirit was attached to it. Without Him, it was just an object. It was not the object of earth alone, but what is behind the veil—in heaven, the unseen in the present time—the Spirit attached to it. Seek what the object represents in heaven. It was an amazingly powerful holy object. There was so much holy energy and power in the ark that it could not be destroyed, and it is possible that the ark simply vanished out of this physical world of earth into heaven. The Spirit or holy angels could have taken it away. Just as the Spirit snatched Phillip away from the Ethiopian, it most likely happened with the Ark. I don't believe anyone on earth possesses this holy, powerful ark.

It is also possible that as a contact or bridge between two realms, it still exists physically in a secret place within this earth until it will be revealed to Israel at the designated time. There is a report of it being discovered in Israel underneath the spot where Yeshua was crucified. If this story is true, then as Israel returns to the land, its discovery is a sign of a coming deliverance, salvation, and exodus from the impending extinction underway on the planet. I do not believe it is a sign of a coming beast with a mark.

Israel returns to the land just in time for its discovery and before life ceases upon the earth.

> Jeremiah found a cave dwelling; he carried the tent, the ark, and the incense altar into it, then blocked up the entrance. Some of his companions came to mark out the way, but were unable to find it. When Jeremiah learned of this, he reprimanded them. "The place shall remain unknown," he said, "until God finally gathers His people together and shows mercy to them. Then the Lord will bring these things to light again." (2 Maccabees 2:4–8)

An idol by itself is nothing. The demons people seek and worship through the idol as a contact are unseen. Some Christians who do not believe demons haunt or possess houses and things—only people and animals—forget about the ark and idols. They forget Deuteronomy 7:25–26 and 1 Corinthians 10:16–22. Spirits become attached, or portals are opened. Idols bring a visitation of darkness, curse, and evil into a natural, earthly space. Hence, the second commandment in Exodus 20:4 (NKJ):

> You shall not make for yourself any carved image, or any likeness of anything that is in heaven above, or that is in the earth beneath, or that is in the water under the earth; you shall not bow down to them nor serve them. For I, the Lord your God, am a jealous God, visiting the iniquity of the fathers on the children to the third and fourth generations of those who hate Me, but showing mercy to thousands, to those who love Me and keep My commandments.

God knew that spirits attach to objects. Those objects and images are the doorway into our natural dimension. The object itself is nothing, but with an entity attached, it changes the atmosphere and causes curses or devastation. God sees this abomination in the midst of people who worship it. When it is His own people, He is jealous. He is jealous not of the object but of the entity coming through it. The Israelites were to destroy, break, and burn these idols to close the door to them.

Out of the ark, the water, and the bread and wine, only two apply to us today: the water and bread/wine. Why establish three witnesses if their testimony has no power or weight? God is not a vain God to establish powerless witnesses with an empty testimony. A powerful God does not establish powerless witnesses that can do nothing but symbolize.

The Body and Blood of Yeshua

Some believe the presence of Yeshua is contained in the bread and wine, but there is no mention of any connection to the unseen realm. They don't deny that it is the body and blood; they believe it is. They believe His presence is within it by faith. They may believe it turns into flesh and blood after they eat it. They view it only from an earthly view, which seems a limited view or limited faith. There has to be a way to make the double heart only one heart, one faith. There has to be a way to make the limited faith much greater. Each must tap into the unseen realm in heaven and on earth.

Yeshua said, "As the serpent was lifted up, so I will be lifted up and draw all men to myself." Some believe in focusing on what happened in the past on earth. It's not about just picturing Yeshua on a cross in the past, which is not wrong; it's about the now in present time in heaven before the Father. *His death on a cross two thousand years ago activated or released the power that permeates the atmosphere on earth and in heaven.*

"Your will be done on earth as it is in heaven" (Matthew 6:10; see also John 3:12–15; 8:21–28; 12:32–36; Acts 1:2, 9–11; Luke 24:50, 51). He was not only lifted up on a cross on earth; he was also lifted up into heaven to go to the Father. Many only understand this from the seen, natural earthly view of His death on the cross. They don't connect this to the unseen, heavenly view. This is where faith must be used (Hebrews 11:1–3; see also 2 Corinthians 4:18).

One's faith should join with what happens presently and with what happens in the unseen realm of heaven. It should not be just any white yeast bread and any red Kool-Aid or drink.

The Hebrews ate unleavened bread because they were in a hurry and couldn't wait for it to rise, but what about the priests who ate unleavened bread and drank the fruit of the vine in the temple for centuries and weren't in a hurry? God specifically commanded His holy priests to eat unleavened bread and have it as the presence in the Holy Place. He says, "Be holy, because I am holy." He did not order or make exceptions to any yeast, which represents sin or evil, in the bread. If you believe Yeshua is sinless and without any form of evil, then let it be represented in the bread/body you consume. Let God's will be done on earth as it is in heaven. If the priests who served before God day and night obeyed the command to eat unleavened bread and drink the fruit of the vine (wine), and they weren't in a hurry, then as priests today, you should take this seriously and follow their example too.

If Yeshua would take it at the Last Supper, we should follow His example. No one can change or make an exception to anything God has commanded. You must follow the example given and obey the command of God, not seek to change it. You have no authority to change His Word; you are only the servant. You then limit people's faith and make them stumble.

Many don't understand that the unleavened bread and wine do the same thing that unholy objects do. This is a mystery. They reduce it to merely a powerless symbol to memorialize the death of our Lord. "Door" and "bread and wine" are not just metaphors.

Be careful to not be counted as one who has a form of godliness but deny its power (2 Timothy 3:5). The bread and wine can be very dangerous—just as dangerous as or more so than the unholy contacts. Paul said we should judge ourselves before eating it so we are not judged by Him and fall sick or die (1 Corinthians 11:23–31). If it doesn't have any power, then how are believers struck by Him for not revering a mere powerless symbol properly? This sounds like more than mere meaning and symbolism. It sounds like a contact.

Again, the Ark of the Covenant struck men with cancer or dead and blessed others. It is a very dangerous point of contact between the dimensions. How does a box containing mere symbols or earthly objects like a piece of wood, bread, and stones with words on them have any power to bless or curse? The ark was not just a metaphor without power. Perhaps there is a connection, link, attachment, contact, or door open from the unseen realm that makes things happen.

The bread and wine are the same as the Rock in the wilderness that followed the Hebrews; it is Yeshua's point of contact with us across dimensions. The Rock follows His people in this worldly wilderness in the form of unleavened bread and wine. Yeshua said, "When two or more gather in my name, there I am in the midst of them." Perhaps there was a point of contact; they took Communion at almost every moment they came together and prayed. The same is said for water baptism. Many believers know there is power in the blood shed on the cross of Calvary, and it is eternal and heals to this very day. The blood is spoken of and written about more than the body of Christ. One is not more important than another.

There was an altar where the blood was shed, but in the temple, there was no blood. In the temple, there was a curtain or door to go through unto the presence of God. They know that pagan methods of divination have an evil power or open doors for evil. However, they don't see the same for the bread and wine or water baptism or other kinds of contact in the Bible established by God, not humans, for us to use. It is to our benefit to understand and use faith to open the door to Him as His holy congregation.

Miracles, signs, and wonders have happened among believers, but so much more could happen in congregations with an understanding of this truth. "Faith is the substance of things hoped for, *the evidence of things not seen*" (Hebrews 11:1). If we only knew what is happening in heaven and earth when congregations partake of it together. There is a presence and powerful manifestation unseen because this is having a form of physical contact with Yeshua. On one side (earth), it is bread, wine, and water. We see this. On the other side (heaven or the unseen earthly realm), it is Yeshua physically resurrected and our cleansing in Him. We don't see Him. He is the door, the Rock that follows, the manna present every morning with us as it was for the Hebrews in the wilderness. It can be a point of constant, daily contact with Yeshua, the Lamb and King, and therefore to the Father if we want or need Him. It is only by the Holy Spirit we can see Him when He opens our spirits' eyes. This is where faith comes in. This is where the power is. Today, people only look at the earthly side and its meaning and deny that there's anything more to it.

Where is the faith? Where's the faith to believe what is not seen, that anything is happening whenever we eat His flesh and blood or get baptized? No one partakes of this with intent, faith, expectation, or an open mind. They partake knowing the meaning, remembering the story, and in thanksgiving, but there is nothing more—no power or manifestation. I don't see why His Spirit would not be attached to this earthly object of contact, which is the bread and the wine. He sends His Spirit to us for rebirth, to counsel, to teach, to comfort, to drive out darkness, and to fill the temple with the glory of God. Why wouldn't the Spirit also attach to the bread and wine that is on earth in our earthly dimension? It represents Yeshua, who is in the unseen realms, including heaven. He was attached to the ark as a point of contact.

Yeshua said the bread is His body and the wine is His blood. If the Master, the Head, said "This is," then as the servant and body, we should follow what He said and not change it. In faith, we should repeat after Him and say, "This is—so let it be on earth as it is in heaven/Amen." We should not say it is like, similar to, only a symbol, or just a metaphor. If it is good enough for Yeshua to say it, why can't we? Agree with Him. If it was good enough for priests in Exodus 29 to eat and drink daily before entry, then why isn't it good enough for priests today to eat and drink as often as they can before coming into the presence of the Father in heaven? Isn't it through Him you meet with God so He speaks to you? Don't explain it or Him away.

Yeshua, the sacrifice, is the door into the presence of the Father. The bread and wine do not turn into flesh and blood as we eat it or change its molecular composition to DNA, but it is our connection and link to His physical, resurrected body in heaven or the unseen dimension. It is the door. He is the door to the Father. The bread and wine are a connection to His presence.

We should also plead the blood over ourselves, our families, our homes, everything. He is the way to the Father and the way into the kingdom of heaven. Wherever you are and wherever He is—in heaven or on earth—we have His phone number. It is opening the door to Him every time we congregate. Even better, every time we formally meet, we go through Him in the spirit realm into the presence of the Father. We tap into a power that speaks and resonates in the unseen dimension by faith, which is the blood.

How are we priests if we don't know how to tap into the power of the blood of Yeshua, the sacrifice? How are we priests if we don't put the holy name on the people in baptism?

Spiritual Intake of His Flesh and Blood

John 6:27–69 and Matthew 15:27–28 are not metaphors. This is what you do in the spirit realm by faith. We are to feed off of Him in the spirit. He is our manna. His flesh is of His spiritual body, not natural body. Spirit consumes spirit. This is by faith. This is what the disciples who left Him did not understand because they could only see the natural and think cannibalism. They had no faith.

Yeshua is God in flesh. We should go to the scripture to hear its witness and learn from it; we should go to Yeshua to obtain life. How? We ask. By faith, we consume His flesh, drink His blood, eat of His fruit, and are covered under the shadow of His wings. We are hidden in Him, the cleft of the Rock in the spirit realm. Our spirits drink and eat differently than our bodies do. This is how we receive. When we have that expectation and are open to receiving from God, we automatically take in and consume. For our spirits, it is natural to do. We don't try to eat and drink. There is no effort—we just do it. For our spirits, it is as natural as breathing or digesting. It is as natural as a heartbeat.

Every person in the Gospels who was healed of diseases and delivered from evil spirits ate bread from heaven and drank of the river in the spirit realm, though the Holy Spirit was not poured out yet. They did a transaction or an exchange with Yeshua in the supernatural by faith. They did not see this exchange in the natural, only the result of it: the manifestation. *What started out in the spirit realm ended in the natural realm. They saw the result in the natural realm.*

When we read the Gospels, we see the results and manifestations in the natural realm. No one spoke of the exchange actually taking place in the spirit realm. It is an exercise of our spirits to see what happened behind the scenes. This is how mountains are moved. This is the same way attacks from evil spirits happen. They begin in the supernatural/spiritual realm and manifest in the natural as bruises, curses, or scratches. Some say it feels like it happens from the inside out. It starts where one's spirit is, and the results come forth in the natural realm.

The people of Israel, the children, and a few Gentiles were eating bread from heaven and drinking living water in the spirit realm as Yeshua took upon Himself their curses, sins, illnesses, and sorrows. These were put on His spirit back at that time. By faith, His blood still speaks over us to remove them. His blood removed these from those who were His in BC times. He became a curse for us. It was later manifested outwardly in the natural realm toward the end of His ministry. He became a man of sorrows and was acquainted with grief.

When we eat bread from heaven and drink His blood, we are in Him and He is inside us. We are in Him in the spirit realm; He is in us in this natural realm as we live our lives (see John 15:1–11). It is written, "Greater is He who is in you, than he who is in the world." (1 John 4:4). We go through Him, the door, to enter the presence of God, and He covers us in the spirit realm. Our spirits and souls are in Him; we consume His flesh, drink His blood, and stand in God's presence by faith when Communion is taken.

In Matthew 15:26–28, was Yeshua speaking of earthly bread or heavenly bread? Didn't Yeshua say she had great faith? It must have been heavenly bread. It was her persistence, humility, asking, and belief that Yeshua's body would heal and cast out evil. She had no Bible or scriptures in scrolls to cling to. She had faith in the Living Word who is Yeshua, and Yeshua was filled with the Spirit. In the supernatural, her spirit consumed bread from heaven and drank water. There was an exchange, and her daughter's spirit ate and drank, which resulted in her healing/deliverance in the natural realm.

"Seek first the kingdom of heaven (unseen/faith) and all these things (seen/food, clothing) will be added unto you." So, seek first what is unseen and above, and then the earthly and what is needed below will be given to you. Stop seeing the Communion meal as only a ritual. This is something "faith" teachers never teach people. Even they don't understand. This is the main, primary focus, and it's most important thing. It is more important than all the other things to have faith for (also read Hebrews 13:15; 10:19–25).

The resurrected saints of the first century who are with Him now do not need to partake of the bread and wine because they are in the same dimension with Him; we are not. We need that link, and we should partake of it until we are joined with Him where He is in the unseen realm of heaven.

Faith in Yeshua's death and resurrection activates the Communion. Yeshua's finished work on the cross activates the power in His blood and remains eternal with unseen power that causes physical and earthly manifestations—just like a nuclear bomb that gives off radiation many years after it has gone off. The act of setting it off was done, but the effects are felt and seen long afterward.

The blood is eternal. In faith, one taps into a radiating power that still resonates two thousand years later. The blood speaks today; it testifies. When anyone drinks radiation-contaminated water, the effects are seen—even though one does not see the radiation. The same applies with the blood of Yeshua. No one sees it, but its power is real and very present today. It crosses the dimensions. Just because you don't see it, that doesn't make it any less real or any less powerful in the act of Communion as a body. When one eats and drinks on earth, something happens in the spirit realm and in heaven. This is why Yeshua said, "This is." Faith is important.

The Blood's Active and Continuing Testimony over Us

What is salvation? It is being pardoned and cleansed from our sins, released from death because the blood of Yeshua covers us and the Father in heaven sees His Son in us so the judgment and wrath we deserve is removed and we are granted life through Him. We are not saved because we are good people. It is important to note that the Father sees His Son, Yeshua. The Father in heaven, the laws of nature and creation, the elements of water and fire, death, and demons do not recognize anyone as a good person, but they do recognize Yeshua. They respond or react to the blood of Yeshua. It is not enough to say, "I am a good person" to any of them. It is severely insufficient for salvation. They will answer, "Who *are* you? I do not know you." They all will say "Yeshua I know, but who are you?" even the Father in heaven.

This is why it is crucial for us to be in Him and Him in us. When they see us, they see Him. If we are not in the cleft of the Rock or under the shadow of Yeshua's wings, all of them will kill us. None of them will recognize us. As a result of being grafted into Him, we become like Him and naturally bear the fruit of the Spirit. It is because of Him we are accepted by the Father, we are righteous and holy before Him bearing fruit, doing deeds of faith, pleasing to Him.

Here is a metaphor: Yeshua was a nuclear bomb. He had a lot of power in Him. When He spoke and people touched Him—or He touched them—power was released. Many things happened in the spirit realm and in heaven even before He was "detonated" or died and rose again. When the bomb exploded—or when He was broken and bled out on the cross—there was devastation for many and good things for others in heaven, the spirit realm, and on earth.

A bomb can bring victory to one side and great devastation to another. For many years afterward, long after the bomb went off or the act of Yeshua was finished, there is still an unseen energy or power that has positive and negative effects on the environment and the people in it who touch or eat things with radiation or this power on it. This power is like what kryptonite is to Superman. Is it any wonder why the devil did not want Him to go to the cross even speaking through Peter? Yeshua knew what was necessary. His act would not be merely a symbol; it would be one of lasting power through many generations with effects and results. It was not just a memorial. The bomb had to be detonated, and Yeshua had to die.

Many people think of the blood as in the past on a cross two thousand years ago. The act of the sacrifice is past, but the blood is also here today. It is active in the spirit realm. By faith, His blood appears out of nowhere in the spirit realm. It still speaks and flows even though no one sees it in the natural realm. To the enemy in the kingdom of darkness, it flows down the walls, dripping down as pools onto the ground. It marks those who plead the blood and call on His name. It is in the cup we drink by faith. Is He sacrificed again? No, He died once for all. The power is still here. Entities in the spirit realm see it and feel it. They feel its radiation as it appears and flows and covers us.

When death, which keeps coming in and out like a tide, turns back from nothing, it sees it, passes over it, or turns back in fear. Passover is the power of the blood of Yeshua, and it turns back a dark, powerful force such as death. Where His blood is, sin is washed away. One is cleansed and covered, one is forgiven, and death can't find an attachment to you because of the blood. Death cannot stay upon you, get a grip on you, or cling to you. A curse cannot find you or cling to you because He became the curse and takes the curse away. If we are found in Him, under His wings, we are saved and healed. The kingdom of darkness is under a meltdown.

Mahesh Chavda writes, "Pleading the blood releases a spiritual cover that protects and delivers us." The blood's power is like radiation: always present by faith, yet unseen. You know something is there. You sense it. The signs of its presence manifested in many ways.

Death can only attach to humans because of sin. "The wages of sin is death." Where there is no sin, there is no death—or there is resurrection from death. Look at the present tense in 1 John 1:7–10. Where the blood of Yeshua is, death has no rights because there is no sin. The blood is the mark of the covenant between us and God. Death has no choice but to submit to, respect, and flee from the blood of Yeshua.

The Passover is not metaphorical or symbolic in the spirit realm. It is not a symbol without any power. Death, or the destroyer, sees the blood and passes over it. In order not to attach to humanity, sin has to be removed. To turn back the tide of death, death has to see and feel something that is a reality to it. People don't see it, but the blood is very real to death. This is how one is resurrected from death or how one avoids death. Death has to release its victim. It cannot claim you. Again, where the blood is, death has no rights because there is no sin. Sin gives death rights over an individual to claim them. The blood of Yeshua gives the Most High God rights to claim those who believe for themselves.

If there is no power in it, why does a demon-possessed person react to the blessed bread and cup when they take it? It affects the demon negatively and manifests angrily. So, something is already active in the spirit since the demon reacts. It is not just a metaphor or merely a ritual. There is something to this, but churches today cheapen and lessen its power. There is little faith in the act. They obey, but they are double-minded and also profess it has no power. If all it was is bread and wine and a metaphor without power, then why do the demons manifest in a person who eats it? Yeshua's soul is testifying in the blood.

Hebrews says that we are a holy priesthood. What is the function of a priest? They are to stand before the Lord to serve Him, to stand between the people and God in prayer and petition, offer the sacrifice, *and apply the blood*. Priests were to stand between the natural world we see and the spiritual /heavenly world we can't see under the shadow of Yeshua's wings because we must be covered. Priests are to have a contact with the high priest who stands before God in heaven. During the first Passover, the Hebrews slaughtered a lamb and *applied the blood to their doorposts*.

By faith and in the Spirit, we are to tap the power of the blood that was spilled once for all two thousand years ago. The cross activated and set it off, but the radiating power still exists and testifies and waits to be tapped into. How many priests today do this? Many people assent and obey in taking Communion, but not many use faith to apply the blood as a priest does. I believe this is one of the secrets of the churches in Acts. The priests' practice was to pray and be in the midst of the witnesses in the temple, being in contact with them as part of their lifestyle, and so should we.

Mahesh Chavda writes,

> The blood of Yeshua is our protection, but we need to apply it. The lamb's blood afforded the Israelites no protection until they applied it to their doorposts. Likewise, we must apply Yeshua' blood to the "doorposts" of our lives … The blood of Yeshua is powerful, and we overcome by living according to what we say we believe. Belief plus action will protect us and give us the victory.

The blood atones or covers. It is living and speaks as a witness. His soul is in the blood, which speaks. It is crippling to demons just as radiation is to humans, rendering them powerless.

According to one's faith and God's will, so it is. The kingdom of darkness, being crushed by the kingdom of God, does not want anyone to understand this. With this knowledge, the saints today have little to no hindrance unlike the saints in the first century. They contended with a beast and Satan; today, they have been judged. They are a snake without a head.

Terror and trembling are happening in the kingdom of darkness at this moment. No, they don't want anyone to understand this and tap into this. The blood is now more dangerous to them without a master in their kingdom to lead them than it was back then. The beast had his time to prevail over the saints, but his time passed long ago. Satan had his time, but it has passed. Now, the children and servants of this evil kingdom in the spirit realm and on earth must go the way of their master. They are at God's mercy, and because you are in Him, they are at your mercy as well.

A powerful weapon is in your hands. Respect must be given to it—or you will get hurt. If miracles, signs, wonders, and the kingdom of God were powerful and distant during the days of the previous worldly empires, how much more are they after they have passed away and God's kingdom has arrived? How much more effectual and powerful will they be with little to no hindrance? Again, it takes faith.

Yours is this kingdom, O God, which has crushed to dust the kingdoms of the world from the Egyptian to the Roman empires and even to the kingdom of the devil and darkness. You have conquered them, and they are in your hands now. They all fear You. What is the sign that His kingdom has come? The fact the Roman Empire fell and is no more. That is a sign.

The cross was on Golgotha, the skull hill. The devil's head suffered a crushing blow, and a hole was punched in by the Rock, Yeshua, as He bled and died on the cross. The devil's head is removed with the sword of the Spirit at His resurrection. He is no longer head of the kingdom of darkness, and his army is afraid and fleeing. They are defeated as Yeshua, the conquering King, takes control of all that was in the enemy's possession. He removes the old and brings in the new. Satan lost power and control over death and Hades, and the keys are now in Yeshua's hands.

When a holy minister, under the shadow of His wings and washed in the blood, battles and casts out demons in the name of Yeshua and through the Holy Spirit, he is crushing and chopping off the heads of the enemy's servants with an unseen sword, the sword of the Spirit that proceeds from his mouth.

If you are in the cleft of the rock (Yeshua), Satan and his entire kingdom writhe and squirm beneath you. He is the Rock of David from God's sling that crushes the enemies' skulls. Take the sword of the Spirit (bullets, oil) and cut off their heads. Take no prisoners.

Do things occur when this is not undertaken? Yes, but I believe the church of Acts had a lot of miracles, signs, and wonders because faith was in the act of baptism and Communion. *The power of the blood is active and constant. Since the Spirit and the blood work constantly and are always active, things can happen in church even when it is not taken.*

The door is open, but how much more will it open when one applies faith in the act? One can be saved before partaking of it, but the saved should not believe with two hearts. Don't profess the blood to save and then profess when eating and drinking that it has no power to save. Their focus is that it is only bread and juice, but they lose focus of the unseen aspect of it; therefore, they lose faith. Also, they deny themselves the miracle, sign, and wonder that is needed in their life with a lack of faith. They must come into covenant with one heart—one profession. They agree with the King and say, "This is" along with Him and "So let it be" by faith.

Yeshua is showing us how to have faith here. Do not be contrary to the King and explain it away as anything other than what Yeshua said it is. Many teachers do this today, which stumps faith and causes many to believe with a double heart. When anyone has to explain it away, they don't take the King at His Word, they don't understand Him, and they don't believe Him. They are doublehearted. Come into agreement and a covenant with the King. This is. Let it be. Period.

Believers and churches should partake of the unleavened bread and wine so much more often than they already do—like every time they meet. Luke 24:35 says Yeshua was recognized by them in the breaking of the bread, His body. Luke 24:30, 31 say their eyes were opened. The eyes of their spirits were opened to recognize who conversed with them. Revelation 3:20 says He stands at the door (the contact/bread/sacrifice) and knocks.

If we open the door (by faith), He comes in to dine with us and us with Him. Dine on what? We dine on the living bread or the bread of heaven. In Acts 1:14 and 2:1–4, believers came together often. No mention of Communion was recorded at this time, but there is an indication that a portal, a door, a King's gate was opened. The sound of a violent rushing wind filled the entire place, and tongues of fire appeared and rested on each head. Who is the door? Yeshua is the door, and they more likely partook of the Communion in faith, which caused a great sign to happen as they gathered. They had a contact in the bread and wine, which is the body and blood of Yeshua: the door and a radiating power source. They tapped into something great in the spirit realm and in heaven. Just as water was poured out from the rock in the wilderness, so the Spirit is poured out from Yeshua in Acts.

This must become a frequent practice among congregants (Acts 2:42, 46; 20:7, 11). Yeshua said, "As often as you eat it, you do it in remembrance of Me." The churches in Acts partook of this often and without Bibles. Today, we read the Bible every day, but we break bread only one or two times per month. In the first century, they broke bread almost every time they met together—weekly, daily—and they heard scripture weekly at synagogues. If we are "hungry for the presence of God," why isn't this practiced with more frequency? In Mark 2:25–26, the bread David ate is called the "bread of presence" in one translation. This implies we should partake often to remember and contact Him. With knowledge of the truth comes faith and action.

One must come eat and be baptized with *an open mind, in faith, and with intent* like the woman with the issue of blood who purposely touched the wing of His garment among the throng of people. The power left Yeshua's body. Just as her faith drew out His power, your faith will draw His power out—or He will give it. His power is drawn out of Him to those expecting what is hoped for. It was her faith, boldness, and belief that Yeshua's body would heal and cast out evil. She had no Bible or scriptures in scrolls to cling to. She had faith in the Living Word, Yeshua, and Yeshua was filled with the Spirit. In the supernatural, her spirit consumed bread from heaven and drank water. There was an exchange, and her spirit ate and drank, which resulted in her healing and deliverance in the natural realm. Churches take Communion in memory and thanksgiving, but using faith to establish contact with Yeshua on the other side would enhance what already is.

These are the things we should believe and speak as we eat and then pray to the Father. "By His stripes we are healed" (Isaiah 53:5). Before and while we eat and drink, we should think of the stripes and piercings of His body. "Jesus is the cleft of the rock where we can hide from the consuming fire of God's holiness."

The blood protects us from the wrath and judgment of the Almighty. His flesh nourishes our spirit bodies. He is our refuge and an umbrella of safety. We are protected and redeemed by the sacrificial blood.

Yeshua takes my sins, curses, and burdens and exchanges them for peace, rest, healing, forgiveness, and blessings. I enter the presence of God through this door, Yeshua. Here, there is no darkness or evil—only His glory and Holiness. Here, I find mercy and grace undeserved. I am holy because He is holy. I am covered by the shadow of His wings. Yeshua, though in another realm, is here with me now, and I am also at the same time in the presence of the Father because of Him. He is my tree of life. He knocks on the door. If anyone hears Him and opens the door (Communion), He will come in and dine with Him (Revelation 3:20).

Through the blood, one becomes a citizen of the kingdom, a son or daughter, and a bride. Calvary was the victory; now, in our time, is the triumph. His blood is His soul, the life is in the blood, and His soul speaks. He testifies even today; the blood is eternal. God sees Yeshua, not me. I am under the shadow of His wing. I am at the door (Yeshua) of the tent of meeting. While at the door (Yeshua), being covered by Him though unseen, I can pray to the Father. He can speak with me. Being in Him before God by faith (heaven) and Him in me by Communion (earth), we are one. This happens simultaneously. Because he is seated in the heavenly realms and we are in Him, we are in the heavenly realms with Him at the present time.

I tap into and draw power from Him because of faith, intent, and expectation. John 15:1–11; 16:33; 17:21–23 talks about being one with Him and bearing fruit. In Matthew 16:18, He states the gates of Hades will not overpower His church. All are under His feet, and if you are in Him and are joined to His body, they are under yours as well—but only because of Yeshua.

I stand before the Father without condemnation in the name of Yeshua to offer up praise and prayers. I am also in heaven with Him. Yeshua was lifted up on the cross (earth), but He also is lifted up now beside the Father (heaven). By faith, I tap into this power of the blood and let my soul hear what His soul speaks. Water speaks too and recognizes His presence. Worldly kingdoms, beasts, death, and the kingdom of darkness are outside of this space and below it. They are subdued, overpowered, and beneath His feet for this is God's doing. These pass away as heaven and earth pass away from His presence.

Worship in the Spirit isn't just about speaking in tongues, making music, and dancing. What do those who don't speak in tongues do? How do they worship in spirit? Taking Communion by faith is worship in the Spirit, not idolatry. There is no image set up to worship. Is it idolatry to worship Yeshua, the King in spirit. He said, "This is my body. This is my blood."

How is this idolatry when He established this as a practice—and it is by faith? In Genesis 22:5, Abraham offered a sacrifice and worshipped. In the sacrifice, he drew closer to God and responded to His presence. We should draw closer to God and respond to His presence. Were the patriarchs idolatrous when they offered sacrifices to God by faith? How is it idolatrous to take of the body and blood sacrifice by faith? Was He not an acceptable sacrifice to God? How is Yeshua now an unclean thing—an abomination? I do not worship what is in the natural. Yeshua resurrected what is in the unseen realm. Eating His flesh and drinking His blood is worship, but it is also intimacy with Him. It is part of the relationship with Him. It is how we come to seek the kingdom—through Him.

- Exodus 12:1–13. Hebrews eat lamb and bread at Passover.
- Leviticus 8:4–6. Moses performed a water baptism.
- John 6:41–58. The priests eat sacrifice and bread.

During Passover, the Hebrews put blood on their doors, but they also ate the lamb with unleavened bread and were healed. The priests ate the lamb and the unleavened bread. In the same way, Yeshua gave bread and water to the people He forgave and healed. Their spirits consumed His flesh and blood when they were open to Him. It wasn't enough to just sacrifice a lamb; the Hebrews had to eat it along with the unleavened bread. The priests didn't just pray and sacrifice the lamb; there was a portion they ate with the unleavened bread too.

The holy sacrifice has already been offered, should we not consume it in the spirit too? Where is our faith? *If we are a holy priesthood, we pray, bless, and plead the blood. However, in the spirit, we must also eat the lamb and bread.* This is what Yeshua meant when He said this to His disciples. *He was speaking about eating the Passover lamb as the Hebrews did—but in the spirit.* Many Jewish disciples did not understand Him and were offended. They did not make the connection and left Him. In the kingdom of heaven, this is not considered cannibalism as is done in the world.

This is synonymous with partaking of the tree of life so that we can live forever. Yeshua is like the tree of life. He sacrificed Himself two thousand years ago and finished the work, but in covenant, we must also apply the blood and eat His flesh too. There is application that many of us, as a holy priesthood, miss. Faith is lacking in the Communion. The Communion we take has a reality our flesh is numb to, but there is healing and deliverance that manifests in the natural/flesh. This is a form of worship to God, not idolatry, when we partake of His flesh in the spirit.

This is tapping into the power of the blood and body of Yeshua in the spirit. The cross was important; salvation cannot happen apart from the act. The act of sacrifice on the cross was the detonating of a bomb, but we must apply the radiation or power that is emitted. This power or radiation affects saints in a blessed way if they keep the covenant and commands. It is a curse that shows the negative, deadly, crippling effects, like radiation, for those of the kingdom of darkness. Demons can't stand up against it; it is to them what radiation is to our flesh. The blood, with prayer, also acts as an electric fence that binds them. Death sees it and must pass over or release.

"The people spoke against God and Moses ... and we (our souls/spirits) loathe this miserable food (manna)" (Numbers 21:5). Do not be like the Hebrews in the wilderness who spoke against God by insulting what represented the bread of heaven, who was the Lord. In certain Bible translations, they said "our souls/spirits" and "food." This represents what happens to all believers since the first century. Ours souls and spirits eat this food. Remember, Yeshua said to His disciples, "I have food you know nothing about" (John 4:31–34). Yeshua's spirit was fed too.

The blood has power to save and to kill. Does the bread and wine save? That is like asking, "Does the body and blood save?" Be careful not to indirectly deny the power of the blood. Don't profess on one hand and then deny on the other. When thought of as a point of contact, it can and does save.

You make contact with the body and the power of the eternal blood of Yeshua in the other world. What is done on earth is done in heaven. When asked if the bread and wine save, the response should be this: "Yes, by faith, this blood and flesh save. Without faith, it won't save." That is what it is in the other dimension.

Yeshua said, "Take, eat; this is my body. Drink ... this is the blood of the covenant" (Matthew 26:26–29). He did not say, "It is only a symbol" or "It is like." He said, "This is." This is the body and blood in the unseen realm we do not see: faith. No one would be lying to say this because, by faith, we have contact with the body of our Lord and go through the door to our Father.

He was instituting a new memorial and giving them—and us—a contact between heaven and earth. It is something tangible for us to touch on one side, but we must have faith in what we don't see on the other. What is done and remembered on earth is done and remembered in heaven. When it is taken without faith as only a memorial ritual, it does not save. Mere rituals and symbols do not save; they have no power. No faith means no power. It remains just bread, wine, and water.

Asking the question, "Does one have to eat the unleavened bread and wine to be saved" is like asking "do we have to consume the flesh of the lamb and cover our doors with blood as the Hebrews did to be saved from death?" It is like doubting and questioning His command to consume His flesh and drink His blood in the spirit. If any of the Hebrews asked this question, then said, "eating this flesh and marking our doors with the blood of the lamb doesn't save us, but only hoping that his grace will be there for us as death passes over will save us", thus refusing to obey the command, their firstborn would have died with the Egyptians on Passover night. "Did He really mean we must eat His flesh to be saved?" Yes, He meant to eat the flesh and blood to be saved. Was there an act the Hebrews had to do by faith and obedience to bring salvation that night to completion? Yes, they had to act by faith, so we must do likewise in the spirit. The sacrifice is offered, but we must eat and drink or we have no part with Him in covenant. A hope in His grace to save without obeying Him is not faith. It shows doubt.

Asking the question, "Should we be baptized to be saved?" is like asking, "do we really have to crossover and have His name placed on us to belong to Him?" Well, given what happens when we make contact in heaven, yes.

This changes things from just a ritual to a contact as we read believers made frequently in the book of Acts. What is done on earth is done in heaven. A contact, a link, a connection happens.

Peter said it saves (1 Peter 3:20, 21). He understood contact must involve faith in what we don't see happening in another dimension. Believers not understanding this now can be led to this truth. One can be saved before even partaking in it, but the saved are drawn even closer to Him when they eat. Draw near to God, and if He is already near you, you get even closer to Him.

The bread and wine eaten (and baptism done) in faith, with intention, and with reverence links us to His door, His broken flesh, and His blood for eternity. This door or portal to the Father—Yeshua's broken flesh—was activated at His death with the signs of dark clouds, earthquakes, the veil of the temple torn without hands, rocks and tombs broken open, and holy people resurrected without man's intervention. It did what the blood of an innocent animal could never really do: cleanse us and allow us entry.

If anyone desires what happened in the Gospels and Acts to happen today in their congregation, I think this is the missing key. What is already happening by the Spirit of God will be manifested more frequently and more powerfully. It will be enhanced. I don't understand we know spirits interact and portals are opened through Ouija boards and other objects, but our God-established objects are powerless. They don't testify, and they don't save. How do evil objects have their manifestations but holy ones don't—unless faith is lacking? Without the cross, Communion would have no power. Without faith, there is no salvation. Believe that He is feeding you His flesh and blood, which is the bread of heaven.

The covering of the bread/flesh has more meaning than a burial. It could mean He can be seen and be unseen. He appears and disappears. We can see Him with circumcised hearts by the Spirit at His will like those of the first century—or we can't see Him with uncircumcised hearts. "The world will no longer see me, but you will."

The disciples saw what the world was incapable of seeing unless God willed it. This is how He comes as a thief in the night, and no one notices. This is how we are in a visitation. This is more powerful than having a cross up to deter evil. The wooden cross He was hung from is not here anymore, but He is.

CHAPTER 24
The Water as a Witness

God Works through Water

"And darkness was over the surface of the deep, and the Spirit of God was moving over the surface of the waters" (Genesis 1:2).

God was about to work over the waters to create the spirit and the natural. Genesis 1:1, 2 and 2 Peter 3:5, 6 both speak of the Holy Spirit, who is the Word of God, and water in the beginning of creation and how the earth and all life were created from seemingly nothing. It seems that the Spirit hovers over the waters in baptism just as He guided Noah's ark to safety and split the Red Sea for the Hebrews to cross.

Genesis 1:20, 24 and Revelation 13 speak of how creation and the beasts came out of the water and earth. Satan seemed to know in Revelation 13 that water can be used as a way to bring the spiritual forth into the natural world. He stood at the sea, and an empire rose, which was a beast, from out of an abyss or a dark, evil unseen realm. In the natural realm, it manifested as the Roman Empire and its emperors.

The following verses can be a picture of baptism in water and Spirit and a reference of John 3 when Yeshua spoke to Nicodemus about being born again or crossing over. It is what happens spiritually from the kingdom of darkness into the kingdom of light and from slavery in Egypt to the Promised Land (Zion):

- Isaiah 43:1, 2, 16. "But now, thus says the Lord, your Creator, O Jacob, and He who formed you, O Israel, Do not fear, for I have redeemed you; I have called you by name; you are Mine! When you pass through the waters, I will be with you; And

through the rivers, they will not overflow you, When you walk through the fire, you will not be scorched, nor will the flame burn you, For I am the Lord your God, the Holy One of Israel, your Savior."
- Psalm 66:12. "We went through fire and through water; Yet You brought us out into a place of abundance."
- Psalm 77:19, 20. "Your way was in the sea and Your paths in the mighty waters, and Your footprints may not be known. You led Your people like a flock by the hand of Moses and Aaron." Does he not do this today spiritually?
- Isaiah 51:10, 11. "Was it not You who dried up the sea, the waters of the great deep; who made the depths of the sea a pathway for the redeemed to cross over? The ransomed of the Lord will return and come with joyful shouting to Zion, and everlasting joy will be on their heads. They will obtain gladness and joy, and sorrow and sighing will flee away."

The Importance of Water as a Witness

It is written in Deuteronomy 17:6; 19:15; Matthew 18:16; and John 8:14–18 that every matter must be established by the testimony of two or three witnesses. How do we accept water and blood but not Spirit? How do we accept blood and Spirit but not water? How do we accept Spirit and water but not blood? They all save. They are all credible and established by God, and He uses them. When we say any one of these "doesn't save," we have become doublehearted and have a form of godliness that deny the power.

"Death and life are in the power of the tongue" (Proverbs 18:21). Be careful what you believe, speak, and teach. If the blood, water, and Spirit are witnesses, they testify. If they testify, they speak. If they speak, they are alive and powerful.

Yeshua stated, "He who has believed and has been baptized shall be saved; but he who he who has disbelieved shall be condemned" (Mark 16:16). Baptism is associated with salvation (Acts 2:38, 39; 22:16; 16:31–34; 1 Peter 3:21).

With Noah's family and Moses and the Israelites, water played a role in the salvation of many and the death of others. There was also faith and obedience. In both cases, they were saved through water, and many were killed (1 Peter 3:20–21 and Acts 2:38).

We can think of the thief on the cross and say he was an exception to the water baptism and was saved. God would understand a deathbed salvation as an exception to not being baptized in water. However, is it just an exception? Does the thief only need two witnesses to speak for him? Was water one of them? *By faith and according to the law, He only needs two out of three witnesses to speak.* Is that enough? The thief had the blood of the Lamb and Yeshua's Word, which is the Spirit who flows from His mouth to the thief's spirit. It was speaking over the thief who preserved and saved him. The King's Word, the living sword, saves him. The King's Word is enough to seal him. Doesn't His Word sanctify? Before the outpouring of the power of the Spirit on the believers, His Spirit saves.

Is it that a deathbed is an exception or that, in cases like his, the thief only needed at least two to speak over him according to the law? This is not to say this applies to everyone and we only need two in situations like his. The blood, the Spirit, and the water are needed for all to be saved. What the thief could get by with is not what others could get by with too.

We can't pick and choose which witness we want to testify over us. We can't say, "I want blood and Spirit, but not water," "I want water and blood, but not the Spirit," or "I choose Spirit and water, but not the blood." He requires all of it from those who are given opportunity and time. The thief was an exceptional case that only needed two. So we shouldn't conclude that because the thief wasn't baptized in water that water doesn't save, but that only two witnesses are necessary.

The priests of the temple could not pick and choose altar and water basin or water basin and anointing or altar and anointing. They had to go through all three baptisms. Otherwise, they would perish in the presence. If we are a priesthood to God, shouldn't we be willing to do the same? If this was an important practice under the Old Covenant, how much more is it under the New Covenant? If a priest could perish under the Old Covenant if this was neglected and devalued, then how do we escape judgment in the fulfillment? Some cry "Grace," but "faith without works is dead." Again, a hope in His grace to save without obeying Him is not faith. It shows doubt.

Elijah and Elisha were at the banks of the Jordan River when the whirlwind came down (2 Kings 2:6–16). After they struck the water with the mantle, it was divided. That sounds similar to Moses and the Red Sea where there was wind, a splitting of water, and the rod to strike the sea open so the Hebrews left Egypt as Elijah left this earth. The Spirit of God was present to take him away. This depicts how the saints' departure from this earth will be: salvation through water into the air to meet the Lord by His holy name.

For the ancient Jew, a bath was a religious ritual. Water was important for religious rites and renewal. The mikvah, the ritual bath, was drawn from a flowing river or spring. There was a spiritual importance to it that was lost through the centuries and became just a ritual or typical washing of dirt off the body without any spiritual significance. Faith is lost.

Some teachers today teach water does not save and that the bread and wine are only metaphors and don't save. Yeshua says, "No one can enter the kingdom unless born of water." He also said, "This is my body and blood." Why are they contrary? If Yeshua didn't mean what He said, why did He say it? He didn't say, "It is like or similar to." Many don't discredit the power of blood and Spirit to save or speak as a witness as much as they do water. Many believe the water in John 3 Yeshua refers to a woman's birth water, but what is natural comes out of it. What is of the flesh is flesh—but what is of the Spirit is spirit.

Faith is lost in not believing what is unseen. Faith is stumped when people equate water baptism to a work of humanity instead of a work of God. People no longer see the work of God; therefore, they do not have faith or very little faith. They desire the miracles, signs, and wonders of the first-century church written about in Acts, but they devalue what God established to be obeyed in faith. If you obey, obey in faith and believe what is done unseen to the natural eye in heaven. Don't obey and then profess there is no power. This is double hearted.

There was something to the pouring out of water in 1 Samuel 7:6 by the men of Israel. This wasn't a bath.

With water baptism, people quote or repeat what He says without actually doing what it implies to do. Most do not "turn the switch on" or invoke the name of the Father or the Messiah. If there is power in the name, why isn't it spoken? It wouldn't be taking His name in vain because people are being saved and sanctified by the name.

Salvation and rebirth are not vain things. They are the work of God. If there was no power in it, why were most people in Acts filled with the Holy Spirit after coming out of the water? It is a point of contact and has power from the holy name. This is how His holy name is put on the people (Revelation 14:1; 7:3; Ezekiel 9:4). Should it be said instead, "Yeshua (who was raised from the dead) bar Yod-he-vau-heh." So, His name and faith are switches.

More is written in chapter twenty-two on baptism as a witness to act for the good of His people or against His enemies.

Crossing Over through Water in the Spirit

Water aids in the literal crossover from a kingdom of darkness into the kingdom of light or between worlds. It is a crossover from slavery to freedom just like the Israelites from Egypt. It serves as a universal medium of sorts in the spirit realm. It is a medium that helps us cross from one kingdom into another literally. It is a gateway to the supernatural. It is a vehicle used by God to leave one spirit world and enter another kind of spirit world in His name.

We cross a spiritual chasm by this. Sometimes water, apart from baptism, can be used between the spirit and natural realms. Yeshua was baptized in water. As Peter stated, "They were brought safely through the water" (1 Peter 3:20).

Baptism now saves you. It is an appeal to God for a good conscience through the resurrection of Yeshua Hamashiach. "Let us draw near with a sincere heart in full assurance of faith, having our hearts sprinkled clean from an evil conscience and our bodies washed with pure water" (Hebrews 10:22). Flowing water is sometimes thought by some as a conduit for paranormal activity because entities can feed off the energy to manifest.

It is here we see fishing for humans in this cleansing by faith of the heart and body. Believers are crossing through water as fish cross from one world (the water) into another (the land). Humans must be crucified and die with Yeshua, becoming a new creation just as the fish die shortly after being caught. This is the calling to baptize because the apostles were literally, not figuratively, fishers of men. The angels rejoice in this crossover as people enter the kingdom of heaven by faith just as fishermen are joyful of their catch in the boat. What is seen in the spirit realm, or behind the scenes, is one's spirit leaving a dark, dead, and evil spirit realm and entering into one with light, life, and goodness.

We come to stand literally under the cover of Yeshua in the presence of the Father in heaven while still in the natural realm of earth. Eternity in the kingdom of heaven begins to walk alongside us while we live on earth. Angels see this and rejoice. The believers can begin to see holy angels more often. This is how you are surrounded by a cloud of witnesses. *It is in the holy realm of the spirit.* This is how we can boldly go before the throne and make our petitions before God through Yeshua. Yeshua said,

"I do what I see my Father do." How does He see the Father do something unless the kingdom surrounds Him in the unseen realms? This is how "to be absent from the body is to be present with the Lord." The natural body is the only thing separating us from a holy world that exists alongside us.

The only thing separating the unsaved from a dark, evil, doomed world is the body. Instead of a dark spirit world that seeps into our natural world to haunt because that is what used to surround us, a holy world full of light—a kingdom of God—seeps into our natural world. When a spirit from the unseen world enters into where we are naturally, the laws that we know are suspended, and the supernatural begins to happen because a door is open. There is a visitation. This is where miracles, signs, and wonders happen. This was Acts.

The presence of God rests on His priests. *They are always in His presence because they are always in His world, under the cover of Yeshua.* The priests enter this holy world through Yeshua, the door, and are covered. God's world begins to surround them. This is being born again and being in Him by blood, water, and Spirit. The atmosphere changes in the natural realm as we live and speak in Him, being covered, because we carry and are also in His presence. When Yeshua taught and spoke in the synagogues and in the temple, the atmosphere always changed. We truly have citizenship in His kingdom as we dwell in this natural world.

The saints of the Yeshua's generation had authority over the powers of darkness, but they were greatly persecuted, and the beast prevailed. In the case of a believer today, though there is still persecution and enmity with darkness, there should be a prevailing of the saints over darkness and a takeover because that is what conquering kings do. The kingdom of darkness is in great fear of the kingdom of God and is subjected to it. A believer has the holy name marked on their forehead, having been baptized in the name of the Father, Son, and Spirit. One is cleansed with blood and anointed with the Holy Spirit.

People fail to see and understand the spiritual, behind-the-scenes aspect of this. They teach and proclaim, "Baptism does not save." There is no faith to see the unseen. Remember that "faith is the substance of things not seen." There is literally something that happens in the spirit realm when one is baptized, but because we do not see this with eyes of flesh, the power of water baptism is discredited. Its testimony is null and void to us.

Godliness denies the power. Remember that the power of life and death is in the tongue. One could simply nullify what they did out of obedience by speaking and believing otherwise. It is doublehearted.

The blood, water, and Spirit testify and save (John 3:5; Acts 2:38; 1 Peter 3:20, 21, 1 John 5:6, 7, 8). If they testify, they speak; therefore, there is a life or power in each of these. This water is not birth water from a woman. That speaks of another kind of birth—one of flesh. This is the one through the name and the Spirit.

How can they speak and have power but not save? How do two save and one does not? That says these are more than merely symbols and rituals we do. Now why do we believe the blood and Spirit save—but not the water when it testifies too and is in agreement with the other two? Why are we willing to be baptized in water and the blood, but we refuse His Spirit to birth us and anoint us to enter His presence?

With the earthly temple, in order for the high priest to enter the most holy place, which is where the ark was and where the Father dwells in heaven, he must offer the sacrifice (blood), wash in the basin, and be anointed. If he made an error in bypassing any of these, he was struck and died. Even Yeshua says that no one can enter the kingdom unless he is born of water and Spirit. There seems to be an exception to deathbed salvation, like the thief on the cross, who only needed two witnesses.

Notice in Acts how often people were baptized in water and Spirit shortly after believing. They did not wait to cross over from one kingdom into another. They did not wait to die and be crucified in Him. They did not wait until they felt like it. There was a sense of urgency with them in Acts and in the baptism of John. There was no complacency. They seem to understand the importance unlike people today who tend to wait. Why do we wait when believers in the first century got in it right away? They obeyed immediately, but we don't. We obey, but we wait and don't understand how important it is.

Perhaps we don't understand how water literally functions, testifies, and saves; therefore, we reduce the significance of it as a witness. It washes away our sins and clears us from the evil conscience (Acts 2:38; 22:16; 1 Corinthians 6:11; Ephesians 5:26; Hebrews 10:22).

Biblical and Nonbiblical Examples of Water as a Contact/Bridge

The blood through Communion is a contact. If wine is a contact, then water is too. Oil can be another one. The Spirit of God moved over the surface of the waters as earth was being created (Genesis 1:1, 2).

Creation came into existence through water. The Spirit is first and then the natural, but the natural came through the water. The Red Sea parted at the command/action of Moshe as he stood on the shore. In Genesis 32:10, Jacob crossed the Jordan with only his staff, which represents a baptism. It reads that Jacob said,

> For with my staff only I crossed this Jordan, and now I have become two companies.

It goes on later in the chapter to describe Jacob's wrestling and seeing God face to face. His name was changed to Israel.

> So Jacob named the place Peniel, for he said, 'I have seen God face to face, yet my life has been preserved.' Now the sun rose upon him just a he crossed over Penuel, and he was limping on his thigh. (Genesis 32:30, 31)

So after Jacob crossed through water, his name changed, he saw God, he was saved or preserved, and the light of the sun rose upon him. This can represent our rebirth in water and Spirit too. After baptism, we cross over from darkness to light, we will see God, He preserves or saves us, and we will have new names, His light shines upon us.

Joshua 3:5–17 speaks of the water splitting for the priests and the sons of Israel because God's spirit was on the ark. This could represent baptism. The earthly temple had a basin of water near its entrance. The Rock was with the Hebrews and released water in the wilderness for them to drink and bathe in. There are stories of blessed holy water sprinkled on people and they were healed and delivered from demons. The well-known river in Lourdes, France, where there is a shrine is known for its healing powers and apparitions that appear there. There are some paranormal accounts of various manifestations of different kinds when water was running or pooled nearby. After baptizing the Ethiopian in water, Philip vanished.

In the Gospel, it was recorded that the angel came down to stir the pool and heal the first one who entered. Many of Yeshua's miracles happened near the Sea of Galilee or a pool, which was not a coincidence. Yeshua made wine from water. The water was used in the multiplying of the fish several times. The wine came through a conduit or contact from His unseen storehouse. Think of Yeshua making mud out of spit and sending a man to wash in water or the man with a legion of demons that was cast into a herd of swine then they jumped off the cliff into the sea. The demons went into another realm with this casting. Think of when Yeshua was baptized in water, a dove appeared, and God spoke of Him. The Spirit hovered over the waters. Yeshua walked upon the waves of the tossing sea. There was probably something holding Him up from the other side, the water submitting under His feet, and water was a conduit or contact of sorts. Again, here is the Spirit hovering over the waters.

In the books of 1 and 2 Kings, many signs and miracles happened near water or oil. Elijah was told that he would drink of the brook, and the ravens would bring him bread and meat as long as the brook was there. When the brook dried up, there were no more ravens, and he was told to go to a widow. He asked the widow for a little water in a jar. The widow had a little flour and a little oil. There was always a supply of oil and flour. Note that water and oil is used here.

A king was healed of leprosy after dunking seven times in the river, according to the Word of God through the prophet. Elijah set up an altar, dug a trench, and filled it with water, which was not only a conduit/contact. It was dried up by the fire that fell from heaven. Elijah had told his servant to go up and look toward the sea seven times as he prayed until a cloud manifested into the natural realm. The widow's oil was increased by the faith of the prophet Elisha. The lost ax-head mysteriously floated and was recovered from the water after a stick was thrown in. *Many miracles, signs, and wonders have water (or a liquid) involved at some point.* I don't think it's a coincidence that God uses it to save and to kill. Many fail to notice how liquid is used in many miracles. Since water is so abundant and a part of life, it's easy to miss how things occur that are out of the ordinary. We are so numb to it.

A cleansing of the soul and spirit actually happens with water and the Spirit (Ephesians 5:26, 27; Acts 22:16; 1 Corinthians 6:11; Titus 3:5, 6). We are sanctified with His name and the Spirit and cleansed. The Spirit (river of heaven) causes this to happen through water on earth as a conduit and contact. This is not symbolic.

The parting of the Red Sea, the ark being guided and protected in the flood at the Word of God, Yeshua walking on water, the angel stirring up the pool for healing, and water turned to wine by His Word are all signs that water is conduit and contact between two dimensions and two worlds. God used it and established it as a contact. *It is no coincidence that water was used in these situations.* It is so subtle and hidden. It is hidden in plain sight. We see, but don't see. Many don't see the connection and reduce water baptism to only a symbol that represents death and resurrection. It is a witness that testifies and a contact. There is energy in the wind and water that He commands and controls. *His name is a switch that activates the manifestation of His Spirit into this world. It is a conduit of His energy and Spirit between two worlds and can bring manifestations into this world.* His Spirit causes the water to move in an unnatural way that is miraculous.

Whatever is done on earth is done in heaven or in the unseen realm (John 7:38, 39; John 4:7–14, 23, 24; and John 3:5). The Spirit is rivers of living water that flow from heaven and from within. The water of earth is the Spirit in the unseen dimension just as the bread/wine on earth is the body and blood in the unseen dimension of heaven and earth.

There must be faith to believe what is not seen with eyes of flesh. The water from the rock that followed the Hebrews in the wilderness represents Yeshua who gives the Holy Spirit. Yeshua came by water (earth) and Spirit (heaven), and rebirth happens by water and Spirit (1 John 5:6–8 and John 3:5). Is this why manifestations of the Spirit happen shortly after people come out of the water? Contact is made and manifestations occur through this conduit (water).

"Baptizing them in the name of the Father, Son, and Holy Spirit" is not a phrase to repeat. It suggests speaking or putting the holy name unto the people. It is for a holy purpose, not a vain one. How are we to call on the name of the Lord to be saved, but we can't say it? When His holy name is invoked, the Spirit comes through it.

Think of it like an electrical current that flows easily through water when the switch is turned on, resulting in electrocution and death. Likewise, His Spirit flows easily through water when the name is invoked, resulting in manifestations of the filling of His Spirit, the birth of a new nature, and the death of a sinful nature.

His holy name marks His people. Does electrical current (or His Spirit) cease to be—or is it limited to water? No, He still works, and there is evidence of Him apart from water. However, God uses water as a contact or conduit and has established it as a witness to testify that "God has given us eternal life, and this life is in His Son" (1 John 5:11), Yeshua, who lives.

His holy name is put on His people, the sheep (Revelation 14:1; 7:3; Ezekiel 9:4). This name on the foreheads is not seen with eyes of flesh, but eyes of the Spirit. It is unseen. That is what was understood in the first century but lost through the millennia. That is why so many sought water baptisms so eagerly after hearing about the kingdom. People today wait to obey; they don't see the connection, the power, or the importance. They only see symbolism without power. This is where their faith stops and is stumped. Is this my work or God's work? This is the work of God. I obey by faith, but it is God who works.

The Power of Water in Creation

Water is powerful in the natural. The miracle of creation is through water. It quenches thirst and hydrates our bodies. It cleanses us, allows life of all kinds to exist and grow, and is used to generate energy. If the seas, lakes, and oceans are polluted, contaminated, and poisoned, life dies off. The marine food chains break down. When life in the oceans is no more, it is not long before humans and other land life are no more.

It has the power to save or kill, and it actually can do both. When water is removed from our area or vanishes, we understand the value it has. We see how important it is and understand its power. We would never say after it has quenched our thirst, revived our minds and bodies, cleansed and healed our bodies, "water has no power". Water is a very precious resource to have. We take water for granted in so many ways, even spiritually, by downplaying its role with these very words. Yeshua and Peter say it saves, but teachers say, "No, it doesn't." They are speaking contrary to what is written and spoken.

We should speak the same way Peter and Yeshua spoke in that it saves. We shouldn't conclude that it doesn't save. It has an important testimony over us—but only through and in His name. If His priests needed water along with the blood and anointing in oil, which is the Holy Spirit, in order to enter His presence, we as a priesthood need it too. We shouldn't downplay its role when Yeshua and Peter didn't. We shouldn't downplay its role because we don't understand by faith what role it plays and how God uses it. We should see its importance in not just the natural but in the spirit.

When the waters of earth vanish and are no more, then there is no more fruit of the vine or grain to make the unleavened bread. This is a sign of the door of salvation closing. When no one can be saved, only judgment and death follow.

CHAPTER 25
The Biblical Pattern of Contacts

With more people and more faith, there are more results—and the glory of God is displayed. Note the pattern throughout the Bible:

Event	Blood/Bread	Water (cleansing)	Door/ Entrance	Few saved/ Many perish
Noah: Genesis 7–8	Altar: Genesis 8:20–21	Flood waters/ Rain	Genesis 7:13–16	Genesis 7:21–24
Sodom and Gomorrah: Genesis 18–19	Meal: Genesis 18:5–8; 19:3, 4	Genesis 18:4, 19:2—feet	Genesis 18:1; 19:6–11	Genesis 19:23–29
Tent of Meeting: Exodus 29–30	Exodus 29:1, 10–28	Exodus 29:4; 30:17–21	Exodus 29:32, 42	Exodus 32:7–10, 27–29
Moses: Exodus 12–14	Exodus 12	Exodus 14	Exodus 12:7, 22	Exodus 14:13–31
Yeshua: Gospels	Death/ Resurrection	Baptism/ from His John 13:5–8—feet wash pierced side/	John 10:2, 9	Matthew 7:13–14, 22; Luke 13:24, 25
Acts and today	Communion activated by the finished act and faith	Baptism/feet wash activated by finished act and faith	Yeshua's body	From first century until now

Another partial example is Acts 27:14–44. There is water, wood, and bread. It represents how one is carried through judgment unharmed while under the cross and in the body of Yeshua through the water to be saved.

Am I saved over and over again? Am I adding to the work of God? No, it is the work of God. No, it is a holy and priestly practice, a lifestyle, making contact with the unseen kingdom by faith, feeding my spirit His flesh or eating, tapping the power of the three witnesses of heaven and earth, and opening the door to Him. These are the witnesses He has established, not me. This is what a priest should be doing as a practice.

Just as the Levitical priesthood had constant contact with the blood of lambs, water, and anointing/light, God's holy priesthood today must have constant contact with the God-established witnesses of heaven and earth. There is a part we participate in with our end of the covenant with Him. It is not just about Yeshua finishing everything on the cross almost two thousand years ago and we do nothing else. We must, by faith, incorporate this into our lives. A priest has a practice, the Lamb was slain, the sacrifice was offered once for all, but you must eat and drink today. We feed off of Him. We partake of the fruit of the tree of life.

As a holy priesthood, we do the function of a priest, which entails more than just praying and fasting. The priests of the temple stood before the Lord to serve Him. They fasted, prayed, and had a lot of contact with the sacrifice (blood and flesh) and the water. They anointed each other (Spirit) passing by the menorah and presence (body and Spirit) to the most holy place.

We must act as well by faith. Faith without works is dead. It is about functioning in a different realm (heaven) through the witnesses as we live in this natural one. Wherever you are, the kingdom of heaven is with you on earth in a sense. With His name as a badge of authority, you are able—and have the right—to operate here where you live.

As one author put it, we are to "transform the environment and impact the world with heavenly light" or with the government of a King. Priests should loose and bind up on earth and in heaven if they are one with His will. This is one aspect of being a priest.

Another aspect is bearing the burdens of others (Galatians 6:1–2). Frank Hammond wrote,

> The deliverance minister must be like the Old Testament priest who ate the trespass and sin offerings. According to Numbers 18:8, only Aaron and his sons were to eat the

flesh of these offerings. "Every male shall eat it." Other offerings could be eaten by the priest's household, but only the male priest could eat the sin and trespass offerings. It was their *duty* to eat them. The "male" represents strength. It takes a strong person to perform this ministry. Under the New Testament all believers are priests. As priests it is our duty to "eat" the sin and trespass offerings of others. What is brought to us in the spirit of confession and repentance is consumed and not shared ... not even with one's household!

CHAPTER 26
The Lord's Prayer (Matthew 6:8–15)

"Give us this day our daily bread" refers to the bread of heaven not so much the bread we make in this natural realm. It is saying to the Father to provide the bread of heaven for our spirits to consume and live. Yeshua said if we "seek first the kingdom of heaven and His righteousness, then all these things (natural/earthly food, drink, and clothes) will be added to us." It makes sense that He meant to ask for the bread of heaven as part of the search for the kingdom. God will provide the bread our bodies need. When we seek God first, who is unseen by faith, in the spiritual realm, then the seen in the natural realm will be provided for us by Him.

"Forgive us our debts as we forgive our debtors" is not just about forgiveness of sin. It is about healing too. Remember how Yeshua said to the many people He healed seconds later, "Your sins are forgiven." There was a manifestation in the natural realm of healing or deliverance. In forgiving the sins, He cleansed the people, taking it from them, and He gave bread and water for their spirits in return. Healing is a sign of forgiveness of sin.

Remember the paralyzed man? "Which is easier to say, 'Your sins are forgiven or rise take your mat and walk? So that you know the Son of Man has authority on earth to forgive sins, rise, take your mat, and walk.'" This is an exchange. Our spirits consume the bread of heaven as the people did where Yeshua ministered, and He takes our sins and transgressions. We are forgiven in the cleansing from and removal of our sins and healed in the consuming or receiving of His flesh and blood. This is the exchange. We are to repeat this with others so that they can be healed too. Is this why we must leave prayer to be reconciled to one we offended unjustly (Matthew 5:23, 24)?

Why do we expect Yeshua to forgive us and heal us, but we don't want to forgive and allow or bring healing to others? Isn't this in the Great Commission? "They will lay hands on the sick, and they will recover." This is not just about healing; it is about forgiveness too. They had gifts of healing, but they were also supposed to forgive or ask for forgiveness. Not everyone may have the gift of healing, but everyone has a type of healing that comes from forgiving others.

You have the power to remove (forgive) sin in Yeshua's name so that death does not approach the offender. If you don't forgive, the offender is led to death. We should turn back one being led to death. One way is by forgiving, which removes sin by blood, and in the name, which turns death away. When we don't forgive, disease and death come to the offender in time. Death is attracted to sin because the wages of sin is death. We must turn the curse and tide of death back with forgiveness. If death comes to the person anyway, we are still free, forgiven, and healed by God for we did our part. God has judged and taken vengeance into His own hands.

"Confess your sins to one another so that you may be healed." In other words, you will be forgiven. Do many Christians suffer illness and weaknesses in their bodies because they have not forgiven someone—or someone hasn't forgiven them?

Yeshua said,

> For if you forgive others for their transgressions, your heavenly Father will also forgive you. But if you do not forgive others, then your Father will not forgive your transgressions. (Matthew 6:14, 15)

This could extend to healing. If we don't forgive others, which could lead to healing or prevent an illness from falling upon them, how can we expect the heavenly (unseen) Father to forgive us, heal our illnesses, and protect us from disease, illness, and infirmity? If we don't forgive and heal, He will not forgive and heal us. We can't seek healing from Him, and there is someone who we have not forgiven. He will not honor our request. Could this be a reason why many Christians are ill, sick, and weak for many years? Have they forgiven those who sought them for forgiveness and refused at some point in their life? Forgiveness extends to healing because there is an exchange.

Another note about Matthew 6:14, 15—if all our sins, not just the past and present—and future uncommitted sins too—are forgiven at once, then why does Yeshua say, "If you do not forgive others, then your

Father will not forgive your transgressions"? I thought all were forgiven when I first came to Him? Why did Yeshua say I will not be forgiven of sins by the Father in heaven if I was already forgiven for my future sins? Why am I not forgiven by the Father even when I don't forgive others, when I am presently forgiven of my future sins?

How do I say, "I won't forgive so-and-so, but even though Yeshua said the heavenly Father won't forgive me for doing this, all my future transgressions and sins are forgiven despite what I did and regardless of what Yeshua said"? How do we go contrary to Yeshua? If what is taught by humans is true, then how can what Yeshua say be true too? How is it possible for us to not be forgiven by the Father in heaven, according to Yeshua, and at the same time be forgiven of every committed and uncommitted sin? Someone is wrong. Yeshua stated it was possible for believers to not be forgiven when they don't forgive. If we are forgiven of every sin in the future, then how is it that many are sick now? Illness may not always be caused by or be the result of sin, but there are too many ill in the churches now for it not to have anything to do with sin at some point. There is sin in the midst, therefore many illnesses, and therefore all sins are not forgiven. Too many people are sick. There is healing, but there are sicknesses too, which indicates possible sin. Another sign of sin or wickedness is the fact many fall in the presence of God. Falling or being slain could be a sign of wickedness or sin.

The entire prayer was spiritual, not parts of it. "Your will be done on earth as it is in heaven" could also be taken as "Your will be manifested in the natural realm as it is in the unseen spirit realm/heaven. "Daily bread" means the body of the Lord taken daily, not the typical bread baked in the oven on earth. Note how this is said after "Your will be done on earth as it is in heaven." He said, "Man does not live on bread alone, but on every word that comes from the mouth of God." Isn't Yeshua the Living Word? Didn't this Word become flesh (John 1:1, 14)? Isn't this the flesh we are to eat to live and never die? Don't we eat this flesh in Communion? When this flesh is eaten, we are living on His Word. Should we eat this during fasts? Yes! We live on the Word of God, His flesh. He is your sustenance. Yeshua is the Word of life (1 John 1:1, 2).

The bread, lamb, and drink refer to Yeshua (John 6:26–40 and Exodus 29:31–46). In the Lord's Prayer, was He speaking of earthly bread when He said to seek the bread of heaven in John?

Note: In Exodus 29:32, the bread and lamb are eaten at the doorway of a meeting tent. This parallels with breaking of bread and wine as a contact for us today and entering the presence of God through Yeshua's flesh and He is the door where God will come and speak to you. Also notice, it was done day and night and not once a month. The miracle of loaves and fish probably has a spiritual meaning. Exodus 30:1–10 speaks of incense offered day and night, which is parallel to His people praying day and night through Yeshua. If one prays day and night, shouldn't one eat day and night too—or at least more often than once or twice a month?

The anointing of oil in Exodus 30:22–33 is the Holy Spirit.

CHAPTER 27

The Gun and the Bullets: The Scripture and the Sword

Let's go back to Yeshua's incarnate visitation upon this earth. The written Word, the scripture, speaks and testifies about Yeshua:

> You search the Scriptures because you think in them you have eternal life; it is these that testify of Me; and you are unwilling to come to Me so that you may have life. (John 5:39, 40, 46–47)

Yeshua spoke of the scriptures not as though He or the Spirit were scripture but as though it was a separate witness of Him. The written Word is good and should be read and listened to often, but it points to Yeshua, the Living Word and tree of life, whose flesh we are to consume so we may have eternal life.

Scripture lifts up Yeshua. What did saints do before the Bible was copied? What did Abraham do before God gave Moses the Law? They had no Bibles or scriptures to refer to and study in their homes, but they had faith and went to the Living Word, and He did great and awesome things for them. The Living Word was with them, led them, covered them, and followed them. Yeshua was "I Am" before the written Word came into existence, which means His Spirit is greater than the written witness since the written witness comes from the Spirit. It lasted for many centuries because of God, and it comes from God—not because it is God. It has His breath on it.

The Bible is the written Word of God. It is a form of the Word of God and is inspired by God (2 Peter 1:20, 21). As men were filled the Holy

Spirit, they wrote/recorded the words of God. What is meant in Ephesians 6:17 is that the sword is the Holy Spirit.

As Peter gave his sermons, he quoted scripture, but these were accompanied by the Holy Spirit that had filled him (Acts 2:14–36; 3:11–26; and 4:8–12). Acts 4:33 has them filled with the Holy Spirit and speaking the Word of God. They were preaching the truth of the Gospel and the kingdom, which included the use of scripture. They were talking to the crowds as the Spirit gave them the words. *As they spoke, there was a sword coming from their mouths—but also living water. They did not use scripture apart from the Holy Spirit.* Yeshua was conceived by the Spirit to a virgin. Yeshua comes forth from the Spirit of God and is His Son.

Why would you take a witness to fight evil and darkness without the Spirit? When He came a second time, there was a sword coming out of His mouth; it was the Holy Spirit He was filled with. He wasn't quoting scripture. The words that came out of His mouth were active and alive.

Demons were driven out of people by the Spirit, not scripture alone. After the temptation of Yeshua, the devil left because Yeshua knew the correct understanding of scripture. He knew the kingdom's constitution and couldn't be deceived or swayed. He was taught well by God, He is God in flesh, and He was filled with the Spirit of God. He resisted the devil, and he left him (1 Timothy 3:15–17).

Yeshua did not face temptations by just quoting scripture; He faced them with the Spirit too. Yeshua did not carry scrolls of scripture with Him. The Spirit was upon Him when He was tempted. The Holy Spirit was filling Him and coming from His mouth as He quoted scripture. It wasn't just that He quoted and used the scripture correctly; *He had power as He spoke scripture. He had bullets, light, and fuel, which are the sword. He had force and holy energy behind what He spoke. This is the sword; the power is the sword.*

Satan uses the gun too, but he has blanks. There are no bullets in the gun he attempts to use. He uses poison to deceive and lead people to their deaths by distorting the scripture. Distortion and deception only happen where there is no Spirit and disobedience.

When Yeshua spoke scripture, it wasn't the same as when anyone else spoke scripture. It was different with Him. When Yeshua spoke, the atmosphere shifted. Everyone in the synagogue, temple, or house could feel it and sense it. The atmosphere shifted with the first word that came out of His mouth. They may not have figured out why at first, but they knew this man had authority and was unique, different, unusual, otherworldly, and powerful. No other man could compare with how Yeshua taught and spoke.

With humans, scripture was just words, but Yeshua exuded peace, love, truth, and power. What He spoke was followed by powerful manifestations all the time because He spoke and taught scripture with power. Living waters filled the room. Light dispelled darkness, and darkness fled. Fire burned the entities hiding in the shadows of the room or in the deep recesses of a person's soul. The secrets of people's hearts were exposed, shaming them, humbling them, or angering them. One either loved the light or hated it.

In the presence of Yeshua, everything in the supernatural realm was touched in some way. Nothing could escape. The same sun that softens the wax hardens the clay. The condition of a person's heart is important in receiving the words He spoke and becoming fruitful. It was seen in the natural realm as miracles, signs, and wonders. No one else could speak the way He spoke, unless they were filled God's Spirit as we see in Acts.

The disciples' hearts burned as Yeshua explained the scriptures to them (Luke 24:35–37, 32). The Spirit that had recently raised Him from the dead accompanied the scriptures. If it were anyone else quoting and teaching scripture, the disciples' hearts would not have burned because there was no Spirit in them.

This is how it should be with His people today. However, with many men and women, even in this day and age, there are many words from the Bible, but no power or light. There is good teaching, but there is still no power or light. There are many words, but they are filled with errors and inaccuracies. Many people carry their guns and their lamps and talk a lot about the Father and Yeshua. They say they have their sword, but they actually lack bullets and oil. Many who speak don't cause the atmosphere to shift on the first word. That is authority, and you either welcome it or despise it.

As He taught about the kingdom in the synagogues, demons perceived by the teaching—and the Spirit accompanying it—said He was the Son of God. There was Spirit flowing out of Him as He preached and taught, which agitated the evil spirits. They were being burned and pushed away as He taught. Demons hate scripture because it testifies about the Holy One and His Son, it is our guide, and it is our kingdom's constitution. They hate it because it is the Word of the King in writing. Yet, when the Spirit of God accompanies it, scripture comes alive—and they are tormented, terrorized, driven out, burned, and bound. They are exposed in the light of the Holy Spirit.

Being filled with the Holy Spirit, He will force the demons to say their names. The Spirit is the sword and bullets, and we fight spirits with Spirit. Why would He force the demon to say its name if He is the sword that drives the demon out? There should be power in the words one speaks if filled with the presence of God. Yeshua didn't just teach and quote scripture; He packed a punch.

Why weren't they exposed and agitated at the teaching of other rulers in synagogues, priests, Pharisees, and Sadducees? They did not have the Spirit of God. Also, they were children of the devil. They were on the demon's side. Yeshua held the people in awe. There was power and manifestations that came with His teaching. There were amazing results. Before Yeshua's incarnation and even today, demons can sit in a synagogue or church where scripture is quoted often and never be exposed; there is no light to burn them.

There's a story of an evil spirit throwing a Bible across the room at someone in their own house; in another story, a hardcover Bible on a table closed itself and flipped over. If the Holy Spirit had been present there, it would not have touched it. In another story, a Baptist man who faithfully read his Bible daily aloud, but a demon caused the ceiling above him to fall on his head, causing great injury. The demon wore this religious man down to the point where he was sick and lost hope. He lost the spark from years earlier. He did not have His sword to fight, oil to light his way, or water to revive him. He had a gun without bullets, and the demon knew it. The Bible was hated by the evil spirit, yet people were not protected from it. They were without a sword: the Living Word.

A paranormal museum contains Bibles that became corrupted "with dark energy or attached with hostile presences." The Spirit, the blood, and the blessed water invoked with the holy name can never become tainted with evil; they are witnesses that save. Evil can't corrupt the Spirit of God, the blood of Yeshua, His body, which is without sin, or the blessed water invoked with His name. Salt, herbs, rosaries, crosses, medals, and statues might work, but they are not God-established things. According to John Zaffis, the tainted Bibles, among many other objects, were "known to be used for weapons used for ills or become trophies of dark forces who demonstrate their power." Dark forces cannot demonstrate their power over the blood of the Lamb, the Holy Spirit, or the blessed water.

Scripture works best with the Spirit indwelling the person who quotes, speaks, and lives by it. *It is the Spirit that packs the punch. It is the Spirit that gives the enemy a mighty blow. The Spirit gives life to what is spoken. There must be anointing with the scripture. When the Spirit (or oil/anointing) is present, one is counseled and taught correctly.*

In John 6:63, Yeshua says, "The words I have spoken to you are spirit and life." False teachings and doctrines and major errors will not occur to mislead people to sin. Many Jews in early times had scripture read and heard in synagogues, but they were still lost and without truth. They quoted scriptures a lot, but what good did it do them without the Spirit of God to teach them? There were the possessed, infirm, blind, deaf, mute, diseased, lame, bound, and tormented in their midst as they read scripture every Shabbat.

As the scripture was read every Shabbat, the written Word testified about Yeshua. It always points to Yeshua. Even the scribes, rulers, and teachers of the law were not taught correctly and did not understand as they should have. They were amazed by Yeshua's teaching. They did not have the Holy Spirit or anointing. Even the anointed high priest of the temple who was taught and memorized the scriptures did not recognize the Living Word, Yeshua, who was anointed with the Spirit of God. There was someone much greater than Him standing before Him, but he failed to recognize Him.

Without the Spirit, much is hidden and misunderstood. Simeon and Anna recognized who He was as a newborn infant before He said a word because the Spirit was with them. The anointed high priest did not have the Spirit.

How did the exorcists at that time drive demons out? They used scripture and the name of God, but they likely had to keep reading and repeating scripture and yelling it over and over again to make it happen. How did Yeshua do it? He only spoke one word or a few sentences, and it was done immediately with little trial or battle and no injuries. He had a sword that the exorcists did not have. Yeshua and the apostles never had to bind a demon-possessed person to prevent an attack. The Spirit bound and arrested the evil spirits before an attack could be unleashed on them.

Yeshua drove them out with the Spirit by a word. It wasn't a long ordeal for Him, and He did not speak to every level of command one at a time specifically. Why is it any different for us? Yeshua alone, without intimidation of the number of demons, dealt with a legion of demons in under five minutes. Why does it take us anywhere from two to ten hours to cast out one or two demons in His name by the Holy Spirit. Sometimes it requires natural bindings and repeating the commands? Perhaps one is given a certain level of authority by God. How long do you think the brief conversation with a legion of demons took? Not more than five minutes. How many times do you think Yeshua repeat Himself? None. Did He have to bind the demoniac as the men in the village did? No, He used a spiritual binding of the Holy Spirit.

Why do we perform deliverances so differently than He did? Is it a matter of faith and fasting? Did Yeshua have to prepare for or clean up vomit? No. If Yeshua can handle six thousand demons all at once, why do we deal with them one by one and for hours at a time? Yeshua had no time for that! I can't imagine casting out six thousand demons one at a time. It was wisdom on His part to ask the demon for the name it used as a group, thereby casting out all six thousand at one time. People's ways may work sometimes, but they are not like Yeshua. It's not the same. If Yeshua was tired, it was because of the volume of people He ministered to and not the hours He spent with each individual He healed or loosed from demons.

One man will put many to flight (Leviticus 26:6–8 and Deuteronomy 32:23–33). This is true in the natural realm and in the spirit realm. His will is done on earth as it is in heaven or unseen realms of earth. The words "to flight" suggest a departure that happens quickly as though running for their lives or from destruction. It is fast. This should be true for His people—even in the spirit realm with a legion or more of demons. That is authority and power.

Yeshua did not have to say things more than once. The people who He has given authority and power to shouldn't have to say anything to the King's captive twice. So how does exorcism take hours to complete? How does Yeshua do it in such a short time with so many demons? This is something to consider. The demons are fearful of His sword. Why do they procrastinate leaving a person or place? Why would they plead to stay if there truly is a fiery sword upon them? They will run! Anything or anyplace else would be better than any contact with His sword—just as the legion of demons thought being cast into swine would be better than His torment and strike. There was no pleading on their part to stay or hide inside the man, especially with a fiery and living sword coming down upon them or driving them out. Yeshua dropped it on them like it was hot! He laid the sword on them fiercely. Evil entities don't want to dance with His sword. Yeshua is serious, and He is not a King to play around with.

Yeshua and His disciples cast out demons wherever they went; they weren't on holy ground in the natural realm. They were on holy ground in the spirit realm—in the heavens. People can go farther and cast out more demons when they are on spiritual holy ground. There is more progress and more accomplished for the kingdom of heaven. When it is holy ground in the natural realm, one is limited. When it is in the natural realm and without ammunition, it is limited and wears one down.

The human method is working harder; Yeshua's method is working smarter for the kingdom of God. Man's method doesn't cover much ground. Yeshua's method covers more ground and gets more accomplished more effectively and more efficiently.

Yeshua sent out the apostles during His ministry, and they cast out demons, but they were under His holy cover in a similar way. The presence of God was with them wherever they went. They carried His name on their foreheads from their baptism in the name of the Father, Son, and Holy Spirit. It was their badge. The kingdom was in the midst of them. In the spirit realm, they were on holy ground. This calls for faith.

The exorcists were without the Holy Spirit and any faith in Yeshua personally. They were beating demons with the gun, but they had no ammunition. They had lamps that were dim or unlit. They weren't covered and in Him as Paul and the apostles were. The apostles had the name too, but they also used swords in His presence and under the covering. They were guided and filled with the Holy Spirit who was the ammunition—the power.

Philip told the Ethiopian about Yeshua from the scripture in Isaiah, but he also had the Holy Spirit with him. The Spirit within Philip shed light upon the Ethiopian, so he could understand Scripture in Isaiah (Acts 8:25–40). In Acts 6:10, the leaders "were unable to cope with the wisdom and the Spirit with which he was speaking." In Acts 7:54–56, the Spirit cut at their consciences and angered them.

> "Lord, Lord, did we not cast out demons in Your name and do many miracles in Your name?" He will say to them, "I never knew you; Away from me, you who practice lawlessness!" (Matthew 7:22, 23)

They were not born again and did not have His Spirit. They did not and could not obey Him as King and Lord.

The Word of God is the Spirit of God or Yeshua. He is the Living Word made flesh. He was before scripture came to be. This sword drove away evil spirits in the Gospels and destroyed the beast in Revelation. The sword that comes out of Yeshua's mouth in Revelation is the Spirit, not the Bible. Scripture is the written word and points to the Spirit of God and Yeshua who was I Am before scripture came to be. *Keep the Living Word behind the written Word you believe and quote. The living waters must be flowing as you speak scripture. This is where the power is.* Otherwise, it is like having a car without gas or a battery. It is like having a gun without any bullets. It is like reading a book in the dark or without electricity or a candle. The Spirit makes the difference.

The Jews in the first century—and before—had the car without the gas. They had the gun without the bullets. They had the book, but they were still in the dark. Darkness saw the void and the weakness and filled it. A light dawned on those sitting in the land and shadow of death (Matthew 4:15, 16; Isaiah 9:1–2; 60:1–3).

With scripture read every Shabbat, how were they still sitting in the darkness and considered lost sheep? The sun does not shine in the spirit realm. Natural light is not there. Doesn't scripture give light? Isn't it a lamp? Isn't scripture the sword? According to these verses, it wasn't enough. It was the Living Word (Yeshua) that came and shone on the people living in the dark. This Living Word, Yeshua, was conceived of the Holy Spirit. He is the light and the power of scripture.

"Thy word is a lamp unto my feet and a light unto my path" (Psalm 119:105). This refers to the written Word, but the Holy Spirit is the oil that keeps the lamp (scripture) shining. If there is no oil, it will grow dark. Understanding of the written Word is hidden or lost. In the light of the Holy Spirit, the written Word directs our steps and guides us. If the Spirit doesn't teach you His word, you read in the dark.

"The Lord is my light and my salvation" (Psalm 27:1). Psalms 19 and 119 are still true of the written Word. The Lord lights my lamp and illumines my darkness (Psalm 18:28). Which is greater, the gun or the bullets? The bullets, but both are needed to make something happen in this realm. The fuel/battery is very important to the car, but both are needed to make something happen in this realm. Would you rather pistol-whip or shoot the gun? Shooting is better.

This was similar to the Ark of the Covenant. When Israel disobeyed, God told them He would not be with them in battle (1 Samuel 4–7). Even though they brought the ark to battle with them, He withdrew His Spirit from it—and Israel was still defeated with the ark present. The attachment of God's Spirit to the ark provided light, power, victory, and energy to the

Israelites when they fought. When God was displeased with them, He withdrew Himself from their midst so that they lost. The battle belonged to the Lord—not to the ark or to the Israelites. Without His Spirit, they had no sword, and they lost the battle even with the ark in their midst. The ark only served as the contact or bridge through which He entered the natural realm.

It is the same way with scripture. The battle belongs to the Lord, not to the Bible. Without His Spirit attached, you have no sword. You can lose the battle even with a Bible in your midst. The ark and the scripture are both holy and established by God, but the Spirit is where the power is. Where there is no Spirit, one will lose the battle even quoting scripture. There is no sword and no bullets in the gun, and the enemy figures this out quickly. The holy objects are needed in this natural realm, but they work best with the Spirit of God attached to the ark or the person He fills. The battle belongs to the Lord, not to us. We fight darkness, but it is the Lord who goes before us, who is in us, who gives us the victory. He wins it as we act or speak according to His will, not ours.

When scripture is taught and understood accurately and in truth, our aim will also be accurate and on target. You will never miss. Yeshua had his gun with his bullets and had good aim. He never missed His target. He could shoot from great distances when the Roman asked Him not to come to his house. He could shoot from anywhere and not just from a certain place because He was in the Holy Place wherever He went. Holy ground was where He was at the time. Many today do not have good aim because their understanding and doctrine have errors or are not accurate or up to date.

When we quote or read Scripture —whether you carry a Bible or not— it is your gun. The Spirit is your endless supply of bullets. If you are filled with the Spirit, you never have to reload the gun. When Peter gave his sermons in Acts, he quoted scripture without carrying scrolls with him. He had his gun, and it was loaded with bullets: the Holy Spirit.

The scripture is the lamp, but the Holy Spirit is the oil that keeps it lit. Again, which is greater: the lamp or the oil? The oil is greater because it is the fuel for the lamp, yet both are needed in this realm. The ten virgins had lamps (scripture), but only half of them had plenty of oil (Holy Spirit). Those who did not have enough oil were left outside to beg to come in with the bridegroom. The Holy Spirit causes us to see the bridegroom and the kingdom of heaven. Apart from His Spirit, there is blindness or darkness and no entry into the kingdom. We need the Holy Spirit with the scripture we read or quote. If we hold our lamp, He will fill it with oil and we will hear Him. If you don't know the Scripture or have a lamp, how will He fill and light it? His light causes us to understand and see.

Scripture comes from the Holy Spirit; the Spirit does not come from the scripture. The Holy Spirit is greater because scripture comes from Him, points to Him, and testifies of Him.

May Yeshua be lifted up, so all of us are drawn unto Him. Like Philip, "We have found Him of whom Moses in the Law and also the Prophets wrote—Yeshua of Nazareth, the son of Joseph" (John 1:45).

If this is how it was for the disciples when He went to the Father in heaven, how will it be after He has returned in fulfillment of scripture in the first century and during this ongoing visitation of the King?

Adonai, pour the oil and fire of Your Spirit into my lamp that it may give me light, light my path, and bring accurate understanding of Your written word which points to and testifies of Yeshua, the Living Word. Without the oil and flame of Your Spirit there is no light so there is a lack of understanding and a distortion of Your laws and commandments to the peril of our souls. Without Your Spirit to teach us, truths also remain hidden from its readers and hearers. Without the light of Your Spirit, we read with a darkened mind. The written word, the Scripture, comes from Your Spirit.

Just as Your Spirit broke the swords and arrows of Your enemies and the arms that were posed against You and Your people in the past, so too break their natural guns and weapons in this day. Their guns are no match for Your sword which is alive. You are above, they are below. Dominate and subdue those against You, glorify Your holy Name just as You did long ago. Let the nations fear You and stand trembling before You again. May they make no mistake of who You are and that You are with those who believe, who are in Yeshua. Let them speak of Your mighty deeds and works which You will do for the salvation of Your chosen people.

You are a great King renowned in the heavens, so too in these last days of earth, may Your great and holy Name be renowned on the earth among every nation. Amen.

CHAPTER 28

The Warning and the Blessed Hope

History supports the fulfillment of prophecy in this interpretation. Everyone must wake up and understand that the signs the entire world are witnessing and experiencing are birth pangs that have continued since AD 70, but they are also a warning. The earthly signs that began in the first century don't stop with Messiah's Parousia; they continue until the passing away of this first heavens and earth.

A futurist interpretation of prophecy just does not align with history and the present reality. The signs are misread prophetically. A futurist sees the signs as an imminent Second Coming of the Messiah. It is beyond a Second Coming; it is either a divine visitation that has been ongoing in the Spirit for thousands of years or another coming at hand, not in fulfillment of Zechariah 12, but a deliverance from the passing away with fire. It is signaling an end to what is temporal. The King traverses to and fro. The signs are of an imminent extinction in the coming decades.

Is God calling Israel back to their land before this extinction? Is it as such a time as this that God is lifting the veil from Israel to believe Yeshua is the Messiah and their brother? Is it at such a time as this that the Holy One of Israel pours out His Spirit upon Israel and Christians?

Many will ignore all the signs and say, "I don't believe it," "That is a long, long way off," or "A loving King would not do such a thing." However, that is the thinking of the unbelieving world in Noah's and Lot's day. They did not believe and were destroyed. He is a loving and merciful King, but He is also holy, just, and faithful. He keeps His Word.

To the skeptic, the doubter, the futurist, the preterist, the believer, the unbeliever, those dwelling in the natural and spiritual places, the governments, and the holy congregations, let it be said: Let God be true and every man a liar. "Heaven and earth shall pass away, but my words will not pass away" (Matthew 24:35).

While I don't consider it condemnable to be a futurist, there are futurists who would condemn me as a preterist. However, for a futurist to see these signs and the deterioration and collapse of economies, governments, worldly systems, ecosystems, and planet earth itself and refuse to acknowledge the truth prevents many from hearing what God is warning everyone. To say what is written in this book disrupts the peace of a synagogue or church is refusing many to prayerfully decide if this is of God or not and act on whatever God would have all of us do. The truth Yeshua spoke and taught in the synagogues unsettled many people and caused a disturbance. He brought division. The truth should not remain hidden from His people to prevent unsettling people; they must know and prayerfully decide for themselves. Telling people to go back to sleep numbs their sensitivity. They put their heads in the sand, ignore the truth, and refuse to face it until it is way too late.

As a preterist, I am trying to inform Apollos (believers today) who only knew about John's baptism, about another baptism. I want believers to come out of the woods and know much more is happening than they think. I want believers to upgrade from Windows 98 to the current one. I want believers to see the footprints of a dinosaur that was present. I am saying a dinosaur, or someone great and renowned in the heavens, was here at certain times in history; look at the footprints, the clues.

Here are more questions to consider: How do the saints visibly reign on this present old earth with little to no life on it? What is left for the saints to return to? Over what will the saints have dominion over if everything is dead? How does Yeshua come after earth's massive die-offs and extinctions? Maybe He comes again just before.

We know the inhabitants of Jerusalem loudly wept and mourned the loss of their temple in AD 70. As the Spirit was poured out, according to Zechariah, who did they see before or even as they perished in the onslaught? They mourned the destruction of the temple and God's lack of deliverance from their enemies. Yeshua was revealed by the Spirit. Who dealt the judgments written and prophesied in Ezekiel to the deceived "Christian" Crusaders who surrounded the holy city, Jerusalem? Who inflicted the nations of the earth today with severe drought according to Zechariah? Before whom do the heavens and the earth begin to pass away? All these things occur in the Day of the Lord. It is Yeshua—before whom all these things came to pass.

Yeshua visited in early AD 70 and again during the Crusades. Now either He is still visiting as a thief in the night in a Parousia or He is coming yet again, not in fulfillment of Zechariah 12, but to reap a harvest and deliver His people out of the world's inevitable, impending destruction with fire and intense heat. Now consider that if He can bring these things to pass, how is the passing away of the heavens and earth not going to happen in coming decades? How can we downplay it as though it won't be that serious or it is not going to happen?

The Day of the Lord has surely come as a thief in the night as many sleep unaware and caught off guard during His Parousia. *The fulfillment of these scriptures was not a coincidence; the words came to pass at the proper time.* There is no time for rebuilding a third temple. Rethink your interpretation. The millennial reign had to have happened, and a reign continues. We don't see it naturally because His kingdom is spiritual, not of this world. *If flesh and blood can't inherit the kingdom of heaven, how do we see it coming with our natural eyes of flesh?*

Earth's resources were given by God for human use. It is expected for the earth to grow old and wear out like a garment. Humankind is to dominate, rule, and subdue the earth; that is what God intended (Genesis 1:26–30). However, we have dominated it in a manner of destruction and sabotage. Humans have proved to be a destructive species. Humankind has dominated earth with a mentality of it being a slave, using it until it dies, or something that has inexhaustible or eternal supply resources that can always replenish and recover despite the damage and pollution we put on it.

Should we have ever behaved and lived as though we were rulers over the earth or as people who coexisted equally with the rest of creation. How has humankind ruled and dominated the earth? Has humankind been good ruling stewards of God's footstool? What is the fruit of a rule (spiritual or natural) that God is pleased with? Does a good ruler carry a responsibility for good stewardship over spiritual and earthly matters?

God has given us charge over caring for the earth. As citizens of an eternal kingdom—and by extension of the millennial reign that already occurred, regardless of having been judged or not—we must understand the authority we have in Yeshua and the ongoing and current reign and rule under the headship of Yeshua.

We shouldn't think Yeshua would not hold us accountable for not just our personal property, businesses, and our witness of Him. What have we done to His footstool? Yeshua would have every right to ask us why He should allow us to inherit and rule on the new earth if we lack the fruit of an acceptable rule on the old earth.

"He who is faithful in a very little thing, is faithful also in much; and he who is unrighteous in a very little thing is unrighteous also in much" (Luke 16:10). This verse can also apply to the faithful stewardship of earth. The first-century generation who ruled in the millennial reign did not damage and destroy the earth; later ones did. Perhaps it will be given to them, leaving us saved but subordinate to them. I wouldn't be surprised if that was His judgment to us. It would be gracious of Him to allow us to inherit the new earth anyway. We don't deserve it.

Given the destruction upon this earth, we should not feel entitled to a new one. This would be akin to the servant in Yeshua's parable feeling entitled to more talents despite his lack of productivity. We should humble ourselves before Him. On one hand, I think believers, who are also stewards of personal property and the planet, should be leading the charge on saving the earth, but on the other hand, Yeshua said it would die. His Word will not be fruitless, and no one can override and make void what He has spoken. Extinction will happen. Earth cannot be saved. We are at His mercy.

We live our lives while denying the reality of earth's imminent, inevitable end. Did Noah or Lot deny the reality of the impending destruction coming to their generations? Did Joseph disregard Pharaoh's dreams and not prepare for the imminent catastrophic famine that was coming? They had to face the reality of destruction as believers in the one true God. They did not panic, but they had to pray, seek God, move, act, and go, go, go.

The people of the AD 70 destruction of the temple and the desolation of Jerusalem, *Titanic,* and the Holocaust also faced the reality of destruction. We are no different from all of them. There are no hills of Judea to flee to. Where do we go? Go to Him, submit under His authority, and obey whatever He tells us to do. Open the door to Him. Be ready because the tide is coming. Wake up!

It is not the beast of a Roman emperor or any other man one must contend with. The beasts the inhabitants of the earth must contend with now are climate change, super volcanoes, and the hidden dangers coming from space that we can't see or detect now, and eternity in hell. Facing an angry God who, as judge, has the power to destroy the body and soul is also a terrifying expectation of what is to come.

Pay attention to the strange and unusual changes earth is undergoing.

The rains in the desert that cause deadly swamps to form, steam and gases pouring out of the ground in a desert indicating a volcano forming, increasing earthquakes and volcanic eruptions, the strange behavior and die off of animals, the dying coral reefs, large sink holes and large cracks forming in the ground, and many more.

Pay attention to the strange and unusual changes the stars in the sky undergo. Remember, it is not just earth, but the heavens that pass away in fire too. Already there are more meteors and fire balls seen beginning to fall upon some areas of earth. Some stars are seen pulsating or twinkling unusually. A piercing star (which I think precedes the formation of a black hole) was recently spotted in 2019.

The Word of the Lord shall stand; heaven and earth will pass away, but what must be done today?

> Be anxious for nothing, but in everything by prayer and supplication with thanksgiving let your requests be made known to God. And the peace of God, which surpasses all comprehension, will guard your hearts and minds in Christ Jesus. (Philippians 4:6)

1. Accept the King's invitation to His feast. Put on your life jacket. Stay in the lifeboat. This is not a time to think, "It's hot in this lifeboat, and this humble lifeboat is beneath my tastes. Hmmm, that water (or world) sure looks good right now. Let me take off this life jacket, get out of this lifeboat, and take a swim." This is the thinking of a faithless believer. Making this decision to leave Him could spell peril for you. A strong, swift current might take you far away from safety or from under the shadow of His wings. A faithful believer should look at the waters (or world) and say, "That water is looking pretty funky, polluted, and foul right now. I will stay clean and dry in this lifeboat."
2. Throw out the lifeline or the life jacket because they are drowning. Invite them to the feast of the great and renowned King of the heavens. He wants guests at His table. Continue to spread the good news of the kingdom of God for salvation because the door is closing.
3. Pray for the harvest because the door is closing.
4. Pray that the Lord will pour His Spirit upon Israel and the Jews' eyes will be opened to see His face as they are gathered.

5. Pray that His Spirit will be poured out upon all believers, Jew and Gentile; so that we may be equipped to accomplish any tasks we are to do in His name related to kingdom and to preserving species of animals.
6. Pay attention to the increasing signs in the earth and in the heavens above. They are birth pangs that began before His coming in AD 70, but they continue until the extinction of life on earth.
7. Ask how you can help preserve the creatures of the earth as it was done during Noah's day. Ask the Lord to be compassionate over the various species of animals as done during the flood and even Lot's sheep. Animals need our help.
8. Your citizenship in the kingdom of heaven must be at the forefront instead of the citizenship of your earthly country. Worldly systems will break down and collapse. All that is natural is being stripped away, fleeing from the presence of Adonai. Democracy is not going to matter anymore. It will pass away along with every other form of worldly government, leaving the only government of God's kingdom. It shall remain when everything collapses and ends.

We put on our most holy faith. We ask God and speak to the "mountains," which are the various disasters and catastrophes arising in the world today due to this extinction and the lack of resources, which are appearing before us.

We have not because we don't ask. We must make our requests known to the King without trying to override, change, or reverse the King's order of this passing because these things must take place and cannot be stopped. We take authority over the conquered kingdoms, and we further or continue to exert the reign that rightfully belongs to the people of God in the earth while we remain here for a short time before the destruction. We must do this while remaining in His will and as a people in one accord.

We also await our salvation. We comfort and encourage each other, we pray for each other, and we help each other get through tough times. These things are necessary in times of great trouble, calamity, loss, and danger. What would the outcome be if Noah and his family stayed on land, trying to encourage the world to get on the boat and pray for them, but never actually got on the ark and allowed God to close the door.

What would the outcome be for Moses if he stayed on the side of the Red Sea with the Egyptians comforting, encouraging, and praying them for their fellow fearful Hebrews without ever actually crossing over to the other side? What would the outcome be for Lot if he stayed and tried to persuade his sons-in-law to leave—and he never left himself? Time would be wasted in each case, and the outcomes would be tragic. Obedience was very important. Danger and catastrophes were approaching, and there was no delay. There was a sense of urgency to leave, get out, and act by faith. As believers, we cannot do this. We must courageously follow what these men did.

Most topics on television and in sermons these days pale in comparison to recognizing, praying, and discussing the passing away. That sign pales in comparison to the kingdom of heaven. If we are not talking in the light of these things, then it's unimportant, trivial, and meaningless. He wants us to take a step or two up. There is a serious lack of immediacy to how people are acting toward this. People say they have things to do—or they are really enjoying themselves—but isn't this what Yeshua said they would be doing? People are building, marrying, buying, selling, traveling, and conducting business before destruction suddenly comes on them.

As it was with Joseph, his brothers, and his father, so it will be with Israel and Yeshua. They will come to Him because of the earth's lack seeking sustenance, He will save Israel, and they will realize He is their brother.

As it was in Acts 11:27–30 when it was prophesied that a great famine was to come, the believers prepared and gave a contribution to provide relief to the brethren in Judea. Perhaps we should take heed to the warning until our departure.

I believe there is about to be an exodus of a different kind. An exodus—a removal or mass migration—of God's people as it was with Noah, Lot, and the Hebrews out of Egypt. At hand, a harvest of wheat and tares, a resurrection of the holy and unholy to be separated. An exodus or migration like that of the survivors of *Titanic* and the Holocaust has to be imminent.

The last days of the temple won't apply to us, but the last days of the earth will. This present earth's story of its end will be legendary, but we have a greater hope of a new heaven and earth in which the saints reign and the meek shall inherit the earth (Isaiah 65:8–25; 66:18–24).

No human has ever seen living dinosaurs, but there are signs and evidence that they existed long ago in the history of time. The signs and evidence we look at are its footprints and bones. They left their mark here. There are clues of their existence and presence upon earth that we put together and make a conclusion on what existed before or in the beginning of humankind's existence. We don't look at the clues, set them aside, ignore them, and never consider or acknowledge the existence or presence of a creature that use to live before its extinction. Likewise, Yeshua has left His footprints, though no one in current generations has recognized His visitation(s). We shouldn't look at the clues, set them aside, ignore them, and never consider or acknowledge the existence or presence of His visitation(s). History and the written record of ancient historians are the clues left behind and both concur with fulfillment of prophecy.

We can see that the events starting from the four worldly kingdoms that are absent and are no more: the temple's destruction in AD 70, the ensigns or idols and sacrifice that defiled the holy temple, Vesuvius's eruption in AD 79, the great earthquake that split the city, a thousand-year period from the end of Domitian's reign (the eleventh horn) and the end of the Flavian dynasty, the Crusades (Gog and Magog), the visions and experiences of people who were taken by Yeshua to heaven and/or hell and coming back to report and testify of what they have seen, and the present and swift deterioration of earth and its inhabitants. This aligns with the prophecy written in scripture. When we remove the gaps that humans have placed in biblical prophecy, we can see Yeshua has fulfilled a lot more than what teachers today proclaim. Human gaps only put a delay on fulfillment and put people to sleep. They give the impression that things are not as serious and dire as they really are. Things will not be good for our current generations in the coming decades. Much of the world is in a panic in regards to climate change, various deadly epidemics, catastrophic natural disasters, wars, conflicts between humans and animals, food and water scarcity, pollution, and government and economic instability. Many "biblical, Noah-like" problems are arising that are unprecedented for current generations and will only grow worse. Scientists have noticed the signs, but they do not connect it to or understand that it was prophesied in Scripture a long time ago. If we don't see Him in the Spirit, in the very least, we must learn to read the signs of fulfillment that occur in the natural accurately. I am concerned many believers fail to connect the signs to prophecy and interpret accurately. Therefore, they do not take the disasters to come seriously and so prepare accordingly.

We must recognize this is also the Day of the Lord, and He has been very much present and traverses the earth and heavens. Who else was fighting against the Crusaders who came to Jerusalem and their spiritual entities Gog and Magog? Who caused the Crusaders' flesh to rot in their mouths and fall off as gangrene? Who did this during a time, and the last time, when the world fought with gear described in Ezekiel at Jerusalem? It is not a coincidence that all these things happened to line up with prophecy. Again, they don't put the pieces of the puzzle together. They miss this footprint, evidence of someone's presence.

Wake up, open your eyes, and read the writing on the wall. Stop allowing teachers to put you back to sleep—or you will be like those of 1 Thessalonians 5:2–10 who sleep during the night and the Day of the Lord comes as a thief closing in on them suddenly and they are unprepared to meet King Yeshua.

Judgment begins with God's house, and then the saints are expected to judge the world, angels, and demons in the second resurrection (1 Corinthians 6:2, 3; Revelation 20).

Stop going with gut feelings, which more likely are the flesh. Just go by the Spirit, the scripture, and the signs given. We, as believers, must come to realize that—just as the book of Daniel was sealed up until the time of fulfillment during the end of the holy temple—this has been sealed and hidden from us until now. The time of heaven and earth's end has come. Life for everyone on the planet will not go on as normal. According to Scripture, many lives, both human and creature, will perish.

While this sobering truth seems bitter, the sweet part is that the kingdom of God has arrived and "the meek shall inherit the earth", a new earth (Matthew 5:5; Revelation 21:1).

Timeline of the Kingdoms

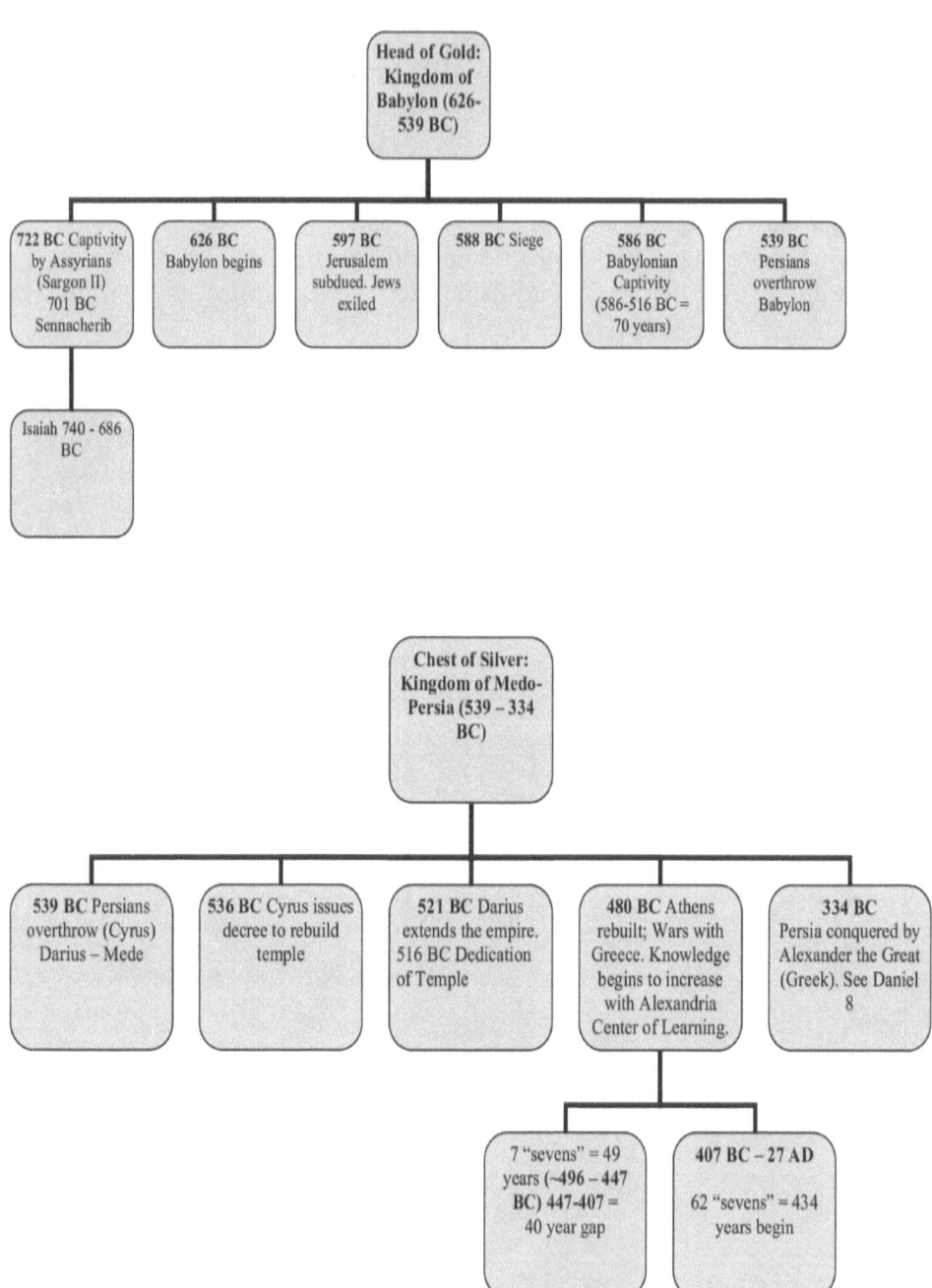

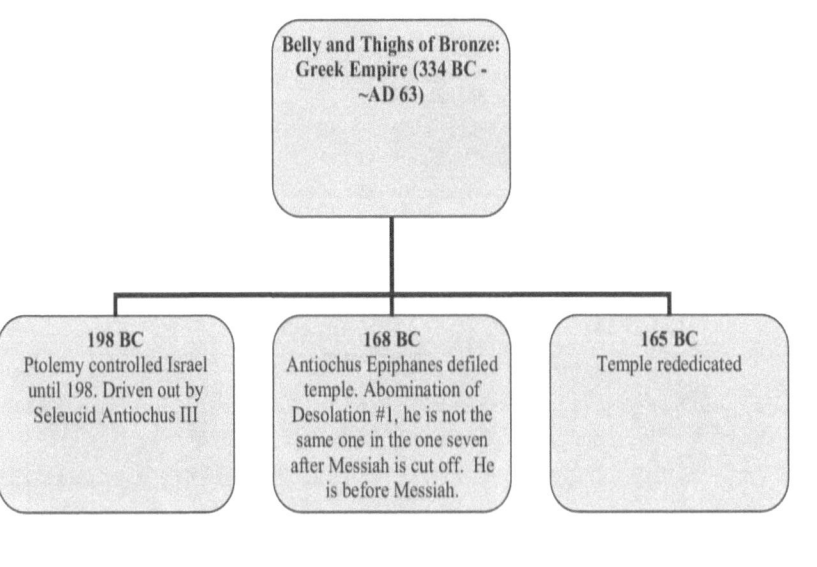
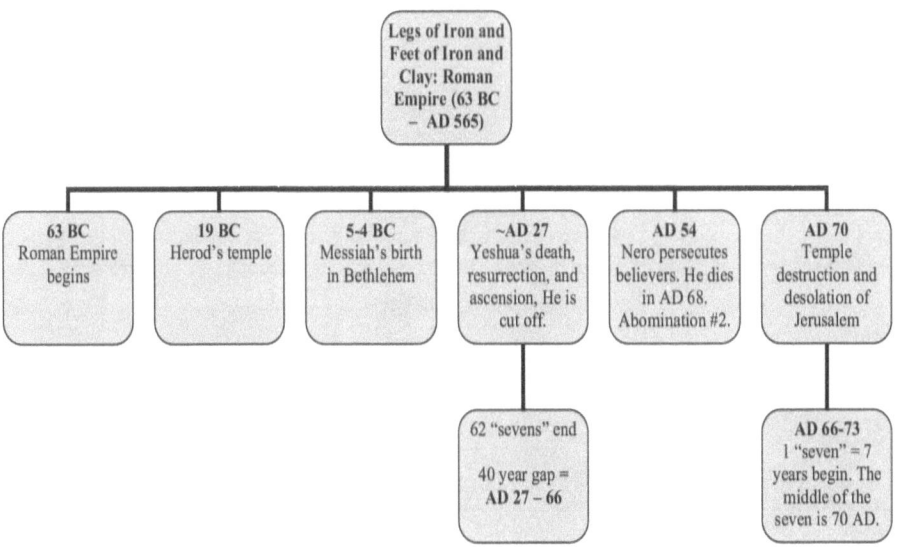

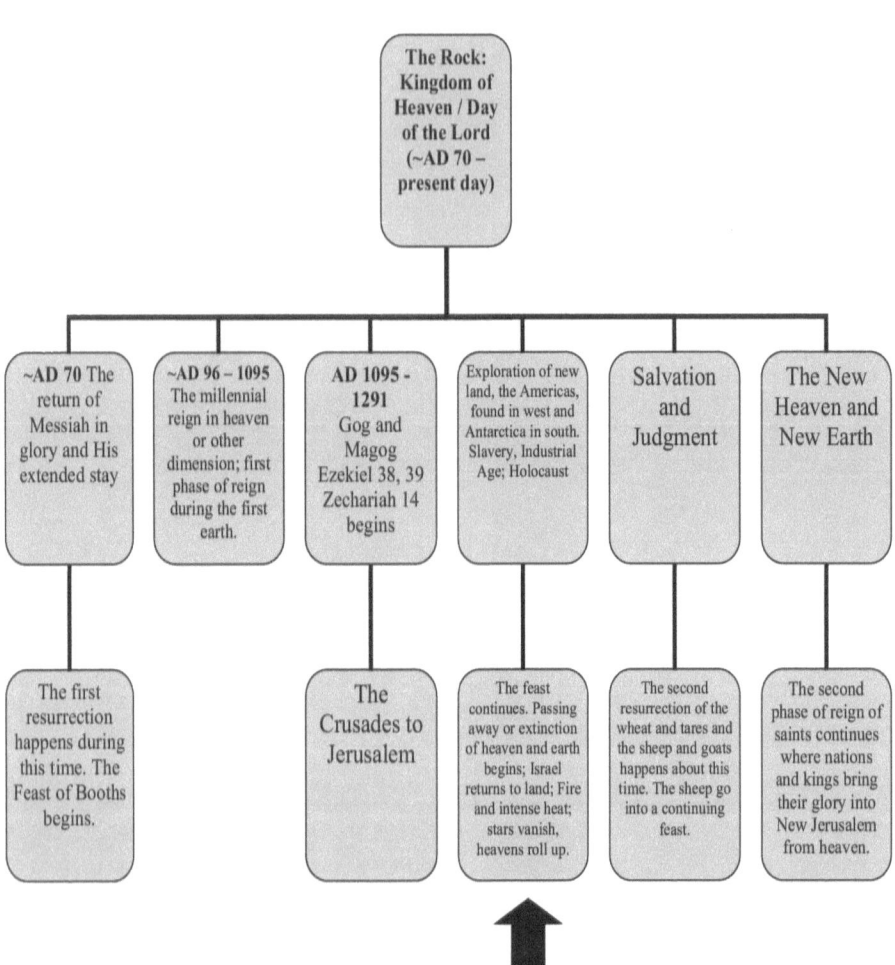

Glossary

preterit. Past.

exist. To continue to be, actual occurrence, in progress, to move forward, continual, ongoing

full preterism. All prophecy is fulfilled. This is the new heaven and earth.

partial preterism. Some prophecy fulfilled. Some believe the Second Coming is still to happen in the future. Some believe it was fulfilled in the first century.

existential or progressive preterism. This can be partial preterism, but there is another element going on. It is in progress now. This is not meant in the sense that God's Word changes and He does not keep His Word, but that it is being fulfilled and He is bringing His Word to pass. Everything written is coming to fulfillment as promised. We witness it now. His Word is in the progress of fulfillment.

Parousia. The physical presence of a person, the prospect of the physical arrival of that person, especially the visit of a royal or official personage and sometimes as an extension of this usage, a formal occasion.

Bibliography

AD 79: A Prophecy Paradox, Lynn Louise Schuldt, 1996, Son Mountain Press.

AD 1000: Living on the Brink of Apocalypse, Richard Erdoes, 1995, Barnes and Noble, Inc.

Demon Haunted: True Stories from the John Zaffis Vault, John Zaffis and Rosemary Ellen Guiley, 2016, Visionary Living, Inc.

The Annals and the Histories, Cornelius Tacitus, translated by Alfred John Church and William Jackson Brodribb, 2003, Modern Library Classics.

The Complete Idiot's Guide to the Crusades, Paul L. Williams, PhD, 2002, Pearson Education Company.

The Complete Works of Josephus, Flavius Josephus, translated by Wm. Whiston, 1981, Kregel Publications.

The Crusaders: Warriors of God, Georges Tate, translated from French by Lory Frankel, 1996, Harry N. Abrams Inc.

The Crusades: Five Centuries of Holy Wars, Malcolm Billings, 1996, Sterling Publishing Co., Inc.

The Discerning of Spirits, Frank Hammond, 2014, Impact Christian Books, Inc.

The Hidden Power of the Blood of Jesus, Mahesh Chavda, 2004, Destiny Image Publishers, Inc.

The History of the Roman Emperors, Robert Lynam, 2017, HardPress.

The Last Two Million Years, 1977, The Reader's Digest Association, Inc.

The Principle and Power of Kingdom Citizenship, Myles Munroe, 2016, Destiny Image Publishers, Inc.

The Twelve Caesars, Suetonius, 1989, Penguin Group.

Bloomberg Businessweek, Caroline Winter, June 10, 2019, "Towing Icebergs from Antarctica to South Africa."

People.com, Georgia Slater, February 7, 2020, "Scientists Warn Bumblebees Might Be Going Extinct Due to Climate Crisis."

Wikipedia.org

Catastrophes and Crises

The followings resources speak of the signs unfolding within the earth. For e-book readers, if link is not active, copy and paste the links into browser to view articles:

Farms Struggle

https://www.agriculture.com/news/kansas-and-nebraska-farmers-keep-planting-praying-for-rain.

http://time.com/4170029/crop-production-extreme-heat-climate-change/.

https://www.fb.org/market-intel/addressing-the-impact-of-prolonged-drought-on-farm-program-yields.

https://www.nytimes.com/roomfordebate/2015/04/07/can-farms-survive-without-drying-up-california-13/california-farmers-have-suffered-enough-from-the-drought..

https://familyspice.com/california-farms-water-crisis/.

https://www.nbcnews.com/storyline/california-drought/california-farmers-near-survival-mode-drought-drags-n332566.

theeconomiccollapseblog.com/archives/total-catastophe-for-u-s-corn-production-only-30–of.

https://www.zerohedge.com/news/2019–05–09/food-crisis-here-trouble-farmers-corn-belt.

https://earther.gizmodo.com/drought-has-wiped-out-130-millions-pounds-of-corn-in-el-1827860076.

Glaciers, Lakes, and Rivers Disappearing, Water Shortages https://www.nytimes.com/2016/02/13/science/two-thirds-of-the-world-faces-severe-water-shortages.html.

https://www.worldwildlife.org/threats/water-scarcity.

https://www.huffingtonpost.com/entry/water-scarcity-study us 56c1eb c5e4b0b40245c72f5e.

https://www.theguardian.com/environment/2015/mar/08/how-water-shortages-lead-food-crises-conflicts.

http://strangesounds.org/2016/06/rivers-and-lakes-mysteriously-disappear-increase-around-the-world.html.

http://mentalf loss.com/article/56732/10-lakes-are-disappearing-or-already-gone.

https://m.youtube.com/watch?v=OWKAq9rb8H8.

https://www.theguardian.com/global-development-professionals-network/gallery/2016/dec/09/the-lakes-of-the-world-are-disappearing-in-pictures.

https://www.newscientist.com/article/2079562-many-of-worlds-lakes-are-vanishing-and-some-may-be-gone-forever/.

https://www.usatoday.com/story/news/world/2018/02/14/water-crisis-cape-town-day-zero-june/337844002/.

https://www.cnn.com/2018/01/24/africa/cape-town-water-crisis-trnd/index.html.

https://w w w.zerohedge.com/news/2016 – 06 –17/las-vegas-going-dry-largest-reservoir-america-reaches-record-low.

https://www.cbsnews.com/news/lake-mead-is-shrinking-and-with-it-las-vegas-water-supply/.

https://truthout.org/articles/arctic-is-thawing-so-fast-scientists-are-losing-their-measuring-tools.

https://www.cnn.com/2019/06/19/india/chennai-water-crisis-intl-hnk/index.html.

https://www.ecowatch.com/greenland-temperatures-above-normal-2638907188.html.

https://www.washingtonpost.com/weather/2019/06/14/arctic-ocean-greenland-ice-sheet-have-seen-record-june-ice-loss/?utm_term=.45209fa9e958.

Animal Mass Deaths

http://www.end-times-prophecy.org/animal-deaths-birds-fish-end-times.html. (The above address has many link buttons to click to see the various animals, areas, and dates that the deaths occurred. Scroll all the way to bottom to see previous years from 2011–2018. YouTube has many videos of the animals, birds, crabs dying mysteriously.).

http://www.latimes.com/science/sciencenow/la-sci-sn-saiga-antelope-dieoff-20150531-story.html.

http://www.foxnews.com/science/2018/01/18/scientists-unravel-bizarre-mystery-mass-antelope-deaths.html.

http://www.dailymail.co.uk/sciencetech/article-3099450/Mass-deaths-hit-Kazakhstans-endangered-Ice-Age-antelope-species.html.

https://www.nytimes.com/2015/06/02/science/saiga-antelope-mystery-disease-die-off.html.

https://www.cbc.ca/news/canada/british-columbia/grey-whales-stranded-west-coast-1.5119056.

Extinction

http://www.dailymail.co.uk/sciencetech/article-4684530/Earth-s-sixth-mass-extinction-underway.html.

https://www.usatoday.com/story/tech/science/2017/07/10/earth-faces-sixth-mass-extinction/465655001/.

http://time.com/3035872/sixth-great-extinction/.

https://www.weforum.org/agenda/2017/08/a-sixth-mass-extinction-is-underway-and-its-our-fault/.

http://www.newser.com/story/208606/mass-extinction-underway-will-kill-off-humans-report.html.

https://www.washingtonpost.com/archive/politics/1998/04/21/mass-extinction-under way-majorit y-of-biologists-say/dc906383 –fc37–41e1–a8e9–2d2f061d8a88/?noredirect=on&utm term=. 60f76d0b5cdd.

https://www.rte.ie/eile/brainstorm/2018/0223/942906–breaking-the-next-mass-extinction-event-is-already-underway/.

http://www.pbs.org/wgbh/evolution/library/03/2/l 032 04.html.

https://grist.org/science/150000 –penguins-have-disappeared-in-antarctica-thanks-climate-change/.

https://ypte.org.uk/factsheets/penguins/penguins-disappearing-from-the-antarctic.

https://www.biologicaldiversity.org/news/press releases/2010/african-penguin-09–28–2010.html.

https://www.newsweek.com/stunning-yellow-eyed-penguins-already-endangered-are-being-drowned-fishermen-723640.

https://planetsave.com/2010/08/24/lizard-species-going-extinct-rapidly-from-climate-change/.

http://www.dailymail.co.uk/sciencetech/article-1278365/Lizards-face-extinction-global-warming-forces-stay-shade.html.

https://extinction.in/content/reptiles-are-going-extinct.

https://www.theguardian.com/environment/2013/feb/15/reptile-species-face-extinction.

https://www.ohio.edu/research/communications/lizards.cfm.

https://www.sciencedaily.com/releases/2013/03/130305200306.htm.

https://gritpost.com/humans-extinct-climate-change/.

https://www.news.com.au/technology/science/animals/koalas-now-functionally-extinct-says-australian-koala-foundation/news-story/1ee81a3bb80b59f22abbbe8f5a50d777.

https://www.nytimes.com/2018/07/09/science/orcas-whales-endangered.html.

https://www.sfgate.com/news/article/2–more-whales-found-dead-in-San-Francisco-Bay-Area-13773155.php.

The Extinction Domino Effect that Could Annihilate Life on Earth Has Already Started: https://m.youtube.com/watch?v=H6EXFpnjXNc.

https://www.theguardian.com/environment/2018/feb/13/a-national-disgrace-australias-extinction-crisis-is-unfolding-in-plain-sight http://www.animalplanet.com/wild-animals/endangered-species/

https://theconversation.com/an-end-to endings-how-to-stop-more-australian-species-going-extinct-111627

www.engadget.com/2019/02/11/global-insect-decline-scientific-review/
https://w w w.sciencealert.com/half-a-million-insect-species-face-extinction-a

Full list of animal and plant species declared extinct between 2010 and 2019:

https://lifegate.com/people/news/extinct-species-list-decade-2010-2019

Heat Waves

http://www.latimes.com/opinion/op-ed/la-oe-stokes-heat-wave-media-climate-change-20180715–story.html#.

https://www.statista.com/statistics/267708/number-of-deaths-globally-due-to-heat-or-cold-waves/.

https://www.princeton.edu/news/2019/05/08/occurrence-back-back-heatwaves-likely-accelerate-climate-change.

http://www.washingtonpost.com/news/worldviews/wp/2018/07/24/

death-toll-climbs-as-japan-wilts-under-a-record-breaking-heat-wave/.

https://www.indiatoday.in/india/story/bihar-heatwave-kills-184–people-section-144–imposed-in-gaya-1550457–2019–06–17?fbclid=lwAR15ZZnPIH0zJq2VmU-j6hfa3zn9ls84n96Sf XvK4wrgmnbl05ph0HTn RGY.

Islands Disappearing

https://www.smithsonianmag.com/science-nature/will-tuvalu-disappear-beneath-the-sea-180940704/.

https://www.theguardian.com/environment/2016/may/10/five-pacific-islands-lost-rising-seas-climate-change.

https://www.motherjones.com/environment/2009/11/tuvalu-climate-refugees/.

Coral Reefs Dying and Fisheries Being Depleted

https://www.nytimes.com/2017/03/15/science/great-barrier-reef-coral-climate-change-dieoff.html.

https://www.nytimes.com/2016/04/10/world/asia/climate-related-death-of-coral-around-world-alarms-scientists.html.

https://www.bing.com/videos/search?q=coral+reef+death&qpvt=coral+reef+death&FORM=VDRE.

https://www.businessinsider.com/great-barrier-reef-death-coral-bleaching-climate-change-2018-5.

https://www.alternet.org/environment/global-fisheries-are-collapsing-what-happens-when-there-are-no-fish-left.

https://news.stanford.edu/news/2006/november8/ocean-110806.html.

https://www.huffpost.com/entry/climate-change-already-sparking-fishing-wars n 5b215152e4b0adfb82706c39.

Climate Refugees

https://www.nationalgeographic.org/encyclopedia/climate-refugee/.

https://www.aljazeera.com/indepth/features/2015/11/climate-refugees-151125093146088.html.

https://www.cbsnews.com/news/climate-refugees-kiribati-cbsn-on-assignment/.

https://w w w.theguardian.com/environment/2009/nov/03/global-warming-climate-refugees.

China's Pollution

https://sploid.gizmodo.com/blue-skies-in-china-can-only-appear-on-screens-because-1458359419.

https://www.cnn.com/2016/12/15/asia/china-air-pollution-study/index.html.

https://thediplomat.com/2014/11/china-pollution-blue-skies-over-beijing/.

https://www.boredpanda.com/blue-skies-military-parade-no-cars-beijing/?utm source=bing&utm medium=orga nic&utm campaign=organic.

Videos

Some videos that are a must-see are and are considered sources for the events previously mentioned include *Years of Living Dangerously* (seasons 1 and 2), *Before the Flood, An Inconvenient Truth: Part II* (2017), *Time to Choose,* and *Mission Blue* (2014).

www.yearsoflivingdangerously.com—there are two seasons of videos out on iTunes, Vimeo, Amazon prime, Hulu, Google Play. Now known as TheYearsProject.com.

Saving the coral reefs: Researchers race against the clock to restore vital ecosystems: https://www.houstonchronicle.com/news/science-environment/article/Saving-the-coral-reefs-Researchers-race-against-13107199.php?utm campaign=email-premium&utm source=CMS%20Sharing%20Button&utm medium=social This message was sent via houstonchronicle.com.

Natural World Disappearing

https://www.theguardian.com/commentisfree/2018/jun/29/natural-world-disappearing-save-it.

https://www.irishtimes.com/news/environment/recent-climate-extremes-indicate-a-global-climate-emergency-on-horizon-1.3575234.

Permafrost Melting

https://www.commondreams.org/news/2019/04/23/we-are-not-moving-fast-enough-study-shows-cost-melting-permafrost-could-total-70.

https://www.counterpunch.org/2018/07/25/methane-deathtrap-threatens-democracy/.

https://thinkprogress.org/arctic-death-spiral-coastal-permafrost-collapse-23d650acea99/.

https://www.counterpunch.org/2019/06/21/permafrost-collapses-70–years-early/.

https://www.theguardian.com/environment/2019/jun/18/arctic-permafrost-canada-science-climate-crisis?fbclid+lwAR1gKXxfqQ15T7KgHU9tZHEabueOxihCTJYvvWsPG4f6G6Z7718p9HbOOz4.

Other

www.thebigwobble.org/2019/06/temperatures-touching-51–deg-c-124–

deg.html.

www.siberiantimes.com/other/others/news/alarming-wildfires-rage-near-giant-mouth-of-hell-gash-in-the-tundra-a -wonder-of-siberia/.

https://www.livescience.com/65721–climate-change-neverending-heatwave.html.

https://www. theguardian.com/commentisfree/2019/jun/10/extinction-rebellion-bubble-denial-climate-crisis.

https://desdemonadespair.net/2019/06/19/video-starving-poar-bear-wanders-into-russian-city-of norilsk-hundreds-of-miles-from-home.html.

https://www.theguardian.com/environment/2019/jun/28/california-mussels-cooked-heat.

https://www.cnn.com/2019/06/27/us/new-york-city-declared-climate-emergency-tmd/index.html.

Video to go with above article: New York City Declares Climate.

Emergency/Extinction Rebellion: https://m.youtube.com/watch?v=XPtAKjhT02s.

https://www.smh.com.au/environment/climate-change/scorching-temperatures-kuwait-and pakistan-among-hottest-measured-20190619–p51z4k.html.

https://www.sfgate.com/news/article/Mega-fire-measuring-1-5-million-acres-forms-in-14965345.php

geologypage.com/2017/05/earthquakes-can-make-thrust-faults-open-violently-snap-shut.html

https://www.space.com/mysterious-gravitational-burst.html Websites

Strangesounds.org.
Livescience.com.
Truthout.org.
Ecoshock.org.

http://revelationrevolution.org

Unverified Report that the Ark of the Covenant Was Discovered https://www.youtube.com/watch?v=S2e5Cf8yt9Q.

Spontaneous Combustion

https://m.youtube.com/watch?v=b1kMBGkT1CA (in another language: Tree Catches Fire After Temperature Reaches 62 Degrees in Kuwait?).

Index

A

abomination of desolation 22, 23, 24, 36, 43, 122, 200
Abraham 17, 65, 73, 254, 277
Antichrist 53, 77, 160, 172, 176, 202
Antiochus Epiphanes 22, 24, 106

B

beast xxv, 4, 5, 24, 25, 26, 27, 30, 31, 32, 36, 38, 39, 41, 42, 43, 44, 45, 46, 48, 49, 51, 52, 53, 55, 64, 69, 70, 75, 76, 77, 84, 85, 98, 105, 106, 107, 111, 125, 152, 172, 176, 178, 189, 194, 201, 202, 203, 206, 212, 230, 240, 250, 251, 259, 264, 284, 290
black holes 76, 77, 78, 80, 81, 82
bubonic plague 135, 136, 137

C

Caiaphas 46, 55, 104, 116, 156, 201
climate change xvi, xxii, xxiv, xxvi, xxvii, 5, 8, 10, 11, 16, 19, 84, 86, 87, 91, 137, 144, 154, 155, 168, 171, 172, 173, 290, 294
Crusades 31, 32, 33, 35, 42, 54, 55, 56, 66, 68, 84, 87, 91, 96, 98, 109, 120, 121, 122, 126, 127, 128, 129, 130, 131, 132, 133, 134, 135, 140, 144, 154, 194, 197, 199, 206, 207, 225, 289, 294, 301

D

Daniel xvi, xxv, 20, 21, 22, 24, 25, 26, 27, 28, 29, 31, 32, 33, 37, 39, 42, 45, 52, 54, 55, 56, 62, 67, 68, 90, 102, 106, 117, 118, 148, 150, 157, 159, 161, 162, 165, 170, 177, 178, 179, 180, 189, 190, 191, 192, 193, 200, 202, 203, 205, 207, 225, 229, 295
Day of Judgment 77, 92, 179, 182
day of the Lord xvi, xvii, 2, 27, 77, 80, 92, 183, 185
destruction xvi, xxv, 6, 17, 25, 26, 27, 28, 29, 31, 37, 38, 39, 42, 44, 51, 58, 60, 61, 62, 64, 69, 73, 74, 76, 77, 78, 79, 84, 88, 89, 90, 92, 97, 98, 99, 106, 107, 116, 130, 133, 140, 144, 145, 149, 154, 155, 157, 158, 159, 162, 164, 165, 169, 171, 175, 176, 177, 182, 183, 184, 192, 193, 194, 195, 206, 207, 212, 214, 221, 222, 224, 225, 228, 229, 230, 231, 232, 233, 282, 288, 289, 290, 292, 293, 294
Domitian 27, 33, 36, 39, 42, 52, 54, 118, 194, 294
Droughts 8
dual fulfillment xv, 79, 103, 109, 147, 197, 211

E

earthquake 14, 52, 79, 124, 219, 294
eclipse 60, 61, 74, 79, 136, 211, 212
endangered 2, 12, 305, 306, 307
end of the age 31, 62, 159, 190
ensign 46, 48, 49, 106
extinction xvi, xxii, xxiv, xxv, 2, 4, 5, 6, 8, 10, 11, 13, 16, 56, 74, 77, 78, 85, 86, 89, 119, 142, 144, 154, 155, 158, 168, 172, 207, 209, 212, 213, 215, 231, 237, 240, 287, 292, 294, 306, 307, 311

F

false Christ 109
false prophet 55, 70, 75, 76, 77, 84, 85, 98, 107, 152
first century generation 165, 201
first resurrection xxv, 32, 59, 62, 79, 175, 183, 184, 200, 206, 209
futurist xxi, xxiv, 4, 5, 118, 126, 147, 166, 188, 189, 197, 204, 287, 288

G

generation v, vi, xvii, xx, xxi, xxiv, 18, 21, 25, 27, 28, 29, 30, 31, 32, 35, 37, 38, 41, 48, 54, 55, 59, 69, 72, 79, 84, 102, 113, 114, 115, 116, 117, 118, 119, 135, 136, 140, 145, 146, 147, 148, 150, 159, 161, 162, 163, 164, 165, 166, 167, 172, 174, 175, 183, 184, 188, 191, 192, 193, 194, 195, 196, 197, 198, 199, 200, 201, 202, 203, 204, 205, 207, 210, 218, 219, 220, 231, 264, 290
ghost 38, 50, 51, 87, 178
Gog and Magog xxv, 5, 31, 42, 55, 67, 68, 84, 87, 91, 98, 121, 122, 126, 129, 131, 152, 172, 194, 197, 199, 212, 220, 294

Great Commission 103, 115, 161, 163, 190, 191, 192, 274

H

Hades 56, 65, 72, 73, 74, 75, 76, 77, 78, 83, 84, 85, 86, 87, 89, 93, 138, 152, 179, 180, 205, 206, 219, 225, 251, 254
Herod 29, 37, 39, 40, 41, 43, 52
Holocaust 137, 194, 224, 225, 226, 227, 232, 290, 293

I

iceberg 16, 220, 224, 231
Israel xvi, xxiii, xxv, xxvi, 14, 15, 21, 22, 23, 27, 37, 42, 46, 54, 56, 61, 64, 70, 83, 90, 98, 103, 105, 108, 109, 111, 115, 118, 119, 121, 123, 125, 126, 127, 128, 129, 135, 136, 137, 156, 157, 163, 169, 170, 173, 192, 193, 195, 205, 207, 212, 218, 230, 231, 232, 238, 240, 246, 259, 260, 262, 266, 284, 287, 291, 293

J

Jerusalem xv, xxiii, xxiv, xxv, 4, 9, 23, 24, 27, 33, 35, 36, 40, 44, 46, 47, 53, 56, 57, 58, 59, 61, 62, 66, 67, 68, 69, 90, 91, 92, 99, 100, 101, 102, 103, 104, 105, 106, 107, 108, 114, 116, 117, 118, 119, 120, 121, 122, 125, 126, 127, 129, 131, 132, 133, 134, 135, 136, 137, 140, 142, 144, 145, 146, 147, 156, 165, 172, 176, 184, 192, 193, 194, 196, 197, 198, 200, 201, 202, 205, 212, 220, 232, 288, 290, 294, 295
John the Baptist 23, 27, 28, 41, 62, 75, 148, 191

Josephus 40, 47, 53, 102, 104, 105, 107, 194, 301

judgment xvi, xxiv, xxvii, 5, 6, 18, 27, 32, 58, 64, 68, 74, 75, 89, 91, 96, 98, 114, 117, 120, 134, 137, 138, 144, 152, 154, 157, 165, 169, 172, 179, 180, 181, 186, 195, 196, 204, 205, 206, 207, 209, 212, 218, 219, 247, 253, 261, 269, 271, 290

K

kingdom of God 21, 23, 27, 28, 29, 30, 33, 63, 67, 68, 93, 96, 112, 113, 115, 149, 187, 194, 223, 250, 251, 264, 283, 291, 295

kingdom of heaven 4, 28, 29, 30, 31, 32, 36, 62, 63, 65, 66, 90, 94, 98, 109, 111, 112, 140, 152, 187, 191, 204, 206, 207, 220, 238, 245, 247, 255, 263, 271, 273, 283, 285, 289, 292, 293

L

lake of fire 7, 56, 72, 73, 75, 76, 77, 78, 80, 82, 84, 85, 86, 87, 88, 89, 154, 179, 186, 206, 207, 209, 223, 227

last days 118, 129, 159, 165, 286, 293

lawlessness 44, 106, 130, 176, 283

M

meteors 60, 74, 78, 79, 210, 211, 291

millennial reign xxiv, xxv, 4, 5, 32, 33, 35, 42, 55, 64, 66, 93, 98, 164, 172, 199, 209, 212, 289, 290

Moses 6, 16, 17, 48, 70, 98, 115, 135, 157, 183, 199, 218, 226, 227, 228, 230, 231, 232, 255, 256, 260, 261, 270, 277, 286, 292

N

nations xvi, xx, xxiii, xxiv, xxvii, 4, 9, 12, 14, 17, 26, 29, 42, 50, 52, 55, 56, 65, 66, 68, 69, 70, 79, 86, 87, 89, 90, 91, 92, 93, 98, 99, 100, 102, 120, 121, 122, 125, 126, 127, 129, 133, 135, 136, 137, 138, 140, 141, 142, 144, 152, 157, 160, 161, 162, 168, 170, 177, 190, 192, 197, 206, 232, 286, 288

Nebuchadnezzar 137, 193, 205, 229

Nero 24, 25, 26, 36, 37, 38, 39, 43, 44, 45, 46, 49, 50, 51, 52, 76, 106, 107, 176, 180, 194, 202, 203, 230

Noah xvii, xxii, xxvi, xxviii, 3, 6, 16, 17, 75, 83, 84, 88, 97, 137, 153, 154, 155, 157, 158, 169, 173, 182, 183, 207, 213, 222, 223, 224, 228, 229, 231, 232, 259, 260, 270, 287, 290, 292, 293, 294

P

Parousia iii, vi, xxii, xxiv, 61, 100, 205, 206, 287, 289, 299

passing away vi, xv, xvi, xxi, xxv, 2, 3, 5, 8, 14, 16, 32, 35, 82, 85, 88, 90, 99, 109, 142, 149, 151, 154, 165, 170, 172, 173, 174, 176, 180, 186, 206, 207, 209, 211, 212, 215, 220, 231, 287, 289, 293

plague 9, 131, 132, 133, 134, 135, 136, 137, 140, 142

Pliny 48, 60

preterist xv, xvi, xxi, 5, 17, 31, 45, 102, 126, 146, 147, 171, 173, 175, 176, 182, 188, 200, 201, 203, 209, 287, 288

R

Red Sea 17, 123, 183, 218, 228, 259, 261, 265, 267, 292
Roman Empire 20, 26, 27, 29, 30, 32, 33, 44, 65, 67, 68, 118, 121, 159, 162, 164, 189, 191, 192, 193, 194, 195, 251, 259

S

Schindler 219, 224, 226, 227, 230
second resurrection xxv, xxvi, 31, 32, 79, 180, 184, 207, 295
stars xvi, xxv, 56, 59, 60, 62, 73, 74, 75, 76, 77, 78, 79, 80, 82, 83, 86, 152, 153, 157, 168, 209, 210, 211, 224, 291

T

Tacitus 102, 104, 301

ten kings 33, 41, 42, 43, 55
thief in the night xv, xx, xxii, xxiii, 2, 17, 32, 39, 55, 61, 67, 98, 109, 112, 114, 133, 135, 149, 151, 157, 158, 169, 171, 177, 181, 195, 198, 220, 226, 258, 289
Titus 24, 25, 37, 39, 42, 46, 47, 52, 54, 267
tribes of Israel xvi, 61, 64, 98, 103, 108, 118, 156, 195
Tribulation 57, 193, 194

V

Vespasian 24, 25, 39, 48, 52, 60
Vesuvius 54, 294
vultures 57, 58, 59

W

worldly kingdoms xvi, xxv, 19, 21, 33, 68, 93, 150, 294

www.ingramcontent.com/pod-product-compliance
Lightning Source LLC
Chambersburg PA
CBHW021422070526
44577CB00001B/21